THE BUSINESS ENVIRONMENT

CHALLENGES AND CHANGES

Ian Brooks and
Jamie Weatherston

Faculty of Management and Business
Nene College of Higher Education

PRENTICE HALL

London   New York   Toronto   Sydney   Tokyo   Singapore
Madrid   Mexico City   Munich   Paris

First published 1997 by
Prentice Hall Europe
Campus 400, Maylands Avenue
Hemel Hempstead
Hertfordshire, HP2 7EZ
A division of
Simon & Schuster International Group

Typeset in 10 on 12 Plantin
by MHL Typesetting Ltd., Coventry

Printed and bound in Great Britain by
T.J. International Ltd

Library of Congress Cataloging-in-Publication Data

Brooks, I. (Ian)
  The business environment : challenges and changes / Ian Brooks and
Jamie Weatherston.
      p.   cm.
  Includes bibliographical references and index.
  ISBN 0-13-376716-7
  1. Industrial management.   2. Business   3. Commerce.
I. Weatherston, Jamie.   II. Title.
HD31.B753   1997
658–dc20   96-32314
                                                            CIP

British Library Cataloguing in Publication Data

A catalogue record for this book is available from
the British Library

ISBN 0-13-376716-7

---

  2   3   4   5   01   00   99   98

For
Hannah, Cara, Connor and Bernie
and for
Dawn, Jack and Alice

CONTENTS

PART I

THE BUSINESS ENVIRONMENT

CHAPTER 1
THE BUSINESS ENVIRONMENT

Ian Brooks

 LEARNING OUTCOMES

On completion of this chapter you should be able to:

- define the business environment and appreciate a number of models of the contextual environment of organizations;
- understand the prime variables which comprise the external environment;
- appreciate that environmental forces acting at a variety of geographical scales and political tiers influence organizations;
- map environmental stakeholder's power/interest;
- understand that the business environment is unique to each organization;
- appreciate that human processes influence our understanding of the business environment;
- appreciate the complexity and dynamism of environmental influences;
- critically assess the nature and value of environmental forecasting techniques and styles;
- appreciate the complex relationship between organization and environment and the influence of the environment on structure and strategy;
- appreciate the nature of the strategy formulation process.

1.1 Environmental forces

Introduction

Whether it is a financial institution, a university or a multinational chemical manufacturer no organization exists within a vacuum. It is very likely, for example, to have a number of competitors, to be subject to local government planning restrictions, obliged to comply with national or European pollution regulations and subject to fluctuations in the fortunes of the local, national or global economy. The business environment comprises an array of 'forces' acting upon organizations often with far-reaching implications. In order to fully appreciate the nature of the business environment it is first necessary to analyse the various forces at play. Only then can we attempt to develop a more integrated and holistic understanding of environmental activity. Thus following this introductory chapter this text unravels these powerful forces and illustrates how each may affect organizations.

The purpose of this introductory chapter, however, is to explain the rationale and scope of the book and to demonstrate the fundamental characteristics of the business environment, its relationship with organizations and the implications for organizational structure and strategy. We start by defining the business environment and by classifying the forces at play. The chapter then develops a model of the business environment which forms the basis of our approach. We briefly explain the diverse nature of organizations and take a closer look at various approaches to environmental forecasting. The chapter then discusses the relationship between the business environment and organizational activity. The role of the business environment in influencing the strategic direction of organizations is addressed and some of the complex issues are debated. Naturally, many of the issues raised are further developed in later chapters and the prime theme of dynamism and complexity is explored in depth in Chapter 9.

The business environment: a definition

The word 'environment' does not merely refer to the natural or ecological environment, although that may be an important consideration for many organizations. Instead, it is a generic concept which embraces the totality of external environmental forces which may influence any aspect of organizational activity. Similarly, the word 'business' is used to imply any type of organization, whether it be a commercial profit-making enterprise, a government agency or a non-profit-making charitable trust. Consequently, we will use the terms 'business' and 'organization' interchangeably. Hence 'the business environment' is a broad and all-embracing term which encompasses any and all influences which are external to the organization in question.

The focus of this book is on the *organization in its environment* rather than on the individual, group or government and their external environments. Figure 1.1 demonstrates that focus; however, these other focal bodies – individual, group, government – are referred to where appropriate and are covered in more detail in the concluding chapter. Additionally, public sector organizations are singled out for special attention in Chapter 8, partly because of the unique and dynamic environmental influences acting upon this sector and partly because more frequent reference is made to commercial organizations throughout the text.

The day-to-day activity of organizations includes interaction with the 'task

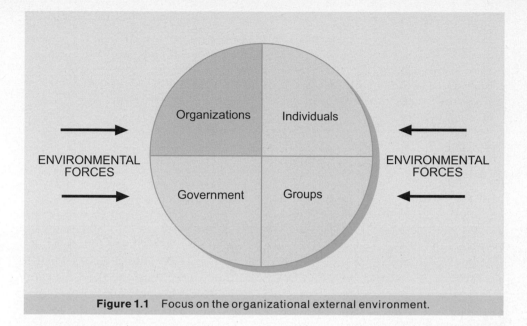

Figure 1.1   Focus on the organizational external environment.

environment' (Dill, 1958). This includes those relationships with its customers, suppliers, trade unions and shareholders. However, this book focuses on the broader contextual environment which permeates and extends beyond the immediate task environment.

However, defining the environment poses an intellectual problem although a number of eminent researchers have categorized the different approaches (see Smircich and Stubbart, 1985; Mansfield, 1990). Wilson (1992) has suggested three broad conceptions of the business environment, each of which is covered in some detail in this chapter. He argues that the business environment may be viewed as:

- an objective fact, a clear, measurable and definable reality;
- a subjective fact, its particular characteristics being dependent on each individual's interpretation and perceptions;
- enacted (Weick, 1979), where the division between organization and environment is not clear and where the environment is created and defined by individuals.

This complex argument is explained further in the section below entitled 'Perceptual filters' (pp. 19–21). It need not overly complicate our understanding of the business environment at this stage, although awareness of the role of human perception when defining environmental opportunities or constraints is useful.

A classification of environmental forces

There have been numerous attempts to model the business environment either in

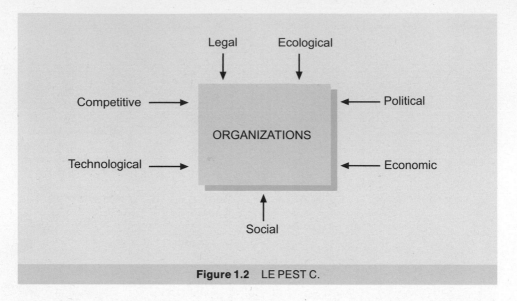

Figure 1.2   LE PEST C.

its totality or in its specific elements. Perhaps the most popular of the former category is PEST analysis.

The simple acronym PEST (standing for Political, Economic, Social, Technological) serves well as an *aide-mémoire* when considering the array of environmental forces influencing business activity. In fact if the acronym is enlarged to LE PEST C (to include Legal, Ecological and Competitive) it encompasses most areas of concern in this field. Figure 1.2 illustrates this categorization of the business environment. This text concentrates on each of these forces and the interaction between them.

PEST analysis enables students or managers to assemble a logical and comprehensive picture of their environment. However, it is the interrelationship between the apparently different factors which adds not only complexity and uncertainty to the analysis but also richness and greater accuracy. Figure 1.3 illustrates a partial PEST analysis of Scania, a multinational, Swedish owned, truck manufacturer.

As is clear, there are a number of important aspects of Scania's environment which will influence the company's activity and its business and strategic decision making. Some of these factors lie within Scania's control while many others, such as fluctuations in the value of the Swedish krone, are beyond its influence.

There are numerous other, sometimes graphic, representations of the business environment. Daft (1992) demonstrates pictorially his typology of environmental forces (Figure 1.4).

This 'dartboard' configuration gives the organization pride of place in the centre while radiating from it are eight categories of environmental concerns. This typology is similar to the LE PEST C acronym suggesting, as it does, that all environmental forces fall within one or more of these specified categories.

Legal

- Block exemption: threatened removal of EU regulation 123/85 leading to possible cancellation of motor franchise arrangements enabling dealers to seek multi-franchises; 'Block Exemption' renewed (1995) temporarily.
- EU transport regulations/harmonization; drivers; hours of work; emissions standards (Euro 1, Euro 2, Euro 3).
- Maximum legal truck sizes likely to increase; may reduce truck demand due to scale efficiencies.

Ecological

- Euro 1, 2 and 3 regulations impose increasingly stringent emissions and noise limits requiring redesign of engines and other parts.
- Environmental transport lobby aim to increase rail freight and reduce the numbers of large trucks on the roads
- Stringent standards require more frequent engine service and emission checks.
- Increasingly aware and active public concern over health issues, quality of life and road congestion.

Political

- Government transport policies; possible change of government.
- Investment in rail freight terminals and other infrastructure following privatization.
- Pressure to regulate road haulage companies further, e.g. truck size, driver hours, registration requirements.
- Reductions in centrally funded road building; toll roads.
- Excise duty on diesel; levels of road tax on trucks.

Economic

- Effects of economic cycles are pronounced in this industry, especially affecting new truck sales (e.g. Scania sales 1992=2900 trucks while in 1995=5500).
- Currency fluctuations: especially of Swedish Krone against sterling, DMark, Ffranc, Guilder.
- Single European currency.
- Interest rates (many trucks purchased on financing arrangement organized through Scania Finance Ltd.)

SCANIA IN THE UK

Social and Demographic

- Societal lobby of governments to reduce or control road traffic and congestion.
- Changing shopping habits influencing rates of growth and geographical distribution of retailers.

Technological

- Complexity in truck design and on-board aids, e.g. on-board computers – engine management systems, trans-European navigation, communications.
- Channel Tunnel: increases in rail freight?
- Continual improvements in fuel consumption and emission control as manufacturers seek competitive advantage while complying with Euro standards.
- Alternative fuels.
- Alternative transportation systems.
- Improved technologies and quality, increasing service intervals.

Competitive

- Changing customer base: from small haulage operators to large fleet management organizations – increased buyer power.
- Growth of rental market and non-manufacturing suppliers, e.g. Ryder, BRS.
- Convergence in design and 'quality' characteristics among main players leads to increasing competition.
- Marque loyalties of declining importance; lifetime cost considerations; aftersales market of increasing importance.
- Whole package concept (e.g. trucks, financing and aftersales services).
- Possible future Japanese or Far Eastern incursion into European truck market.
- New entrants' excursion into large and lucrative aftersales market (as in motor car industry, e.g. Kwik Fit).

Figure 1.3 PEST analysis: Scania in the UK.

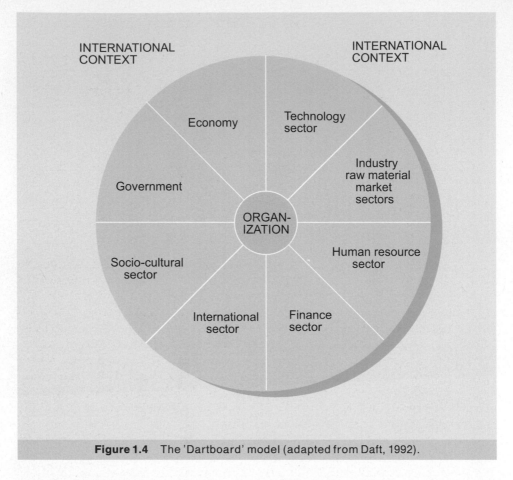

INTERNATIONAL
CONTEXT

INTERNATIONAL
CONTEXT

Economy

Technology
sector

Government

Industry
raw material
market
sectors

ORGAN-
IZATION

Socio-cultural
sector

Human resource
sector

International
sector

Finance
sector

Figure 1.4   The 'Dartboard' model (adapted from Daft, 1992).

For analytical purposes Peace and Robinson (1994) separate a firm's external environment into three categories. They refer to:

- the 'remote environment', such as global and domestic political, social and technological concerns – this is akin to the contextual environment outlined above;
- the 'industry environment' or its competitive forces;
- the 'operating environment', which comprises a rather mixed group of actors including suppliers and customers – similar to Dill's (1958) task environment.

It is not the intention of this book to focus, in any detail, on the internal or operating environment of the organization. Robbins (1992) suggests that the prime forces for change within organizations derive from forces acting within its environment. Specifically, he suggests a typology of forces which are: the nature of a workforce, technology, economic shocks, social trends, world politics and competition. These and other dynamic environmental forces will be explored within this book.

Classifications of the type outlined above attempt to model the environment, and although they tend to simplify reality, they help us to identify and understand what are complex environmental processes and forces, and serve as useful tools to aid our analysis of the environment. The 'real' environment is a complex array of interrelated forces; we merely compartmentalize them for simplicity and to gain insight. Often, in reality, a number of forces within the environment combine to influence an organization. It is when reading and analysing case studies of other 'real' organizations that the complexity of the business environment becomes apparent, yet understanding of the individual elements of that environment will enable you to better appreciate the nature and dynamism encountered.

Environmental stakeholders

All organizations, whatever their size, have a number of stakeholders. A stakeholder is a person, organization, interest group or other body which holds a 'stake' in the business. In addition to having an interest in the activities of the organization, some stakeholders have power to influence those activities. Institutional shareholders, for example, are powerful stakeholders in many commercial companies and consequently have considerable influence, if they wish to use it, upon the nature of company objectives. Governments often hold a controlling influence over public sector bodies and hence are vital stakeholders in those organizations. Our prime concern with the stakeholder concept is to identify which, if any, of these power groups can be categorized as part of the organization's business environment.

The concept of an 'environmental stakeholder' is very real for most organizations. In the National Health Service (NHS), hospital management and medical personnel regard the Department of Health and the particular government of the day as very important and powerful stakeholders. Whether they, as managers or medical professionals, like it that way is a debatable issue but the fact remains that the government, via the Department of Health, provide the funds and the legal framework within which hospitals and other NHS facilities operate. However, in addition to the Department of Health each hospital trust has other 'environmental stakeholders'. These include the local community which the hospital serves. One might argue that this customer base is the most 'important' stakeholder. Of course, not all stakeholders will hold equal power or influence over the affairs of the organization. For example, the community may have less influence over hospital strategic activities than does the Department of Health; for instance, many regional health authorities no longer undertake free cosmetic surgery, except in severe cases, at the expense of the NHS, despite a not inconsiderable demand from the general public. The Department of Health therefore effects a cost saving. It is often the case, for example, that small shareholders in companies have little power or influence in the organization.

TABLE 1.1   Environmental stakeholders: higher education

Environmental stakeholders	Power to influence strategy	Level of interest in activities
Government: Department of Education	High	Low
Students	Medium	High
Quality assessment bodies	High	Medium
Local government	Low	Low
Local residents	Low	Medium
Funding body	High	Medium
Other regional HE institutions	Medium	Medium
Taxpayers	Low	Low

However, a large institutional investor might have many millions of pounds of its clients' funds invested in the company and may wield its power of influence to determine organizational performance. In 1995 many small shareholders in British Gas plc objected to pay and bonus increases awarded to the chief executive, Cedric Brown. However, their collective action was insufficient to combat the power of large institutional investors who were less inclined to object.

By way of further illustration, Table 1.1 lists some of the environmental stakeholders of a typical Higher Education college or university in the United Kingdom. It indicates whether the stakeholders have 'high', 'medium' or 'low'

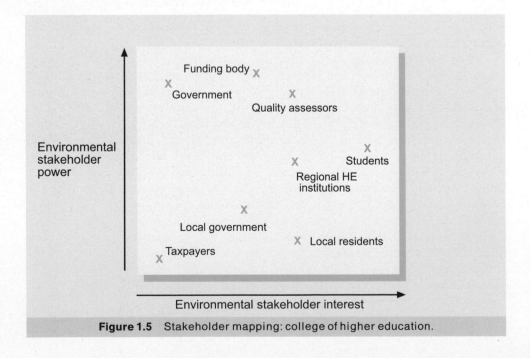

Figure 1.5   Stakeholder mapping: college of higher education.

power over the college and whether they have a relatively 'high', 'medium' or 'low' interest in the activity and strategic direction of the organization. The analysis involves judgement; however, it can be carried out for any organization with which you are familiar. It should also be noted that, due to volatility in the business environment, stakeholder power and interest is itself dynamic.

Figure 1.5 shows how one might 'map' stakeholder power and interest in an organization using the data from Table 1.1. This graphically illustrates the stakeholders that wield most power and influence.

This analysis provides a useful analytical tool for managers to assess the relative power and influence of each of their environmental stakeholders. It may prove invaluable in the strategic management process.

Geo-political scales

This book studies the business environment at a range of geo-political scales. The 'geo' in this case refers to 'geographical' scale while the political implies levels or tiers of government. Hence, at the local level in most countries there is a tier of government which is responsible for certain activities within a relatively small area. Similarly there is a tier of government, often very important and influential, at a national scale. In Europe the European Union (EU), and in South-East Asia ASEAN, form a further level of government. International developments may exert a powerful influence, either directly or less overtly, on most organizations. The EU, for example, has created enormous change, not least in trading relations, patterns of trade and alterations in product specifications, to name but a few. It is a dynamic force in organizations across Europe and indeed elsewhere.

Most organizations are influenced by environmental forces operating at different geo-political levels, as illustrated in Figure 1.6. For example, Scania interact with their environment at a variety of scales. At the local level in the United Kingdom their head office is located in Milton Keynes, England, and a move to an alternative location within the town is imminent. The decision where to locate will be subject to local government planning restrictions which will, in turn, be influenced by national laws and EU directives. Also, Scania employs a large number of skilled, experienced and professional staff who currently live in or near Milton Keynes. Hence factors within the local environment (i.e. local government and local labour supply) are important to the activities of Scania (GB) in Milton Keynes. However, Scania is also subject to environmental dynamism at the national, European and global scales. Table 1.2 illustrates two influences upon Scania (Great Britain) at four geo-political scales. It also categorizes these forces into legal, ecological, political, economic, social, technological and competitive (LE PEST C). Many environmental issues, such as EU engine emission regulations, are themselves the outcome of a diverse range of influences acting in cohort. Hence, as illustrated in Table 1.2, the nature of the laws governing truck engine emissions within the EU is influenced by a complex consortium of ecological, social, technological, political and legal forces. Conflicting pressures are brought to

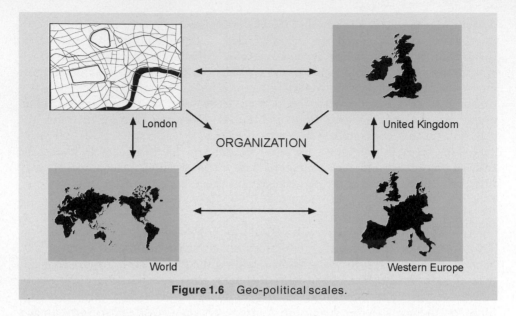

Figure 1.6   Geo-political scales.

bear on the European government from ecological pressure groups, social and political philosophies and organizational lobbyists. The outcome is, in this case, a compromise 'solution' enshrined in law.

It is not always simple to identify the precise scale at which an environmental

TABLE 1.2   Factors operating within Scania's business environment at four geo-political scales

Geo-political scale	Environmental issues, for example:	Environmental forces
Local	A: Milton Keynes town planning regulations (Scania GB headquarters)	A: Political, legal, social, ecological
	B: Local skilled labour supply conditions	B: Social, economic, competitive
National	A: Value of sterling against the Swedish krone	A: Economic, political
	B: Government freight transport policy	B: Political, social, competitive
European Union	A: Emission control and truck size regulations	A: Ecological, technological, political, social, legal
	B: Trading relations and concessions to non-EU countries	B: Political, competitive
Global	A: GATT negotiations to pursue free trade agreements	A: Political, legal, competitive
	B: Rio Conference CO_2 emission targets	B: Ecological, social, political

force operates. Some forces will operate at a number of different levels and manifest themselves in a variety of ways. Hence it may fall upon local government to enforce pollution controls that originated at global governmental conferences. Even many small, local companies are increasingly aware that forces operating at the European level, such as product specification directives emanating from Brussels, have a direct and often profound influence on their business. For example, many local butchers' shops are finding it increasingly difficult to comply with European Union health and safety regulations. For some it is proving to be the proverbial last straw.

Unfortunately, it is not always practical to distinguish between the business environment at various geo-political scales as these influences are often so interrelated and complex that they can only be fully appreciated collectively.

Not all organizations are influenced equally by the business environment. In fact what may prove to be a real threat for one organization could be a wondrous opportunity for growth and profitability for another. For example, the technological advances made in the design, production and marketing of personal computers, and the consequent reduction in their cost and improvement in quality, have led to enormous increases in their demand for household and business use. These technological forces have, however, virtually proved a death blow to the manufacture of mechanical and even electronic typewriters and have reduced the demand for mainframe computers for certain applications. In reality, every organization has a complex array of environmental influences with which it interacts and which are, in their entirety, unique.

Hence the business environment is a complex array of forces acting with often unpredictable and unequal force upon organizations at a variety of geographical and political scales.

The organization–environment relationship

The relationship, or direction of influence, between environment and organization is not uni-directional, simple or static. Organizations have tentacles of influence which help form and give shape to the business environment. In other words there is not a one-way causal relationship between environment and organization. We have argued above that it would be rather naïve to assume that organizations themselves do not play a major part in influencing their own environment. The reality is that many profoundly shape their own environment and that facing numerous other organizations. The simplest example is that of a number of competing companies in an industrial sector. The activity of one, say the introduction of a new product range, will influence the activity and success of another. Figure 1.7 indicates this two-way influence between organization and environment.

Each organization forms part of the business environment of other organizations, as competitors, allies, suppliers, buyers and so forth. No organization is so isolated that it has no influence on its own environment and that of others. Many organizations, especially sizeable and/or influential ones,

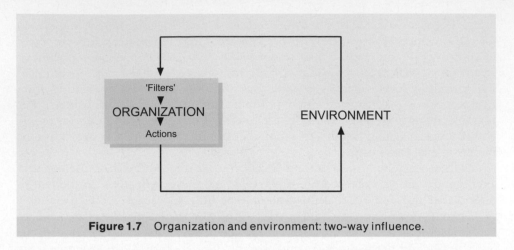

Figure 1.7   Organization and environment: two-way influence.

exert considerable pressures for change in their business environment. Hamel and Prahalad (1994) argue that companies can only control their future if they know how to influence the destiny of their industry. For example, the Direct Line Insurance company in the United Kingdom have revolutionized the motor and household insurance business. They have effectively marketed and delivered a quick and efficient 'telephone line' insurance service. This has reduced their overheads, when compared to normal broker and insurance services, rapidly increased their market share and enabled them to maintain highly competitive rates which have 'squeezed' more traditional competitors. They, and the numerous companies now mimicking them, have changed the business environment for all motor and household insurance companies. They are now employing their methodology to various financial services, hence they will encroach upon the environment of still more organizations.

Sometimes organizations within a business sector collaborate with each other in order to maintain a stable environment within known competitive conditions. For example, many European motor manufacturers have recently succeeded in persuading the European Union to extend the 'block exemption' scheme for motor distributor dealerships. That is, manufacturers can still demand that their dealerships distribute, service and repair solely their vehicles. Hence motor manufacturers maintain control over their distribution channels which act as a strong barrier to entry for any new makes that might want to enter the market. The investment required to establish a comprehensive distributor network is immense and effectively deters many potential entrants and limits the penetrative capabilities of others. The conditions of competition are thus maintained – business as usual.

A model of the business environment

The model, illustrated in Figure 1.8, indicates how the various environmental forces, acting at a variety of scales, pass through what we refer to as 'perceptual

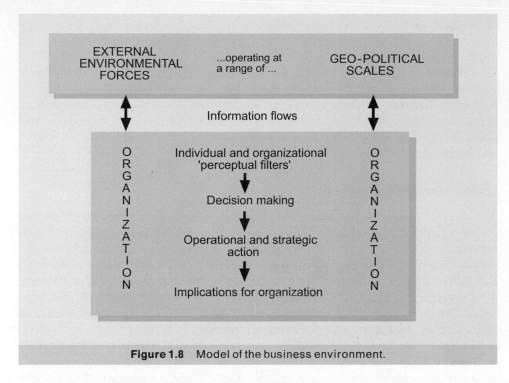

Figure 1.8   Model of the business environment.

filters'. These filters are explained below but briefly comprise all the internal mechanisms within organizations which enable managers to construct their own view of environmental realities. For example, an organization may not have an active environmental scanning capability and hence may literally miss numerous potential opportunities, while another may be managed by eternal optimists who are convinced of their organization's invincibility even when faced with hostile environmental influences. For all intents and purposes, these perceptual filters actually change and shape 'reality' for organizations. They influence the way organizations look at their environment and what they see. Consequently, we must not underestimate their power and influence. The failure of the United Kingdom motorcycle industry, which has been virtually wiped out in the post-1945 era, was in large part due to its inability to accept that its business environment was rapidly changing. Design, product and process changes, largely developed in Japan, were ignored by British manufacturers who failed to perceive and react to both these environmental changes and evolving customer requirements.

Information about an organization's environment may take a variety of forms; for example, it may comprise sophisticated data from a strategic management information system or, conversely, an apparently minor snippet of information gleaned by a powerful senior manager. There is little evidence to suggest that organizations are more likely to act on concrete data than on the opinion or impression of the senior personnel. Environmental information is always the result of 'human' analysis. It has passed through the complex perceptual filters which exist within every organization. However, this information will not influence all organizations equally.

Managers at all levels utilize environmental information to facilitate their decision making in order to enable the organization to operate successfully. A thorough awareness of the nature of an organization's environment is an essential prerequisite for strategic management. The environment often determines, and always influences, the future course of action of organizations. It acts as a force for change in organizations.

Dynamism and complexity

Throughout this book we stress the dynamic nature of environmental forces; however, we recognize that the degree or extent of dynamism is not equal for all organizations or environments. For example, at present the extent of environmental flux affecting a high street solicitor, although not negligible, is less than that influencing BP or General Motors. It may be the case, of course, that BP have a far greater influence over their environment than does the solicitor's office, so dynamism is not necessarily a handicap, especially if that very dynamism preserves and enhances the competitive strengths of the firm.

Complexity in the environment is a product of a number of interrelated factors. Firstly, the degree of environmental uncertainty plays a major part. An

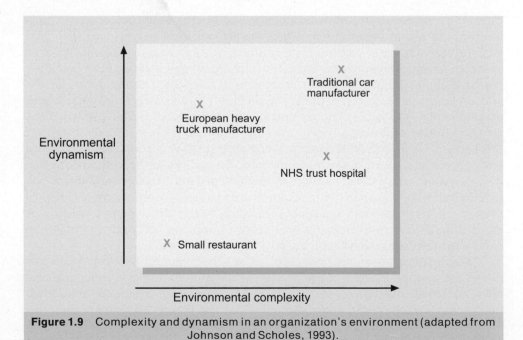

Figure 1.9 Complexity and dynamism in an organization's environment (adapted from Johnson and Scholes, 1993).

organization faced with an uncertain environment is, other things being equal, in a less advantageous position than one facing stability. However, yet again all is not straightforward, for many organizations become complacent when faced with a set of known environmental parameters. A significant change in one or more of those characteristics often leaves the inflexible organization unable to cope. Environmental complexity also tends to increase for organizations operating at a variety of geo-political scales. A transnational manufacturing and marketing organization is likely to encounter dynamic environmental forces at local, national, continental and global levels. Figure 1.9 can be used to 'map' an organization's position according to the levels of complexity and dynamism in its environment. By way of illustration we have located the approximate position of a number of 'generic' organizations.

When faced with a complex, uncertain and dynamic environment some organizations and many individual managers attempt to simplify that environment, at least in their own minds. Bourgeois (1985), however, recommends that organizations face up to and actively confront that difficult environment. Other researchers have argued that attempts to reduce environmental uncertainty may lead to poor long-term organizational performance. The themes of dynamism and complexity will be developed throughout this book and the consequences for organizations, government, individuals and groups further explored in Chapter 9.

QUESTIONS

1. Using the information in Figure 1.3, identify three variables in Scania's environment (a) which are totally outside the organization's control, (b) in which Scania have some, albeit minimal, influence, and (c) which Scania may attempt to alter and further influence for the benefit of the organization.

2. For an organization with which you are familiar (e.g. workplace, university, school, a case study from this book) identify two environmental forces for each of the LE PEST C categories. Establish the geo-political scale(s) at which each force may operate.

3. Carry out an environmental stakeholder analysis of an organization with which you are familiar. Place this information on a grid (as shown in Figure 1.5). What may this tell you about management priorities and their chief concerns?

1.2 The organization

Types of organization

The term 'organization' or 'business', as used in this book, embraces a wide range of legal entities with diverse objectives. Table 1.3 lists, with examples, the prime

TABLE 1.3   Types of organization in the United Kingdom

Types of organization	United Kingdom examples	Global examples
Government civil service departments and agencies	Ministry of Agriculture Food and Fisheries	Ministero Scuola Ed Educatione (Italy)
Local government organizations	Gloucestershire County Council	
Incorporated by Royal Charter or by Act of Parliament (public corporations)	BBC (by Royal Charter) Post Office (by Act of Parliament)	Air France
Quasi-autonomous non-governmental organizations (Quangos)	Higher Education Funding Council Executive (HEFCE)	UMNO (Malaysia)
Sole trader	The King of Balti's	Kobayastri Electronics (Japan)
Partnership	Peat Marwick McLintock	
Charity organizations	Oxfam	International Red Cross
Private limited company	Virgin Atlantic	
Cooperative	Cooperative Retail Society	Cooperativa Di Consumatori
Public limited company (plc)	BP	Heineken
Building societies and friendly societies	Bradford & Bingley Building Society	

types of organization in the United Kingdom. Each country will have variations upon these, yet in many ways they are similar.

As organizations fundamentally differ from one another in their legal status and prime objectives it is not surprising that the environmental forces which influence them also vary. In fact environmental pressures may encourage some organizations to actually change their legal status and objectives. For example, deregulation and increasing competition in the financial services industry is influencing the activity and success of building societies. Due to over-capacity, technological changes and further potential for economies of scale, some building societies have merged with one another while others have been swallowed up by larger banks. Merger activity may, in turn, lead to a change in legal status. For example, in August 1995 The Halifax and The Leeds building societies formally merged; they now intend to become a public limited company, as did the Abbey National before them, with its shares quoted on the London stock exchange. This loss of mutual status is also being considered by some insurance companies, such as Scottish Amicable.

Organizational objectives profoundly influence an organization's activity and strategic direction. Knowledge of these objectives will help determine the importance of different environmental forces and changes. Table 1.4 gives a flavour of the range of objectives that exist between just three types of organization.

TABLE 1.4 Organizational objectives

Type of organization	Prime objective
Commercial company (e.g. Hanson plc)	To maximize shareholder value
Charity (e.g. Oxfam)	To relieve poverty, distress and suffering in any part of the world
General hospital (e.g. Kettering General Hospital NHS Trust)	To provide quality health care provision for the local community

In addition to the legal status and prime objectives of organizations there are numerous other factors which may profoundly affect the nature of the organization–environment relationship. These include:

- organizational structure;
- size of the organization;
- type of technology used;
- cultural and political context of the organization;
- organizational and individual perceptual filters.

These and other factors will, subtly or otherwise, alter the importance of any particular environmental variable. For example, a large and diversified organization may cope better with a sudden rise in the price of an important raw material than a smaller more specialized firm which is heavily dependent on that input. Conversely, it is frequently argued that small firms tend to be more flexible and able to cope with environmental uncertainty than large, sluggish organizations.

Perceptual filters

This section will explain how organizations and their employees can assist in the 'creation' of their own business environment such that the actual nature of the business environment remains as much one of human interpretation as of hard 'reality'. It will suggest that different organizations in the same industry often 'view' environmental forces quite differently from one another, even though those forces may in fact be very similar. Finally, it will explain how organizations 'filter' and 'interpret' incoming information about the environment and how managerial cognition and organizational culture and politics can influence this process.

Decision makers in organizations receive and assimilate incoming data from the environment. That data is, however, incomplete. Even the most sophisticated environmental scanning and forecasting activities can only hope to collect and process a small proportion of all important environmental information. Most strategic decision makers are primarily concerned to learn about those changes which might influence their activity and, as such, they continuously make decisions regarding the importance or significance of 'new' information. It is quite possible, therefore, that person A will ignore data or dismiss it as unimportant while person B, even in the same organization, may take this same information on board and 'allow' it to influence his or her decision-making process. This difference in 'reception' may be attributed to differences in the manager's background, his or her position in the organization or how 'welcome' or potentially threatening the information is to the receiver. Just as individuals differ so do organizations and whole industrial sectors.

Our individual and collective perception only enables us to 'see' and interpret in certain ways. It is these perceptions that drive individual and business actions. Weick (1979) suggests that individual and organizational actions might in turn influence change within the environment. A hypothetical example will help to illustrate this phenomenon. Let us assume that Forefront, a computer software house, perceive that the competitive environment in which they operate is changing. These perceived changes encourage them to develop a technologically superior Windows^{TM} environment software product. They also perceive that numerous smaller software companies may begin to encroach on their other activities if they do not focus research and development (R&D) activity in these areas. Faced with a decision, Forefront decide to increase their efforts in R&D in the Windows^{TM} market. This entails reducing their R&D spend and management attention elsewhere. After two years, Forefront have successfully produced and marketed their Windows^{TM} product. They remain the market leaders with almost unassailable strength. However, there has been a cost. The neglect of their other software products has meant that competitors have overtaken them in terms of market share in these other product lines. Their original perception of their environment led them to a particular strategic management decision. As a result of that decision Forefront, in this example, have enacted their environment; that is, their actions have assured that their perceptions became a reality. Their actions – i.e. to focus on the Windows^{TM} environment at the expense of their other products – have led other 'environmental actors' (that is, their competitors) to adjust their strategic policy to take advantage of the opportunity. Forefront's perceptions and subsequent actions have become a self-fulfilling prophecy.

Miller (1988) argues that managers' perception of their environment has a greater influence on organizational decision making and eventual strategic direction than does more objective information. He is not alone in this belief. Boyd et al. (1993) suggest that this raises some major concerns regarding the reliability and validity of managers' perception. They argue, for example, that managers often make broad generalizations based on a small number of cases. Huber (1985) contends that these and other shortcomings are inevitable owing to the perceptual and cognitive limitations of managers. When facing an uncertain business environment, some managers and organizations actually perceive their environment as more certain than it actually is. This is particularly true of those managers who have a low tolerance for confusion or ambiguity.

In summary, the main influences upon individual and organizational perception are:

- characteristics of individuals, such as background, education and duration of employment within the organization;
- organizational culture;
- organizational politics, structures and control mechanisms;
- history and devlopment of an organization;
- industrial sector–sector norms.

We have argued that managers' perception influences their vision and assessment of the business environment. These processes are based on subjective judgements of the environment; however, many organizations attempt to form and utilize more objective environmental measures. The following section explores some of these objective, and other more perceptual, measures, while the role that culture and outlook plays in influencing an organization's 'view' of the environment is discussed in the final section of this chapter.

QUESTION

Discuss why two organizations in the same sector might 'see' their environment in quite different ways.

1.3 Environmental forecasting

Forecasting in a dynamic and complex environment

Managers with strategic responsibilities in organizations are often frustrated by the difficulty of predicting or forecasting changes in the environment. It is frequently the case, especially in smaller organizations, that little formal long-term forecasting takes place. It is viewed as such an uncertain science that time is not spent attempting to foresee what is often regarded as the unforeseeable. Instead managers prefer to be influenced by a combination of information resulting from their accumulated experience in business and a variety of perceptual measures of their environment. This may, however, prevent organizations from acting proactively. Such organizations are always in a position of having to react to a change thrust upon them.

There are many examples of companies who have failed owing to their reliance upon incorrect forecasts or to the inability of management to react accordingly to environmental evidence. One of the better examples is that of the car industry in the USA in the 1970s. Over 20 per cent of its market share had, by 1980, been lost to foreign manufacturers who produced smaller, more fuel-efficient vehicles. The American manufacturers had failed to appreciate that global political and economic conditions would lead to large increases in oil prices, and that social factors, such as greater female economic and geographic mobility, were 'conspiring' to create a preference for smaller cars. In the early 1980s, US car companies made losses in excess of \$5 billion (£3.1 billion). Japanese car manufacturers, on the other hand, had anticipated the future need for fuel-efficient cars with lower servicing costs or, as many commentators have argued, they planted the idea in consumers' minds.

At best, assessing the potential impact of likely changes in the environment offers organizations an advantage over their competitors by enabling decision makers to narrow the range of options. Measures will always entail some element of subjectivity, if only in the processes involved in collecting the data. The accuracy and, therefore, the value of such forecasts will often depend on the 'richness' of data, itself a product of managers' choice of communication media. Boyd *et al.* (1993) argue that 'richness' is a product of the speed of feedback, the variety of communication channels utilized and the 'personalness' of the information. Nevertheless, it is clear that in a dynamic and complex business environment attempting to forecast sometimes discontinuous trends is fraught with difficulty. One need only look at the frequent inaccuracies of United Kingdom Treasury predictions of medium-term inflation and GDP growth despite that agency's 'closeness' to the economy and privileged access to data. However, to do nothing is also a dangerous course of action for an organization as is over-reliance upon internal sources of information rather than external channels. It is quite possible, in such circumstances, that a state of inertia could set in which would ill-equip organizations to make accurate forecasts of changes in the environment, which may in turn lead to poor quality decision making and organizational under-performance.

Approach to forecasting

Peace and Robinson (1994) suggest that strategic managers need to take a step-by-step approach to forecasting. Their model outlines five steps:

1. Selection of environmental variables that are critical to the organization.
2. Selection of sources of information about those variables.
3. Evaluation of forecasting techniques.
4. Integration of the results of forecasting into the strategic management process.
5. Monitoring and evaluation of the critical aspects of these forecasts.

Some variables may be so obviously important to the well-being of the organization that they become, in a sense, self-selecting. For example, a company which smelts aluminium will be concerned about likely changes in the price of electricity as this forms a major cost in the production process. Other variables will be identified, usually by senior managers with experience in the organization and within the sector. However, it is critical to select variables that may be important in the future and not just rely on those which have been critical in the past. It is not a difficult task to select the key variables, although a little lateral thinking may prove useful. It is likely that you could select many key variables for each of the case study organizations at the end of this book. In order to keep the list of variables manageable it is recommended that you omit factors that have little chance of occurring.

There are numerous sources of information about the business environment. These include government statistics and forecasts regarding economic variables such as inflation and growth rates, research findings estimating changes in commodity prices, informed opinions on political, social or technological changes, and so forth. A considerable amount of information is merely 'picked up' by managers keeping their eyes and ears open and continually scanning their business environment for opportunities or threats resulting from imminent change. Although quantitative measures of environmental variables carry a certain credibility it is likely that more judgemental and subjective approaches prove more practical and even more accurate. You will note from our discussion of perceptual filters that subjectivity impinges on all human activity, not least upon the manager when sensing changes in the business environment.

Forecasting techniques

Using sophisticated computer techniques and relying primarily on numerical data, some companies and many governments attempt to model changes in the environment. These models often utilize economic data and attempt to estimate future economic variables, such as interest rates and the external value of currencies. There are many private consultancy companies that specialize in developing such models for government and commercial clients. However, as environmental stability is very much a phenomenon of the past, modelling of this type has been subject to considerable 'bad press'. Such models find environmental flux and discontinuity difficult, if not impossible, to predict.

Far less expensive to develop, and often just as accurate, are time series and judgemental models. Time series models attempt to identify trends in variables based on historical data or cyclical factors and extrapolate this into the future. For example, a simple time series model may look at the population of a country at five-year intervals over the past one hundred years then use this evidence to predict future demographic changes. This method does not, however, allow for environmental discontinuity where the 'rules' of the past no longer apply. A slightly more sophisticated model may add additional variables, such as likely changes in birth rates and predictions concerning the migration of people which may have a bearing on the population of the country in question. The resulting demographic forecasts may prove useful for strategic planners in government and some organizations.

Judgemental models are those based upon the informed opinion of people in the relevant field. For example, salesforce personnel may be asked to estimate likely future trends in sales potential taking into consideration all likely variables. Their experience 'on the ground' may prove invaluable and lead to more accurate forecasts than sophisticated modelling techniques could achieve.

Brainstorming is another common, rather creative, method of generating ideas and forecasts. Brainstorming can usefully be employed to estimate future trends in technology development, for example. A number of informed people are encouraged to generate ideas and forecasts in a group setting. Many of these ideas may appear fanciful but trends in technological development often lead to 'fanciful' outcomes! Such techniques can generate useful, judgemental, ideas about potential future events.

The Delphi method of forecasting is a more systematic technique than brainstorming. This method attempts to gain consensus among a group of people, such as a senior strategic management group. For example, a company senior management team may meet and aim to forecast their likely competitive position in five years' time. They will discuss all relevant variables and start to agree on as many points and issues as possible in an attempt to develop the most likely and most widely held 'view'. This can then be used in the strategy process.

Scenario development recognizes judgemental and non-quantitative information such as changing fashions. Scenarios are 'pictures' or 'stories' of what might be the case some time in the future. They draw upon both subjective and more objective data. Hence a company may develop two or three likely scenarios for some future date and take these into consideration in their planning process. They may develop contingency plans to cope with each scenario should it arise. The multinational oil giant, Shell, have made extensive use of scenario 'planning'.

Finally, a number of organizations and consultancies have developed 'political risk' ratings for countries around the world. These take into consideration the stability and predictability of nations and their governments, and advise commercial organizations and governments on the risks involved in overseas investment.

Impact analysis

One simple, yet effective, type of forecasting the effect of environmental changes on organizations is to conduct an impact analysis. This involves ascertaining a series of potential environmental changes and assessing the probable effect of these on a range of organizations, usually direct competitors. Table 1.5 illustrates a simple impact analysis of the heavy truck industry. The effect of a change is firstly assessed as either a positive (+) or negative (−) influence. Positive influences are those where there will be a benefit to the company financially or otherwise. Changes which may lead to strongly positive effects are given a + + or even + + + rating. The impact analysis may then involve a brief explanation of the plus/minus score.

It can be seen from the impact analysis (Table 1.5) that changes in environmental regulations will adversely affect all truck manufacturers; however, some are better prepared owing to a history of concern for such issues. A depreciation in the external value of the Swedish currency, however, will not affect all three companies in the same way. As both Volvo and Scania are Swedish

TABLE 1.5   Impact analysis in the truck industry

Environmental scenario	Scania	Leyland DAF	Volvo Trucks
Ecological Strict new European Union environmental protection legislation	– Track record in R&D on environment-friendly engines and truck design features; nevertheless changes will require extra investment	– – – Less invested in R&D in environmentally friendly technology; may require longer to 'catch up'	– – R&D expenditure on enviroment-oriented technology but without outstanding quality reputation of Scania
Economic Depreciation of the Swedish krone	++ Should reduce the cost of exported trucks and increase sales; however, it will also increase costs of imported parts	– Will have little direct effect (its trucks will be more expensive in Sweden); Swedish competitors will reduce their prices in the UK	++ Same effect as for Scania; Volvo is a Swedish company and most of its trucks are manufactured there
Political Governments enforce movement of freight to railways and restrict the use of heavy trucks	– – – Will adversely affect the sale of trucks, servicing and parts sales as Scania do not produce light trucks and vans	– Will adversely affect the sale of trucks, servicing and parts sales, but may increase the sales of smaller trucks and vans	– Volvo is protected to a degree by having sizeable market shares in motor vehicles of all sizes but heavy truck sales would suffer

owned, and most of their trucks are wholly or partly manufactured in Sweden, a fall in the external value of the krone will mean that these trucks may be less expensive in other countries. This should increase sales of both Scania and Volvo trucks and increase company profit margins.

Impact analysis enables managers or analysts to assess the effects of environmental change on an organization and upon its competitors. Clearly, where such changes are likely to adversely affect an organization more than its competitors then contingency planning needs to be considered.

QUESTIONS

1.   Select an organizational case study and identify an array of environmental variables which influence that company.
(a)   Which of these variables may management be able to forecast?
(b)   What are the likely sources of information to facilitate forecasting?
(c)   What approaches and methods of forecasting might be employed?

(d)   What would be some of the difficulties in accurately forecasting changes in these variables?

2.   Conduct an impact analysis for a sector of industry with which you are familiar.

3.   Using library and other information sources and accessing historical data, assess whether previous predictions of environmental parameters were accurate. For example, the United Nations and the OECD predict all manner of economic, technological, social and demographic trends. What are the causes of any inaccuracies?

1.4 Environmental analysis and strategic process

Strategy and structure: environmental influence

Most early organizational theory and management research assumed a largely stable business environment. Hence proponents of the Classical School and of Scientific Management argued that organizations should be machine-like and feature centralized authority, clear lines of command, specialization and the division of labour and numerous rules and regulations. However, such mechanized and bureaucratic organizations, typified by hierarchical structures and a fervent adherence to the power-control role of management, are poorly suited to dynamic and complex environments. By the 1940s in North America, and increasingly so in Europe, the deficiencies of the 'classical' organization became apparent. Technological changes, increasingly complex markets and social, political and cultural changes created new demands on organizations which many were ill-equipped to manage. Although many of the basic principles identified by classical management theorists, such as Fayol and Taylor, remain entrenched within many 'modern' organizations, other environmentally sensitive changes have occurred. The Human Relations School (late 1930s onwards), typified by the work of Chester Barnard and landmark studies by the Tavistock Institute, together with the Hawthorne studies, signalled change. In the search for greater effectiveness and flexibility within organizations, emphasis has shifted towards the consideration of 'people' issues such as motivation and leadership. A better motivated and well-led workforce will prove to be more flexible and capable of coping with environmental change and complexity.

A study of electronics companies in the United Kingdom by Burns and Stalker (1961) attempted to establish why some companies were able to cope with changes in their environment – specifically dynamism in their product markets – while others were inept in this regard. They argued that successful innovators had developed an 'organic' structure while those with 'mechanistic' structures were less able to adapt. Lawrence and Lorsch (1967) found a similar relationship between the business environment and the internal structure of the firm in the

United States. They differed in one respect from earlier researchers: they did not believe that organizations or their environments were uniform or unchanging, and postulated that the more turbulent and complex the environment the greater the degree of difference between sub-parts of the organization. Hence, they argued that successful companies were those that developed appropriate degrees of differentiation between specialist departments while simultaneously promoting integration calling on common goals.

In environments that are certain and stable, organizations will tend to develop a form and structure which is most efficient in relation to that environment – probably one with a high degree of managerial control and mechanistic structures and systems. If an organization's environment is uncertain and complex, managers design structures with greater in-built flexibility. However, perception may play a part in this process; that is, managers in organizations which have an organic structure may perceive the environment as being dynamic and uncertain, while those in more mechanistic structures may perceive their environment as being more certain, yet the reality may be quite different. Nevertheless, the company graveyard contains many firms whose managers 'perceived' their environment as being stable and certain when in fact it harboured destructive dynamic forces.

There has been considerable research in more recent years concerning the relationship between groups of organizations and their collective environment. Grinyer and Spender (1979), for example, argued that organizations in a particular industry sector, such as the motor vehicle industry or the higher education sector, have a tendency to develop 'recipe knowledge' about how to operate in that business. This recipe knowledge influences their collective view of the industry environment. They argue, however, that companies who continually develop their recipe knowledge in line with changes in the environment are likely to succeed and prosper at the expense of their more sluggish competitors. These organizations are not imprisoned by the recipe.

As argued in the section above on environmental forecasting, it is often suggested that the success of commercial firms depends on their ability to foresee and subsequently act upon environmental information. Miles and Snow (1978) have identified various types of organization which possess quite different capabilities and motivations in this respect. Their typology of organizations refers to the 'style' in which they operate strategically. This style influences their relationship with the business environment and is, in turn, influenced by that environment. Hence 'defender' organizations, they argue, attempt to create a stable environment which suits their non-dynamic structure and strategy, while 'prospectors' view their environment as ever-changing and seek continual strategic and structural adjustments to cope with those changes. They are continually searching for new opportunities and in the process may create change and uncertainty for others within their competitive environment. They identify two other categories of organization, 'analysers' and 'reactors'. The former are capable of acting in both stable and unstable environments; a quality of considerable value.

'Reactors' act only when environmental change 'forces' them to do so. They are not 'proactive' organizations. Boyd *et al.* (1993) state that 'given these differences in internal versus external focus, one would expect a greater potential for environmental misperception among defenders or reactors, relative to analysers'.

All four types of organization, it is argued, 'enact' or create their environment. What they choose to see and how they choose to interpret that environment is unique to each organization. Hence a defender may view ostensibly the same environment as a prospector yet see stability and continuity all around, while the prospector sees only change and opportunity. Clearly each organization filters data to suit its own capabilities and concerns. As such, executives selectively misinterpret aspects of their environment. These filters include individual manager's cognitive processes, organizational culture and politics, other group or team factors and the strategic orientation of the organization. Therefore, as stated above, it is quite possible for two organizations to view the same environmental change as either a glorious opportunity for growth and prosperity or, depending on their perception, a catastrophe threatening organizational survival.

More recently the development of Chaos Theory has stressed that because of the unpredictability and constant flux which characterizes the business environment, organizational structure and strategy need to be fundamentally reappraised. This interesting development is further developed in the final chapter of this book.

Strategic planning

The strategic planning process in organizations is the subject of considerable attention in the field of business and management. The academic and, increasingly, the practitioner worlds are engaged in lively debate over issues such as the nature of strategy formulation. To put it rather simplistically, there are two broad schools of thought: the rationalist and the subjectivist approaches.

The rationalist approach argues (although, to be fair, often only as a pedagogic framework) that strategic planning is, or certainly should be, undertaken in a logical and largely linear fashion. It is suggested that organizations monitor their business environment and analyse their internal resource position in order to assess what strengths and weaknesses they have which might facilitate the exploitation of environmental opportunities and the avoidance of environmental threats. A stakeholder analysis is also important at this stage.

PEST analysis, or the many variants upon it described above, is usually undertaken within organizations as a prelude to a more strategically orientated technique – a SWOT, which stands for Strengths, Weaknesses, Opportunities and Threats. As part of a strategic process of analysis an organization may assess its strengths and weaknesses from an internal resource perspective. For example, it may conclude that it is in a sound financial state and that it utilizes modern, effective technology. However, its weaknesses may, for example, be an under-trained and poorly motivated staff.

The latter two elements of the SWOT acronym are of particular relevance here, for the business environment is where both opportunities and threats can be found. As a vital strategic tool, businesses often attempt to identify such opportunities that they may seek to exploit and threats that they attempt to avoid.

Similarly, a popular, primarily pedagogic, model suggests that the initial stages of strategy formulation lie in gaining an appreciation of the degree of uncertainty in the organization's environment. This is proceeded by an audit of environmental influences. The strategic planner then conducts a structural analysis of the immediate competitive environment of the organization before analysing the organization's strategic position (Johnson and Scholes, 1993). Johnson and Scholes explain that, 'the aim of such analysis is to develop an understanding of opportunities which can be built upon and threats which have to be overcome ...'. Organizations can then adapt to their environment and by actively managing environmental relationships can, in turn, shape the changes that are occurring. The task of rational strategic management in this scenario involves reading the environment and then 'creating initiatives that will resonate with the changes that are occurring' (Morgan, 1989).

Senior management generate a series of strategic options from which choices are later made after due analysis and consideration of all parameters. The chosen strategies are then implemented.

Thus it is assumed that actual or predicted changes in the environment lead to planned strategic change in organizations. Strategic planning, therefore, is an attempt to match organizational capabilities with environmental opportunities. Hence the dominant paradigm is that organizations are in a state of 'dynamic equilibrium' continually adapting to their environment. These planning activities, it is argued, are essential if organizations are to cope with environmental dynamism.

Strategic planning often tends to adopt a three- to five-year time scale during which time the business environment of most organizations will alter significantly. However, it should be mentioned that proponents of the rational approach do stress the need for 'reality embellishments' such as feedback loops (for example, to enable further environmental scanning to influence decisions at a later stage) and consideration of the role of organizational culture, politics and other contextual, non-rational, issues in the planning process.

This argument brings us to an alternative perspective on strategy formulation. These alternative views are often based both on empirical research and intuitive judgement and attempt to explain the actual processes that take place in organizations. They tend to be less prescriptive. As argued above, organizations are not entirely rational or logical in their environmental sensing or decision-making processes. Organization level filters of an intensely 'human' nature disrupt mechanical linear planning processes, influence the nature and quality of information available and severely limit the range of strategic choices likely to be entertained. They also add an inescapable richness and reality to organizational activity. It is rather pointless to assume, as some traditional rational models imply, that organizational culture, politics and other human processes can, somehow, be easily managed, ignored or prevented from fundamentally influencing organizational activity.

Hamel and Prahalad (1989), in a study of numerous organizations in Europe, America and Japan, question the almost taken-for-granted assumption that successful organizations adapt or seek to 'fit' their environment. They argue that firms that do seek adaption to their environment are prone to imitation and repetition as competitors do likewise. Many successful organizations use resources more creatively and challenge environmental assumptions. They are able to influence the environment of their competitors and, in part at least, create their own environment. This process, referred to as 'enactment', is discussed above. However, the simple rational model of strategic planning pays little attention to the notion of enactment or the way in which organizations influence their business environment.

We have argued above that organizations and individuals enact their environment and may view similar information in quite different ways. This is a non-rational process. When we make this assumption we suggest that environments are not fixed and measurable in a strict sense. They are ever-changing and open to multiple interpretations. Additionally, internal processes of strategic planning are not as the Rationalist School would suggest. Often crucial business decisions are based on very limited data, moulded by personal considerations or cultural norms and implemented by political expediency. Some organizations will have sophisticated planning departments, others will be strategically 'led' by a dominant stakeholder such as the managing director. There is not a great deal of evidence to suggest that one style is a guarantee of greater success than the other.

Although interesting, this subject is complex. You are very likely to investigate it in further detail if you are engaged on a structured business or management course which leads to considerations of strategic management or corporate policy. It is, however, wise at this stage to appreciate the arguments of both schools of thought and develop a broad understanding of organizational processes and academic debates.

Chapter 9 explores the essential nature of the business environment in more detail, continuing many of the debates above. It argues that rapid and sometimes discontinuous change calls for major alterations in strategic planning processes and demands organizational flexibility.

QUESTIONS

1. What is the relationship between the degree of uncertainty in the business environment and organizational structure? Attempt to explain this relationship.

2. What is an organic structure? How might an organic structure make an organization more able to cope with environmental change and with product innovation?

CONCLUSION

Having set the scene and defined the parameters within which we will study the business environment, this book now takes a closer look at the individual environmental forces which influence organizations. Chapters 2–7 run through the LE PEST C forces while Chapter 8 focuses on the somewhat unique aspects of the public sector environment which is so often neglected in business environment texts. Each chapter will explore the forces at play and the implications of these for organizations. The final chapter revisits many of the themes discussed above and further develops and explores them, focusing in particular on the influence of the business environment on organizations, individuals, groups and governments. The case studies at the end of the text support this material.

SUMMARY OF MAIN POINTS

This chapter has aimed to 'set the scene' on the business environment and to delineate the scope of this book. A number of vital issues and concepts have been covered. The key points are:

- There are a number of interrelated forces acting upon organizations which emanate from the external environment of the organization.
- For the purpose of analysis, these forces can be placed in distinct categories but in reality they form an interrelated and complex whole.
- Environmental forces act at a number of geo-political scales.
- The relationship between organization and environment is not clear-cut as information flows from the environment to the organization but also from the organization to the environment.
- There are a variety of types of organization which can be differentiated by, for example, their prime objectives or their legal status. The environment influences different types of organization in different ways.
- Individual perception and organizational filters influence how the business environment is viewed.
- Forecasting the business environment is problematic due to change and complexity, yet many methods exist and are widely used.
- There is a relationship between the business environment and both the structure and strategy of organizations.
- There is considerable debate concerning the nature and process of strategic policy formulation, but an understanding of the business environment is essential for successful strategic management.

References

Bourgeois, L.J. (1985) 'Strategic goals, perceived uncertainty and economic performance in volatile environments', *Academy of Management Review*, vol. 28, pp. 548–73.

Boyd, B.K., Dess, G. and Rasheed, A.M.A. (1993) 'Divergence between archival and perceptual measures of the environment: causes and consequences', *Academy of Management Review*, vol. 18, no. 2, pp. 204–26.

Burns, T. and Stalker, G.M. (1961) *The Management of Innovation*, Tavistock, London.

Daft, R.L. (1992) *Organisational Theory and Design*, West Publishing.

Dill, W.R. (1958) 'Environment as an influence on managerial autonomy', *Administrative Science Quarterly*, vol. 2, pp. 409–43.

Grinyer, P. and Spender, J.C. (1979) 'Recipes, crises and adaption in mature businesses', *International Studies of Management & Organisation*, vol. 9, p. 13

Hamel, G. and Prahalad, C.K. (1989) 'Strategic intent', *Harvard Business Review*, May–June, pp. 63–76.

Hamel, G. and Prahalad, C.K. (1994) *Competing for the Future*, Harvard Business Press, Boston.

Huber, G.P. (1985) 'Temporal stability and response-order biases in participant descriptions of organizational decisions', *Academy of Management Journal*, vol. 28, pp. 943–50.

Johnson, J. and Scholes, K. (1993) *Exploring Corporate Strategy: Text and Cases* (3rd edn), Prentice Hall, Hemel Hempstead.

Lawrence, P.R. and Lorsch, J.W. (1967) *Organisation and Environment*, Harvard Graduate School of Business Administration, Cambridge, MA.

Mansfield, R. (1990) 'Conceptualizing and managing the organizational environment', in D.C. Wilson and R.H. Rosenfield (1990) *Managing Organizations: Texts, Readings and Cases*, McGraw-Hill, London.

Miles, R.E. and Snow, C.C. (1978) *Organizational Strategy, Structure and Process*, McGraw-Hill, New York.

Miller, D. (1988) 'Relating Porter's business strategies to environment and structure', *Academy of Management Journal*, vol. 31, pp. 280–308.

Morgan, G. (1989) *Creative Organisational Theory: A Resourcebook*, Sage.

Peace, J.A. and Robinson, R.B. (1994) *Strategic Management: Formulation, Implementation and Control* (5th edn), Irwin, Chicago.

Robbins, S.P. (1992) *Essentials of Organisational Behaviour* (3rd edn), Prentice Hall, Hemel Hempstead.

Smircich, L. and Stubbart, C. (1985) 'Strategic management in an enacted environment', *Academy of Management Review*, vol. 10, no. 4, pp. 724–36

Weick, K. (1979) *The Social Psychology of Organizing*, Addison Wesley, Reading, Mass.

Wilson, D.C. (1992) *A Strategy of Change*, Routledge.

CHAPTER 2
THE COMPETITIVE ENVIRONMENT

Jamie Weatherston

 LEARNING OUTCOMES

On completion of this chapter you should be able to:

- recognize the difficulties that businesses face in a dynamic and changing competitive environment;
- understand the traditional microeconomic view of competition and be aware of the structure–conduct–performance paradigm;
- understand the classification of markets and appreciate how competition in markets differs;
- be aware of the factors on which competition is based;
- understand and be able to use some of the tools and models of competitive analysis;
- be familiar with the role of government and regulatory authorities in the market at different geo-political scales;
- be aware of the public interest aspect of market activities.

2.1 Introduction

In this chapter we will seek to identify the competitive environment and determine how its dynamic nature affects both the level of competition that an organization faces and the future profitability of organizations. It has been suggested by Thompson and Strickland (1995) that when crafting an organization's strategy one of the major tasks facing decision makers is an assessment of the company's external environment, in particular the industry and competitive conditions in which the organization operates. The structural characteristics of an industry play a key role in determining the nature and intensity of competition within it (Grant, 1995). Using the traditional microeconomic approach we will outline the basic economic problem, the approach of economic systems to that problem and examine how resources are allocated in differing economies. We will identify the conditions that determine the level of complexity in a market and investigate each of the market structures to which these conditions apply. An exploration of market structures and an understanding of the differences between the structures presented by economists provide a useful starting point for this analysis.

Organizations will always attempt to reduce the dynamism and uncertainty of the market in which they trade. Many tactics, both fair and foul, can be employed in this endeavour. A major part of this chapter will be devoted to the identification and analysis of the tactics displayed. The huge sums of money that some organizations invest in research and development and advertising may be necessary to maintain the organization's position in the market and raise a barrier to prevent others from entering that market. Other activities, for example entering into agreements that restrict competition, may have a similar effect. This type of collusive activity may be against the interests of consumers. If that is the case then regulatory authorities need to become involved. We will examine the role and the activities of these bodies at various geo-political levels. The concept of contestable markets will provide the reader with an additional interpretation of the market.

Michael Porter's (1980) structural analysis of competitive forces (the five-forces model) establishes the factors which determine industry profitability and competitiveness. This model originates from the traditional approach and provides a useful basis from which strategists can begin to build a picture of their competitive position. Competitor analysis can also be used in conjunction with the five-forces model to create a more in-depth analysis of the position. Throughout the chapter we will be identifying the tools and techniques which are needed to carry out an investigation of the competitive environment. The starting point for our analysis is the traditional economic view.

2.2 The traditional economic view

The basic economic problem is how to allocate scarce resources among the almost limitless wants of consumers in society. Choices have to be made about what and how to produce and for whom goods and services should be produced.

An examination of the theory as it applies to two theoretical types of economy is useful: that is, the command economy and the market economy.

The command economy

In a command economy the questions of allocation are answered by the state. The state decides on the volume of production, the types of goods and services produced, the type of work each citizen will do, the ways in which they will be rewarded, the level of pollution control and many other aspects of life. Individual citizens must accept a large measure of direction in their daily life.

The market economy and the price mechanism

The market economy is at the other end of the spectrum. Within this system the consumer is 'king'. Choices made by consumers directly affect the allocation of resources in the economy. Consumers aim to gain the maximum 'utility', or satisfaction, from the goods that they purchase, and are therefore concerned about the price they have to pay for items they consume. They express their choices by the prices they are willing to pay for goods.

In the market economy firms choose the methods by which to produce goods and services. They are concerned, primarily, with the costs of making their products or providing their service and the revenues they receive. In this situation firms aim for the greatest return on their investment.

Ideally, the price mechanism allows people to buy what they want, subject to income constraints. The nature and quantity of what is produced will be influenced by consumer preference, expressed through buying behaviour. The ways in which goods are produced will be decided by competition between producers who will seek to produce at lowest cost. The number of people who are able to buy the goods and services will also be decided by the market. Those whose specialist services are in greatest demand will receive the greatest rewards, in terms of wages, and so have the greatest buying power. This mechanism registers people's preferences and transmits them to the firms who produce the goods for consumers to buy.

The consumer is central to the system via the operation of supply and demand. Demand influences price and price influences supply; therefore, demand influences supply. (A full analysis of demand and supply is given in Chapter 6.) Ultimately the use of scarce factors of production – that is, land, labour and capital – is dictated by the demands or wants of individuals. When consumers want more of a good than is being supplied, price increases, resources are attracted to the industry and supply expands. When demand falls the opposite effect occurs. There is obviously a time lag involved in the operation of the price mechanism. The speed of the effect varies depending on the situation. In a manufacturing context it is very difficult to transfer production quickly from one good to another in response to a change in consumer demand, because of the specific nature of machinery or the need to retrain labour.

The traditional microeconomic view of competition concentrates on the role of market structures in the market economy.

A market is a set of arrangements by which buyers and sellers are in contact to exchange goods and services. (Begg *et al.*, 1994)

This view is based on the structure–conduct–performance (s–c–p) paradigm which

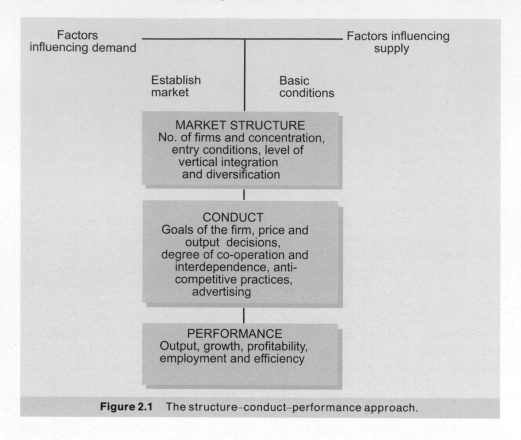

Figure 2.1   The structure–conduct–performance approach.

tells us that demand and supply establish the basic conditions of the market. This, in turn, prescribes the market structure, conduct of the organization in the market and its performance, for example its turnover and profit (see Figure 2.1).

Readers may be unfamiliar with economic theories relating business activity to market structure. As competition is based on these theories it is necessary to have an understanding of some of the concepts raised by microeconomics.

Economists distinguish between various types of market which are classified into four general types: perfectly competitive, monopoly, oligopoly, and monopolistic competition. The classification and correspondingly the level of competition is based largely on:

- the nature of the product that is supplied, which in turn is determined by demand and cost conditions facing the market;
- the number and concentration of firms in the market;
- market entry conditions including the existence of barriers to entry and the level of information available to firms and customers.

We will now look at each of these factors.

The nature of the product or service

It is important to differentiate between the product or service offered as its nature will affect competition. It is usual to distinguish between homogeneous (the same sort) and heterogeneous (different sorts) products.

If a number of organizations are selling an identical or homogeneous product then the ability of producers to set the price of that product is reduced. One small grocer is constrained in the price that can be charged for a litre of pasteurized milk by prices charged by other small grocers in the locality. Competitive behaviour is limited because the individual organization has no market power. If the product is differentiated in some way, for example if the grocer was also the supplier of goat's milk or flavoured milks, then the seller has an increased ability to decide the price, and other aspects of competition, because the product is differentiated.

This ability to differentiate products is recognized as essential and is used widely by organizations. Marketing is an important differentiating tool that is effective in promoting brand image. Brand recognition and customer loyalty are often important advantages possessed by incumbents. The car industry produces heterogeneous products since each model is different, though each still has the fundamental characteristics that distinguish it as a car. Even if different models look very similar it may be possible for manufacturers to create a difference through marketing. The world market for soap powders is dominated by two companies, Procter & Gamble (P&G) and Unilever. They do not sell only one homogeneous product each, but have a range of differentiated products, targeted at particular segments of the market. This process of differentiation has increased recently. From 1937 to 1980 P&G launched only seven new fabric washing products onto the market. This compares with the introduction of fourteen new lines from 1989 to 1994. The effect of this upsurge of launch activity was to further fragment the market. In both of the industries above, because organizations have the power over their market, it is inevitable that they will compete actively with each other in all respects.

This aspect will be considered in more detail when looking at the market for goods and services below.

Number of firms and concentration

If there is just one organization in the market then there is no competition. That organization is a monopolist and capable of making substantial profits. BT's monopoly position in the telecommunications market has allowed it to make enormous profits since privatization, reaching over £2.5 billion in both 1993/94 and 1994/95, despite having to meet substantial redundancy costs. The level of profit from its activities in the home market has increased BT's ability to compete in international markets, utilizing its size in an extremely competitive environment. As the number of organizations in the market rises, competition increases and the ability of organizations to protect their profits declines. Hamburger stalls at any festival or sporting event, or ice-cream sellers on a beach, for example, face intense competition as consumer choice is multiplied.

It is not only the number of organizations that decides the extent of competition in a market. The level of concentration also affects the nature of competition. Concentration measures the share that the largest companies have of the total market output and reveals the extent of the domination by those large companies. Market concentration can be measured by the concentration ratio (CR).

> *The n-firm concentration ratio is the market*
> *share of the n largest firms in an industry.*

Let us take an example of an industry with a turnover of £50 million where the five largest organizations have a combined share of £35 million. The concentration ratio of the five largest organizations is the output of the five largest firms divided by the total market, that is

$$35/50 \times 100 = 70\%.$$

The five firm concentration ratio is 70 per cent, that is CR5 70.

The most commonly used measures are the four- or five-firm concentration ratio. Table 2.1 denotes two hypothetical five-firm concentration ratio (CR5) calculations, one representing the cigarette industry and one the shoe industry in the United Kingdom.

In this example the five biggest organizations in the cigarette industry have 84 per cent of sales (CR5 84). In the shoe industry the top five firms account for only 7 per cent of the market (CR5 7).

TABLE 2.1 Concentration ratio

Cigarette manufacturers	Sales (£m)	Shoe manufacturers	Sales (£m)
Joggy PLC	300	Sole Ltd	4.2
Hobby PLC	270	Heel Ltd	3.8
Lobby PLC	195	Tongue Ltd	3.5
Groggy PLC	170	Instep Ltd	2.9
Smoggy PLC	120	Toe Ltd	2.0
Top 5 sales	1055	Top 5 sales	16.4
Other firms	200	Other firms	200.0
Industry sales	1255	Industry sales	216.4

Five firm concentration ratios:

Cigarette manufacturers	1055/1255 = 84%
Shoe manufacturers	16.4/216.4 = 7.6%

The concentration ratio should give an indication of the amount of competition within an industry. Industries with low concentration ratios, shoes in this case, may be more competitive because each organization is competing with similarly sized rivals. No one organization in this market wields more market power than the others. It is also apparent that the less concentrated an industry, the lower the barriers to entry (and vice versa). If there are few barriers to entry then new organizations can enter the market relatively easily and capture market share. This effectively increases competitive pressures in that industry. (See below for further explanation of barriers to entry.)

Alternatively, a high concentration ratio may indicate a smaller degree of competition, as in the cigarette industry where, because of fewer organizations in the market, it should be possible for each organization to protect its share. This is particularly likely to occur if the market is still growing. We will analyse this in more detail when looking at the market for goods and services.

Evidence suggests that market concentration increased sharply until the 1970s, since when there has been little change in most sectors. One sector which has seen substantial change in market concentration is that of building societies, where merger activity and the abandonment of mutual status is ongoing.

The number of organizations and their concentration is not the only important factor to consider when analysing an organization's competitive position. Table 2.2 shows two markets, each with a CR5 80. In market A the second largest organization has a market share of just 44 per cent of that of the largest organization. In market B the second largest organization is much closer in size, and the rest of the market is more evenly distributed among the top five. The competitive nature of these markets is likely to be very different, even though the CR5 is identical.

The CR3, that is the market share of the top three producers, in the United Kingdom cigarette market was estimated in 1994 to be 90. If this concentration ratio is used as the only measure it would be inferred that the UK cigarette market was not particularly competitive. However, this could not be further from the truth. The concentration of a market is only one indicator which should be appraised in conjunction with others when assessing the competitiveness of a market. These examples illustrate a basic problem with the concentration ratio measure, that it gives no information about inequality or the relative market share within the group of organizations selected.

TABLE 2.2   Relative size within a market

Firm	Market A	Market B
1	43	23
2	19	16
3	10	16
4	5	13
5	3	12

Herfindahl–Hirschman Index (HHI)

An alternative indicator which attempts to overcome the problem of the concentration ratio measure is used in the United States where concentration and market dominance are measured by the Herfindahl–Hirschman Index (HHI). This measure is used by regulatory authorities in the USA, particularly when considering merger activity.

The HHI measures not only the number of organizations in the market but also the inequality between them, in terms of market share. A score of over 1800 points on the HHI represents a highly concentrated market. A merger which creates a market with this level of concentration will raise concerns (Fishwick, 1993).

The 1992 US guidelines specify that the score on the post-merger HHI has to be less than 1000 for the merger not to have an adverse effect on competition in the market.

In 1993 the US cigarette market scored 2900 on the HHI, thus representing a highly concentrated and competitive market, with no room for merger activity. Clearly, the impression that is conveyed using the HHI is more accurate than that given by the CR3, described in the United Kingdom example above. Yet it is doubtful that the UK cigarette market differs greatly from that of the United States in terms of the level of competition.

Market entry conditions

Many markets present severe barriers to entry to prospective competitors while in others barriers are almost non-existent. It is clearly easier to open a small restaurant than to establish a Formula One racing team! The barriers in each case are very different. Barriers to entry can be categorized into two groups, so-called innocent barriers and those deliberately erected to prevent entrants.

Barriers erected deliberately

In some cases incumbents may take action to restrict entry. This could involve increasing expenditure on R&D, the introduction of new technology, advertising or by rewarding customers through fidelity rebates. Barriers founded on reputation – for example, the use of predatory pricing which lowers the price paid by the consumer – can be very effective in making new entrants think twice about the attractiveness of the market. Brand proliferation, as has happened in the soap powder market (see above), also acts as a barrier to entry. Multiple brands, produced by the same manufacturer, compete against each other but also present an effective barrier to new products. It is difficult for a new entrant to establish a large market niche with only one product.

Unilever raised strategic barriers in the United Kingdom ice-cream market by providing freezers free of charge to shops who stocked their brands. Retailers could only store Unilever products in those freezers; competitors were 'frozen out'.

Innocent barriers

Innocent barriers arise when an organization has absolute cost advantages. In this case the incumbent organization is able to produce at such a cost that it is uneconomical for another organization to try to enter the market because its unit costs are, in comparison, much higher. The unit cost is the cost of producing one unit of output. In this situation organizations are said to benefit from economies of scale.

   Barriers to entry will be investigated in more detail below.

Economies of scale

Figure 2.2 shows that average costs per unit of production fall as output rises (average cost is total cost divided by output, i.e. TC/O). Costs fall, not at a uniform rate but at a declining rate, producing the typical U-shaped long-run average cost curve. When the curve becomes horizontal this output is known as the minimum efficient scale of production (MES), in this case 80 million units per year. In some industries economies of scale are substantial, for example in telecommunications and car manufacture.

   If the MES is large in relation to the total market demand, then it will be almost impossible for a new entrant to enter the market successfully. An organization trying to enter the industry at lower levels of output, e.g. 30 million units per year, would be at a severe cost disadvantage to the incumbents (see

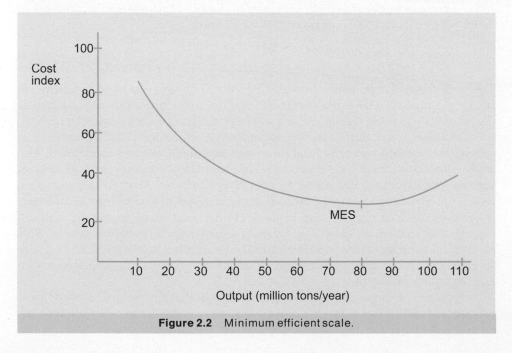

Figure 2.2   Minimum efficient scale.

Figure 2.2). The price that the new entrant would have to charge to break even would be much higher than the incumbent organizations that are experiencing economies of scale, and so it would be very difficult for the new organization to attract customers.

The possibility of successful entry into the market is slim, unless the organization were able to target a particular segment of the market that is regarded as unimportant by the incumbents. The new entrant would still face a tough struggle as it would be a formidable task to establish a brand image and customer recognition over a very narrow product range. Japanese motorbike manufacturers Honda, Yamaha, Suzuki and Kawasaki managed to achieve this when they entered the American and United Kingdom motorbike markets, selling only small-capacity machines. The incumbents in the market did not realize the subtle changes that were occurring. Rather than operating in a secure, stable, national market, protected from competition by the high costs of transportation and communication or by the ignorance of foreign companies, they were now in an international market competing against knowledgeable and efficient overseas rivals. The result of this inability to recognize change resulted in the almost total collapse of motorcycle manufacture in Europe and America (see Honda mini case in this chapter). The only survivor was the Italian industry which was protected by government protectionist measures. Global competition can wipe out previously concrete advantages. Organizations need to be able to respond to change quickly if they are to survive in the fiercely competitive global market.

It is not only economies of scale that confer advantages on organizations. We can use the experience curve phenomenon to further illustrate how advantages of incumbency can accrue to organizations (see Figure 2.3).

Experience curve

The experience curve effect provides additional insight into the problems of entering a market. The experience curve was first described and popularized by the Boston Consulting Group (BCG), an American consultancy company, in 1968.

BCG observed, during studies of company performance, that incumbents in any market segment benefited from the experience that they had accumulated. The study showed a direct and constant relationship between aggregate growth in volume of production and declining cost of production. That is, as production volume increased the company became more efficient at producing the product, the cost per unit of that production therefore declined. At first cost per unit fell rapidly and then more slowly as learning opportunities were exhausted. This resulted in a progressively declining gradient exhibited in the experience curve (Figure 2.3). It has been claimed that costs fall by around 15 to 30 per cent with each doubling of output.

Experience curve savings are particularly important if price levels for a product are relatively similar, because what makes a company more profitable than its competitors is the level of its costs. If an organization can increase output

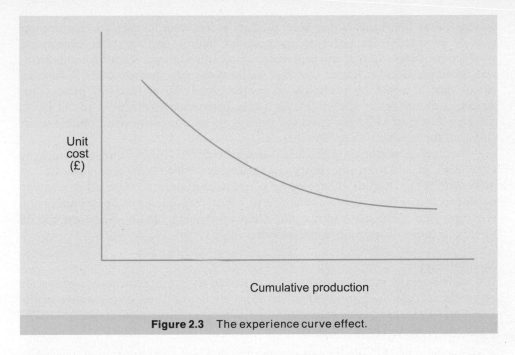

Figure 2.3   The experience curve effect.

relative to its competitors then it will move down the experience curve more quickly, reducing costs, and thus widening cost differentials.

BCG put forward three reasons why this fall in unit costs may occur. These were due to learning, specialization and economies of scale. We have examined the last of these reasons above and will explore the first two here.

Learning
It is important to understand that organizations as well as individuals learn. As tasks are undertaken more frequently individuals can learn and become more proficient at their work. Labour costs should decline. Similarly, an organization should be able to learn and put in place efficient systems and procedures which should also translate into cost savings. Learning is likely to be the most important component in the experience curve for organizations in high technology industries. Maintenance of learning and its conversion into organizational knowledge is a key element of competitive advantage for many high-tech companies. Japanese companies have been at the forefront of the global learning process, adapting American philosophy of total quality management and advancing the ideas. This has led to the development of 'quality circles', 'kaizen' or continuous improvement, 'just-in-time manufacturing', 'right first time, every time' and many more management techniques which some Western companies are still coming to terms with.

Mansfield (1994) illustrated this point by reference to Texas Instruments, a major producer in the highly competitive global markets for semiconductor chips and other electronic products. When the semiconductor industry was relatively young, Texas Instruments priced its product at less than its then current average cost of production in order to increase its output and its total cumulative production. Believing that the experience curve, through the learning component, was relatively steep, it hoped that this would reduce its average costs to such an extent that it would be profitable to produce and sell at this low price. This strategy was extremely successful. As Texas Instruments continued to cut price, its rivals began to withdraw from the market, its output continued to increase, its costs fell further, and its profits increased.

Boeing's domination of the world aircraft market is in part due to learning by experience, gained from early entry into the market, which has been translated into more efficient operations. That Boeing's dominant position in the market seems to be under threat may, in turn, be due to other manufacturers, particularly the relatively young European competitor Airbus Industrie, having closed the gap on Boeing in terms of learning and experience.

Specialization

It usually becomes increasingly possible to design narrow and focused jobs as scale of production grows. Ford's car plants were at the forefront of this move in the 1920s and 1930s. Increasing specialization through the division of labour should bring advantages. These are summarized by Beardshaw (1992):

- increase in skill and dexterity means the task can be carried out more expertly;
- time saving through reducing down time, the time in which a worker is idle, and the time saved on training;
- individual aptitudes can be utilized so that individuals can concentrate on what they do best;
- machinery can be further utilized – modern production techniques, starting with the Ford Motor Company's own production line, are able to make full use of machinery because of specialization of the workforce;
- breaking down the process into separate tasks allows for closer management control.

The ease of entry into a market is probably the major force influencing competition. If organizations can enter a market at relatively little cost then entry will occur. Various strategies, as we have seen, are available to organizations that enable them to construct barriers that prospective competitors find difficult to overcome. One of the main deterrents to organizations entering a market is the risk of losing valuable funds in the venture. We explore this further by examining the contestable market approach below.

At this stage it is useful to undertake a closer examination of the market for goods and services. As in the business world very few organizations operate within perfectly competitive markets, we can concentrate our analysis on the monopolistic, oligopolistic and monopolistically competitive markets. We will draw on the ideas introduced in this section in the analysis.

QUESTIONS

1.   In what ways have car manufacturers used product differentiation to create a barrier to entry?

2.   How does concentration in a market affect its competitiveness?

3.   Using market research data, calculate the CR5 for building societies for 1985 and 1995. Comment on your findings.

4.   The single European market has been accused of creating a 'fortress Europe'. How is the European Union limiting the entry of competition from outside its boundaries? What may be the long-term impact of such a strategy?

2.3 The market for goods and services

In this section we will investigate the different competitive environment that organizations will face in monopoly, oligopoly and monopolistic competition and probe some of the issues surrounding each configuration. Table 2.3 summarizes the characteristics of these markets.

Monopoly

The economist's view

Economists view monopolists as the sole supplier of an industry's output, producing goods and services for which no substitute is available. In this extreme case a monopoly is said to have a concentration ratio of 100, it being the only organization supplying the market. Those monopolies that enjoy massive economies of scale are called natural monopolies, in this case there is only room

TABLE 2.3   Models of market structure

Characteristics	Perfect competition	Monopolistic competition	Oligopoly	Monopoly
No. and size of sellers	Many, small	Many, small	Few, large	One; no close substitutes
Type of product	Homogeneous	Differentiated	Differentiated or homogeneous	One
Entry barriers	None	None	Low, some	High
CR (%)	0	Low	High	100
Example	Fruit and vegetable markets	High street clothes retailers	Airlines, car manufacturers	Regional Water Boards (UK)

for one firm producing at minimum efficient scale – for example, water, gas and electricity suppliers. Monopolies can arise because of barriers to entry that prevent competition. These barriers may be due to actions taken by incumbents or innocent barriers. De Beers' very strong position in the supply of diamonds relies on its central selling organization controlling 80 per cent of world trade in rough diamonds.

Monopolists, because of their protected position, need not be overly concerned by the threat of new organizations entering the industry in the short or medium term.

It is possible for the monopolist to make monopoly or abnormal profits in the long run, unlike in a competitive industry where profits are eroded by new organizations entering the market. Indeed companies which hold monopoly positions, and are able to maintain large profits, are not uncommon. The utilities, privatized in the United Kingdom during the 1980s and 1990s, on the whole enjoy monopoly positions in their home market. Their annual reports are widely reported in the media, and profit announcements are often accompanied by a furore from consumer groups who are concerned that profits are being made at the expense of the consumer.

The view of the authorities

An alternative view of monopoly is employed by the competition authorities. In the United Kingdom an organization is said to be a monopoly if it has over 25 per cent of the relevant regional or national market. In 1995 Sega had a 38 per cent share of the United Kingdom combined video games console and games software market and is, by this definition, a monopoly. Its main rival, Nintendo, had a share of just under 25 per cent. Although an organization does not control the whole of the market, its market position may confer on it enormous power.

Problems associated with monopoly

Lack of competition in the market may mean that there is a danger that a monopolist can take action that may adversely affect the consumer. Results could include:

- restriction of output as the monopolist can create a shortage, depriving consumers while increasing its profits;
- price fixing as the monopolist can restrict supply to those who can afford to pay higher prices;
- regulation of terms of supply as the monopolist can impose harsh terms on consumers;
- removal of consumer choice – for example, the situation for consumers buying cars in the former communist states of Eastern Europe was dire.

The mini-case below illustrates some of these potential problems.

The video games market

Following complaints about the price of games cartridges and video games consoles, particularly from parents, the Director General of Fair Trading announced an investigation into the £500 million market in January 1994. The report, published in March 1995, found considerable evidence of anti-competitive practices.

The market is dominated by two major Japanese games companies, Sega and Nintendo. They were found to:

- be sole suppliers of games cartridges, controlled through the licensing conditions they have with software writers;
- be able to make excess profits because agreements with retailers restrict the rental and part exchange of games software;
- deter potential competitors by holding down the price of games hardware (the two companies supply 99 per cent of all games consoles used in the United Kingdom) and impede the entry of new games systems;
- operate a discriminatory pricing policy to maintain and exploit their monopoly situation.

The report recommended changes in the licensing conditions operated by the companies, in particular the control of the manufacture of games cartridges. The entry of Sony into the market in 1995, with their play station console, may add a vital competitive element.

Because monopolists may try to manipulate the market against the wishes of the consumer, it is necessary for other forms of control to be applied to the market.

Control of monopoly power

The imposition of strict controls provides a challenge to the monopolist's position and its ability to make profits. Control of monopoly can take a number of forms. In an effort to limit the dangers of monopoly power many monopolies have to be regulated by the government or its agencies. Control of monopolies is not only the province of national government but is increasingly coming under a higher tier of control, that of the European Union. The main regulating body in the United Kingdom is the Monopolies and Mergers Commission (MMC), founded over forty years ago. References are made to the MMC by either the Secretary of State for Trade and Industry (sometimes known as the President of the Board of Trade) or the Director General of Fair Trading.

In the United Kingdom the privatizations of the 1980s and 1990s also spawned the growth of regulatory bodies such as OFTEL, OFGAS, OFFER, to provide a framework to control those newly privatized monopolies. (Further examination of this can be found in Chapter 8.)

References to the MMC can be made on a number of counts. Mergers are subject to an investigation if they involve 25 per cent or more market share, or the takeover of assets valued at £30 million or over. Other areas of activity that could necessitate referral include:

- newspaper mergers;
- general references – involving general practices in an industry;
- restrictive labour practices;
- competition references – involving anti-competitive practices of individual organizations;
- public sector references – the regulator, in the case of the privatized industries, has the power to refer to the MMC;
- functions under the Broadcasting Act 1990.

Between March 1989 and March 1992 the MMC published 74 reports, 34 of which had adverse findings (MMC, 1992). The MMC has to determine whether the referred monopoly or proposed merger operates against the public interest and recommend action to ensure the maintenance of competition. In 1995 Stagecoach Holdings and Go-Ahead, two large bus operators, were strongly condemned for their anti-competitive behaviour and predatory actions. A number of recently proposed mergers, involving the regional electricity companies (RECs), have not been referred to the MMC. The takeover of Manweb by Scottish Power created a vertically integrated company. The Secretary of State for Trade and Industry, however, signalled in November 1995 that there may be some objection, in principle, to the merger of electricity generation and distribution companies, by referring the bid by National Power for Southern Electric and PowerGen's bid for Midland Electricity to the MMC. The MMC found in favour of the bids. However, in April 1996 the President of the Board of Trade overruled the decision of the MMC by not allowing the two bids to go ahead.

Other RECs have also been subject to takeover and takeover speculation, which is evidence that this once stable preserve of a public monopoly is now a dynamic market with an international perspective. Eight of the 12 RECs face an imminent change in ownership. South Western Electricity was sold to Southern Company of the United States; Eastern group are now under the control of the transnational conglomerate Hanson; Seeboard have agreed a bid by Central and South West Corporation of America; and Norweb were taken over by North West Water.

Regulation of monopolies can also have a detrimental effect. BT is restricted by government legislation from entering the market for cable television. The rapidly changing technology and the ability of other domestic and foreign competitors to enter the market may be to the long-term disadvantage of BT. The ability of the United Kingdom's biggest telecommunications company to compete in the world market might be harmed.

It is evident from this brief analysis that the competitive environment facing a monopolist is likely to be benign. However, monopolists do not have free rein over their market. It is up to organizations within the market to be particularly aware of how changes in the regulatory regime are going to affect them in the future and design organizational responses to meet those changes. Of increasing importance is the response of consumers to monopolists. For example, the drought in some areas of the United Kingdom in 1995 provoked an outcry from consumers and consumer groups. It is in the interests of the water companies to listen to the problems of their consumers or the government may be forced to take action. Being proactive and implementing self-control is often considered beneficial in the long run, as opposed to being constrained by tight regulation.

The economist Joseph Schumpeter (1883–1950) also recognized the transient nature of the monopolist's position. A monopoly, he suggests, will eventually be circumvented by technology and innovation and that barriers to entry are not a serious problem to a competitive market in the long run. The position of BT, for example, has substantially altered from its position as a monopoly provider of telecommunications in the United Kingdom prior to privatization in August 1984. Not only have regulations resulted in more competition, but the development of mobile phones, and more recently the Internet, will have enormous implications for BT as it strives to maintain its position (see case study 'Telecommunications: a changing industry' on p. 381). Similarly, the position of Sega and Nintendo in the computer games market is coming under threat from Sony's new games hardware.

Oligopoly

Oligopoly is defined as a market in which a small number of producers compete with each other. In some cases two organizations dominate – for example, in the detergent market where Procter & Gamble and Unilever are dominant, or in the UK mobile phone market where Vodaphone and Cellnet hold sway. This form of oligopoly is known as a duopoly.

Because of the small number of competitors each organization has to consider how its actions will affect the decisions of its competitors. Organizations are interdependent, which means that action by one organization will solicit a response from its competitor(s). This is particularly important in regard to pricing decisions. It is likely that any change in price will be copied by competitors, with the effect of reducing profits for all organizations. Freedom of manoeuvre for an organization is very restricted, not because of fear of entry into the market, but because of this interdependence of organizations within the market. The consequence of this is relative price stability in the market, with competition based on quality, branding, advertising and service. For example, advertising expenditure in the soap and detergents market in 1991 was £125 million (Key Note, 1992).

The music industry provides a good example of an oligopolistic market in operation, where a handful of organizations account for the bulk of sales. Each company must take account of the reaction of the others when it formulates its price and output policy, since its optimal strategy will depend, in part, on the response of competitors. The almost simultaneous release of recordings by Oasis and Blur, perhaps the most important artists, in the summer of 1995 created huge interest. Bets were placed on which would top the charts. It was clear that the

TABLE 2.4   Market share of top five manufacturers measured by new car registration in the United Kingdom and Western Europe, January to June 1993

	United Kingdom	Western Europe
Ford Group	21.75	11.33
General Motors Limited	17.07	12.80
Rover Group	13.60	
Nissan	4.67	
PSA	12.44	12.00
Volkswagen Group		16.70
Fiat Group		11.30

Source: Adapted from Key Note Report 1993.

competition to get to the top was a major factor in pushing sales. Clearly, the actions of the record companies in releasing the product at the same time created extra interest. To come second, as Oasis did in this case, was probably more profitable than going to the number one slot had the rivalry not existed. This was a clear case of joint optimization as each organization was doing the best it could, given the behaviour of its rivals.

Economists usually distinguish further between those oligopolies that sell homogeneous products, for example oil companies, and those producing differentiated products. In reality all oligopolists try to differentiate their products either in substance or by marketing, advertising and image creation. In markets where products are differentiated by advertising – for example, the fabric conditioners market – it is possible to erect substantial barriers that new entrants cannot overcome. In 1993 P&G and Unilever's two leading brands each held around 36 per cent of the market, leaving very little room for new entrants.

The concentration ratio in this sort of market is typically high, with each organization holding a substantial share of the market. Market share figures for the top five car manufacturers in the United Kingdom and Western Europe are shown in Table 2.4. The top five in each market retain a substantially larger market share than their smaller niche rivals.

It is in the interest of firms to erect barriers to entry to make it difficult for new organizations to enter the market. Barriers can be created in many ways (see below). However, in some markets it may be possible for organizations to enter and exit at no cost, increasing the effect of competition greatly. The number and geographical diversity of manufacturers in the car market reflects the ease of entry and the weakness of restrictive barriers. One way organizations can manufacture barriers to entry is by entering into agreements, known as collusion.

Collusion

Organizations in an oligopolistic market may have much to gain from some form of collaboration or collusion. This can be implicit or explicit. The aim is to jointly reduce uncertainty, prevent entry into the market and maximize profits. Collusion has a distorting effect on the market. It tends to raise prices and control output, both of which adversely affect the consumer. Because of the likely impact on consumers, both explicit collusion (the operation of cartels) and implicit collusion are illegal. One of the roles of the MMC and Directorate General for Competition, Directorate General (DG) IV, is to ensure that markets do not operate against the public interest.

Explicit collusion

Under this form of collusion, usually referred to as a cartel, prices are fixed and output or sales are allocated to each member of the cartel. The cartel is able to act as a monopolist. Allocation decisions are usually the result of negotiation between the organizations. Often decisions are made in relation to the sales each organization has had historically, or on a geographical basis. The Organization of Petroleum Exporting Countries (OPEC) successfully ran a cartel from 1973 until 1986. The oil price rises instituted by the cartel in 1973 and 1979 resulted in a huge boost in the income of the countries within the cartel and caused severe problems in all non-oil-producing nations. Price rises caused significant inflationary pressures. Oil producers outside OPEC also benefited from an increase in oil prices. Marginal fields in the North Sea, belonging to Norway and the United Kingdom, which had been deemed too expensive to exploit, became viable propositions for development by the oil companies as the price of crude oil rose. It is unlikely that these fields would have been developed as quickly had it not been for the action of OPEC.

There have been instances where explicit collusion has been given official sanction. An example is shown in the mini-case below.

Cartels are not restricted to Europe. Japan's construction industry has long been criticized for the way the cartel, or dango, organizes the resolution of contract

Explicit collusion: official sanction

A cement cartel had been in existence with the official blessings of the government. In 1983 the Minister of Trade and Industry overruled Office of Fair Trading concern that a price agreement was operating against the public interest. John Camden, then the chairman of RMS, a major manufacturer, suggested that 'the common price agreement has generally served Britain well over the last 50 years or so' (*The Times*, 16 June 1983).

However, the cement cartel came under investigation by DG IV of the European Commission. Investigations centred around price fixing by 33 members of the £5.3 billion a year industry who were accused of making agreements to rig the market over a 10-year period.

The commission found evidence of anti-competitive practices and in November 1994 imposed fines of Ecu 248 million, which represented 6 per cent of the 1992 industry turnover.

awards, to the detriment of foreign competitors in particular. The dango routinely decided which company would win a contract and the price to be offered. The recession in Japan from 1991 to 1995 led to a reduction in the number and power of cartels. TNT and Ansett Transport Industries of Australia were fined $A5 million for price fixing and collusion in the air freight business in 1994 (Tagaza, 1994).

Implicit collusion
In the case of implicit collusion a price leader may materialize within an industry and other organizations tacitly follow. Alternatively, agreements may have some form of official sanction. The price of transatlantic air fares from European destinations is fixed through IATA. It has been suggested that the existence of this type of system will encourage anti-competitive behaviour. Evidence seems to suggest that airlines have colluded through IATA to block cut-price fares. Understandings over fares also prompted the Civil Aviation Authority, in 1994, to suggest that collusion and price fixing on transatlantic air routes had blocked competition and held those fares at artificially high levels. Because agreements are often tacit rather than explicit it is difficult to find evidence of such arrangements. The European Commission may be forced to take action to stop this kind of price fixing.

   An example of the role of competition policy and how difficult it is to identify implicit collusion can be seen in the example of the UK music market in the mini-case below.

UK compact discs

The UK market represents 8 per cent of global music sales. It is possible to examine the industry from two perspectives, that of the record companies and of the retailers. The British Phonographic Industry has around 150 members, the major record companies: EMI records, Polygram, Warner Music, Sony music and BMG records between them account for approximately 70 per cent of the UK market. On the retail side WH Smith (which includes Our Price and Virgin), Kingfisher and HMV dominate (CR3 54).

Compact discs (CDs) were first introduced into the UK market in 1983. Over the years the industry has been accused by consumers and the Consumers Association (through its *Which?* magazine) of keeping the price of CDs at artificially high levels in the face of decreasing production costs and lower priced CD players. Following from these initial rumblings the Office of Fair Trading (OFT) felt that a cartel had been created in this market on three counts:

*   the companies' pricing policies;
*   agreement restricting imports;
*   terms of contract with artists.

The result of this concern was the National Heritage Committee's 1993 report, published on 11 May, which addressed three issues:

- the price difference between CDs in America and Britain;
- the price difference between CDs and cassettes;
- the absolute price of CDs.

The inquiry found no evidence of collusion in their investigation though they did consider that major record companies and retailers were effectively cartels that had created a market in which there was 'no serious price competition' and recommended a £2 cut in the dealer price of CDs to move in line with prices in the United States. The OFT decided to refer the question to the MMC for further investigation.

In response to this report an investigation by the Monopolies and Mergers Commission (MMC) was launched in May 1993 by the then Director General of Fair Trading, Sir Brian Carsberg, who was not satisfied with explanations given for the high price of CDs. He stressed that the price of CDs was relatively high in comparison to other formats and in comparison with CDs in the United States. The typical price of CDs in the United Kingdom at that time was £13.49, with cassettes and LPs retailing at £9.99. This contrasted with prices in the United States, where typically CDs retailed at $14.99 (approx. £9.99 – at £1 to $1.50).

The commission, reporting in June 1994, found that although the market was dominated by the three major retailers it did not operate against the public interest. A scale monopoly (a situation in which one company/group supplies at least one-quarter of the market of all products of one description) did exist in favour of WH Smith which supplied over 26 per cent of the market. However, this situation was judged to be justified on the grounds that the retail market is very competitive, though not as competitive as in the United States, where the CR10 is 30.

Similarly, the record companies were found to compete to gain the support of retailers and were thus unable to exert market power to the disadvantage of customers.

The commission found that United Kingdom CD prices were the lowest in Europe and, although more expensive than in the United States, this difference was comparable with the price of other consumer goods.

This may or may not be a satisfactory conclusion to this issue. It does, however, highlight the problems facing regulators whose job it is to ensure that markets operate in the public's interest.

The breakdown of collusion

A major problem associated with collusion is the temptation for organizations to 'cheat' and so ignore any agreement. By doing so it is possible for the organization, in the short run, to increase profits at the expense of other parties to the agreement. As a result it may be difficult to sustain any agreement for a prolonged period, particularly if there are a large number of organizations. The Japanese construction cartel seems to have collapsed because of increasing competition in the market.

The demise of OPEC was due largely to cartel members selling too much oil, that is, above their quota level. Excess supply flooded the market forcing prices downwards. The break-up of the cartel contributed to the increased tension between Iraq and Iran which culminated in war and later in Iraq's invasion of Kuwait.

Oligopoly is the dominant form of market structure found in all market economies. We have seen that in some oligopolistic industries, for example the car industry, competition is intense and car manufacturers have to fight hard to maintain their market share. In others the nature of the industry, or the existence of agreements, means that organizations can come close to joint-profit maximization. However, high profits will attract competitors, so organizations must devote a lot of time to maintaining and defending the barriers to entry. Competition authorities are also active in limiting the amount of collusive activity (see mini-cases).

Monopolistic competition

Monopolistically competitive markets include a large number of organizations with differentiated products, and no barriers to entry. There is, therefore, freedom of entry into a market where firms cannot make super profits in the long run. Organizations act independently, because their market share is likely to be small and their actions are of little concern to others. If one organization changes price, for example, this is unlikely to affect prices throughout the market. The large number of organizations, combined with their correspondingly small size, means that the concentration ratio will be low, which increases competitive pressures.

The retail trade is often cited as an example of this type of market. For example, a T-shirt is a product that no one has a monopoly on selling. They are not all the same, but differentiated by each seller. A price rise in one store will not result in price rises everywhere else (though it is suggested that neighbouring shops may respond).

One of the features of monopolistic competition is the high level of advertising as organizations attempt to maintain or improve their position in the marketplace. Product differentiation may exist because of imaginary differences in the mind of the consumer brought about through advertising, branding and the service provided by an organization. Logos on T-shirts enable organizations to sell the same material with a more desirable logo for a higher price.

Product innovation is also constantly sought after, as new products may provide a temporary competitive edge and an opportunity to raise prices and increase profit.

The health food industry is dominated by numerous small companies and a few large multinationals with health food interests. Because organizations are small, expensive forms of advertising, for example the use of television commercials, are avoided. Organizations concentrate on below the line advertising, e.g. competitions and point of sale material. Advertising expenditure has increased substantially in the main sector of this market since 1988 – see Table 2.5.

TABLE 2.5   Main media advertising expenditure on vitamins and dietary supplements, 1988–94

Year	Expenditure (£)
1988	7.2
1989	7.9
1990	9.2
1991	8.6
1992	10.5
1993	10.3
1994	11.6

Source: Register-Meal.

The real or perceived differences created by advertising and innovation mean that it is possible for an organization to charge a higher price. If organizations in the market are seen to be obtaining high profits, new organizations can enter the market because of the low barriers to entry. The monopolistically competitive market is therefore liable to see high levels of competition between incumbents and entrants to the market. There will be enormous pressure on organizations to reduce their costs and improve their efficiency as a way of preserving margins and thus profitability.

Many economists maintain that this type of market is almost never found in practice. It is suggested that all firms in the market have to take account of their competitors at some level.

QUESTIONS

1.   It is suggested that a vertically integrated industry, such as that established by the integration of the electricity generating and supply industry, can afford gains to the industry and the consumer.

(a)   How can such merger activity benefit the consumer and the organizations involved?

(b)   Why did the DTI refer the bid to the MMC?

2.   Identify organizations that have lost monopoly positions due to new innovation. Analyse, using available sources, how the loss of market came about.

3.   Analyse competition in the video games market since the entry of Sony into that market.

4.   The data on advertising expenditure in the health food industry (Table 2.5) does not show a continuous rise. How do you account for this?

2.4 The European Union and competition policy

Competition policy in the United Kingdom is increasingly influenced by the European Union. When Swiss-owned Nestlé acquired Rowntree in 1988 the bid was not referred for consideration by the MMC, despite creating a new entity with over 25 per cent market share. The new enlarged company had less than 25 per cent of the European market. In this situation European Union policy, under Article 85, took precedence over United Kingdom competition policy.

Competition policy in the European Union is the remit of Directorate General (DG) IV of the Commission of the European Communities (CEC). The specific objective of the CEC (1993) is to:

> prevent any agreement or practice that may distort competition. Accordingly, any restrictive practice that affects or is liable to affect trade between Community countries is prohibited, and any agreement between organizations having such characteristics is null and void.

Competition policy is governed by a number of rules. Articles 85, 86 and 92, in particular, have an impact on competition. Article 85 focuses on concerted practices between two or more organizations, Article 86 is concerned with exploitation of monopoly power and Article 92 with the role of governments in distorting competition through the provision of aid. European competition law is in place to prevent the abuse of monopoly power. Over recent years it has become more rigorous in its pursuit of the free market and the diminution of monopoly power.

The tough line of the Commission has been illustrated by recent clamp-downs on two of Europe's largest industries. Investigations in the steel and paper industries (see mini-cases below) mark the latest in a series of drives by Brussels to stamp out uncompetitive activities by EU-based companies. If found guilty of anti-competitive activities companies can be fined up to 10 per cent of their world-wide annual turnover.

European clamp-down: steel

In February 1994, following investigations going back to 1991 into activities during the 1980s, 16 European steel manufacturers were fined £79.2 million for operating a price-fixing cartel contrary to European competition law. The biggest fine of £24.3 million was levied on British Steel for its role in the cartel. The inquiry uncovered evidence of price fixing, market sharing and illegal information exchange in the steel beam market, and suggested that 'the companies had been involved in a clear cut and systematic cartel over a number of years'.

In defence, the steel producers claimed that the Commission had failed to indicate how they could move from a legal cartel (which existed between 1980 and 1988) that allowed the producers to share information and markets, and move back to an open market. The Commission said that even when the market picked up the cartel did not close down and so was in breach of EU law.

A further investigation started in November 1994 into additional price fixing allegations in the heavy duty steel tubes sector. Of the eight companies implicated, two – British Steel and Thyssen – were involved in the earlier case. The companies were suspected of colluding in price fixing and sharing out contracts in the gas and oil industry.

The European Commission has not been afraid to use its powers under Article 92 to investigate state aid to companies. In the United Kingdom, aid to Rover, the car manufacturer, came under the spotlight when it was sold off. In 1994 the Commission held an official inquiry into the French government's planned injection of capital (its fourth since 1991) into the loss-making Air France to examine whether the injection violated competition rules. Conversely, the European Commission is also able to approve aid to companies without raising high levels of opposition. In the autumn of 1994, Groupe Bull, the French computer group, was given aid totalling £1.3 billion. The Commission said 'subsidies can have a positive effect on employment and competitiveness in Europe without damaging other business'. The competition commissioner said that Bull passed five key tests on which he based his decision to allow the aid to be paid (Tucker and Riding, 1994). These are:

- the company must be restored to profitability within a 'reasonable' time;
- measures must be taken to offset any adverse effects on competitors;
- the aid must be kept to the strict minimum needed;
- the restructuring plan must be implemented in full;
- there must be detailed reports to monitor progress.

In May 1994 there was a move to support the European Union's 'open skies' policy, a policy aimed at liberalizing the airline industry and fostering competition. The monopoly position enjoyed by Air France at Paris's Orly airport was lifted by the European Commission when BA were granted landing rights. Later in the year

Paper and cardboard

Following investigations lasting over three years in July 1994 the European Commission imposed what was then the largest fine in its history, totalling £101 million (Ecu 132 million), on 19 European cardboard producers for running a price-fixing cartel. The cartel met as the Association of Product Group Paperboard, ostensibly for legitimate reasons. The board producers were described by the Commission as 'the most pernicious price-fixing cartel'.

the European Court of Justice further signalled a move to a more competitive market by ordering the French government to abide by the ruling of the European Commission and open up both the Orly–Marseilles and Orly–Toulouse routes, thus ending the monopoly enjoyed by Air Inter.

The European Union is also seeking to secure equality of treatment and opportunity for organizations bidding for public works contracts. Eight public works directives had been issued by the European Commission, for incorporation into the laws of member states, up to mid-1994. The directives require that all public contracts of more than Ecu 200 000 should be advertised in the *Official Journal of the European Communities*. The Commission is eager to ensure that companies from all member states have the same prospect of winning a contract as those from the home country. In 1990 public procurement in the European Union totalled Ecu 595 billion, 98 per cent of which was awarded to companies from the home country.

Agreements that restrict competition

An example of EU competition policy can be seen in the control of oligopolies by the regulation of agreements covered under Article 85. In general terms agreements are liable to be prohibited if:

- they have the object or effect of restricting competition;
- they have an appreciable effect, either actual or potential, on trade between member states.

Agreements that prohibit competition can be placed into two categories: horizontal or vertical. In this section we will investigate both types of agreement.

Horizontal agreements

Horizontal agreements are between actual or potential competitors, that is, organizations at the same stage of production. The examples of the steel, paper and cardboard industries in the mini-cases above are useful illustrations of this type of agreement. Horizontal agreements are restricted if they lead to (CEC, 1993):

- joint fixing of prices by competitors;
- market sharing;
- setting of production quotas;
- tie-in sales clauses;
- discriminatory sales practices;
- joint purchasing by competitors;
- joint sales;
- sales promotion which restricts participation at commercial fairs or joint labels or trade marks, where this leads to an alignment of commercial strategy;
- exchange of information if this may lead to collusion.

Vertical agreements

Vertical agreements are between organizations operating at different levels in the distribution process. This may be an agreement between a manufacturer and a retailer. As a general principle policies in Europe presume that collectively imposed vertical restrictions are harmful, unless proved otherwise, even though economists can produce evidence that vertical agreements may, in some cases, actually promote inter-brand competition.

Vertical agreements are restricted if they lead to (CEC, 1993):

- a compartmentalization of the market through an exclusive or selective distribution agreement or a franchise agreement (for example, export bans);
- restrictions in the choice of suppliers or customers;
- prices not being set freely;
- an exclusive purchasing obligation for an unlimited period and in respect of a broad range of products;
- discriminatory exclusion of certain types of retail outlets through an exclusive retail agreement.

Summary

We have now applied the traditional economic model of industry structure as a basis of analysing competition. To what extent is this model of use? Caves and Porter (1980) suggest that if structural change within an industry, particularly changes of concentration and entry, appears to be slow then the traditional model will be applicable.

However, in other circumstances the model may present only a partial view of the competitive conditions facing an organization. In some industries the rate of change may be rapid with, for example, technology transforming the industry structure by changing both process and products. One only needs to look at the demise of products like electric typewriters and the changes forced on IBM to cope with the market for personal computers to see the influence of technology (refer also to Chapter 4). It is in these circumstances that the value of using industry structure as a basis for analysing competition may be diminished. A survey of the computer industry 'Within the Whirlwind' published in *The Economist*, 27 February 1993, gives a very good examination of this question.

Other economists, too, have put the structure–conduct–performance approach under the microscope. The Chicago School has taken an alternative view that concentrated markets are not necessarily evil in themselves. Markets that exhibit extremes of concentration may gain benefits such as economies of scale or greater efficiency. The Chicagoans believe that barriers to entry are more apparent than real and that competition is powerful enough to prevent organizations from controlling markets. The conclusion is that conduct and performance of the market is not related to its underlying structure. Competition in a highly concentrated market could be fierce. This obviously has a significant impact on businesses operating in these type of markets.

2.5 Contestable markets

A valuable addition to the theory of industry structure is provided by Baumol (1982). He suggests that it is possible for organizations to enter a market without incurring costs because these costs can be recovered when the organization exits. There are no sunk or unrecoverable costs. This situation is known as a perfectly contestable market. Sunk costs can include the cost of building, advertising and R&D. If the sunk costs of entry are lower, then the market is more contestable or more competitive. Contestable markets are vulnerable to hit-and-run entry. There has been a proliferation of stores on UK high streets offering all of their goods at less than £1. In this case they are able to operate efficiently, keeping their costs to a minimum. Shops tend to remain in operation for a relatively short period of time. The organizations take advantage of having low sunk costs, so entry into and exit from the market is relatively fast and painless.

It is doubtful whether a perfectly contestable market exists. In most cases some sunk costs are incurred in market entry. It is the scale of the sunk costs which may, or may not, dissuade a potential entrant from attempting a hit-and-run entry.

The risk that Virgin Atlantic took to start an air service from London to Japan was lessened because the sunk costs were relatively low. If the route proved to be unprofitable, aircraft could be transferred to other routes, rental of terminal space could stop and ground equipment switched to another airport. In June 1995, Virgin Atlantic started a service on the London to Sydney route, the so-called kangaroo route, in partnership with MAS, using MAS aircraft – a strategy further designed to eliminate sunk costs of entry. The main block to contestability of the airline industry seems not to be sunk costs but regulation (see below). The construction of the Channel tunnel presents a completely different story. If the operators fail to gain market share from ferry or airline operators, then the whole cost of construction may represent a sunk cost, resulting in enormous losses to shareholders and the consortium of banks currently funding the business.

2.6 Structural analysis of competitive forces

Despite criticism, the structure–conduct–performance model may still be a useful foundation for the analysis of a rapidly changing business environment. Porter (1980) argues that 'understanding industry structure must be the starting point for strategic analysis'. Strategic analysis focuses on identifying the basic, underlying characteristics of an industry which is rooted in its economics and technology. It is these characteristics that shape the competitive environment that the industry faces (Porter, 1980).

To enhance understanding it is advisable to examine Michael Porter's 1980 model more closely. The model illustrated in Figure 2.4 brings together many elements discussed above as it is based on the s–c–p paradigm.

Porter suggests that the collective strengths of five forces determine the state

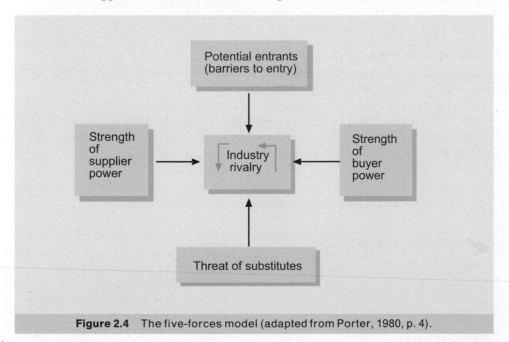

Figure 2.4 The five-forces model (adapted from Porter, 1980, p. 4).

of competition and therefore the ultimate profit potential within an industry. The five competitive forces identified by Porter are:

- rivalry among competitors;
- threat of entry;
- threat of substitution;
- bargaining power of buyers;
- bargaining power of suppliers.

We will briefly explore each one.

Rivalry among competitors

This is Porter's central force. Increased rivalry will lead to increased competition and reduced profits. Intensity of rivalry between competitors will depend on several factors.

The number and relative size of competitors within an industry

If there are many organizations of a similar size, as in monopolistic competition or oligopoly, then rivalry will be intense. Organizations in the industry are likely to try to gain market share through all possible means. Witness the situation in the petrol retail market where new deals to consumers are continuously being introduced. In industries with relatively few organizations, or where one or two organizations dominate, rivalry tends to be much less and the market much more stable.

The rate of growth in an industry

It is important to recognize that the growth rate of an industry is dependent upon a number of factors and that sectoral differences abound. Market growth in industries where product innovation and displacement are dominant is likely to be very different from that of the more traditional sectors, for example ship building. Geographical differences also need to be taken into account. Cigarette smoking is increasing in some areas of the world and declining in others (see mini-case below).

Decline in cigarette smoking

BAT industries have, for some time, sought to diversify away from their core business of tobacco into the financial services and insurance sector. This is largely in response to the decline in the cigarette market. In the United States the proportion of adults that smoke has fallen to 25 per cent, and in the last 10 years sales have been declining at a rate of 2–3 per cent a year. In the United Kingdom the market fell by 11 per cent, in volume terms, between 1989 and 1994 and is forecast to fall at least a further 6 per cent by 1998 (*source*: Mintel). The situation is no better for the manufacturers in Western Europe. Competition is clearly becoming more intense as manufacturers have to fight to maintain sales in a declining market.

The cigarette market may well be in a mature or declining stage of its life-cycle in these particular geographical regions. As a consequence, manufacturers have attempted to expand the market elsewhere, particularly in Africa and South-East Asia. A feature of declining markets is the intense price competition that exists. This has been intensified by the introduction, in many markets, of cut-price own brand cigarettes. An unmistakable manifestation of this price competition was witnessed in 1993 when American tobacco giants Phillip Morris severely marked down the price of its leading brand, Marlboro, in an effort to recoup lost market share. This episode became known as 'Marlboro Friday'.

When an industry is growing slowly competition will be more intense. The only way an organization can expand is by taking market share from competitors. The early 1990s saw a fall in European car sales, a phenomenon referred to as negative growth. The only manufacturer to prosper in this cut-throat market was Rover who managed to increase its market share, albeit from a low starting point.

It is important for organizations to be aware of the product life cycle (PLC) that their products face as competitive conditions can be very different at each phase of the life cycle. Figure 2.5 shows four stages in the PLC, each with its own characteristics.

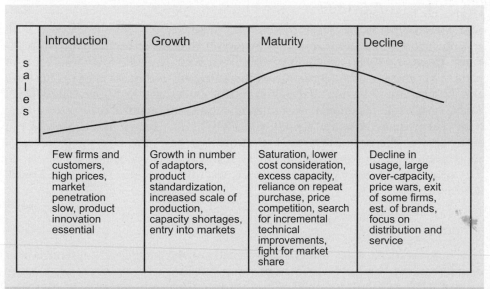

	Introduction	Growth	Maturity	Decline
s a l e s	Few firms and customers, high prices, market penetration slow, product innovation essential	Growth in number of adaptors, product standardization, increased scale of production, capacity shortages, entry into markets	Saturation, lower cost consideration, excess capacity, reliance on repeat purchase, price competition, search for incremental technical improvements, fight for market share	Decline in usage, large over-capacity, price wars, exit of some firms, est. of brands, focus on distribution and service

Figure 2.5   The product life cycle: competitive environment.

Cost conditions

The relationship between fixed and variable cost is important. If organizations operate in a business with relatively high fixed costs it will be in the interests of that organization to cut its prices in order to sell its output. The world steel industry, for example, saw savage price competition in the 1970s and 1980s as companies attempted to increase sales at the expense of competitors. Train operators are willing to reduce prices at certain times of the day and different days of the week to attract customers. British Rail offers discounts for off-peak users and a range of discount cards for students, families and pensioners. The variable cost of selling a ticket is very low, the fixed cost of operating a railway high. Staff have to be employed and trains have to be in service. Organizations in this situation will seek additional business, that is, increased ticket sales, as long as the revenue from sales covers the variable costs of those sales.

The battle to attract valuable inward investment from multinational companies is often augmented by substantial offers from governments that cover significant proportions of the start-up cost. The United Kingdom has been very successful, in the face of widespread international competition, in attracting this type of investment. In 1995 Samsung and Siemens announced the opening of plants in the United Kingdom in preference to many alternative sites (see Chapter 7 on regional policy).

Lack of product differentiation

If there is little to distinguish one product from another, competition will be intense (see the nature of the product or service above).

High exit barriers

Exit barriers can be measured by the costs organizations incur when they leave an industry. Exit barriers are said to be high if the cost of leaving an industry is high. These costs can include redundancy payments and the low scrap value of plant. Exit barriers in the form of emotional barriers and government policy may also be in place. The fact that more football clubs have not been closed down owes much to the emotional, as well as financial, support that they receive from their, often long-suffering, supporters. That more car manufacturers did not close down in the early 1990s may reflect the high cost of leaving the industry. A short period of losses may have been easier to sustain than complete closure. In the case of Renault, financial support was forthcoming from the French government.

Threat of entry

New organizations enter a market, attracted by the high level of returns that incumbents receive. New entrants bring new capacity, new resources and a desire for market share. The result will be more competition and so a fall in profit for all organizations.

Threat of entry depends on the potency of barriers to entry. The higher the barriers, the lower the threat of entry. BT's repeated price reductions on some of its UK telephone calls is not only to satisfy its regulator, or to pressurize its main terrestrial competitor, Mercury, and various mobile phone companies, but also represents a higher barrier to others with ideas of entering the market. The main sources of barriers to entry are:

- product differentiation;
- economies of scale and absolute cost advantages;
- legal barriers;
- capital requirements;
- access to distribution channels;
- threat of retaliation.

Many of these have been discussed above. We will briefly explore those hitherto unmentioned.

Economies of scale and absolute cost advantages
Economies of scale were discussed in detail above. No matter what economies of scale exist, other cost advantages may also exist, so-called first-mover advantages, which cannot be replicated by potential entrants. These could include:

- access to raw materials – it is extremely difficult to establish a nuclear industry without access to raw material as many countries have discovered (for example, Iran and Iraq);
- favourable locations – it would be an almost impossible challenge for an overseas bank to set up a wide branch network to compete with the established networks of the home-based organizations, unless, like HSBC, it takes over a United Kingdom bank;
- product know-how and experience curve advantages (see above).

Government subsidies can be used to reduce absolute cost advantages. The launch aid received by Airbus Industrie helped it to compete effectively against America's Boeing. The support for sunrise industries, those emerging new industries of the future, may also be a legitimate use of subsidies.

Legal barriers
Legal barriers, such as government licence, charter or a patent, may also be used. A licence is required in many fields of business including the taxi cab, banking and broadcasting sectors. The 1986 Financial Services Act requires that all sellers of investment products are authorized by the Securities and Investment Board. Glaxo and other drug companies are able to protect their new products from competition by use of patents. Environmental and safety standards also place barriers in the way of new organizations entering some industries. Inefficient public monopolies have in the past been accused of being protected from competition by government funding, especially the power, transport and

telecommunications sectors in the United Kingdom and telecommunications and postal services in France and Germany respectively. The Japanese government has long been criticized in Europe and North America for imposing barriers that protect Japanese manufacturers and farmers and drastically limit the import of a wide range of goods, such as rice, cars and Scotch whisky, into the Japanese market. Action was taken in mid-1995 by the US government in response to Japan's conduct, and the increasing trade deficit between the United States and Japan, to limit the number of Japanese exports to the United States. Measures proposed included 100 per cent tariffs on Japanese cars entering the US market.

Capital requirements
The need for capital is linked closely to our earlier discussion of sunk costs. It may be too expensive for an organization to enter a market. The London evening newspaper market has not had a successful new entrant for many years. One attempt at entry ended with the incumbents starting a price war and forcing its new rival out. The newcomer could not sustain its position.

Access to distribution channels
A barrier can be created by the inability of an entrant to gain access to a distribution channel. Mercury was given the right to rent access to BT's phone lines, otherwise it would have been impossible for them to enter the market. Sega and Nintendo control distribution of their computer games which limits the number of distributors offering the product.

Threat of retaliation
The effectiveness of barriers may be in part reliant on the expectations that entrants have of the possible retaliation of incumbent organizations. Porter (1980) suggests that entrants into an industry can be deterred if:

- there is a history of retaliation against entrants; e.g. it has recently proved difficult to establish new newspaper titles because of the aggressive nature of price cutting used by incumbents;
- established organizations with substantial resources fight back; e.g. the cross-Channel ferry operators are very aware of the threat posed by the Channel tunnel and are marshalling their resources in a bid to keep their market share;
- established organizations are heavily committed to the industry and have assets which cannot be employed in other sectors; e.g. British Steel have become one of the most profitable steel makers in the world and it is in their interests to maintain barriers to ensure a continued growth in profits;
- the industry is undergoing slow or zero growth, as new organizations cannot be absorbed so easily.

Threat of substitution

Substitutes are those goods or services, offered by another organization, that can be used in place of the good or service a company supplies. The American Express charge card, for example, faces competition from cash, travellers cheques, cheque books and credit cards. The threat of substitutes imposes a price ceiling as high profits will attract substitutes. The extent of the threat will depend on:

- the propensity of the buyer to substitute;
- switching costs;
- the relative price and performance of substitutes.

The propensity of the buyer to substitute

A critical factor is the propensity, inclination or tendency of a buyer to substitute. If the propensity of a buyer to substitute is high then substitutes will present a great threat. Some products have a low propensity of substitution because of the brand loyalty that has been established. This may apply to certain brands of cigarette. New discount stores like Netto and Aldi, and own brand offerings, are bringing cheaper, non-branded goods to British shoppers. Consumers may switch from their usual brand of, for example, baked beans to a cheaper alternative, thus increasing their propensity to substitute. If this is the case it will create a problem for the manufacturers of branded goods.

The wider economic environment is an issue in this case. The recession has brought job losses and lower real income which must have an impact on the buying patterns of individuals.

The situation is further complicated because substitutes may be difficult to identify and, hence, to keep out. What is the substitute for a newly released CD? Is it another CD from a different artist released by another label, or can substitutes come from outside the industry? Organizations compete for discretionary expenditure – a record company may compete with a sports wear manufacturer, for example.

Switching costs

The one-off cost that faces a buyer when switching from one supplier to another is important. Where the switching cost is high then transfer of allegiances is less likely, and vice versa. A company can quite easily switch to a different supplier of stationery, allowing a new entrant into the fray. However, the cost of switching to a new lift or elevator company might impose huge costs and encourage a closer relationship with the existing supplier, thus closing the door on a competitor.

The relative price and performance of substitutes

The ability of some of the Japanese high-volume car manufacturers to gain market share in the sports car segment of the car market, largely reflects the relatively lower price of the Japanese vehicles in comparison to their performance and the value that they offer in comparison with competitors.

Bargaining power of buyers and suppliers

Suppliers are those individuals or organizations from whom another organization purchases items that are needed to carry out business activities. These are the inputs to the organization and include raw materials and components. Supplier power can reduce prices, increase quality and increase service level demands, all of which will reduce margins.

Buyers are those individuals or organizations who purchase an organization's outputs. Bargaining power of buyers can reduce prices, increase quality and increase service level demands. It could be argued that the fall in price and higher level of service offered by some of the recently privatized utilities, for example BT, is a direct result of buyers gaining more power from increased choice.

The examination of supplier power is analogous to that of buyer power (the factors that contribute to greater buyer power will decrease supplier power) and so we will concentrate on buyer power in this section.

Buyers depend a great deal on the quality and timeliness of information they receive. Full information means that a buyer is in a better position to negotiate a price. Buyers are powerful and more sensitive to price if:

- their switching costs are low – it is easy to go for a drink to the pub next door, no costs are involved;
- the product is important to the buyer. This could be the case if:
  - the product represents a high proportion of total costs – buyers of major pieces of capital equipment are likely to have a strong hand when it comes to contract negotiations;
  - the product is purchased in high volume (see below);
  - the profitability of the buyer industry is low, which may mean that the buyer will want to reduce the price of goods that are bought in to protect its own margins.

Products are undifferentiated and substitutes are available

We have already outlined the problems that firms face if products are homogeneous and easily substituted. Buyers can simply play one company off against the other. The decline in building construction in the United Kingdom has resulted in fewer sales of materials, particularly bricks. The homogeneous nature of the product means that construction companies can shop around for the best prices and, consequently, reduce the sales and profit for builders merchants.

Buyer concentration is high

If your product is bought by only one buyer then concentration is at 100 per cent. In this case buyers have total power, not only over price but all other aspects of the relationship, including quality and delivery time. Toyota in Japan are able to gain almost 100 per cent reliability on the light bulbs for their cars because many are provided by a network of small family companies who rely on Toyota for all of their sales. Marks & Spencer have many exclusive agreements to buy the whole of the output of an organization. If they withdraw their order then plant closure may be the result.

Threat of backward integration

In some cases a buyer has the ability to move into that particular business itself. Typically, car manufacturers in the past reduced their dependence on their suppliers by taking them over. In 1995 Rover, the UK car manufacturer, was involved in a bid to regain control of Unipart, its former parts subsidiary. The big food processors have recently seen their sales hit because of moves by their buyers, the big grocery chains – for example, Tesco and Sainsbury – into cheaper own brand labels which have displaced some of the better known branded products.

Porter's five-forces model provides organizations with a model for analysing their competitive environment. Unless a company can analyse its competitors it will never be in a position to compete effectively. The benefits to be gained from having an intelligence-gathering system are immeasurable. A capable system may ultimately ensure survival.

2.7 Competitor analysis

The proliferation of different types of washing powder such as enzyme rich, enzyme free, biological and non-biological is a tactic used by the two major manufacturers to put in place a barrier to entry, as described earlier. However, the multiplicity of types arises from the need of one company to match the innovation of the other. If the companies in the market are unaware of their competitors' direction then a rival may be able to increase its market share.

Competitor analysis is another way of achieving an insight into the activity of competitors. This type of behaviour exists in industries as diverse as the car industry and software design.

Competitor analysis involves an investigation of competitors' goals, assumptions, strategy and capabilities (Porter, 1980). Not only do existing competitors need to be examined but there is also a need to put potential competitors under the microscope. Add to this a dose of self-analysis and a picture of the behaviour of the market comes into focus. Figure 2.6 shows the competitor analysis model.

Porter (1980) proposes that competitor analysis can answer questions such as:

1. What are the implications of the interaction of the probable competitors' moves?
2. Are organizations' strategies converging and likely to clash?
3. Do organizations have sustainable growth rates that match the industry's forecast growth rate, or will a gap be created that will invite entry?
4. Will probable moves combine to hold implications for industry structure?

The Honda mini-case below provides an illustration of how competitor analysis can help the market entry strategy of an organization.

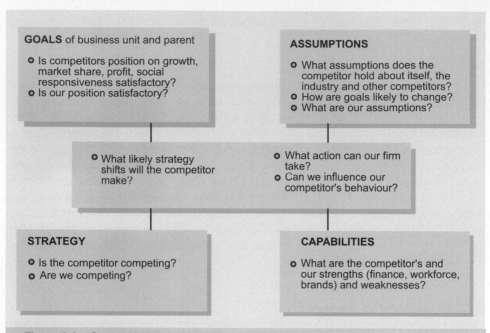

GOALS of business unit and parent
- Is competitors position on growth, market share, profit, social responsiveness satisfactory?
- Is our position satisfactory?

ASSUMPTIONS
- What assumptions does the competitor hold about itself, the industry and other competitors?
- How are goals likely to change?
- What are our assumptions?

- What likely strategy shifts will the competitor make?

- What action can our firm take?
- Can we influence our competitor's behaviour?

STRATEGY
- Is the competitor competing?
- Are we competing?

CAPABILITIES
- What are the competitor's and our strengths (finance, workforce, brands) and weaknesses?

Figure 2.6   Components of competitive analysis (adapted from Porter, 1980, p. 49).

Honda's infiltration of the UK and US motorcycle markets

In 1959 Honda made its first moves into the United States motorcycle market. Initially it targeted large cubic-capacity (cc) machines. Honda failed to gain a foothold in this market segment as there were no customers for these machines. According to Pascale (1984) Honda had not carried out any market research prior to this move. Expansion into the United States was not even part of Honda's long-term plan.

Honda was keen to assess why its attempt to sell in the United States had failed and sent a team to evaluate the lack of market success. The team noticed that people were interested in the small machines that they were using for their own transport. One particularly important person was a buyer for Sears, a large US retailer. In response, Honda decided to focus on selling at the smaller end of the market, and entered that segment with their 50 cc Super Cub range. This range found buyers immediately.

Honda's success went a long way in redefining the image of the motorcycle in the United States to a practical, inexpensive mode of transportation for the urban commuter. With new US volume Honda was able to reap substantial global economies of scale in motorcycle production (Porter, 1980, p. 289). By 1964 Honda was making inroads into the small machine market in both the United Kingdom and the United States.

Honda used its established position in one segment of the market to establish a dominance in the large-capacity segment and also used competitor analysis to investigate the competition and concluded that (Grant, 1995):

- both companies, BSA in the United Kingdom and Harley-Davidson in the United States, pursued medium-term financial goals rather than market share goals;
- both organizations were benefiting from an upsurge in motorcycle demand.

Therefore, the companies would not be unduly alarmed at forfeiting market share as:

- both organizations believed that due to their own customer loyalty and brand image, the Japanese producers were not a serious threat in the big bike market;
- even if their rivals did act aggressively, the effectiveness of their response would be limited by their weak financial positions and by their lack of innovation and effective manufacturing capabilities.

The result, as we know, was the domination of the world motorcycle market by Honda and the other Japanese manufacturers.

QUESTION

Using the models that have been developed in the chapter, examine how Honda were able to successfully enter the motorcycle market in the late 1950s and early 1960s.

CONCLUSION

We have seen, in this chapter, that the structure of the market has a direct impact on the competition that an organization faces. It is, however, evident that market structure does not remain static. Today's monopoly could be tomorrow's competitive cockpit. Organizations face a dynamic and changing competitive environment. International competitors are becoming the barometer by which we measure the success of all organizations.

Organizations cannot rest and remain satisfied with their past achievements. It is important to develop and maintain mechanisms with which to sense environmental change. In this chapter we have introduced you to some of the tools and models that can assist organizations to understand their own position and that of their competitors. We have also shown that there is a role for government at all scales. Markets left to their own devices may become anti-competitive, so intervention may be needed.

Governments can also provide support for new, fledgling industries to allow them to grow and become competitive in the international arena.

The next chapter explores the macroeconomic environment.

SUMMARY OF MAIN POINTS

Competition is influenced by a wide range of factors. In this chapter we have investigated a range of these factors and introduced you to models to aid your analysis of the competitive environment. The chapter has shown:

- The basic economic problem, of allocation of resources, is resolved in quite different ways within the command and market economies.
- Competition is influenced largely by the nature of the product, the number of firms and their concentration, and the market entry conditions.
- Some organizations are protected from competition by barriers to entry and may be capable of making above normal profits in the long run.
- A strong competitive position is likely to be eroded by, for example, the use of technology and innovation.
- Oligopolists are interdependent and must consider the actions of rivals when making business decisions; because of the lack of freedom of manoeuvre, competition is based largely on quality, branding, advertising and service.
- Some organizations act to reduce uncertainty by entering into agreements which may be anti-competitive. Regulations need to be in place to monitor such agreements and to protect the public interest.
- Contestable markets exist where there are no sunk costs of entry. In such markets competition will be intense.
- Porter's five forces are:
  - rivalry among competitors
  - threat of entry
  - threat of substitution
  - bargaining power of buyers
  - bargaining power of suppliers.
- The collective strengths of the five forces determine the state of competition and therefore the ultimate profit potential within an industry.
- Competitor analysis involves the investigation of organizations' goals, assumptions, strategies and capabilities.

References

Baumol, W. (1982) 'Contestable markets: an uprising in the theory of industry structure', *American Economic Review*, March.

Beardshaw, J. (1992) *Economics: A Student's Guide* (3rd edn), Pitman, London.

Begg, D., Fischer, S. and Dornbusch, R. (1994) *Economics* (4th edn), McGraw-Hill, London.

Caves, R. and Porter, M.E. (1980) 'The dynamics of changing seller concentration', *Journal of Industrial Economics*, vol. 19, pp. 1–15.

CEC (1993) *Small Business and Competition: A Practical Guide* (10th edn), Commission of European Communities, Brussels.

Fishwick, F. (1993) *Making Sense of Competition Policy*, Kogan Page, London.

Grant, R.M. (1995) *Contemporary Strategy Analysis: Concepts, Techniques, Applications*, Blackwell, Oxford.

Key Note (1992) *Report on Soap and Detergents* (8th edn), Key Note, Hampton.

Mansfield, E. (1994) *Applied Microeconomics*, Norton, New York.

MMC (1992) *Fact sheets 1–6*, Monopolies and Mergers Commission, London.

Pascale, R.T. (1984) 'Perspectives on strategy: the real story behind Honda's success', *California Management Review*, vol. 14, no. 3, pp. 23–31.

Porter, M.E. (1980) *Competitive Strategy: Techniques for Analyzing Industries and Competitors*, The Free Press, New York.

Tagaza, E. (1994) 'World Trade News', *Financial Times*, 11 August.

Thompson, A.A. and Strickland, A.J. (1995) *Strategic Management: Concepts and Cases* (8th edn), Irwin, Chicago.

Tucker, E. and Riding, J. (1994) 'Brussels approves £1.33 billion rescue for Bull', *Financial Times*, 13 October.

CHAPTER 3

THE INTERNATIONAL ECONOMIC ENVIRONMENT

Mark Cook

 LEARNING OUTCOMES

On completion of this chapter you should be able to:

- appreciate the changing nature of production in the major international economies;
- appreciate the role of government in influencing macroeconomic activity;
- recognize the changing nature of growth in the major international economies and the implications that flow from this;
- consider the methods of control and impact of inflation;
- understand the reasons for the changes in unemployment within Europe;
- understand the development of trading blocs;
- recognize the importance of international trade between countries and trading blocs;
- understand the interrelatedness of the major European economies;
- appreciate how exchange rate regimes have developed and their possible implications;
- consider the impact of the Single European Market on countries inside and outside of the European Union;
- consider the implications for the European economies of the development of a single currency.

3.1 Introduction

On one level it is possible to consider organizations as having control over their own actions. They can decide upon the kinds of resources they require, relate these

75

to forecasts of demand, the current goals of the organization and the organization's long-term strategy. However, organizations do not exist in a vacuum. They are affected and respond to changes in both short-term and long-term economic conditions. It is fairly easy to see how interest rates, the level of inflation and competition policy have an effect on the organization but there are other economic forces at play. For example, changes in government policy towards training will have a direct impact on organizations both in the short term and the long term and could lead to a shortage of skilled workers, reducing the organization's productivity and allowing competitors to gain an increasing share of a previously safe market.

Changes in the external environment with regard to trading blocs can affect the ability and desire of organizations to be involved in export markets. Economic problems with the home economy can result in policies by a government to control its expenditure, leading to a downturn in general economic activity. Poor underlying strength in an economy can lead to changes in interest rates and exchange rates, both of which may inhibit the performance of the organizations in an economy. This chapter, therefore, considers the changes that have occurred in the macroeconomic environment. It will consider the structural changes that have taken place in the major economies of the world, the move towards growing international integration, the development of trading blocs, and the role and evolution of international capital flows. In addition, the chapter will address issues such as: growth, the coordination of macroeconomic policy and the changing power structures of the major economies. Throughout the chapter it is important to bear in mind the impact that such macroeconomic environmental changes have upon the organizations that lie therein.

Any account of the macroeconomic environment needs to be selective. We have included those features which are believed to be most relevant. It should also be borne in mind that although the macroeconomic environment can be viewed from a number of perspectives we have, in the main, concentrated on a European one.

3.2 Macroeconomic accounts

There is much debate as to how the level of economic activity in the major economies of the world can be compared. A standard approach is to consider Gross Domestic Product (GDP) or Gross National Product (GNP) figures for the different countries.

GDP measures the level of economic activity produced in a country in any one year. GNP measures income from all sources, including net property income from abroad. This income is made up from previous investments abroad and is income earned by United Kingdom citizens or commercial organizations. GDP can be measured by adding:

- all the expenditures that are made on final products during the year – National Expenditure;
- all the output of final products/services produced in that country during the year – National Output;
- all the incomes received by the factors of production in the making of the final products during the year – National Income.

Table 3.1 shows the GDP figures for the United Kingdom measured by the three approaches in 1994; each gives approximately the same result.

TABLE 3.1   Gross domestic product measured at factor cost (1994)

Approach	£ (million)
Expenditure	
(a) Consumers' expenditure	363 882
(b) Central government final consumption (G)	133 979
(c) Gross domestic capital formation (I)	95 695
(a)+(b)+(c) give Total domestic expenditure	593 556
(d) Exports of goods and services (X)	166 189
(d)+Total domestic expenditure equals Total final expenditure	759 745
Less Imports of goods and services	−180 729
Statistical discrepancy	124
Gross domestic product	579 140
Income	
(a) Income from employment	362 758
(b) Income from self-employment	63 655
(c) Gross trading profit from companies	91 189
(d) Gross trading surplus of public corporations	4 529
(e) Gross trading surplus of general government enterprises	486
(f) Rent	56 793
(g) Imputed charge for consumption of non-trading capital	4 051
(a)+(b)+(c)+(d)+(e)+(f)+(g) gives Total domestic income	583 461
Less Stock appreciation	−3 880
Statistical discrepancy	−441
Gross domestic product at factor cost	579 140
Output	
Agriculture, hunting, forestry and fishing	11 548
Mining and quarrying	13 078
Manufacturing	121 272
Electricity, gas and water supply	15 458
Construction	31 035
Wholesale and retail trade; repairs; hotels and restaurants	83 472
Transport, storage and communication	49 039
Financial and business activities	154 550
Public administration, national defence and social security	38 797
Education, health and social work	69 116
Other services	22 044
Less Adjustments	−30 269
Gross domestic product	579 140

Source: National Income and Expenditure Blue Book, 1995.

TABLE 3.2   GDP and GDP per capita, various countries (dollars)

Country	GDP 1992 (Billions US$)[1]	GDP per capita 1993
Austria	186	23 510
France	1338	22 490
Germany	1763	23 560
Italy	1226	19 840
Japan	3699	31 490
Spain	580	13 590
Sweden	246	24 740
Switzerland	244	35 760
United Kingdom	1039	18 060
United States	5881	24 760

[1] Current prices and exchange rates

Source: Adapted from OECD (1993) and World Bank Report (1995).

It is also useful to make comparisons between countries. Table 3.2 compares the United Kingdom with other major industrial countries.

There are a number of factors to consider when a comparison is made of inter-country GDP figures. Larger countries tend to have higher total GDPs, therefore a better comparison is GDP per head or GDP per capita. As Table 3.2 indicates, some of the smaller countries, such as Switzerland, have the highest GDP per head. GDP per head can be used as a comparison of inter-country performance. However, GDP needs to be considered in real terms rather than nominal terms. That is, account should be taken of the varying rates of inflation between countries. Secondly, GDPs need to be converted into a common currency – for example, American dollars.

There may be times when one currency is weak against the American dollar, while others are strong. This will tend to overvalue or undervalue some countries' GDP figures. For example, in converting Japanese yen into US dollars during 1995, the exchange rate of 1 US dollar has varied between 97 and 105 yen. Secondly, GDP figures can only include factors on which there is information. For some activities in the economy data is not collected since these are not measured in monetary terms, e.g. housework. Other countries may not be in a position to collect enough 'quality' information; their GDPs may be understated. Moreover, many products in less-developed countries may not actually be exchanged for money but operate in the barter economy and, therefore, these transactions will not be included in any figures on expenditure. For the developed countries one major source of information is the tax authorities. Firms report sales, individuals report incomes and data is collected in the European Union on Value Added Tax. Herein lies a problem. How certain can we be of the accuracy of these figures? Often income is not reported, being part of what has become known as the hidden or underground economy (see Table 3.3).

Accurate figures on the hidden economy are difficult to collect. One measure

University of Chester, Queen's Park Library

Title: The business environment :
challenges and changes / Ian Brooks and
Jamie Weatherston.
ID: 01047623
Due: 19-11-15

Total items: 1
29/10/2015 17:51

Renew online at:
http://libcat.chester.ac.uk/patroninfo

Thank you for using Self Check

248

TABLE 3.3   Estimates of the underground economy (%)

Canada	France	Germany	Italy	Netherlands	Norway	UK	USA
3–8	4	4–24	5–52	6–16	4–17	2–15	2–26

Source: Economie et Statistiques, November 1989.

used by *Economie et Statistiques* (1989) has been to compare the estimates of GDP measured by the income and expenditure approaches to national income. Another indicator is the sales of intermediate inputs in certain activities: there is a wide discrepancy, for example, between the purchase of construction materials and reported construction activity. In addition, we need to consider the time factor. Data from the tax authorities is subject to a level of time delay and estimates need continual revisions as more accurate information comes to hand. The inaccuracy of data can pose significant problems for policy makers, who may consider expanding the economy when the data suggests some downturn in economic activity, only to find that the expansion was not required when the actual data arrived. This approach obviously has implications for organizations which may be affected by changes in government policy.

GDP figures do not make reference to the distribution of income between countries. The unequal distribution of income and wealth can lead to changes in the overall expenditure patterns of a country's citizens and this has implications for the business communities both within and outside that country. Finally, GDP figures make no reference to the social costs of production. Thus, changes in the perceptions about environmental damage and the resulting policies that may follow can have important implications for organizations.

In some countries, GDP has grown at a faster rate than in others. This tendency for unequal growth between countries and within trading blocs has implications for government policy, interest rates, exchange rates and the optimal conditions for the growth of businesses within those countries.

 QUESTIONS

1.   GDP is often criticized as a measure of well-being since some public goods are inherently difficult to price. Which goods fit into this category and how can the GDP data be improved or adjusted to account for this problem?

2.   How do changes in the level of GDP affect the performance of domestic organizations?

3.3 Macroeconomic goals

In general, most countries have a range of economic goals, not all of which are mutually compatible. These economic goals include:

- a high level of economic growth;
- a strong balance of payments;
- a low level of inflation;
- a low level of unemployment.

Some of these goals may be conflicting. For example, it may not be possible to have a low level of inflation together with a low level of unemployment. Higher levels of economic growth can lead to increases in the rate of inflation. Thus in achieving one goal, governments may have to forgo others. Governments, too, have a raft of economic policies which they can use to achieve their targets. For example, a government which wishes to improve the sales of its domestic industries could try to stimulate its domestic economy by:

- reducing taxes (fiscal policy);
- increasing the amount of money available or lowering interest in the economy (monetary policy);
- erecting trade barriers to encourage domestic consumers to buy more home-produced goods.

For all these policies the outcome may be a short-term increase in business activity in the domestic economy, but the long-term impact may be different. Reducing interest rates may lead to higher levels of inflation in the domestic economy, which then encourages domestic consumers to purchase substitute foreign goods. The introduction of trade barriers may lead to other countries imposing retaliatory trade barriers on the country's exports and so damage business sales abroad. What the above indicates is that policies can be implemented to achieve a particular goal, but the long-term side-effects may well be different.

QUESTION

What do you consider to have been the main economic goals of the economy over the last
(a) 5 years?
(b) 20 years?

3.4 The circular flow

Before we consider the specifics of various countries and trading blocs, a useful starting point is the more general approach to changes in economic activity that can be seen through the circular flow of income in Figure 3.1.

At the centre of Figure 3.1 are two groups, households and firms. Households provide services to firms in exchange for wages, and firms sell products to households in exchange for income. Figure 3.1 also indicates that some income leaves this circular flow (leakages) while other income (expenditure) is

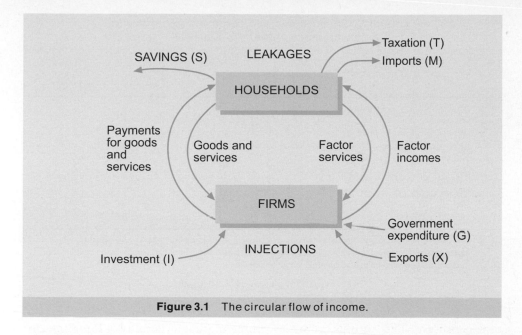

Figure 3.1   The circular flow of income.

added (injections). Both firms and individuals are subject to taxes, and this money is withdrawn from the circular flow. Much, if not all, of this will be put back into the circular flow through general government expenditure on, for example, road building and social security payments. Savings undertaken by firms, individuals and governments also represent leakages from the model, and corresponding to this are inflows into the circular flow from investment. Finally, very few economies are 'closed' – that is, not involved with international trade and capital flows – thus exports are seen as foreign money entering the domestic economy and are a further injection into the circular flow, while imports can be viewed as money leaving the national economy and thus a further leakage.

For selected major economies Table 3.4 indicates the components of GNP during the 1980s.

The circular flow model indicates, among other things, the role of the government in the economy. Government steers the economy through the budget, delivered each year in November. It is a reflection of the government's income and expenditure. If the government has expenditure which exceeds income then it needs to borrow this money from elsewhere. This may come from the sale of government securities (gilts) or by borrowing from external sources such as the International Monetary Fund (IMF). In the United Kingdom the amount that the government borrows is called the Public Sector Borrowing Requirement (PSBR). As we shall see later, with regard to a single currency within Europe, the European Union has set guidelines on the upper level of borrowing that a government should not exceed if it wishes to participate in a single currency.

Alternatively, it is quite possible that government revenue exceeds the level

TABLE 3.4   Components of GNP: expenditure and income (averages over 1981–85. % of GNP)

	Expenditure			Gross taxes	Income transfers	S^h	Memo: GNP growth
	C	I	G				
Australia	64	25	20	35	13	6	0.3
France	60	20	18	47	26	8	1.5
Germany	57	20	20	45	21	8	1.2
Italy	58	22	16	37	20	14	1.6
Japan	58	29	10	30	13	11	4.0
Norway	49	26	20	54	22	2	3.4
Sweden	54	19	29	60	25	1	1.8
Switzerland	59	22	13	32	16	8	1.4
UK	60	16	21	41	17	4	1.9
USA	64	18	19	31	12	6	1.2

C = consumption expenditure; I = gross private capital formation; G = government purchases of goods and services; S^h = household savings. C+I+G may not add up to 100%, the remainder being related to net exports

Source: OECD National Accounts, IMF.

of expenditure. This surplus on the government account is called a Public Sector Debt Repayment (PSDR). Such a situation occurred in the United Kingdom during the 1980s. Revenue rose from the increased tax paid by more individuals in work and from receipts from the sale of privatized industries. Some European countries, such as Luxembourg, have consistently run surpluses on their government account while others, such as Italy and Belgium, usually have very high levels of government debt and borrowing.

QUESTIONS

1. Why do some countries appear to run surpluses on their government account while others appear to run consistent deficits?

2. If there is an increase in the amount of injections entering an economy what effect may this have on the organizations?

3.5 Structural changes in the major economies

The circular flow depicts, in a clear way, the flows between two groups in the domestic economy – households and firms – and the external forces that impinge upon them. In macroeconomics there is a tendency to treat all firms as one and the same yet, over time, there have been important changes in the structure of industry. By structural change we mean how the sectors in an economy have changed. It is useful to give some broad definitions of these sectors:

1. The primary sector includes activities directly related to natural resources, for example farming, mining and oil extraction.
2. The secondary sector covers production industries in the economy such as manufacturing, the processing of materials produced in the primary sector and construction.
3. The tertiary sector includes all private sector services, for example banking, finance, computing services and tourism as well as public sector services such as health and defence.

Generally there has been a convergence of economic activity in structural terms; that is, the developed economies have become more oriented towards the service sector. As Table 3.5 indicates, almost 60 per cent of the economic activity in many countries is in the service sector, when measured as a contribution towards GDP and in terms of employment. Agriculture plays a bigger part in the economies of some European countries, such as Ireland, Spain, Portugal and Greece.

Consideration of the sectors overall may hide important changes within sectors. For example, the decline in the primary sector in the United Kingdom is almost entirely attributed to changes in mining during the 1960s and 1970s and to the subsequent rise and fall in activity in oil and gas production (see Cook and Healey, 1995).

Within the secondary sector it is manufacturing which has felt the full force of any structural change, though once again there are differences by country, as Table 3.5 indicates.

The United Kingdom has seen a fall in its share of world manufacturing exports and a fall in manufacturing employment. For other countries, such as Japan and Germany, the picture is somewhat different. In fact, between 1964 and 1992 Japan continued to see its manufacturing employment grow, while at the same time Italy lost 8.6 per cent, the Netherlands 6.1 per cent and the United Kingdom over 50 per cent. Consideration of such a long time period also disguises other changes that have taken place. Since 1979, the Netherlands has actually gained in industrial employment; so, too, have Austria and Japan. The United Kingdom is the biggest loser with an absolute loss in industrial jobs of around 33 per cent.

These changes in employment between the various sectors of the economy are, to some extent, overstating the problem since many manufacturing firms used to undertake service sector activities themselves and the employment would have been included under the manufacturing heading. More recently these firms have begun to contract out this type of activity (such as marketing), thus the jobs now appear under the service sector employment heading. Although the data in Table 3.5 indicates important differences between countries it also shows that a number of countries are alike in terms of their economic structure. Some countries appear to stand out from the others as having less-developed service sectors, in particular Germany and Japan.

TABLE 3.5   Sectorial contribution to GDP and employment, 1991, percentages

	Agriculture		Industry		Services	
	GDP	Employment	GDP	Employment	GDP	Employment
Belgium	1.8	2.6	30.1	28.1	68.1	69.3
Denmark	3.9	5.7	24.4	27.7	71.7	66.6
Germany	1.5	3.4	38.7	39.2	59.8	57.4
Greece	13.5	23.9	24.1	27.7	62.5	48.4
Spain	5.3	10.7	35.0	33.1	59.7	56.3
France	3.1	5.8	28.7	29.5	68.2	64.8
Ireland	9.0	13.8	33.4	28.9	57.6	57.2
Italy	3.3	8.5	32.1	32.3	64.6	59.2
Luxembourg	1.4	3.3	33.7	30.5	64.9	66.2
Netherlands	4.2	4.5	31.5	25.5	64.2	69.9
Portugal	5.8	17.3	37.8	33.9	56.4	48.7
United Kingdom	1.3	2.2	30.0	27.8	68.7	70.0
Austria	2.8	7.4	36.3	36.9	60.9	55.8
Finland	4.8	8.5	27.0	29.2	68.3	62.3
Norway	2.9	5.9	35.5	23.7	61.6	70.4
Sweden	2.6	3.2	29.5	28.2	67.9	68.5
Switzerland	–	5.5	–	34.4	–	60.1
US	2.0	2.9	29.2	25.3	68.8	71.8
Japan	2.5	6.7	41.8	34.4	55.7	58.9

Source: OECD in Figures, Supplement to OECD Observer, June/July 1993.

Industrial structure

Not only has the overall structure of economies changed, but within the various economic sectors, countries have tended to specialize in producing certain products. The United Kingdom is more specialized in extractive industries, chemicals and financial services; France in food products; Germany in engineering and chemicals; and Italy in clothing, textiles and footwear. Of the smaller European countries, Sweden specializes in wood products, paper and furniture; Spain in leather goods and tourism; and Belgium in iron and steel. These differences may explain some of the variances in trading patterns, an area that will be considered later. It is useful to note that if we disaggregate the various areas of manufacturing into slow, medium and fast growth sectors, as noted by Sharp (1992), then the majority of countries in the OECD had equal proportions of these. There were exceptions, however: Germany, Japan and the United States had a higher concentration of manufacturing in the high-growth sector, particularly in capital goods. Conversely, countries such as Spain, Portugal and Greece have traditionally had a higher proportion of their manufacturing industries in slow-growth sectors of the economy, such as textiles. This suggests that when there are upturns in economy activity, these countries will have improvements in growth which are less than in those countries which have sectors which exhibit high-growth performance.

3.6 Economic growth

As we have seen already, GDP figures differ between the various nations; if these are considered over time then this provides an estimate of the long-run growth of the economy. Growth brings improvements in real incomes and a greater variety of goods and services to all sectors of the economy. The generation of growth may follow from a highly motivated, highly skilled and highly productive workforce, coupled with innovation, quality capital investment, and a high level of skill training and education.

Table 3.6 describes growth in real output per worker, a good proxy for growth in real income per person, of five of the world's major industrial countries, and provides a comparison of the post-1945 years with earlier eras.

The United Kingdom has a long-standing peacetime tendency for a slower growth in labour productivity and, therefore, slower growth than its major competitors. Moreover, the table reveals that there has been a general slow-down in productivity growth since 1973. Reasons cited for UK performance are:

- the short-termism of United Kingdom industry;
- the poor labour relations between unions and management;
- its less skilled and qualified workforce;
- the role of North Sea Oil, as noted by Forsyth and Kay (1980), which served

TABLE 3.6   Growth rate of real output per worker employed (% per annum)

	UK	USA	France	Germany	Japan
1873–99	1.2	1.9	1.3	1.5	1.1
1899–1913	0.5	1.3	1.6	1.5	1.8
1913–24	0.3	1.7	0.8	−0.9	3.2
1924–37	1.0	1.4	1.4	3.0	2.7
1937–51	1.0	2.3	1.7	1.0	−1.3
1951–64	2.3	2.5	4.3	5.1	7.6
1964–73	2.6	1.6	4.6	4.4	8.4
1973–79	1.2	−0.2	2.8	2.9	2.9
1979–87	2.1	0.6	1.8	1.5	2.9

Sources: Matthews, R.C.O., Feinstein, C.H. and Odling-Smee, J. (1982), *British Economic Growth, 1865–1973*, Stanford University Press, p. 31; as Organization for Economic Co-operation and Development (OECD) (1988), *Historical Statistics, 1960–1987*, OECD, Paris.

to drive up the United Kingdom's exchange rate during the early 1980s making its exports less competitive and imports more attractive to purchase;
• its poor record on non-defence research and development.

Table 3.6 further indicates that after 1979 there was a relative improvement of the United Kingdom in the growth league, although in absolute terms productivity growth did not regain the level of the 1960s.

The pattern of growth has been very uneven since the second oil shock of 1980/81. If we take the early part of the 1980s through to 1985, the overall growth rate of the European Union was very slow at around 1.4 per cent per annum (economies need a growth rate of at least 2 per cent per annum to keep unemployment from rising). Some European Union countries did perform a little better, such as Denmark and the United Kingdom, while in the latter part of the 1980s almost the reverse appeared to be true – that is, Germany, Spain, Ireland and Portugal had growth rates in excess of the European Union average of 2.8 per cent, while the United Kingdom, Denmark, Sweden and Greece were the poorer performers. During the 1990s the growth performances of most Western economies have come more into line, though there were still indications of countries in the European Union whose level of economic growth was out of phase with others. For example, in both 1993 and 1994 the United Kingdom registered significant improvements in its real GDP, while other European Union members were slower to come out of recession.

What factors affect growth rates?

If countries knew precisely which were the important factors affecting economic growth then remedial action could be taken and we would notice a large number of countries with extremely high and similar growth rates. The factors that are .believed to influence growth can either have an individual country dimension or constraints to growth might involve policies at a wider level, such as that of the trading bloc (for example, the North American Free Trade Association) or the economic bloc (the European Union).

On a European level it has been suggested by Cook (1996) that four factors lie behind the poor growth performance of the European nations during the 1980s:

• the changed structure of growth;
• the constraints caused by the size of the welfare state;
• aggregate supply imbalances;
• the interaction of exogenous shocks and macroeconomic policies.

Growth and structural change

The 1950s and 1960s saw the growth rates of the European economies at unprecedented levels. There was an abundant supply of labour, moving from agriculture into other sectors of the economy. Oil discoveries in the Middle East ensured cheap oil supplies, particularly as oil production was in the hands of a few major Western European companies. Further, technology transfer from the United States enabled the relatively backward industries of post-war Europe to make rapid improvements in productivity. Increasing real incomes improved market sizes and, coupled with the removal of trade barriers through the development of the European Free Trade Area (EFTA), the development of the European Community (EC) and the successes of the General Agreements on Tariffs and Trade (GATT), conditions were ripe for high levels of sustained growth.

By the early 1970s conditions were beginning to change. The movement of labour from agriculture to manufacturing had begun to decline, labour relations deteriorated. The 1973/74 oil price rise led to a period of more expensive and less secure energy, and exchange rate movements led to European commodities losing some of their competitiveness. In addition, there was increasing competition from Japan and the newly industrialized countries (NICs) of Singapore, Hong Kong, South Korea and Taiwan in shipbuilding, steel and car manufacture – areas in which the Europeans had regarded themselves as pre-eminent.

At the same time Japan, in particular, had begun to adopt different working practices which implied that the old labour rules needed adjusting, a feature which was heavily resisted by the trade unions in Europe. In other words, inadequate adjustment of its industry had reduced Europe's ability to compete in global markets. Free marketeers believe that the weakness of governments and the strength of trade unions allowed real wage rates (the amount of items that take-home pay will purchase) to soar. Thus, products became more expensive within Europe and government policy only served to safeguard jobs rather than improve output. The much more *laissez-faire* approach adopted by the United Kingdom government, since the early 1980s, has attempted to address the problem of the high price of labour through legislation, designed to limit the power of trade unions, and encourage private sector involvement through its privatization policy.

Another factor linked to the slower growth rates of the European economies was the level of government involvement in the economy, a subject to which we will return later in this chapter. A high level of government expenditure, Bacon and Eltis (1976) argued, has tended to 'crowd out' private sector investment. Thus one of the reasons for the slower growth rates in Europe during the 1970s/80s was that the private sector had been rationed of investment funds. In addition, the actual behaviour of the welfare state was deemed to have stifled innovation providing a 'cosy safety net' for some groups. Government involvement may also have propped up ailing industries, led to lower efficiency through the spread of state-run enterprises, and increased both consumer and industry tax burdens. As a result, public spending took an ever-larger share of GDP during the 1980s, a part of which can be related to the growing underlying upward trend in European unemployment. The period of retrenchment during the 1980s saw governments unwilling to increase their fiscal deficits in order to reflate their economies, relying instead on export-led strategies to improve their growth records.

TABLE 3.7   Estimates of real GDP growth rates for selected South-East Asian countries

Country	Annual average rate 1984–91	GDP growth rate (%) 1992	GDP growth rate (%) 1993	GDP growth rate (%) 1994
Hong Kong	6.9	6.3	5.8	5.5
Singapore	6.8	6.0	10.1	10.1
Taipei	8.4	6.7	6.3	6.5
China	9.8	13.2	13.4	11.8
Indonesia	6.0	6.5	6.5	7.4
Malaysia	6.2	7.8	8.3	8.5
Philippines	1.1	0.3	2.1	4.3
Thailand	8.9	7.9	8.2	8.5

Source: World Bank, *The World Bank Atlas 1995*; Asian Development Bank.

Finally, within the Western economies, we need to consider how external shocks affected growth. The oil price rises of 1973/74 and 1980/81 resulted in very tight monetary policies coming into operation making investment expensive. Fiscal policy (the use of government expenditure changes or tax changes) was an option, but many policy makers believed that either expanding government expenditure or reducing taxes would only serve to drive up the inflation rate rather than having any long-term effect on production and output. Having successfully reduced their debts during the 1980s governments were loath to push them up again by borrowing more. There is an extensive belief that only export-led growth is an acceptable means by which growth can be re-established.

Although these factors may underlie the poor growth performance of the major Western industrialized nations, not all countries have experienced slower growth rates during the 1980s/90s. South-East Asian countries have performed remarkably well, as we can see from Table 3.7. Some saw this as the result of a much more *laissez-faire* approach by governments to their economies, while the notion of an unfettered, cheap labour market and economies which were also growing from a lower base level have also been advocated as reasons.

The BMW mini-case below illustrates the effect that growth rates can have on business.

The economic environment and BMW

In their 1994 annual report, BMW, the German car manufacturer, highlighted the changing nature of growth patterns around the globe and other changes in the international order and the effects these were having on their company sales.

World economy recovers

In 1994, the strong expansion of world trade decisively boosted recovery of the world economy. For the first time this decade, North America and Europe both benefited from an upward trend. In contrast, Japan lagged behind.

North America and Great Britain recorded the strongest growth among the traditional industrial countries. Continental Europe came out of recession, but continued to have structural problems. In the United States during 1994, 3.5 million new jobs were created, capacity utilization was at 85 per cent but, nonetheless, inflation was kept under control at 2.7 per cent. It followed that sales to the United States picked up appreciably. For some Latin American countries growth was even more dynamic, at 3.5 per cent. BMW recognized that this was a potentially lucrative market, not only in which to sell their cars but also in which to invest to take advantage of the lower cost structures there.

Although the Japanese market was fairly subdued, the Asia–Pacific region continued to be the focus of world economic growth. On average, the growth rates of the South-East Asian 'tiger' countries grew by 7 per cent. Investment continues to grow in these markets and foreign companies like BMW can take advantage of access to these burgeoning sales markets.

In their home market, BMW were forced, like many other German companies, to increase productivity via job-shedding. Competition in the home market is growing and private consumption increased very little during 1994. General improvement of the economy should not obscure the fact that Germany still has structural problems. Companies, including BMW, have made efforts to break through outdated structures and cut unnecessary costs, but they still have a long way to go.

The costs of growth

An assumption that has been made is that growth brings only benefits. However, there is a view that growth has a number of negative aspects in terms of environmental damage and that the process of achieving higher growth may not be worth the effort.

Firstly, to achieve a higher growth rate some consumption expenditure may have to be forgone today and resources switched to investment goods so that future consumption may be higher. We can illustrate this concept using Figure 3.2.

The initial consumption level is shown as C_1 and the growth path as G_1. Suppose the government wishes to push the economy onto a higher growth path, shown as G_2. To enable this growth path to be reached requires more investment, which could be financed through more savings or higher taxes, both of which reduce current consumption. As Figure 3.2 indicates, it takes until time T_x before the two growth paths coincide. Whether or not the sacrifice is worth while depends upon the amount of extra consumer goods produced in the future and how long it takes to make up for the sacrificed goods.

Secondly, growth may cause negative externalities; it is the developed countries which produce the greatest amount of pollution and 45 per cent of greenhouse gases (and consume around 70 per cent of all resources) – see Chapter 6 for a discussion of the environmental costs. Many of these costs are likely to be

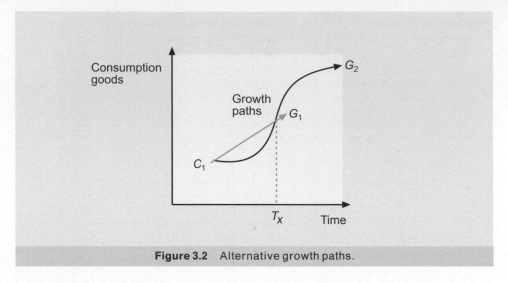

Figure 3.2   Alternative growth paths.

understated, since precise measurements are not available. If, as Meadows and Meadows (1992) suggest, the costs of growth are included in the estimates of real national income, then the benefits of economic growth may be overstated.

Growth also has an impact on resources, particularly non-renewable ones. If growth is stimulated today we are just bringing the day forward when non-renewable resources will disappear. Growth also brings technical progress, which may create jobs but, at the same time, destroy others by making skills redundant. People may be forced to take low-paid, unskilled work or migrate. The results of this process can be seen in the structural changes outlined earlier.

Whether governments should pursue the goal of growth depends, therefore, on the costs and benefits of growth and how much weight individual groups in society attach to them. Perhaps constrained growth is the solution, where growth is sought, but subject to, for example, levels of environmental protection, minimum wages, and maximum rates of resource depletion.

There are individuals who suggest that we do not have to worry about using up finite resources. In their view, as the resource is depleted so its price will rise and consumers will purchase less of it. It is possible, too, that resources which were not profitable at the old price will come into use, as was the case in the development of North Sea oil and gas reserves. These marginal resources may be used efficiently if technology can provide a means of increasing the capacity usage. Suppose, however, that there comes a point when technology cannot make marginal resources as effective as those that have been depleted. It follows that the prices of materials would rise; this would feed through to inflation, and a wage price spiral would ensue, reducing everyone's standard of living. Alternatively, resources could be rationed.

Although these arguments seem a little improbable on first viewing, the notion of resource depletion did receive support at the Earth Summit in Rio de

Janeiro in May 1992. The call was for controlled growth. A constrained growth rate is easier to bear for the developed countries, but for many less developed countries (LDCs) or newly industrialized countries (NICs) the development of indigenous natural resources is seen as a prerequisite for escape from low levels of GDP per capita. Their acceptability of this constrained growth scenario depends upon whether the developed nations provide increased aid to finance any difference between sustainable growth and their 'normal' level of growth.

QUESTIONS

1. What factors are seen as the prominent drivers in the growth process?
2. What can governments do to stimulate growth in their economies?

3.7 Inflationary pressures

Inflation may be defined as a persistent increase in prices over time – in other words, the rate of inflation measures the change in the purchasing power of money.

There are a number of ways in which inflation can be measured. One method is by measuring changes in the Retail Price Index (RPI). The RPI measures the change in prices from month to month in a representative basket of commodities bought by the average consumer. The commodities in the basket are weighted differently to indicate the proportion of expenditure made by the average consumer on various items. As Table 3.8 indicates for the United Kingdom, the weights change over time as goods change in relative importance in the average basket of commodities purchased by consumers.

In the United Kingdom, since mortgage interest payments are included in the RPI, changes in interest rates will alter the RPI. If it is the government's intention to reduce inflation by increasing interest rates and thereby reducing consumer expenditure, the opposite effect will occur. Higher rates of interest serve to push up mortgage rates which feed through into the RPI and increase the rate of inflation. Since the RPI was the index which was usually used as a basis for wage claims, this led trade unions to ask for higher increases. These would then increase the costs of industry, causing further price rises.

Other European countries, for example France and Italy, exclude owner-occupation from their consumer price index.

In the United Kingdom a new measure of inflation has been developed which does not include the costs of mortgages, RPIX. A further method for measuring inflation has also been developed called RPIY. This measure of inflation excludes both mortgage interest rate payments and indirect taxes such as VAT and excise duty. This is a measure, therefore, of the true underlying rate of inflation.

TABLE 3.8   General index of retail prices: group weights

Category	1987	1994
Food	167	142
Alcoholic drinks	46	45
Tobacco	76	76
Housing	157	158
Fuel and light	61	45
Household goods	73	76
Household services	44	47
Clothing and footwear	74	58
Personal goods and services	38	37
Motoring expenditure	127	142
Fares and other travel costs	22	20
Leisure goods	47	48
Leisure services	30	71
	1000	1000

Source: Employment Gazette (1988, 1994).

Why the concern about inflation?

From 1950 to 1970 prices were fairly stable in Western nations. The first oil price rise in 1973/74 changed this. The increase in the price of oil pushed up energy prices, transportation costs and increased the prices of all goods that were oil related. The response of the Western nations was to try to squeeze inflation out of the system. Figure 3.3 shows how inflation has changed in the United Kingdom since 1972, and indicates the price rises following the 1980/81 oil shock and the further rise in inflation towards the end of the 1980s.

Inflation is said to have redistribution effects. If money wages rise at the same rate as inflation, then real wages remain constant. However, if tax bands and tax thresholds do not rise in line with inflation a greater proportion of income is subject to tax. Inflation also reduces the real value of the debt to the government, thus redistributing income from the people to the state.

The redistribution effects of inflation not only take place from individuals to governments but also affect individuals and businesses. Inflation favours debtors rather than creditors, as it erodes the value of debt.

Inflation also has external consequences, making domestically produced goods more expensive and less competitive on world markets and imported goods cheaper on the home market. In this case the balance of payments position will worsen and pressure will mount for the exchange rate to fall. As the exchange rate falls it will make imports more expensive and reduce the price of exports, thereby restoring equilibrium in the balance of payments. Governments, however, may pursue a policy of managed exchange rates which prevents the market from restoring equilibrium in the balance of payments. In these cases controlling the effect of inflation by other means, rather than letting the exchange rate do the correction, may be a better approach.

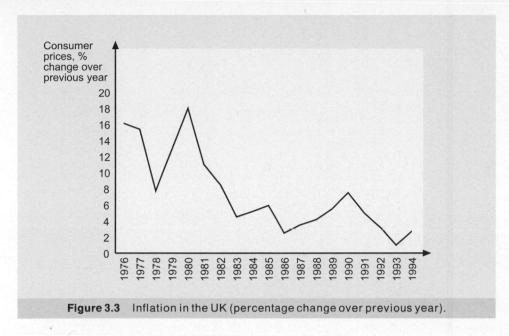

Figure 3.3   Inflation in the UK (percentage change over previous year).

Government policies throughout Europe shifted, during the 1980s, from reducing unemployment to controlling the rate of inflation. Policy makers argue that this is the correct approach since, once inflation is beaten, unemployment will fall. The arguments are stated as follows. High and variable inflation makes future income streams from investment projects uncertain. Thus firms may reduce investment or may only consider undertaking investment projects which yield a high rate of return in the short term. However, the positive link between inflation and unemployment is somewhat tenuous with Friedman (1977) supporting the relationship and Higham and Tomlinson (1982) finding no general evidence.

High inflation may lead to governments imposing wage and price controls which inhibits the working of the market mechanism. Some firms, which may be relatively more efficient or in markets where the demand for their products is rising, may be prevented from offering their employees better rewards because of the controls put in place by government. In addition, the more efficient firms may be unable to offer rewards high enough to entice staff from other sectors of the economy. High inflation may also lead to industrial unrest as unions seek money wage increases in order to prevent a deterioration in their real wages. It may also be expected that high inflation depresses saving as consumers purchase products from organizations before their price increases once again.

Inflationary expectations also take time to adjust downwards. A reduction in current inflation may not lead to an improvement in the amount invested since it is possible that investors may feel that the inflation rate will remain high in the future.

Given the problems that can arise from inflation it would be easy to suggest

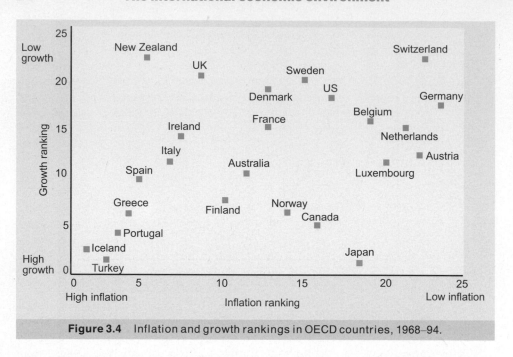

Figure 3.4   Inflation and growth rankings in OECD countries, 1968–94.

that countries which have relatively higher rates of inflation perform less well than countries with lower levels of inflation. As Figure 3.4 indicates, this is not always the case. Thus a government which pursues a policy of low inflation as a means of improving the economy's growth performance cannot always be guaranteed of this outcome.

The causes of inflation

Inflation can be damaging both internally and externally and it is not surprising that governments have used a variety of means to control inflationary pressures.

   The more traditional view was that inflation could be due either to 'cost–push' or 'demand–pull' factors. In the former it may be due to:

- increases in costs of labour that are not linked to increases in labour productivity;
- increases in the costs of raw materials which could come about in buoyant stages of the economic cycle, where the demand for raw materials may outstrip supply in the short term;
- a deterioration in exchange rates which tends to cause import prices to rise.

   In the demand–pull scenario, it is the excess demand for goods that pulls up prices. If aggregate demand increases, the increased demand for labour would bid up real wages rates. If unions in other sectors of the economy attempted to keep their members' wages in parallel, then it is possible that, even though there is an

TABLE 3.9 The UK and world economy since 1979

	Inflation (% rate)		Unemployment (% level)		Real GDP (% growth rate)	
	UK	OECD	UK	OECD	UK	OECD
1979	13.4	8.7	5.0	5.0	2.8	3.5
1980	18.0	11.3	6.4	5.7	−2.2	1.5
1981	11.9	9.5	9.8	6.6	−1.3	1.7
1982	8.6	7.2	11.3	8.0	1.7	−0.1
1983	4.6	5.5	12.5	8.5	3.5	2.7
1984	5.0	4.9	11.7	8.0	2.1	4.8
1985	6.1	4.3	11.2	7.8	3.7	3.4
1986	3.4	2.7	11.2	7.7	3.6	2.7
1987	4.2	3.4	10.3	7.3	4.7	3.5
1988	4.9	3.3	8.6	6.7	4.5	4.4
1989	7.8	4.3	7.1	6.2	2.3	3.6
1990	9.4	4.7	6.8	6.1	1.0	2.5
1991	5.9	4.5	8.9	6.8	−2.2	1.1
1992	3.7	3.5	9.9	7.4	−0.6	1.5
1993	1.6	2.9	10.3	7.8	2.0	1.0
1994*	2.0	2.4	9.5	8.5	2.9	2.2

* Estimated

Source: OECD Economic Outlook, June 1994.

the United Kingdom, world inflation, the exchange rate and its effect on import prices have all played an important part in explaining the changes in its inflation record. We should also consider the United Kingdom's 'temporary' membership of the Exchange Rate Mechanism (ERM). Under fixed exchange rates organizations cannot rely on the exchange rate to restore competitiveness in their prices if their relative inflation rates are too high. In the short term, if labour seeks too high a wage claim, then the loss of competitiveness that follows from any increases in prices would lead to job losses. Thus, the ERM was seen as providing discipline for the labour market.

At this stage let us consider the arguments. Inflation is costly both domestically and internationally. Many reasons have been put forward to explain why inflation occurs and almost as many remedies. For the latter there does not appear to be any consensus. However, in seeking to bring down inflation, countries have often deflated their economies and in doing so worsened the conditions for business. For Eastern European countries the scenario is somewhat different. By Western standards, inflation has remained high in most parts of the region, as Table 3.10 indicates.

Part of the explanation for the relative poor inflation performance of many Eastern European countries has been the introduction of market forces into many sectors and the reduction in state management of prices. Nonetheless, there are signs that inflation is being controlled, though high levels of inflation probably have affected business formation and development.

TABLE 3.10   Consumer price inflation (% per annum) in selected Eastern European countries

Year	Bulgaria	Czech Rep.	Hungary	Poland	Romania	Slovakia
1989	5.6	1.4	17.0	251.1	1.1	1.3
1990	23.8	9.7	28.9	585.8	5.1	10.4
1991	338.5	56.6	35.0	70.3	174.5	61.2
1992	79.4	11.1	23.0	43.0	210.9	10.0
1993	59.1	25.2	22.5	35.3	256.1	23.2
1994	55.1	10.0	16.8	30.8	265.3	15.5

Source: *Employment Observatory, Central and Eastern Europe*, No. 6, 1994, European Commission.

QUESTIONS

1. How does monetary policy affect the behaviour of organizations?

2. If the United Kingdom had an independent central bank, then inflation would be under greater control. Discuss.

3.8 The role of the state in the economy

Table 3.11 indicates that European Union governments' spending is around half of GDP. The top six spending governments are Sweden, Denmark, the Netherlands, Belgium, Norway and Italy, all of which spend over 55 per cent of GDP.

Government spending by all European Union governments exceeds that of both the United States (38 per cent of GDP) and Japan (31 per cent of GDP). There is no single reason to explain why some countries have higher proportions of

TABLE 3.11   Government expenditure 1991

Country	Total government expenditure as a proportion of GDP	Country	Total government expenditure as a proportion of GDP
Belgium	57	Portugal	44
Denmark	60	Spain	43
France	52	United Kingdom	43
Germany	49	Austria	49
Greece	52	Finland	48
Ireland	44	Norway	57
Italy	56	Sweden	64
Luxembourg	51	EU-16	51
Netherlands	59		

Source: OECD National Accounts.

GDP devoted to government expenditure than others. The six European countries listed above are not all the highest spenders in terms of government projects. Expenditure on social security is paid for by central government in Denmark and Sweden for example, while in Germany and the Netherlands the majority of social security is paid for by social funds. Therefore, the two former countries would be expected to have higher government expenditure figures, as a percentage of GDP. In addition, European Union countries differ, quite markedly, in their expenditures on housing, education, defence, roads, recreational and cultural facilities.

These different levels of government activity occur for a variety of other reasons. Part of the spending represents a redistribution of income among its citizens. Governments may also play an active role in macroeconomic stabilization of the economy, using government spending to prevent excessive fluctuations in income and unemployment, thus smoothing out business cycles in the economy.

Government expenditure is a very important part of total expenditure in most economies. Governments are big consumers, spending around one-third of the total that all households spend on goods and services. Like many households they are prone to over-expenditure and are forced to borrow money from the private sector or from abroad. The level of this debt can reach almost unmanageable amounts and, as Table 3.12 indicates, for some countries like Greece, Italy and Belgium this burden of debt can be in excess of a full year's domestic product.

Interest payments on these debts is an important problem for countries, particularly those with debts in excess of 100 per cent of GDP. Interest payments

TABLE 3.12   Government debt as a percentage of GDP

Country	1988	1993	Change
Belgium	132	139	7
Denmark	61	80	19
France	34	46	12
Germany	44	48	4
Greece	80	115	25
Ireland	118	96	−24
Italy	93	119	26
Luxembourg	10	8	−2
Netherlands	79	81	2
Portugal	75	67	−8
Spain	42	60	18
United Kingdom	50	48	−2
Austria	58	57	−1
Finland	17	62	45
Norway	43	45	2
Sweden	54	84	30

Source: European Economy, Supplement A, 11/12 November 1994; European Commission, OECD, Economic Outlook.

TABLE 3.13   Government receipts as a percentage of GDP (1992 figures)

Country	Indirect taxes	Direct taxes	Social security contributions	Other	Total
Belgium	13	17	18	2	50
Denmark	17	30	3	7	56
France	14	9	21	4	48
Germany	13	12	19	4	47
Greece	19	7	11	3	40
Ireland	17	16	6	3	41
Italy	11	15	15	3	44
Luxembourg	15	16	14	5	49
Netherlands	13	16	18	5	52
Portugal	16	11	11	4	42
Spain	12	12	14	5	42
United Kingdom	16	12	6	2	36
Austria	16	14	12	5	47
Finland	15	18	6	3	42
Norway	17	18	12	9	56
Sweden	18	20	15	7	61

Source: Commission of the European Communities.

in 1991 for example, were:

- 10.6 per cent of GDP in Belgium;
- 12.8 per cent of GDP in Greece;
- 10.8 per cent of GDP in Italy.

In these countries higher taxes, both on the business sector and on consumers, may have to be levied, for a long period, to finance the interest payments and to repay the debt.

Another way to reduce the debt is to curtail government expenditure. However, this may be difficult, since as unemployment rises there is often a concomitant rise in state benefits and reduction in tax revenue. It may, of course, be possible to reduce the deficit through increasing tax revenues. Table 3.13 shows the main sources of revenues for governments in the European Union as a percentage of GDP.

The proportion of revenue obtained from the various sources differs from country to country. For the European Union as a whole the proportion of revenue raised by direct taxes matches that from indirect taxes. However, in the United Kingdom, Portugal, Greece and France indirect taxes are a more important source of revenue, while in Belgium, Denmark, Finland, Italy and the Netherlands the reverse is true. These differences between the burdens of the various forms of taxation can have an impact on company location, level of profits, consumer behaviour and the incentive to work harder, all of which have important consequences for business (see mini-case below).

Tax cuts or not?

In the run-up to the November 1995 budget most commentators suggested income tax reductions. A decade ago such a move would have been universally popular in the Conservative party and among the electorate. At that time there was a consensus that reducing the basic rate made both political and economic sense. However, in 1995 there appeared to be little scope for substantial tax cuts since government ministers pointed to the uncomfortably large public sector borrowing requirement, heading for approximately £27 billion in 1995.

The chancellor was concerned that tax cuts which were not matched by equivalent reductions in public spending would be greeted with alarm in the City. The last thing he wanted was a budget that precipitated a fall in sterling and rising interest rates.

If tax cuts were to take place then some business sectors, such as the roads programme, grants for housing associations (and therefore the construction industry), would have to bear the brunt of the cost reductions. Government spending plans for 1996/97 were reduced by £3.7 billion with further cuts planned in subsequent years. Spending on schools, police and the NHS was increased and the money was saved by cuts in social security and the civil service.

The main changes in direct taxes in the budget included:

- a reduction in corporation tax to 24p for small companies;
- a cut in National Insurance contributions by 0.2 per cent and by 10 per cent from April 1997;
- basic rate of income tax reduced to 24p;
- the 20p lower rate band increased by £700;
- increase in personal allowances and married couples allowance above inflation;
- taxes on savings income cut from 25p to 20p;
- inheritance tax threshold increased to £200,000;
- capital gains tax; relief extended.

The main changes in indirect taxes included:

- cigarettes up 15p for a pack of 20;
- duty on spirits down 4 per cent;
- car tax up by £5 and petrol up 3.5p per litre.

Some ministers were of the view that an increase in the 20p threshold would not be noticed by voters while a reduction in the basic rate to 24p, at a cost of £1.6 billion in 1996/97 and £2 billion in 1997/98, was harder to ignore. Therefore, the impact of tax reductions on business may be influenced by the 'feel good' factor.

Economic cycles

It could be argued that one role of government is to reduce the fluctuations that occur in the economy. Often these fluctuations are not random but follow a cyclical pattern. There are long and short cycles in the economy. The long cycle,

(Kondratief cycle) is estimated to have a period of 50 years and to be associated with technological breakthroughs (see case study: 'Small and medium-sized enterprises', p. 406). Other cycles are observable, such as the business cycle (trade cycle) and political cycles. We would expect to find that in the boom periods of the cycle economic activity is buoyant and organizations find it much easier to sell their goods and services. At the same time there may be pent-up pressures beginning to appear which serve to drive up prices. At this stage the government may seek to dampen economic activity. Conversely, at the bottom of a cycle, economic activity is subdued, there may be high levels of unemployment, less pressure on prices, and the government may perceive that they need to step into the economy more directly and stimulate the level of economic activity.

Over time markets have become more internationalized and countries have increasingly been involved in closer trading groups so that the phases of their cycles are more concurrent. Thus, when one trading bloc or area goes into depression, it may cause other trading blocs to do the same. One national government cannot, on its own, stimulate its economy while others in its trading bloc do nothing. It is now necessary for groups of countries to coordinate economic intervention.

We should not discount that governments sometimes attempt to drive their economy out of its normal business cycle for political reasons such as re-election. Alesina (1989) suggests it is politically risky for governments to approach an election with deteriorating economic conditions.

Table 3.14 shows that during election years the budget tends to deteriorate relative to the previous year, and that the growth rate of the economy is relatively higher. For this scenario to occur it is necessary for governments to introduce

TABLE 3.14   Budgetary and economic conditions in election years, OECD countries, 1972–84

Country	Does the budget deteriorate in election years?		Is output growth higher in election years?		Is unemployment lower in election years?	
	Yes	No	Yes	No	Yes	No
Austria	1	2	1	2	0	3
Belgium	4	0	3	1	0	3
Denmark	3	1	2	2	1	3
Finland	3	0	2	1	0	3
France	2	1	0	3	0	3
Germany	0	4	2	2	2	1
Netherlands	2	1	2	1	0	3
Norway	1	2	0	3	2	1
Sweden	2	2	3	1	3	1
United Kingdom	2	1	3	0	2	1
United States	2	2	3	1	3	1
Total	22	16	21	17	13	23

Source: Alesina (1989).

expansionary policies before an election, leading to higher levels of employment and sales, thus companies are likely to see inventories fall and may increase their demand for labour. After elections it is possible that corrective actions are taken and the economy suffers from depressed demand conditions which leads to lower levels of sales for organizations, increased inventories and lower levels of employment. The economic cycle's effect on the paper industry is given in the mini-case below.

It is relatively easy to see the impacts of economic cycles on international economies, but explaining why they occur is much more difficult. The political business cycle can be explained, though not fully, by the behaviour of domestic governments, but the trade cycle is much more difficult to interpret. Some suggest that an economy begins to fall from its peak of activity because exports fall. This

Economic cycles and the paper industry

Demand is down and prices are weakening (November 1995). Is this a blip in the pulp and paper cycle, or the start of the next downturn?

Judging by the sharp drop in pulp and paper shares in recent months, many investors see a gloomy scenario. Their confidence was not helped by adverse profits at Arjo Wiggins Appleton, the Franco-British paper group, and KNP BT, the Dutch group.

The slowdown has circled the world, starting in Europe this summer, moving onto the USA and now starting to hit the previously buoyant Asian market.

The immediate cause of the problem is a build-up of stocks, driven by the unprecedented rate at which prices for pulp and paper have risen over the last two years. The resulting overhang has curtailed demand and is starting to affect prices. Companies in North America and Europe are cutting production to stop prices from slipping. Many North American container board and white paper mills, for example, have shut machines for two or three weeks at a time and have scheduled longer-than-usual Christmas breaks. Other producers have not been as cooperative, such as those in Korea, Taiwan and China.

Whether the current difficulties amount to a blip in a still rising market or the first signs of a downturn will depend greatly on how the world economy performs in 1996.

However, if this is the start of a downturn, the hope is that industry consolidation, restructuring and limited new capacity addition will create a soft landing.

Analysts are taking no chances and have marked down some pulp and paper stocks by more than 30 per cent since mid-1995, apparently anticipating a repeat of the last cycle, when companies aggressively cut prices to retain market share and ended up suffering large losses.

The sell-off shows the pulp and paper industry will only regain investors' confidence when it proves it can make profits even in cyclical slumps.

suggests that trading partners have experienced a decline in demand conditions. But from where? Others have suggested that expectations play a major role in the swings of the business cycle such that at the peak of the cycle business people and consumers believe that the current conditions cannot remain at their present state and they have the expectation that things will be worse in the future. In this case consumers may reduce their levels of expenditure and organizations may postpone making some investment decisions. It follows that expenditure levels fall and the level of economic activity declines (see mini-case on economic cycles and the paper industry). However, if this was the case then governments could step in and restore the general level of economic activity through their use of increased government expenditure. Even though some governments have tried this response, their economies have still gone into decline. Thus the real reasons behind economic cycles are still waiting to be discovered.

QUESTIONS

1. Why did fiscal policy (the use of government budgets to control the level of economy activity) go out of favour during the 1980s?

2. What is the crowding-out effect? How is this likely to affect organizations?

3. If different types of cycles exist in the economy then the government are powerless to affect the overall level of economic activity. Discuss.

3.9 Unemployment

From the end of the Second World War until the 1970s control of unemployment was the main goal of most European governments. During the 1970s and 1980s control of inflation assumed greater importance. Phillips (1958) argued that low inflation is not compatible with low unemployment. Nonetheless, a number of governments saw that low relative inflation could lead to higher competitiveness and provide the conditions for improvements in employment.

Although unemployment has fluctuated with the general level of economic activity there has been a slow upward trend in the natural level of unemployment since 1945. For example, the estimate of the natural unemployment rate in Germany is 1.1 per cent of the workforce between the years 1971–76 but by the period 1983–87 this had increased to 6 per cent. In the United States, however, the picture was somewhat different: the estimate of their natural rate of unemployment by the OECD was 5.4 per cent in the period 1971–76, and this marginally increased to 6.0 per cent in 1983–87.

The OECD's estimate for the United Kingdom for 1996 is about 8 per cent. Although this is slightly lower than a decade ago, suggesting some progress on supply-side measures in the labour market, it does suggest that the UK economy is getting dangerously close to full capacity.

So why has there been a general rise in the natural rates of unemployment in Europe in particular? Firstly, there is some evidence from Burda and Wyplosz (1993), though not conclusive, that where the safety provisions, such as benefits, for the unemployed are more extensive then unemployment levels are higher. Yet there is counter-evidence from Sweden and Norway to this relationship. What might be the issue here is that benefits do allow some people to stay out of the labour market. Their skills become inappropriate for the needs of the market and they become part of the long-term unemployed.

Secondly, a further difference between the United States and Europe is the process of wage bargaining. Trade unions have been more militant in Europe.

Thirdly, labour costs consist of more than wages: they include labour taxes (social security and retirement contributions) and these, too, have risen steeply. Fourthly, regulation of the use of labour, for example length of the working week and dismissal procedures, is also of importance. In addition to these factors, productivity must also be examined. As labour becomes more productive less employees are required to produce a given quantity of output. Furthermore, part of the answer to higher unemployment will be related to the sectoral changes that have taken place in a number of European economies as they have moved from labour-intensive manufacturing-based industries to service-oriented ones.

In the remaining years of the decade further job creation in the United Kingdom is possible. This is unlikely to come from a simple boost in demand but rather from a longer-term emphasis on investment in infrastructure, training and education (Begg, 1995).

For more than a decade the UK government has been acutely aware of the lack of training taking place, a shortage of skills and a general failure to keep pace with the rapidly changing world of work. The world of education has seen the development of a new National Curriculum and vocationally oriented qualifications. The government's response to the skills shortages that have appeared in UK industry, even though unemployment has been relatively high, include, for example, NVQs, Investors in People, and Modern Apprenticeships.

The emphasis has been on employer involvement in skills training. Some employers, however, during the recessionary period, have cut their training budgets and sought to obtain new employees from the unemployment register who already possess the skills they need.

To emphasize the situation, Studd (1996) finds the United Kingdom:

- 18th out of 25 in the world prosperity league, with an identified skills shortage;
- 18th out of 48 in overall competitiveness;
- 40th out of 48 in motivation of the workforce:
- 35th out of 48 in the adequacy of its education.

Therefore, although the United Kingdom has successfully tackled some of its supply-side problems such as state ownership and trade union issues, it has still to get to grips with deficiencies in the skill base of its workforce.

3.10 International trade

Since the Second World War markets have become increasingly internationalized and it follows that economies have become more 'open', that is, more heavily involved in international trade. But why do countries trade? Clearly, much trade takes place because one country is better able to produce particular products and services than its trading partners. For example, a country situated closer to the equator than the United Kingdom is better able to produce tropical fruit, while it is possible that, because of its manufacturing base, the United Kingdom is better able to produce some manufactured goods. Countries, by specializing in the products in which they are more efficient, can gain by trading these products for other products produced more efficiently elsewhere. These concepts of efficiency and specialization lie behind two of the oldest theories of international trade, those of Absolute Advantage (Adam Smith) and Comparative Advantage (David Ricardo).

These two theories tell us why trade takes place but perhaps do not provide us with the complete picture as to why there has been a growth in international trade. The role of mutual benefit is certainly one driving force. Businesses and governments are unlikely to engage, voluntarily, in international trade if they do not expect either to improve their economic situation or to achieve any material gain in return. Variations in the costs of production constitute another incentive for international trade to occur. In particular, international trade may lead to domestic firms achieving economies of scale which were not available in their domestic markets alone. Changes that have taken place in international markets are of great importance in the trade debate. Many markets have recently become deregulated with reductions in the barriers to trade, and this has enhanced trading opportunities. New patterns of organization and business location have emerged, including the use of foreign suppliers, foreign direct investments, joint ventures and international cooperation. These have arisen to obtain better access to markets and to enhance competitiveness by exploiting specific local production factors such as:

*   favourable labour costs;
*   labour skills;
*   tax situations.

Increasing trade has intensified competition in both foreign and domestic markets (see mini-case below).

Closer international markets in the Latin American brewing industry

Argentines may not drink beer to the extent of their United Kingdom, North American or even Venezuelan counterparts, but from a brewer's point of view they are on the right track: consumption of beer in Argentina has quadrupled since 1982. Much of the increase is due to the efforts of Quilmes, 85 per cent owned by Luxembourg-based Quinsa and 15 per cent by Heineken. Quilmes, which also operates in Bolivia, Chile, Paraguay and Uruguay, has spent years aggressively marketing beer as a light, modern drink and an alternative to wine.

Although competition has been growing in its domestic market, the company has pushed hard to boost sales in neighbouring countries. In Paraguay, where market share had fallen because of a shortage of capacity, the company opened a plant near Asuncion in January 1995 and saw its market share for 1995 increase by 6 per cent.

In Chile, where Quilmes produces Becker and Baltica, market share has increased from almost nothing in 1990 to 12.5 per cent in 1994. In Uruguay, a relatively sluggish market, the company has maintained its dominant position, while this year it has moved into Bolivia with the purchase of 50 per cent of a Santa Cruz-based brewery. This only leaves Brazil and Mexico as the two biggest markets yet to crack.

If the theories of Smith and Ricardo are to be believed, then countries should specialize in those products which they are better at producing. By doing so total world production of goods increases. In other words, by encouraging trade to take place the world may be better off in terms of total production of goods and services and in terms of the efficiency with which resources are used. However, countries taking this 'specialization' route could end up being dependent upon a small range of products or services. In this case if another country is able to produce one of these items more cheaply then the former country may see a large reduction in demand for its good or service. This could lead to balance of trade problems, reductions in sales and increases in unemployment. Therefore, countries may consider producing items which they are less efficient at providing.

Before we consider barriers to trade and the attempts made to reduce trade restrictions, let us appraise the importance of trade in the international arena.

Exports by country

The importance of international trade continues to increase. Trade in goods from European OECD countries increased from 14.3 per cent of GDP in 1962 to 21.6 per cent of GDP in 1992. However, there is increasing evidence of the Europeanization of international trade with the trade between European countries taking an ever greater proportion of total European trade. This intra-European trade rose from 61.5 per cent in 1962 to 71.8 per cent in 1992. Table 3.15 shows evidence of both 'intra' and 'extra' exports of the European Union countries.

TABLE 3.15   Destination of exports by EU-12 and EFTA-4, 1992 (%)

Country	Intra EU-12	Extra EU-12
Belgium/Luxembourg	75	25
Denmark	55	45
France	63	37
Germany	54	46
Greece	64	36
Ireland	74	25
Italy	58	42
Netherlands	75	24
Portugal	75	24
Spain	66	33
United Kingdom	55	44
EU-12	61	38
Austria	64	36
Finland	53	47
Norway	67	33
Sweden	56	44
EFTA-4	61	39

Source: Eurostat.

The main target markets for European Union exporters are other European Union markets and, in particular, those of neighbouring countries. This is especially true for smaller countries within the European Union such as the Netherlands. Larger European Union members are more likely to possess a greater number of large-scale enterprises which can address global markets, thus their proportion of intra-European Union trade will be lower. Other smaller European Union countries such as Denmark, by being on the periphery of the European Union, will have a greater proportion of their trade directed to countries fringing the European Union. During recent years countries situated closer to Central and Eastern Europe, for example Germany, have also seen an increasing proportion of their trade directed towards Hungary, Poland and the Czech Republic. Trade figures are in a constant state of flux. A strong situation in one year can often be overturned by factors beyond the control of individual organizations (see mini-case below).

Belgium's exports

At first glance Belgium's exports appear to be in good shape. In 1994 the current account surplus of the Belgium–Luxembourg Economic Union (BLEU) was an impressive $12.3 billion and this is expected to rise in 1995.

But, healthy figures hide a harsh reality. While the current account remains buoyant, Belgium's exports have been losing market share to their main competitors in the United Kingdom, France, Germany, the Netherlands and Italy. The surplus on the current account has been influenced by the weakness of domestic demand for imports, particularly for consumer goods. Meanwhile, Belgium's traditional important exports of chemical products, transport equipment and machinery have also begun to lose their competitiveness in external markets.

Many factors combine to put the small country's exports at a disadvantage. These include high wage costs, relative to neighbouring countries, and the strength of the Belgian franc whose fortunes are tied to the D-Mark.

While many exporters support the strong currency policy, believing it to be in the interests of the overall Belgium economy, they are less happy about government fiscal policy. In particular, they point to the high non-wage costs, which pay for a comprehensive social security system, but weigh down industry.

Many Belgian exporters are concentrating their hopes on government efforts to meet the economic convergence criteria set out by the Maastricht Treaty (see later in this chapter) as necessary pre-conditions for participation in a single currency. However, in their attempt to reduce the high level of government debt the Belgian government will be unable to reduce employers' social security contributions, the costs of which will have to be borne fully by Belgian employers.

Composition of international trade

In the United Kingdom there has been increased emphasis on trade with continental Europe. But what of the composition of its trade outside of Europe? Trade with North America has remained relatively constant, but this hides the fact that the majority of trade is now with the United States, and only a small proportion is now with Canada. The share of trade with Australia and New Zealand has also fallen, but trade with Japan has increased, particularly exports. There has been a rapid fall in the United Kingdom's percentage of trade with the rest of world, most notably with other Commonwealth countries and with the Latin American states. However, there is growing evidence of increased trade with the newly industrialized countries (NICs) such as Hong Kong, Singapore, Malaysia, South Korea, Taiwan and Thailand.

The United Kingdom imports less food and beverages, basic materials, minerals and fuel, as a percentage of all imports in 1993 than it did in 1960. However, imports of manufactured goods or semi-manufactured goods represent a much higher share of imports. This decline in the United Kingdom's manufacturing sector can be seen more starkly when we examine the United Kingdom's share of exports of manufactures (see Table 3.16).

The table indicates a substantial fall in the United Kingdom's share of world manufactures which does not appear to have been replicated by any of its major competitors. But is the decline sector specific? Table 3.17 indicates that, in terms of exports, the United Kingdom is the only country to have fared worse in all

TABLE 3.16   Share of world export of manufactures of major OECD countries (%)

Country	1960	1969	1979	1993
United States	22	19	16	19
Japan	7	11	14	18
France	10	8	10	11
Germany	19	19	21	18
Italy	5	7	8	8
United Kingdom	17	11	9	9
Others	21	23	22	18

Source: National Institute of Economic and Social Research, OECD.

export markets segments. Increased import penetration (the increased flow of imports), particularly in high- and medium-technology sectors, may indicate a lack of competitiveness by United Kingdom manufactures (see OECD, 1994).

United Kingdom manufacturers are, therefore, responding less well to changes that are taking place in the international business environment. It is not only the United Kingdom that is suffering, as the mini-case on Greek tourism shows.

TABLE 3.17   Export market shares and import penetration in manufactures

Country	High technology		Medium technology		Low technology	
	1970	1990	1970	1990	1970	1990
France	7.7	8.8	8.5	10.0	10.7	12.1
	(21.6)	(31.6)	(19.7)	(34.1)	(10.7)	(21.4)
Germany	17.7	16.2	23.1	24.7	15.0	17.9
	(14.9)	(37.0)	(17.2)	(29.5)	(11.1)	(20.9)
Italy	5.5	5.1	7.1	7.7	8.5	12.8
	(16.2)	(22.8)	(23.6)	(28.9)	(11.8)	(15.7)
UK	10.5	10.2	11.9	8.5	8.9	8.5
	(17.4)	(42.2)	(22.1)	(39.4)	(12.4)	(19.8)
Japan	13.2	21.1	8.5	16.9	13.2	7.1
	(5.2)	(5.4)	(4.5)	(5.9)	(3.0)	(6.6)
USA	31.1	26.3	21.7	15.4	13.4	13.3
	(4.2)	(18.4)	(5.6)	(18.5)	(3.8)	(8.8)

Note: Figures in brackets refer to import penetration.

Source: OECD (1994).

Greek tourism: a declining empire?

When Greece was 'discovered' in 1956, a mere 218 000 tourists spent $31.2 million. In 1994 there were 11.3 million visitors who spent $8 billion. Tourism contributes substantially to Greece's balance of payments. However, the figures for 1995 show tourist arrivals 20 per cent down on 1994. This downturn will deprive the Greek economy of an estimated $2 billion in much needed foreign exchange and reduce employment in the tourism industry. Why has Greece lost this comparative advantage as a holiday destination? A number of factors have been suggested:

- lack of diversification to attract the more up-market tourist;
- the imposition of a special airport tax in 1994 which led to tour operators, who were already working on tight margins, to remove some Greek holidays from their brochures;
- the Greek government has insisted on maintaining an over-valued drachma against the main European currencies;
- strikes at Greek airports;
- some dubious hotels.

In addition to these self-imposed penalties, there has been a series of adverse developments in some of Greece's traditional markets:

- the British have seen the purchasing power of the pound fall following its depreciation outside of the Exchange Rate Mechanism;
- the problems of the former Yugoslavia have reduced the numbers of people driving to Greece;
- Spain, Portugal, Italy and Turkey have become better tourist bargains after devaluing their currencies.

Greece's tourist profile is, therefore, under pressure and this will have adverse effects on its balance of payments. It remains to be seen if the Greek government will tackle the underlying problems of the tourist industry or whether it will develop some other sector from which it can obtain foreign currency.

Trade barriers

The evidence indicates that:

- there has been a growth in trade, especially over the last four decades;
- trade has become increasingly focused on particular trading blocs;
- there should be specialization through trade;
- some countries may lose from trade as their particular historic advantages are eroded.

With regard to the last factor in particular, and because of the costs of economic change, countries have sought to protect their industries, using such devices as:

- subsidies on products produced in the domestic market to reduce their prices down to world competitive levels;
- tariffs to push up the price of imports;

- quotas to limit the supply of imports into the domestic market;
- Voluntary Export Restraints (VERs) to prevent the free flow of goods between countries and enhance their own goods and services.

These types of measure may appear to protect a country's domestic firms but may not bring long-term advantage as other countries may respond. Table 3.17 shows that Japanese market import penetration is low. This could imply that the Japanese do not wish to buy foreign imports, but it could suggest that there are various barriers to entry into the Japanese market.

The growth of tariffs would lead to economic inefficiency as companies would find it difficult to export their products and world activity levels will fall. The General Agreement on Tariffs and Trade (GATT) was set up in 1946 in an attempt to reduce tariffs which had been ratcheted upwards between the two world wars.

There have been eight rounds of GATT trade talks which have become increasingly complex, given the rise in membership from 23 countries in 1946 to 125 in 1995. Moreover, the original trade talks focused on reducing tariffs, particularly those on manufactured goods since manufactured goods were those more likely to be traded, while the last GATT round, the Uruguay Round, considered much wider trade issues including the trade in services and agricultural products. While GATT has been successful in reducing tariffs generally, countries have still sought to limit the free flow of trade via other means. In particular, barriers such as quotas, voluntary export restraints and non-tariff barriers such as the use of red tape, government legislation and health and safety factors have come increasingly into play. Thus, the protracted Uruguay Round (1985–93) sought to address these issues for the first time, most notably because the developed countries are becoming predominantly service-oriented economies and there was an urgent need to consider the flow of services between countries.

A final conclusion to the Uruguay Round was agreed in December 1993 and involved 28 separate accords devised to extend fair trade rules to agriculture, services, textiles, intellectual property rights and foreign investment. Tariffs on industrial products were cut by more than one-third and were eliminated entirely in 11 sectors. Non-tariff barriers were to be converted into tariff barriers and these would subsequently be removed. GATT itself was wound up and replaced by the World Trade Organization (WTO) which would, in addition, govern the new accord on services and intellectual property, as well as codes relating to government procurement and anti-dumping. A streamlined disputes procedure was also to be set up.

Trading blocs

The GATT rounds were a series of multilateral trading agreements, which have now been paralleled by a process of regional trade agreements. These trading agreements can be of various types, such as:

- those that involve reducing tariffs between member countries;

- those that involve reducing tariffs among member countries together with a common external tariff against non-members;
- those that are similar to the second but promote much more commonality than trading arrangements and can cover other rules and regulations such as common currencies and defence/social policies.

Table 3.18 indicates the number of these regional trading agreements operating as at January 1995.

The European Union is one of the oldest and best known trading blocs. More recently the United States has become increasingly focused on the issue with the

TABLE 3.18 Reciprocal regional integration agreements notified to GATT and in force as of January 1995

Europe
- European Community (EC): Austria, Germany, Netherlands, Belgium, Greece, Portugal, Denmark, Ireland, Spain, Finland, Italy, Sweden, France, Luxembourg, United Kingdom.
- EC Free Trade Agreements with Estonia, Latvia, Norway, Iceland, Liechtenstein, Switzerland, Israel, Lithuania.
- EC Association Agreements with Bulgaria, Hungary, Romania, Cyprus, Malta, Slovak Rep., Czech Rep., Poland, Turkey.
- European Free Trade Association (EFTA): Iceland, Norway, Switzerland, Liechtenstein.
- EFTA Free Trade Agreements with Bulgaria, Israel, Slovak Rep., Czech Rep., Poland, Turkey, Hungary, Romania.
- Norway Free Trade Agreements with Estonia, Latvia, Lithuania.
- Switzerland Free Trade Agreements with Estonia, Latvia, Lithuania.
- Czech Republic and Slovak Republic Customs Union.
- Central European Free Trade Area: Czech Rep., Poland, Slovak Rep., Hungary.
- Czech Republic and Slovenia Free Trade Agreement.
- Slovak Republic and Slovenia Free Trade Agreement.

North America
- Canada–United States Free Trade Agreement (CUFTA).
- North American Free Trade Agreement (NAFTA).

Latin America and the Caribbean
- Caribbean Community and Common Market (CARICOM).
- Central American Common Market (CACM).
- Latin American Integration Association (LAIA).
- Andean Pact.
- Southern Common Market (MERCOSUR).

Middle East
- Economic Cooperation Organization (ECO).
- Gulf Cooperation Council (GCC).

Asia
- Australia–New Zealand Close Economic Relations Trade Agreement (CER).
- Bangkok Agreement.
- Common Effective Preferential Scheme for the ASEAN Free Trade Area.
- Lao People's Dem. Rep. and Thailand Trade Agreement.

Other
- Israel–United States Free Trade Agreement.

Source: W.T.O. *Focus, Newsletter*, May–June 1995, No. 3, p. 9.

development of the North American Free Trade Agreement (NAFTA), signed in 1993, which includes the United States, Canada and Mexico. Chile has also opened negotiations with the United States and by the year 2010 it is forecast that a free trade area will exist which will cover the whole of the Americas.

A further, ambitious, project is under way to create an Asia–Pacific Economic Cooperation Forum (APEC) which includes America, Japan, China, Taiwan, Malaysia, Australia and other countries with Pacific coastlines. The European Union is looking for closer ties with its Eastern European neighbours and there is even talk of a free trade area being set up between the European Union and North America.

To what extent do free trade areas affect companies? We need to consider the concepts of trade creation and trade diversion. When a free trade area is set up it encourages trade between member countries. This is trade creation and occurs because previous barriers to trade will be reduced giving each of the countries' industrial sectors reduced costs and therefore encouraging inter-country trade within the free trade area. Countries now outside the free trade area may find it more difficult to sell their products to countries which used to be outside but are now inside the free trade area, since they often face external tariffs barriers. Thus trade is diverted away from the countries outside the free trade area because the price of their products will increase as they face external tariffs, and countries inside the free trade area which do not face any of these external tariffs are more likely to trade between themselves.

There are also problems with rules of origin. Is a Japanese car made in Europe Japanese or European? The definition may depend on the proportion of parts that are provided by the European country. If it is European, then it can be exported within the free trade area subject to no additional tariffs.

What appears to be happening gradually is the development of trading areas or zones. These might lead to significant reductions in trade barriers which then get transmitted throughout the rest of the world in a kind of domino effect, the result of which is that many firms are likely to be winners. On the other hand, trading blocs can lead to some firms being excluded from markets, thereby damaging exports.

Exchange rate systems

Within the context of the growth in trade we should consider how different exchange rate regimes affect business behaviour.

Fixed exchange rate
The advantages of a fixed exchange rate are twofold. Firstly, the stability that it provides for businesses encourages long-term contractual arrangements between businesses. Secondly, since the exchange rate cannot be altered to restore a country's competitiveness if it runs a balance of payments deficit, it imposes a disciplined fiscal and monetary policy, which means a tight grip on inflation.

Floating exchange rate

At the other end of the possible set of exchange rate regimes lies the floating exchange rate. If there are differences between the demand for, and supply of, the domestic currency the price of the currency, the exchange rate, should automatically adjust. Thus one of the great advantages of this type of exchange rate is that it does not require any government intervention; market forces undertake the adjustment. The problems with floating exchange rates are that there are increased uncertainties for traders which may lead to a greater proportion of short-term contracts. In addition, if import prices rise then the balance of payments deteriorates, leading to a depreciation in the value of a currency. This restores the competitiveness of exports, but further raises the price of imports and these increased import costs can feed through into domestic inflation levels. The mini-case of the Italian textile industry shows that the exchange rate is an important factor in the competitiveness of a company.

Italian textiles and the devaluation of the lira

Marzotto, the Italian clothing and textile company, has until recently seen success building on success. Net profits grew from L10.2 billion in 1984 to L50.3 billion in 1988, only for the recession to cut profit back to L10.2 billion in 1994. The 1992 and 1993 results were also a disappointment when many analysts expected Marzotto, a big exporter in the internationally competitive clothing sector, to lead the way for all Italian exporters, on the back of the devaluation of the Italian lira after its removal from the Exchange Rate Mechanism.

Marzotto's other businesses – cloth, threads and yarns – did benefit from the lira devaluation. Thread and yarn exports increased by 32 per cent, more than offsetting a slight fall in Italian turnover, and cloth sales increased by the same amount abroad, against a decrease of 12 per cent on the home market.

So what went wrong in the clothing sector? According to analysts, the 1992 devaluation merely returned the Italian exporters to normal competitiveness, which they had lost during the 1988–92 period when all Italian companies were fighting to keep costs down. Now there is the basis on which to start growing exports again, and the process appears to have already started with a rise in orders for the new winter collection.

However, when it comes to talking about origin of garments, the term is more difficult to define. Of the group's 10 000 employees, although three-quarters are still to be found in Italy, it is this country which is bearing, increasingly, the costs of unemployment. A recent acquisition in the Czech Republic may well have lower productivity levels but labour costs are a tenth of those in Italy, while in Tunisia labour costs are 8 per cent of Italian costs. Thus, the company is increasingly selling its clothing on the basis of its label rather than on where the garment is made. The next two years are likely to provide the answer to the question as to whether Marzotto has benefited truly from the devaluation of the Italian lira or whether its recovery lies in its heavy emphasis on expansion abroad.

The history of exchange rates, since the end of the Second World War, is one of movements between relatively fixed and relatively floating exchange rates. But what about the impact of the various exchange rate regimes on businesses? Evidence suggests that fluctuations in the exchange rate are more likely to have harmful effects on investment; that is, both international investment and domestic investment may be reduced, with concomitant effects on exports in general and output in particular. It follows that any move to a fixed exchange rate system within Europe reduces this uncertainty and improves businesses' expectations. However, separating out the effects of an exchange rate regime from the impact of inflation, interest rates and level of aggregate demand is somewhat difficult. Under a fixed exchange rate system uncertainty is reduced but if, as in France in 1995, the currency is being pegged at a level beyond its real market rate then this will involve high interest rates. Moreover, there may be structural weaknesses in its economy which result in some parts of its economy unable to compete – a factor which may have been prevented with a flexible (floating) exchange rate system (see Higgins (1993)). With regard to whether flexible exchange rates lead to more imported inflation it was notable that when both Italy and the United Kingdom left the European Exchange Rate Mechanism (ERM) in 1993 the depreciation in the value of their currencies did not lead to higher inflation and higher interest rates as might have been believed. In fact we had quite the reverse.

The decision, therefore, to adopt one exchange rate system in preference to another may not be taken purely on economic grounds, but the result of the need for closer political ties and it is to this area of closer integration and commonality of policy within Europe that we now turn.

QUESTIONS

1.   Give examples of the various forms of non-tariff barriers countries use to limit the free flow of trade. How successful has GATT been in tackling these various forms of non-tariff barriers?

2.   Consider the advantages and disadvantages of both fixed and flexible exchange rates for organizations.

3.   What are the implications of the growth in trading blocs for export-oriented businesses? Are the implications the same for companies which do not export commodities?

3.11 Europe as one

The establishment of the European Economic Community in the 1950s was a major step towards helping trade within the European 'six' at the time. The widening of membership to the 12 member states by the early 1980s, the further reductions in trade barriers and the setting up and development of pan-European forums appeared to move the major Western European countries to a stronger economic position. In the 1980s there were, however, signs to suggest that the European Union 12 were experiencing some difficulties. Firstly, their growth rates had begun to slow and, secondly, unemployment levels had begun to rise. There was also a distinct lack of cooperation between Community members and a weakness of common policies. Since a number of countries appeared to be pulling in different directions the European Community appeared to be paralysed. In addition, the massive technological changes that had taken place in the world had, to some extent, left Europe behind. It was importing increasing amounts of high-technology products. The Community's external position, to some extent, was weakening and it was becoming increasingly dependent on foreign suppliers. The fragmented home market in the Community was seen as a main reason for this development and there was a desire to speed up integration between the various member countries. It was argued that a single European market would stimulate the scale of production, marketing, research and development and also strengthen competition, enhancing the efficiency and competitiveness of European industry. A necessary condition for the successful creation of the 'internal market' was a change in the Community decision-making procedures, which until then required unanimous decisions in the Council of Ministers. This condition was met by the adoption of the Single European Act in 1987 whereby in matters concerning the internal market, qualified majority voting was permitted. The SEA included the provision that the internal market should be completed before the end of 1992.

Mergers and acquisitions in the Single European Market (SEM)

Assessing the outcome of the Single European Act is difficult, since, as Kay (1993) and Swann (1992) note, it is likely to have effects in the long run as well as those in the short run. The removal of barriers between markets was expected to encourage competition yet there was an upsurge in merger and acquisition behaviour as firms previously in protected markets sought to reduce the competitive edge in the Community by merging or taking over their rivals.

Table 3.19 indicates that cross-border mergers became increasingly important during the late 1980s. As Cook and Meredith (1994) note, in terms of sectors, the majority of mergers were in chemicals, electrical and mechanical engineering, food and paper. It is not only United Kingdom firms that are involved: German, French, American, Japanese and South-East Asian firms were also very active, the latter three all seeking to gain a foothold in Europe before any barriers to external trade were in place. A major factor in the European merger boom was the strengthening of market position. Firms have been specializing more in the activities at which they are best and disposing of assets related to activities in which their competitive position is weak.

To some extent this merger boom goes against the expectations of the SEA,

TABLE 3.19   Cross-border acquisitions of EU companies (£ million)

Bidder country	1989 value	1990 value	1991 value	1992 value	1993 value
United States	10 040	2 257	2 755	3 592	3 094
United Kingdom	2 651	4 894	1 536	4 435	2 676
Germany	3 152	1 085	1 635	1 061	1 693
France	5 470	6 270	3 328	3 658	1 528
Sweden	680	6 486	683	986	956
Switzerland	1 337	516	902	350	620
Netherlands	458	603	1 217	3 273	406
Italy	762	886	1 153	2 207	400
Luxembourg	n/a	114	1 007	367	185
Japan	515	1 768	559	229	83
Others	4 787	9 986	4 539	8 949	3 785
Total	29 816	34 865	19 314	29 107	15 426

Source: Peat Marwick.

yet the newly established economies of scale enable these pan-European firms to be more competitive in global markets.

The SEA has not achieved a fully integrated internal market. Although it has removed trade barriers for many products, there are still barriers that exist through culture, tradition and consumption patterns. Moreover, economic analysis cannot predict exactly what will happen to each industry in each country, following the SEA. We might be able to say what will occur at the aggregate level, but as Nugent and O'Donnell (1994) note, at the more micro level precise details become fuzzy. It may well be that the successful organizations will be supranational rather than just pan-European. Nonetheless, the SEM may establish conditions where R&D can be regarded as European wide rather than on a national level and this may lead to the European Union taking a more proactive role in high-technology products. In addition, European nations have begun to face up to the fact that no single government is strong enough to shape international projects and agreements. Europe must work as one.

Maastricht and beyond

The SEA can be viewed as a major step towards an economically united Europe, but it is not the ultimate step. If Europe is to be truly united then some argue that there is a need for Economic and Monetary Union (EMU) which coordinates both monetary and economic policies. Monetary policy, presently the jurisdiction of each country, would be transferred to a European central bank and national currencies would be replaced by a single currency. Fiscal policy would be in the hands of national governments, but subject to common policies and restrictions. The move towards monetary union, as enshrined in the Treaty of European Unity 1992 (the TEU or Maastricht Treaty), is to proceed in three stages and a useful outline of this process is given by Arrowsmith

(1995). The TEU also includes a number of other important issues, detailed in Chapter 7.

EMU Stage 1 (July 1990–31 December 1994)
Completion of the internal market, including totally free movement of goods, capital and persons (before 31 December 1992). Countries will begin their economic convergence programmes and are expected to enter the narrow band of the Exchange Rate Mechanism.

EMU Stage 2 (1 January 1994–between 1997 and 1999)
The establishment of a new European Monetary Institute (EMI) to enhance cooperation between European Union central banks, coordinate monetary policy and prepare for the setting up of a European Central Bank. The EMI will seek to establish the convergence of the European Union member economies. The convergence criteria, as set out under Maastricht, are as follows:

1. *Price stability.* The inflation rate should not exceed the average inflation rate of the three countries with the lowest price increases by more than 1.5 percentage points.
2. *Currency stability.* The exchange rate should not have been subject to devaluation within the narrow band of the exchange rate mechanism of the European Monetary System during the last two years before the date of entry in EMU.
3. *Public deficit.* The budget deficit must not exceed 3 per cent of GDP.
4. *National debt.* The public debt must be lower than 60 per cent of GDP.
5. *Interest rates.* The nominal long-term capital interest rates should not deviate by more than 2 percentage points from the average of the long-term interest rates of the three countries with the lowest inflation rates.

The TEU dictates that the EMI should specify, by the end of December 1996, the regulatory, logistical and organizational framework for the European System of Central Banks. It should also set a date for the beginning of the third stage, and if this date is not set before the end of 1997, then on 1 January 1999 EMU will automatically begin for those countries fulfilling the criteria set out above.

EMU Stage 3 (starts between 1997 and 1999)
Founding of the European Central Bank (ECB) and the European System of Central Banks which will incorporate the ECB and the national central banks, responsible for the implementation of the monetary policy set by the ECB; replacement of national currencies of the member states admitted to the EMU by the Euro.

Implications of EMU for businesses

From a purely economic standpoint, a single currency appears to be attractive for at least some of the stronger countries within the European Union because:

- inflation and interest rates should be lower;
- all countries will participate in the setting of interest rates (rather than relying on German interest rates);
- a strong currency area will put companies on a par with the United States and Japanese competitors;
- a single currency removes the transaction costs and uncertainties of operating in different currencies and makes it easier to compare prices between two countries;
- the European Commission have suggested that 11 million new jobs would be created;
- the ability to use competitive devaluations to enhance the sale of their exports is lost; therefore, countries which have relatively higher rates of inflation will need to address the underlying problems of their lack of competitiveness rather than disguising the weaknesses in their economies through exchange rate reductions;
- the currency environment is more stable, improving business confidence.

There will, however, be negative side-effects from a single currency:

- the cost of the initial conversion to a single currency;
- individual country's will hand over their monetary policy to the ECB and they therefore have to remain with the interest rate and exchange rates determined for the whole currency area.

It follows that a country faced with a shock to its economy may not have the option of reducing interest rates as before, and this can lead to higher unemployment. It is now possible that areas which become uncompetitive for whatever reason will experience economic dislocation and increases in unemployment.

This scenario would impose strains on monetary union and would require fiscal transfers from the better-off countries to those which are finding it more difficult to cope with the external shock. Thus this provides for the need for the European economies to converge in terms of performance, as outlined above, before they enter monetary union.

It has also been suggested that improvements in employment are more likely to be in the longer term, with some jobs actually lost as countries try to achieve the criteria for entry into the EMU.

For the United Kingdom, the benefits are less clear. The United Kingdom probably has greater exposure to external shocks simply because (a) it has a greater proportion of its trade with countries outside the European Union, (b) it is a major financial centre and (c) is a net oil exporter.

In terms of internal shocks felt by all Union members, the United Kingdom is more sensitive to changes in short-term interest rates, not least because this affects mortgages. In addition, the United Kingdom has a worse record for keeping wages in line with productivity. However, being outside the EMU may be more of an issue since United Kingdom interest rates will be linked to EMU interest rates whether the country likes it or not. In this case the United Kingdom would not be in a position to influence EMU rates. The United Kingdom's ability to achieve its objectives in other areas of economic policy may also be impaired.

After Maastricht

The optimism that followed the Maastricht Treaty has waned somewhat. In particular, there has been some difficulty, given the world recession, in countries meeting the criteria set out for a single currency. It is likely that there will be a two-stage or multi-speed approach to EMU. But how many nations might be in a position to fulfil membership of the EMU? Table 3.20 gives us some idea of the task in hand.

Forecast data for 1996 suggest that only Germany and Luxembourg would meet all the quantitative tests. In the light of this and other problems it seems that monetary union will not occur in 1997, but will be postponed until 1999. EMU members will be a small 'hard-core' of countries such as France, Germany, Luxembourg, the Netherlands and Austria. Five other countries then seem plausible future members: Belgium, Denmark, Finland, Ireland and Sweden. Will being a member of EMU alter trading patterns, and where does it leave voting arrangements in the European Union between countries inside and outside the EMU?

TABLE 3.20   Economic performance according to Maastricht: convergence criteria: 1996 projections (%)

Country	Inflation	Long-term interest rate	Lending (+) or borrowing (−)		Gross debt ratio	
	1996	1996	1994	1996	1994	1996
Belgium	2.6	8.0	−5.5	−4.0	140.1	136.0
Denmark	2.4	8.7	−4.3	−2.2	78.0	78.2
Germany	2.4	7.3	−2.9	−2.0	51.0	58.9
Greece	9.0	20.8	−14.1	−12.9	121.3	128.1
Spain	4.4	8.8	−7.0	4.7	63.5	66.1
France	2.1	7.5	−5.6	−3.9	50.4	55.6
Ireland	2.7	8.5	−2.4	−1.5	89.0	79.1
Italy	3.5	11.7	−9.6	−7.9	123.7	128.6
Luxembourg	2.7	6.4	3.1	2.0	9.2	9.9
Netherlands	2.5	7.3	−3.8	−2.7	78.8	78.0
Portugal	4.4	10.4	−6.2	−4.8	70.4	72.3
UK	3.3	8.1	−6.3	−3.4	50.4	53.1
Austria	3.1	7.5	−4.4	−4.2	65.0	68.1
Finland	2.7	8.7	−4.7	−2.3	70.0	85.1
Sweden	3.1	10.8	−11.7	−7.3	81.0	95.4
Benchmark	2.3	7.8				
Ceiling	3.8	9.8		−3.0		60.0

Source: The Community Economic Outlook 1994–96, The European Commission, OECD Economic Outlook, OECD, December 1994.

Business almost as usual

The shock of European Union membership has been most keenly felt by the more inefficient industries of Austria, Sweden and Finland. These companies are facing problems as prices in the newest member states are aligned with the rest of the European Union and remaining trade barriers are removed.

The impact of moves towards monetary union could also be marked, but for most exporters it has been business as usual in the three newest member states. Most companies have had plenty of time to adjust, and having sold into the European Economic Area (EEA) since 1 January 1994, very little of their business has changed. European Union entry has consolidated long-standing ties for the new member states. More than half of Finland's trade has gone to the European Union since the 1970s. The pulp and paper sector provides a substantial proportion of this trade. The vice-president of Enso Publications Papers (EPP) of Finland suggests that European Union membership has provided several benefits for his company. The free movement of labour means that red tape has disappeared for visa requirements and there have also been reductions in other administrative burdens. One Austrian banker felt that the benefits which some people expected have not materialized. Austrian, Finnish and Swedish exporters now enjoy a proxy seat at the table where policy is devised and standards are set. This may mean that investment decisions are easier since they are now able to influence decision making directly.

Analysts also point to macroeconomic effects, as European Union membership should bring down long-term interest rates. However, companies in Sweden and Finland that have prospered through substantial currency devaluations will be forced to become more competitive as the European Union moves towards some form of monetary union.

The European Union is the main export market for Sweden's Volvo and whether Volvo is still as successful in the European Union may depend on the impact on the company of the Swedish government's attempt to reduce its budget deficit as a prerequisite for EMU. Swedish companies may benefit, however, from a more consistent investment climate once the option of competitive devaluations is ruled out.

However, in Austria the continued strength of the Austrian schilling, tied to the D-Mark, has affected those companies which have not been operating outside the European Union. Thus, for all three countries the impact of entry into the EU has been slight in the short term, but in the longer run as their governments respond to changes in the requirements of the EU these companies may see some dramatic changes in the costs that each of them face.

Further enlargement of the European Union

Although the European Union has agreed that enlargement of the Community will not be considered until economic and monetary union has been securely established after the year 2000, the question of enlargement of the European Union is likely to return to the agenda. The countries seeking admission are: Cyprus, Malta, Estonia, Latvia, Lithuania, the Czech Republic, Hungary, Poland, the Slovak Republic and Slovenia. On present data, the admittance of the Visegrad Four (Hungary, Poland, the Czech and Slovak Republics) would increase the population of the European Union by one-sixth, but would only increase the GDP by one-twentieth. In terms of population, the Visegrad Four are larger than the United Kingdom or France. Turkey has a population as large and as poor as Poland and all these countries have inflation rates at least four times the Community average. It has been estimated that by allowing even the Visegrad Four to enter the European Union would cost Euro 58 billion and represent a budget increase of 68 per cent. If these new countries are allowed into the European Union then it provides a challenge for each of the current participants. In particular, it poses questions about levels of taxation needed to raise the revenue for the budget increase that is required, and the impact of this on firms and individuals. Moreover, organizations in the newly admitted countries will gain access to lucrative European Union markets which may pose further problems in terms of competitive pressures for current European Union firms.

QUESTIONS

1. What could be the advantages, to organizations, of a country joining a single currency? What may be the costs?

2. What are the implications for organizations in the current EU-15 from widening the membership of the European Union?

3. Using the mini-case study, 'Business almost as usual', how might governments affect organizations by moving towards the convergence criteria for a single currency?

CONCLUSION

Business has always been aware of the impact of the economic environment on its performance and behaviour, but whereas United Kingdom businesses would have paid heed to changes in their own domestic economy, the years since 1945 have seen markets becoming increasingly internationalized and changes in the international economic environment may now have more impact. Some of these changes – such as alterations in environmental legislation, agreements about the provisions for labour and corporate tax changes – have a direct impact on organizations; other changes alter the environment in which the firm exists, and although not aimed at organizations directly, potentially have greater influence on the organizations' behaviour. Here we would include, on an international level, the Single European Market legislation, the movement towards monetary union and external trade policies.

Over the last two decades closer cooperation between countries in pursuing macroeconomic policies and the internationalization of markets has been evident. Such moves require coordinated actions among countries. Of course not all industries are uniformly affected by international macro policy changes; companies which undertake much of their business in the domestic market are perhaps less affected by exchange rate changes than those which are exporting a proportion of their output abroad. In addition, as we have seen in other chapters, the impacts of technology are not equally borne by the different sectors in our society. Nonetheless, businesses cannot ignore the changes that are taking place in their domestic, European and international environment. If they do so it is highly likely that, in the longer term, their position in the market will be weakened to such an extent that their businesses are placed at a competitive disadvantage.

SUMMARY OF MAIN POINTS

We have seen that organizations are influenced by the many forces at play in the wide economic environment and therefore need to be aware of these forces and to be able to react to any changes. The main points made are:

- GDP can be used as a measure of economic growth and it can be used to compare the performance of countries.
- Governments have four main economic goals: a high level of growth, a strong balance of payments, a low level of inflation and low unemployment.
- The goals of the government may conflict.
- Governments may steer the economy and smooth economic cycles through the use of fiscal and monetary policy.
- The industrial structure of an economy is not static but open to continual change.
- Generally Western industrial economies are seeing a shift to the tertiary sector.
- Growth can bring with it improvements in real incomes and a greater choice of goods and services.
- Growth in the European Union has been under pressure.
- Growth also brings with it costs to society.
- Inflation can be caused in a number of ways: through excess demand in the product market, through increased costs of the factors of production, and through slack monetary policy.
- Inflation causes both internal and external problems. It makes exports less competitive and therefore imported goods more competitive with

domestically produced goods. Internally to the economy it harms those groups on fixed incomes, can cause disruption in the labour market, can lead to even higher levels of expected inflation and favours debtors rather than creditors.

■ Government expenditure plays a key role in the functioning of all countries.

■ There has been a slow upward trend in unemployment in the EU countries.

■ The UK economy still has a number of skill gaps which prevents the economy operating efficiently.

■ Countries have become more open which has stimulated international trade.

■ Evidence suggests an increasing Europeanization of trade and the establishment of trade blocs which could limit trade.

■ Exchange rates affect trade and competitiveness.

■ The Single European Market provides opportunities to businesses.

■ The process of integration, rising from the TEU, is likely to continue and gather pace.

References

Alesina, A. (1989) 'Politics and business cycles in industrial democracies', *Economic Policy*, vol. 8.

Arrowsmith, J. (1995) 'Economic and Monetary Union in a Multi-Tier Europe', *National Institute Economic Review*, May.

Bacon, R. and Eltis, W. (1976) *Britain's Economic Problem – Too Few Producers*, Macmillan, London.

Beckerman, W. (1985) 'How the battle against inflation was really won', *Lloyds Bank Review*, 15 January.

Begg, D. (1995) 'The anatomy of a recovery: the UK since 1992', *The Begg Update*, McGraw-Hill, no. 5, Summer.

Burda, M. and Wyplosz, C. (1993) *Macroeconomics: A European Text*, Oxford University Press, Oxford.

Cook, M. (1996) 'Economic growth and the UK economy', *Economics and Business Education*, Summer.

Cook, M. and Healey, N. (1995) *Growth and Structural Change*, Macmillan, London.

Cook, M. and Meredith, C. (1994) 'European mergers and takeovers', *Business Studies*, December.

Economie et Statistiques (1989) Institut National de la Statistique et des Etudes Economiques, Paris.

Forsyth, P. and Kay, J.A. (1980) 'The economic implications of North Sea oil revenue', *Fiscal Studies*, vol. 1, pp. 1–18.

Friedman, M. (1977) 'Inflation and unemployment', *Journal of Political Economy*, vol. 85, no. 3.

Higgins, B. (1993) 'Was the ERM crisis inevitable?', *Federal Reserve Bank of Kansas City Economic Review*, Fourth Quarter.

Higham, D. and Tomlinson, J. (1982) 'Why do governments worry about inflation?',

National Westminster Bank Review, May.

Kay, N. (1993) 'Mergers, acquisitions and the completion of the internal market', in K.S. Hughes (ed.) *European Competitiveness*, Cambridge University Press, Cambridge.

Meadows, D. and Meadows, D. (1992) *Beyond the Limits*, Chelsea Green Publishing, London.

Nugent, N. and O'Donnell, R. (1994) *The European Business Environment*, Macmillan, London.

OECD (1994) *Manufacturing Performance: A Scoreboard of Indicators*, OECD, Paris.

Phillips, A.W. (1958) 'The relationship between unemployment and the rate of change of money wages in the United Kingdom', *Economica*, vol. 25, November.

Sharp, M. (1992) 'Technology and dynamics of integration', in W. Walker (ed.) *The Dynamics of European Integration*, Francis Pinter, London.

Soteri, S. and Westaway, P. (1993) 'Explaining price inflation in the UK: 1971–92', *National Institute Economic Review*, no. 144, May.

Studd, S. (1996) 'The training challenge', *Leisure Opportunities*, May.

Swann, D. (1992) *The Single European Market and Beyond: A Study of the Wider Implications of the Single European Act*, Routledge, London.

CHAPTER 4
THE TECHNOLOGICAL ENVIRONMENT
Stephen Swailes

LEARNING OUTCOMES

On completion of this chapter you should be able to:

- contrast the differences between technology and innovation;
- understand how different business sectors use technology;
- describe some of the generic technologies that are affecting many organizations;
- outline how different countries support research and development;
- describe how technology affects organizations, people and jobs;
- describe how technology can be managed in an organization.

4.1 Introduction

Elsewhere in this book the effects of other macroenvironmental forces on organizations are explained. Economic forces impact upon the organization through factors like exchange rates, interest rates and consumer spending. Social forces affect the availability of labour or the demand for products. Political forces set a broad framework for all organizations and are particularly influential upon public sector organizations.

This chapter examines the technological environment and how it affects organizations. Unlike political, economic and social forces which are mostly beyond the influence of organizations, managers have much more control and influence over technological forces. After all, technology is developed by organizations, for organizations, who may adopt a technology early or late in its life cycle.

This may be about to change with the advent of the information superhighway and the huge political force that exists behind it.

The uptake of technology by organizations may be affected by attitudes and behaviour of employees. We can also see that some organizations are unable to respond to technological shifts and eventually fail.

We should not see technology as divorced from other macroenvironmental forces. The health of the economy will influence the amount that organizations invest in technology. Political decisions can have a strong bearing upon government-sponsored research and development or upon assistance programmes for organizations. In contrast, governments have to respond to the changes that new technologies bring to society. Political control over news and information is now harder to achieve in an era of satellite communications.

While all the primary macroenvironmental forces discussed in this book wax and wane in their intensity and impact over time, the technological environment is currently witnessing a 'new wave' of information-based change. Recent trends towards deregulation in Western markets and intense cost-centred competition have highlighted the role of technology in helping to maintain and build competitive advantage.

4.2 Why is technology important?

What is technology?

We need a definition of technology if we are to understand the relationship between organizations and their technological environment. Technology is not the same as knowledge or innovation. Knowledge is a theoretical or practical understanding of a subject such as chemistry, mathematics, sociology or language. Knowledge about a subject is usually added in very small increments, usually following hypothetico-deductive research and reasoning.

Technology is the application of knowledge into some practical form, typically applied to industrial and commercial use. There can be a prolonged period between the early development of technologies and their evolution into widely usable formats. Galbraith (1967) defines technology as 'The systematic application of scientific or other organized knowledge to practical tasks'. Monck *et al.* (1988) developed this view: 'Technology is both a body of knowledge concerned with the solution of practical problems, what we might term know-how, and also the tools and artefacts which are used to achieve those solutions: it is both software and hardware'. Gillespie and Mileti (1977) define technology as 'the types and patterns of activity, equipment and material, and knowledge or experience to perform tasks'. This latter definition suggests that all organizations use a technology and that only the intensity varies. A useful summary of some of the definitions of technology can be found in Berry and Taggart (1994).

TABLE 4.1   Examples of knowledge, technology and innovation

Knowledge	Technology	Innovation
Identifying a particular gene (1980s)	Tests for specific genes, gene-sensitive compounds	Gene-modifying drugs
The accumulator (late nineteenth century)	Alternator and electric turbines	Power stations
Hydrocarbon chemistry (early twentieth century)	Internal combustion engine	Automobiles, aircraft

Innovation is the spread and diffusion of technology into society and organizations. Freeman (1982) saw technical innovation as the introduction and spread of new and improved products and processes in the economy. This definition includes the design, manufacturing, and management activities involved in the marketing of a new or improved product.

Three examples of the links between between knowledge, technology and innovation are shown in Table 4.1. A knowledge of genetic structure, for example, has led to the development of tests for specific genes and, possibly, will lead to the proliferation of gene-modifying drugs.

A historical perspective

Technology has been problematic for entrepreneurs and managers for at least the past two hundred years. Throughout the nineteenth century businessmen and labourers generally did not see science as being applicable to their world and treated new machinery simply as labour-saving devices (Coleman and MacLeod, 1986). The synthetic dye and electronics sectors declined in the face of German and American competition because British attitudes to management stood in the way of firms responding to technological innovation from competitors (Shiman, 1991).

In the nineteenth century the British cotton textile industry had no international competitors although domestic competition was intense. When corporate economies such as America and Japan became serious threats British cotton textile firms were unable to respond with appropriate technologies, because of the particular industry structure that had evolved (Lazonick, 1981, 1983). This example highlights a link between industry structure and technological change. Structure can impede change, yet we will see later that technology can be a driver of structural change.

A study of Japanese firms from 1929 to 1984 identified that the Japanese economy shifted from mining and light industries to heavy and chemical industries and (post-war) to automotive and electronics. Companies able to absorb Western technology into efficient production systems quickly established market dominance (Yamazaki, 1988). Hence, technology can help create industries but can also be instrumental in their decline.

Technology and modern organizations

While some technologies are associated with harmful effects such as pollution and use of the earth's resources, the overall benefits of technological change to mankind are well documented. Indeed, technologies are being sought to break the link between economic growth and pollution. Governments are anxious to raise living standards which, in turn, requires a sound economy in terms of job availability, working conditions and public spending. Technology impacts on these factors. In the same way that products pass through a life cycle then so do firms and industries. Sometimes technology accelerates the decline of an industry, as word processors signalled the end for mechanical typewriters. Technology also adds new sectors, such as electronic games, to the total toy and game industry.

Faced with intense competition from low-cost countries, some sectors decline in terms of output and employment although often a core of efficient producers remains. Leather manufacture is an example where, faced with intense competition from southern Europe and South America, output in North America and the United Kingdom has fallen as a consequence. In this example, tanners in high-cost countries have access to manufacturing technologies that improve both firm efficiency and working conditions. The long-term problem, however, is that, when the manufacturing infrastructure (a network of machinery and component suppliers and distributors) of low-cost producers is more developed, they will also be able to install the same technologies. Thus a cycle occurs in which developed countries attempt to stay ahead of competing nations through continual renewal of their technological base.

Thus technology can help to extend the lifetime of certain industries facing strong competition. It also contributes to economic development, through new sector growth, which may arise because technology contributes to achieving competitive prices in world markets. This could arise from technologies that allow quick response to orders, consistent quality and cost reduction. To support regeneration, growth and competitiveness firms need to invest. The amount of spending on technology is huge – about 40 per cent of all capital spending in the United States is on technology (Courtenay, 1995).

One of the biggest trends affecting businesses is globalization, that is the convergence of consumer tastes and product designs on a world-wide scale. Consider, for example, the world automobile market where manufacturers seek scale economies by marketing the same designs across many countries. It reduces costs, so makes good business sense. As newly industrialized countries (NICs), like Thailand and Indonesia, develop their economic and social infrastructures, technology greatly assists the process. Technology is a major change agent in world markets and the pace of technological change is rising.

It is widely believed, by managers, that investment levels go some way to explaining productivity levels and, in turn, the ability to be competitive in world markets. Arguably the most successful business product ever, the photocopier first introduced by Rank Xerox, was the foundation for that company's domination of the copier market for upwards of 20 years until patent protection expired. Investment by Canon in copier technology later allowed them to develop their own strong position in the copier market.

Genetic science

Recent advances in genetic knowledge mean that it will soon become possible to develop self-administered screening tests for faulty genes, in the way that pregnancy or blood cholesterol levels can now be tested with over-the-counter kits. These tests will be applicable to unborn babies and to adults to see if there is a gene defect or an increased likelihood of developing a particular condition such as Alzheimer's disease or Huntingdon's Chorea. Furthermore, our improved understanding of genetics will accelerate the production of new drugs to treat conditions such as cystic fibrosis.

Genetic technologies will pose some fundamental questions for certain types of businesses, as well as society in general. How might insurance companies react to the widespread availability of gene testing? Would persons identified as having an increased risk of developing a particular condition in life be able to get insurance? Not under present arrangements perhaps. Hence, insurers will need to re-evaluate long-held views about personal eligibility for policies with inevitable consequences for the portfolio of policies offered.

The spread and use of genetic information will need tight control by responsible agencies (such as the police) and by government. At the moment, scientists are ahead of society in the understanding and use of genetics. Society somehow needs to catch up so that restraints and restrictions are enforced and acceptable uses of genetic science become clear.

Thus we can build a picture of technological development underpinning national growth and consumer living standards. Incidentally, while the British are often stereotyped as being good inventors but poor innovators, the problem might not be as bad as is sometimes made out (Edgerton, 1987).

Emerging technologies present some thorny problems for society, as illustrated by the case of genetic science above.

QUESTIONS

1. To what extent do you agree with the statement that British businessmen are not as effective at exploiting new technology as our major competitors?

2. Can Europe and North America sustain a technological lead ahead of newly industrialized countries? Will the NICs eventually catch up?

4.3 Funding of research and development in industrial countries

National differences

Technologies do not simply evolve by accident: they are the fruits of dedicated research projects that had clear objectives. In our look at the technological environment we need, therefore, to examine how research and development (R&D) is organized in industrial nations. Research spending in the European Union from public funds was Ecu 50 285 million, equivalent to Ecu 145 per capita (1993). The European Union publishes details of the research it wants undertaken and organizations are free to bid for contracts. Usually, at least two different European Union countries must be represented in the bid. At national level, individual governments operate a structure for managing and funding R&D. The Department of Trade and Industry in the United Kingdom manages the funding of government-held research laboratories and non-profit-making research and technology organizations. Funding for projects is also provided through research councils such as the Natural Environment Research Council and the Economic and Social Research Council. The main types of research activity are Basic or Fundamental Research, Applied Research and Experimental Development which are defined below.

Types of research and development

Basic or fundamental research is experimental or theoretical work undertaken mainly to acquire new knowledge. Such work would be undertaken without a particular end use in mind. An example would be the synthesis of new chemical compounds but without any notion of what use they might have.

Applied research is undertaken with some application in mind, for example investigating the usefulness of innovations to medicine or materials technology.

Experimental development is the use of both basic and applied research in the development of materials, processes and synthesis and would typically extend to the prototype or pilot stage.

Source: Adapted from 'Research and Experimental Development (R&D) Statistics 1992', *Economic Trends*, 490, August 1994, HMSO.

The main sources of R&D funding are government and business enterprises. Universities and non-profit organizations also carry out some of the work. Expenditure on R&D changes along with the general state of the economy. When an economy is buoyant, central government's revenues from taxation support

TABLE 4.2   Gross expenditure on R&D in the UK (£m, at 1990 price levels, figures show expenditure by performing sector)

Performed by	1986	1987	1988	1989	1990	1991	1992
Business enterprise	7730	7814	8000	8267	8099	7305	7182
Higher education	1673	1800	1820	1825	1873	1900	1939
Government	1575	1559	1572	1658	1566	1767	1840
Non-profit	411	400	428	449	481	465	467

Source: Economic Trends No. 490, August 1994. Crown copyright 1994. Reproduced by the permission of the Controller of HMSO and the Central Statistical Office.

public spending, a small part of which goes towards R&D. In a buoyant economy, business enterprises may enjoy relatively higher profits which, in turn, can be invested in R&D. Table 4.2 shows gross expenditure on R&D in the UK in 1992 at £11.4 billion, 6.3 per cent less than in 1989 when total spending was at its highest level for some years. Note, Table 4.2 shows spending by the sector performing the R&D, not the sector funding it. There are some important differences between the two.

The government typically funds over twice the amount it spends in its own research centres. This extra funding goes to universities, who typically only contribute about 5 per cent of the research spending in the higher education sector, and business enterprise which contributed about 80 per cent of that sector's R&D spending in 1992. Government funding of British enterprise R&D has fallen from 23 per cent in 1986 to 14 per cent in 1992. Firms compensated for the fall by increasing their own share of funding and attracting funding from overseas.

Table 4.3 shows the gross expenditure on R&D from 1987 to 1992 for several countries expressed as a percentage of each country's gross national product (GNP). The United Kingdom spent 2.12 per cent of gross national product on R&D compared to 2.36 per cent for France, 2.53 per cent for Germany, 2.68 per cent in the United States and 2.8 per cent in Japan. All countries shown in the table reduced the share of gross national product given over to R&D during the period 1990–92.

At first glance, the percentages appear similar, but it is important to recall

TABLE 4.3   Gross expenditure on R&D as percentage of GDP

	UK	Germany	Japan	USA
1987	2.22	2.88	2.63	2.48
1988	2.18	2.86	2.67	2.81
1989	2.20	2.87	2.80	2.76
1990	2.19	2.75	2.89	2.74
1991	2.13	2.65	2.87	2.76
1992	2.12	2.53	2.80	2.68

Source: Economic Trends No. 490, August 1994. Crown copyright 1994. Reproduced by the permission of the Controller of HMSO and the Central Statistical Office.

TABLE 4.4   Gross domestic expenditure on R&D in the European Union

	Per cent of GDP
EU-12	1.98
Germany	2.65
France	2.42
United Kingdom	2.13
Netherlands	1.92
Denmark	1.69
Belgium	1.67
Italy	1.24
Eire	1.04
Spain	0.87
Portugal	0.56
Greece	0.46

Source: Basic Statistics of the European Union (32nd edn), 1995, Table 2.11b.

that gross national product values are huge, e.g. £3730 billion for the United States in 1992 compared to £904 billion for Germany and £594 billion for the United Kingdom. Small changes to the percentage of gross national product spent on R&D thus translate to large sums in absolute terms. For instance, 0.01 per cent of the United States' GNP is around 630 million dollars. Table 4.4 shows gross domestic expenditure on R&D for European Union countries. For Mediterranean countries it is less than 1 per cent of gross national product.

Countries also differ in the way they fund and perform R&D. Governments in the United Kingdom, Germany, France and Japan typically fund over twice the amount spent in their own research centres. The United States funds about four times as much. Business enterprise typically funds about 80 per cent of the R&D it performs whereas Japanese firms seem to fund all of the R&D that they undertake. Also noteworthy is that, despite reduced spending on defence-related R&D, as a percentage of gross national product, the United States, British and French governments were spending much more on defence than Germany and Japan. While it is impossible to make any causal link between defence spending and industrial competitiveness, indeed United Kingdom defence spending secures many jobs in aerospace for example, this observation provides a good discussion point. The Japanese government, for example, spent only 0.03 per cent of GNP on defence spending in 1992 compared to 0.68 per cent in the USA.

An examination of R&D spending by socioeconomic objective sheds more light on this point. Table 4.5 shows the main objectives for government-funded R&D in 1992. While some allowance should be made for the difficulty of categorizing R&D projects to particular socioeconomic objectives, Japan and Germany appear to target around 50 per cent of government-funded R&D at the advancement of knowledge without necessarily having clear practical applications for the research in mind. The British, and the Americans in particular, seem less comfortable with the notion of 'blue sky' research. This might reflect political and cultural norms in the United Kingdom and the United States, such as the Anglo-

TABLE 4.5   International comparison of government-funded R&D by socio-economic objective, 1992 (per cent)

Objective	UK	Germany	France	Italy	Japan	USA
Defence	43	10	35	7	6	59
Advancement of knowledge	25	48	31	44	51	4
Industrial development	8	13	8	16	4	0.3
Energy	2	5	4	4	21	5

Source: Economic Trends No. 490, August 1994. Crown copyright 1994. Reproduced by the permission of the Controller of HMSO and the Central Statistical Office.

Saxon capitalist tradition, pushing funders into a pragmatic mindset when R&D funding is allocated to objectives.

Another factor to consider is the cost of borrowing money. In the United Kingdom the cost of capital is high, compared to Germany and Japan, and businessmen are pushed towards a short-term outlook on investment and risk taking (Rassam, 1993). In contrast, UK companies regularly pay out higher percentages of net earnings to shareholders than German and Japanese businesses (Foster, 1993). Cheaper borrowing is thought to encourage longer term planning horizons.

Comparing countries on the basis of percentage gross national product spent on R&D is a crude but useful measure. To give us a clearer comparison we need to take into account the nature of industry in a country, whether it is labour or capital intensive and the average size of firms.

As noted elsewhere in this chapter, some industrial sectors are less research intensive than others, so if one country spends less than another on R&D we ought to account for the labour intensity and capital intensity of their respective industrial sectors. In a labour-intensive business the main vehicle for value added is labour. In a capital-intensive business, plant and machinery are the main vehicles for value added. Labour-intensive sectors like footwear and clothing manufacture tend to have low fixed costs and high variable costs. Capital-intensive sectors like electronics and chemicals have, in comparison, high fixed costs and low variable costs and tend to spend proportionally more on research and development than labour-intensive sectors. Average firm size could also play a part in explaining the differences in national spending patterns.

Research on sector differences (e.g. Small and Swann, 1993) suggests that large UK firms perform adequately and in some cases above average when compared to other countries in terms of R&D/sales ratios, but less well when R&D per employee is compared. However, ratios based on employee numbers do not make the best indicators with which to compare firms or countries. In reporting the size of their workforce organizations may or may not include part-time employees and they may not include persons employed in subsidiary organizations. Comparison on a per capita basis does not account for the differing skill levels that may exist between organizations.

TABLE 4.6   Research and development expenditure as percentage of turnover for selected companies

Company	1994	1993	1992
Glaxo Holdings	15.2	15.0	14.5
Zeneca	11.6	11.7	11.5
GEC	4.0	4.2	4.2
Volkswagen Group	3.5	3.9	3.5
Volvo Group	3.0	3.9	7.4
Courtaulds	1.8	1.9	1.9
British Telecom	1.9	1.9	–
Anglian Water	0.7	0.6	0.5
Shell Transport and Trading	–	0.8	0.9
British Petroleum	0.6	0.6	0.9

Source: Calculated from Annual Reports. Data relate to financial years which do not always represent calendar years.

Value-based ratios are much better indicators of performance but are still vulnerable. Since sales revenues from an organization's many business units are aggregated into a single group turnover figure it would be problematic to compare a single product organization, where all R&D supports all sales, with a multi-product firm where R&D might only support some of the product lines. We should also recall that some sectors prefer to channel much of their R&D activity through an industry Research and Technology Organization rather than conduct it in-house. One of the strongest figures to use in inter-firm comparisons is added value, rather than sales. This is a more robust measure of an organization's performance and can be related to R&D spending to get a good measure of R&D productivity. Added value is more complex to calculate, however. R&D to sales turnover ratios are given for selected companies in Table 4.6. The highest spending firm, a pharmaceuticals manufacturer, devoted about 15 per cent of turnover to research. Auto manufacturers spent about 3.0 to 3.5 per cent and oil companies spent around 0.7 per cent.

Expenditure by business enterprises has increased overall for the past two decades. According to Dussauge *et al.* (1994) there are three possible reasons for this increase in corporate funding of R&D. Firstly, the Crisis Hypothesis which asserts that major technologies such as petrochemicals have life cycles. The oil shocks of 1974 and 1979 signalled the end of this major technology and increased R&D spending by petrochemicals firms could be a search for cost reductions in the face of rising cost of oil-based products, or searches for replacement technologies. Secondly, the Sustained Progress hypothesis which suggests that the time lag between discovery of new knowledge and commercial application is shortening, thus the funds needed to generate new technologies have increased. Thirdly, the Global Competition hypothesis which suggests that newly industrialized countries (NICs) compete strongly in low technology industries, for example textiles, clothing and footwear, and that some technologies are easily transferred to NICs. Thus organizations in the industrialized countries such as Japan, the United States

TABLE 4.7   National breakdown of the top 200 companies by R&D expenditure, 1994

USA	67	General Motors	(£4497m)
Japan	60	Hitachi	(£3102m)
France	18	Alcatel	(£1261m)
Germany	16	Siemens	(£3096m)
UK	12	Glaxo Pharmaceuticals	(£858m)
Switzerland	7	Asea Brown Boveri	(£1504m)
Sweden	7	Ericson Telefon	(£1152m)
Other countries	13		

The R&D expenditure of the highest spending company in each country is also identified.

Source: Adapted from *The R&D Scoreboard*, Department of Trade and Industry.

and northern Europe have been forced into funding high-technology programmes as a way of competing.

Table 4.7 shows the world's top 200 R&D spenders grouped by country. The dominance of Japan and the United States in the table reflects the number of large companies in those countries. The highest spending company in 1994 is also identified in the table along with its R&D expenditure.

Sectoral differences

Not all business sectors use technology to the same extent, and technology is not equally important to all sectors. Some sectors, such as small local service providers or organizations providing care services, may use little or no technology in meeting their customers' needs. Such organizations require considerable know-how to underpin their business operations, for example the know-how needed to provide care to persons with special needs.

Table 4.8 shows research and development expenditure as a percentage of turnover for leading firms in several sectors. Only high-spending sectors are reported.

TABLE 4.8   R&D expenditure as a percentage of sector turnover, 1994

Pharmaceuticals	12.3
Computer software	12.0
Health care	9.6
Electrical and electronic engineering	6.4
Chemicals	5.8
Engineering	5.0
Telecommunications	4.8
Vehicle manufacture	4.2
Food manufacture	1.3
Oil exploration and refining	0.8

Percentages calculated by dividing total R&D expenditure by total turnover for companies in the top 200 international list.

Source: Adapted from *The R&D Scoreboard*, Department of Trade and Industry.

Some sectors such as textiles, clothing and footwear manufacture invest relatively small amounts of turnover in new plant and equipment. This is not to say that they are somehow worse off than sectors with higher spending levels. Labour-intensive sectors are characterized by small firms which individually are not large enough to justify their own research and development department. They have tended to centralize their R&D efforts in industry research centres as this has been the most efficient way of conducting research and development for the sector. Developments then transfer from the research centre to individual firms. Technology remains important to labour-intensive sectors but on a different scale. Technology tends to be used for incremental process improvements such as:

- combining two or more operations so that labour can be released from the production process;
- automating some processes such as cutting garment sections and cutting multiple layers of fabric;
- developing new fabrics or polymers that can be cut and moulded to give enhancements to the manufacturing process or the final product.

It is partly because of the difficulty of achieving radical technological breakthroughs that some sectors remain labour intensive. In sectors such as clothing and footwear manufacture, some of the manufacturing operations needed to assemble the products require manual manipulation and joining of parts. Until solutions are found to the immensely complex problems of manipulating irregularly shaped components in three-dimensional space and joining them to very high accuracies, such sectors will continue to await breakthrough technologies that will alter the cost structure of the industry.

By contrast, in pharmaceutical manufacture, it is by the development of a new drug or by new ways of synthesizing a compound that firms can gain a distinct advantage over their competitors. Developments of this complexity require dedicated in-house research for two reasons: firstly, to keep control over very complex projects so that research spending is managed effectively; secondly, to keep industrial secrets (intellectual property) within the organization to retain a competitive advantage. However, we will see later that collaboration with other organizations may be an important way of supplementing in-house activities.

Pharmaceutical research has a large appetite for new molecules with medical applications. Finding these molecules among the millions of potential molecular structures is costly. Even when drugs have been trialled and approved for use, damaging side-effects can be identified. Boots Pharmaceuticals had to withdraw their Manoplax treatment for heart conditions for this reason.

An emerging technology to identify the likely properties of different compounds is known as combinatorial chemistry. The UK pharmaceutical company, Glaxo Wellcome, purchased a US company specializing in this technique for $533 million in 1995 as a way of rapidly integrating the new technology into its operations (Cookson, 1995). Mergers and acquisitions are widely used ways of acquiring technology. Glaxo Wellcome itself was formed in 1995 from the merger of Glaxo and Wellcome. Part of the rationale for the merger was a drive for greater economies of scale in R&D in an increasingly competitive sector.

QUESTIONS

1.   To what extent are low defence budgets in Germany and Japan and their high spending on pure research linked to their status as leading economic powers?

2.   If you were comparing firms in different countries in terms of their spending on R&D, what indicators could be used? (Hint: think of company financial statements and link certain figures to R&D spending.)

3.   What indicators could be used to measure the effectiveness of a company's R&D department?

4.4 Some general technologies

It is not the purpose of this book to explain individual technologies in detail. They are well covered elsewhere and are so many and varied that to focus on any one would be of little use. However, there are some technologies that are having a big impact on many business sectors. These are highlighted below along with examples of some specific technologies in different sectors.

Information-based technologies

Information-based technologies have had a tremendous impact upon financial services such as banking, insurance and mortgage services. In this case technology is applied to the capture, storage, manipulation and retrieval of information. Much of the impact of technology in this sector has been to accelerate processing times, to replace labour and to change the nature of work that employees need to do. Technology's impact on financial organizations has arguably been revolutionary when compared to the more incremental impact seen in other sectors. Job losses have been severe and the technology has de-skilled the decision processes such that junior staff can be trained quickly to take responsibility for complex customer enquiries. An interesting question about these relatively recent changes, however, is whether the extensive labour cutbacks have caused a large loss of organizational knowledge that will have negative effects in the long term. There are grounds for thinking that in the long run decision making will be poorer, staff loyalty will stay low and customers will be unable to differentiate between providers.

In addition to labour substitution, information technologies have blurred the boundaries between formerly distinct sectors (Porter and Miller, 1985).

Developments in information technology, coupled with deregulation of financial markets in the 1980s, have allowed building societies to enter the market for insurance services and high street banks to offer mortgage products. Because of trends towards longer working hours and busier social lives, the banking service First Direct was set up to offer people 24-hour telephone banking.

Decision making in organizations is another broad area bolstered by information technologies. Corporate databases allow storage of product-market data on a massive scale. The era of an organization's data 'warehouse' and the concept of data 'mining' have arrived (Gooding, 1995). Because sophisticated IT systems have been used by organizations for perhaps 10–15 years, longer in some sectors, some organizations have created a data archive concerning sales, costs and operations management. An example would be to identify the demographic profile of a retailer's customer base and the way different products appeal to customers according to their position in the profile. Trends within the data archive are explored so that managers can:

- make short-term decisions, for example whether to withdraw a product or to extend a product into new outlets; and,
- make long-term decisions about the best location of a new outlet, for example a new supermarket site, or optimum timing and content for a forthcoming promotion or campaign.

Information technologies allow much closer scrutiny of individual products in retail outlets. Traditionally profit margins were thought of in terms of the difference between sales price and purchase price. But products come in different sizes, weights and pack quantities. These variables, and others, affect the actual cost of ordering, transporting and stocking products and thus actual profit margins can be less or more than simple selling price and purchase price would suggest. This concept, Direct Product Profitability, is brought to life with database software and is now important to retailers selling many different lines in a wide range of weights and sizes.

Advanced manufacturing technology

Historically, a manufacturing production line contained a sequence of processes arranged to add to or change a partly made item in some way. Machines were not connected or integrated and often performed only one process or, at best, only a few processes. When a new product passed down the line, each machine might have required substantial time to change settings. For example, changing the die in a press to stamp-out body parts for cars might have taken up to a day.

Manufacturers have always preferred long production runs of the same product since the unit cost of producing the product falls as volume rises. This occurs through:

- buying materials and supplies in bulk at lower unit costs;

- gaining experience of making a single product so that problems and break-downs can be quickly overcome;
- operators becoming more skilled and efficient at making the product.

Collectively, these factors combine to produce an experience curve, on which unit costs continually fall as volume output rises. This experience curve effect (see Chapter 2) lies behind some of decisions made by organizations when they take over or merge with another organization. By integrating with another organization's experience, the total experience of making a product is increased and, in theory, unit production costs will fall. It is right to point out, however, that there are many reasons why mergers and takeovers are not as successful as originally intended, and the experience curve benefits do not always accrue.

Market-led change runs counter to the production department's desire for long runs of the same product. It requires product innovation and renewal to be a key part of an organization's marketing strategy. Companies that rely on long production runs to minimize costs may find their cost structures compromised by consumer demand for product innovation. Shorter production runs are required and some organizations are unable to respond to the challenge. Flexible manufacturing systems have helped manufacturers make that response by making shorter production runs more cost-effective, by reducing both set-up costs and changeover times for machines. Decision making and tooling-up times are also reduced. For example, to tool-up for a new product traditionally involves:

- manual design drawing;
- making patterns for new component or tools;
- manufacture of tools to cut or mould a new component;
- retooling of machines to cope with new products or components.

Advanced manufacturing technology (AMT) has opened up new possibilities. Firstly, machines can be easily reprogrammed so that a single machine can cope with changes to processing requirements of different components as they pass through a production line. For example, on a car production line, different fixings are tightened to different levels by the same machine depending on the model of car being worked upon. Secondly, machine resetting is faster. Thirdly, machines can share and exchange information about the specification and processing needs of different products so that a machine informs the next process in the sequence. Fourthly, many different processes can be combined and undertaken by one machine.

AMT typically involves computer-aided design (CAD) and computer-aided manufacturing (CAM). CAD allows clothing or engineering patterns, for example, to be designed on a computer screen and stored for easy alteration and reuse. CAM systems receive and interpret CAD data to coordinate the production process.

Designs can now be built on a computer screen. When the design is confirmed the digital information is fed into the next stage so that components are generated from the computerized design and the information used to engineer new tools or moulds, for example. Designs can be transmitted from European or North American headquarters to offices and factories in low-labour-cost countries where the product is manufactured. Processes that would have taken several weeks have been reduced to a few days. Levi Strauss are experimenting with the next phase, mass customerization. Instead of buying jeans off-the-peg, women customers are being given the opportunity, in certain stores, to order their own size and style of garment. The order is passed, electronically, to the factory, made up and returned to the consumer the following day. This service is available at a small $10 premium. National Panasonic of Japan have also installed a similar system for customers to select their new bicycle.

Technological initiatives vary widely between different industrial sectors. Some of the key initiatives currently being followed are shown below.

Some current technological initiatives

Chemical industry

- Waste reduction, recovery of chemicals used in manufacturing processes (intermediate chemicals).
- Reduction of harmful emissions.
- Formulation of novel pesticides and fungicides.
- More ecologically friendly fuels and lubricants.
- Replacements for harmful products such as CFCs.
- Water-based rather than solvent-based products.

Energy

- Developing clean technologies.
- Recovery and recycling.
- Control systems for energy production.

Information technology and electronics

- Mobile communications.
- Novel optical fibres, optoelectronic communications.
- Development of new services, e.g. video-on-demand.
- Semiconductor services, printed circuit board design.
- Imaging technologies (image scanning, storage and retrieval).

Manufacturing and materials

- High-speed manufacturing coupled with precision and automation.
- Innovations in joining technologies (adhesives, welding).
- New polymeric materials with enhanced processing and properties.

Adapted from *The Industry File*, Oakland Consultancy, Cambridge. With permission.

Supply chain management

Installation of AMT has also coincided with a major remodelling of the manufacturer's supply chain. Traditionally, buyers dealt with many suppliers of materials who tended to be treated in an adversarial way. Suppliers were often switched to enable the buyer to obtain the lowest cost for an item. This relationship evolved in the time of long production runs and relatively long product life cycles. When market changes pushed in the other direction, retail buyers pushed manufacturers to find ways of making smaller quantities of more items and to deliver them much more quickly. This was made possible with AMT and IT. Point-of-sale data capture in retailers is analysed to identify the quantity of stock items to reorder. This data can be transmitted to a manufacturer who is able to tool-up rapidly to make the item. Manufacturers have similar links with suppliers so that the materials needed to make a product can be ordered and delivered. Thus time has been eliminated from the total supply chain. Meeting customer needs in a just-in-time (JIT) environment has also altered the relationship between organizations in the chain. Because of the need to share information and better understand the customer's needs (customers are all those in the supply chain, not just the final consumer) organizations have tended to be much more careful about how they select suppliers. Supplier selection is a much more rigorous procedure with customers seeking assurances that supplies can consistently meet price, quality and delivery targets. However, once selected, the relationship between suppliers and customer is more secure, organizations work for mutual benefit and long-term relationships are sought. This is in stark contrast to the adversarial, stand-off type of relationship that commonly used to exist. The automotive sector is a good illustration of where supply partnerships have been forged. Life in the garden is not all roses, however, as supportive relationships do not exist in all sectors.

Electronic data interchange

Electronic data interchange (EDI) allows documents like invoices and orders to be transmitted between organizations who are established trading partners. Where suppliers are located near to their customers, EDI supports just-in-time operations since orders can be placed just a few hours before components are needed on a production line.

The Internet is poised to take the advantages of EDI a step further. We are already seeing suppliers publicize details of their product range, e.g. technical details, availability and prices, on their web site. Suppliers can publicize their goods on a global scale and this is likely to lead to even greater competition between them. The time may come when a buyer can easily search the Net to locate suppliers of particular items and, if satisfied with the specifications, confirm an order and make payments through the Net. Potentially the Net could revolutionize the way organizations purchase materials but it seems the Net needs to become more secure for this to become commonplace. Apart from speeding up purchasing, there could be changes ahead for the close relationships that exist in some supply chains if the Net allows firms, who are not established partners, to securely and reliably trade with each other. The Internet could pressurize the closer supply chain relationships that have evolved between manufacturers.

Other types of communication between organizations are also boosted by the Internet. International and global companies require extensive communications between decision makers in various countries. Travelling to meetings is costly and yet alternatives such as video conferencing have achieved only limited use. The Net offers an alternative as, by posting information on a web site, communications can be bolstered. Functional areas in global businesses, e.g. research and development or design, can communicate ideas and concepts and drawings quickly. Technical and scientific conferences can be held on the Net if authors post their papers on a web site for browsers to read and respond to. While this is an important breakthrough, travel to face-to-face meetings will not stop. Humans are social animals after all. Potentially, the Internet could revolutionize shopping habits by enabling customers to compare and scan a store's product range and order for home delivery. This seems more likely to appeal to professional and managerial classes more than other groups who might have lower motivation to shop electronically and who, conversely, could be motivated to adhere to more social shopping habits. We should take a cautious view of such possibilities, however, as our desire to rationalize the future fails to foresee other trends that have a bearing on the issue. When computers began to proliferate in businesses there was much talk of the paperless office. In fact, the opposite happened because computers made printing much easier and because business trends moved towards greater documentation to support business objectives, e.g. quality management systems.

The Internet can also be seen as an early development in what is potentially a revolutionary transformation of business communications. Governments of advanced nations are encouraging the development of information superhighways as potential wealth creators and a series of initiatives at European and G7 level exist.

QUESTIONS

1.   If trading on the Internet becomes secure, what would the implications be for suppliers of goods and services?

2.   How could close ties between manufacturers be affected if a buyer is easily able to identify cheaper suppliers of components with the same quality and delivery times?

3.   What impact could the Internet have on business organizations?

4.5 Technology and organization

While technology, particularly IT, is often seen as a solution to an organization's problems the view that IT for its own sake will yield benefits is receding (Coffey, 1995). Managers need to be clear about the total impact that will come from investment in technologies. Understanding the impact is a complex task because cost–benefit analysis needs to account for much more than changes to incomes and expenditure, yet the non-financial costs and benefits are difficult to estimate. The difficulties of managing the best out of technology are illustrated by two particular problem projects. The TAURUS project, a computer system for the London Stock Exchange, was abandoned after about £500 million had been spent. The United Kingdom government, reportedly, became very concerned about a defence contract being handled primarily by GEC–Marconi (Gray, 1995). The Phoenix low-flying, unmanned reconnaissance aircraft was six years late in 1995 because of technical problems after over £200 million had been spent on the project.

A key problem in managing large technology projects is their vast size and the high numbers of people and organizations involved. Adcock *et al.* (1993) note that managers can have expectations of IT that exceed its capabilities. Technology installations need to be backed up by strategies for other critical factors, such as customer service and product delivery.

Information technology in particular has been linked to workplace stress levels (Cooper and Payne, 1990) caused by job and workstation redesign, worries about job losses or worries about retraining needs. As well as directly affecting individual jobs, other employers can be indirectly affected by the change that the introduction of new technology causes. Managers and supervisors, for example, have to plan and implement change and deal with the human issues arising, including their own fears about loss of control (Hughes, 1995). Because improvement policies are continuous in organizations, they lead to continuous change and the pressure on employers and managers can seem never ending. Simons (1986) identifies several human resource issues that need reviewing as a result of technical change:

1. Job evaluation and grading.
2. Career development and training.
3. Remuneration policies and working conditions.
4. Personnel planning.
5. Labour relations.

Technology and organization structure

According to Souder (1991) the vehicle for innovation is the organization and the organization of the firm 'has not kept pace with demands of modern technology ...'. He argues that classical management philosophies, which can be summarized as managers planning, organizing and controlling the work of

TABLE 4.9   Characteristics of organic and mechanistic organizations

Organic	Mechanistic
• No rigid rules	• Many rules/low individual freedom
• Participative/internal	• Bureaucratic/formal
• Views aired openly	• Written communications
• Face-to-face communications	• Functional separation
• Interdisciplinary teams	• Long decision chains
• Creative iteration	• Slow decision making
• Outward looking	• Hierarchical
• Flexible adaptor	• Information flows up the organization
• Non-hierarchical	• Directives come down the organization
• Information flows up and down the organization	

Source: Adapted from Rothwell (1992).

others, through a hierarchical chain of command in which people from different specialisms have been organized into separate departments (for example, F.W. Taylor and H. Fayol), are not conducive to innovation.

An assumption of the classical approach is that organizational efficiencies are best achieved through specialization of tasks and subdivision into specialist units. This notion extended to individual jobs being clearly defined and distinct. Many people might have done the same job, but there was little overlap between jobs.

By the early 1960s this form of organizational structure was recognized as being a significant barrier to the innovation process. Burns and Stalker (1961), in one of the most influential books on innovation management, called the classical organizational structure 'mechanistic' and argued that a different 'organic' organizational structure was much more conducive to innovation. The main differences between mechanistic and organic structures are shown in Table 4.9.

In essence, organic structures are less burdened by rules and restraints upon employees, tasks are less rigidly defined and creativity is assumed to come from cooperation and exchange of ideas and information, facilitated by a less hierarchical chain of command. Managerial control is present of course, but the climate is one of involvement and participation and sharing rather than close supervision and demarcation. Horizontal cooperation across an organization rather than vertical authority relationships are stressed.

Burns and Stalker (1961), however, also related organization structures to the organization's environment. Where environments were essentially stable – that is, the past tended to repeat itself and predictions could be made with high degrees of confidence – the mechanistic form of organization could be successful. Confectionery and insurance companies, at the time, fitted this category. Where environments were more dynamic – that is, less easy to understand and harder to predict – organic structures were more successful at supporting innovation processes.

This finding, that mechanistic organization structures could be successful in a stable environment, is likely still true today. However, far fewer sectors still enjoy a stable business environment. The first oil shock of 1974 signalled the vulnerability of Western oil-based product markets including transport, energy and plastics. Higher energy costs resulted thereafter and the search for non-oil-based energy sources began in earnest. Political deregulation of the financial services market in the United Kingdom in the early 1980s had major impacts upon the stability of business environments for banks and insurance companies. Privatization of the UK water, gas and electricity utilities has dramatically increased the rate of change and degree of uncertainty in those sectors. The increasing complexity of markets evidenced through continuing cost pressures and pressure for internationalization or globalization of firms' products and activities have affected once stable professional partnerships. Accounting and legal partnerships, for instance, which formerly operated in a stable environment have seen their clients' environments become more complex. KPMG, one of the world's largest financial consultants, found that it could no longer function with a structure based on historic lines, for example separate audit and tax divisions. Clients' business affairs were becoming more complex through merger, acquisition and internationalization, and so 'complete' consulting packages for business growth were sought. These complete solutions required integration of previously distinct business areas and in general a shift towards the organic organization (Johnson, 1993).

We might now begin to expect that organization structure needs to change with the business environment, to continually evolve to cope with fresh demands upon it. This idea of constant metamorphosis has been advocated by Greiner (1972). Whether environmental change is driven by new technology or not, Greiner's notion is worth remembering. Over short periods (up to a few years) organizational restructuring may be small and incremental in nature. During this time there will be periods when structure will not change at all. Every few years however, a major transformational change is needed to realign the organization with its fast-moving environment.

Technology and jobs

It is true that technological change does lead to a loss (or displacement) of jobs. Yet this statement is too simple since it is the net effect of job losses and job creation that is more important. Job loss does occur but, simultaneously, new jobs are created in firms making and supplying new technologies. Studies of the impact of IT on organizations point to very little job displacement in manufacturing caused by innovation in production processes (Campbell, 1993). Job losses from organizational change have much more impact across all occupations than losses from technological change. Production and professional workers have, mostly, not been badly affected although clerical staff have proved more vulnerable. These findings have been supported by Matzner and Wagner (1990) who found that diffusion of new technology favours better quality labour, although there is a small net negative loss when considering jobs in both technology providers and adopters.

It seems likely that there are several variables that can intervene between technological change *per se* and job change. The attitude of management to the job security of the workforce is one, the ability of workers to negotiate protection from job loss is another.

In a large public-owned organization, technology, until recently, has consistently displaced labour from specific jobs but public funding of the organization allowed the displaced workers to be absorbed elsewhere. Given the tightening of public spending, now evident, and the threat of privatization to public sector organizations, capital expenditure can now only be justified if savings can be demonstrated. Because future budgets in the organization are set on the basis that savings will be realized, it is no longer possible for displaced labour to be reallocated. If this stricter regime affects other organizations, then the belief that technology is not, on balance, a thief of jobs may have to change.

Technology and productivity

Conventional wisdom holds that technological change is a driver of productivity although it is not the only one. Yet there are reasons why organizations may not enjoy fully all the potential benefits from technological change. A study of the footwear manufacturing industry found that while technological change was a source of productivity growth, the industry had been slow to exploit the gains available to it (Guy, 1984). Technology had not diffused fast enough. Footwear is historically a low profit industry and a brief consideration of the sector using Porter's (1979) five-forces model shows why. Barriers to entry are small, scale economies occur at low volume, there are many competitors who use price as the basis of competition. Much of the output is purchased by large retail chains with high power. In contrast, supplier power is weak and there is no substitute for footwear. The continuing low profit levels that this position brings to most footwear manufacturers act as a brake on investment which tends to be sporadic, following relatively good profit years, rather than as part of a long-term investment strategy. The returns on investment in these circumstances are limited (Guy, 1985).

Technological change is a major agent of productivity growth in the food and drink sector although other causes are returns to scale and short-term overmanning (Clark, 1984). In chemicals, a highly research-intensive sector, both technology and the state of demand for chemicals are major productivity drivers (Clark, 1985). A study of paper manufacturing found three main ways of raising labour productivity: intensification, technological change and rationalization. Intensification refers to the reorganization of workers into a more efficient arrangement and does not necessarily involve technological change.

Teleworking

The growth in information technology applications has caused some organizations to rethink the traditional notion of offices and desks for all employees. Sparked off by the recession of the early 1980s, organizations began to look very closely at the cost of overheads like personnel services and data-processing departments. There was a general trend to eliminate these functions from corporate structures such that they were bought in as needed. Often, displaced employees would establish a bureau and work for their former employer. When savings from overhead reduction had mostly been achieved, organizations turned their attention to the remaining employees. Organization structures were 'flattened' by moving away from pyramid-like structures. Layers of management were eliminated, remaining managers had larger spans of control and there were fewer grades of employees. Job security declined as the number of fixed-term and part-time contracts grew. The trend was towards a core of decision-making managers and a platform of flexible employees. The latest focus for cost cutting is the cost of occupancy, that is, building costs, rents, rates and maintenance. Where employees are able to use IT at home or while travelling, the need for permanent office space is reduced. An organization of 400 employees could exist with space for 100 knowing that 300 will be working at home, with customers or travelling. Some arrangements have to be in-place for meetings and similar but these are easily handled by a coordinator who monitors the movements of employees. Teleworking has arrived!

Yet this vision of the future is not without its problems. What will be the impact on interpersonal relationships between employees? How will employees relate to the organization in terms of loyalty and commitment? How will customers relate to an organization that has a slimline administrative centre rather than an impressive headquarters? Do customers need to identify with prestige premises if they are to have confidence in an organization?

While answers to these questions are unclear, it seems likely that a major shift in attitudes is needed if teleworking is to spread. Managers will have to increasingly accept that employees can be as effective at home as in an office. This will require a revolution in the mindset of many people. Employees will need to acquire general information technology skills and act as if 'self-employed', looking after their own pension and sickness arrangements as there will be little likelihood of reliable employment with a single organization for more than a few years.

QUESTIONS

1. What factors might intervene to minimize the impact of technological change on job losses in an organization? What other factors could cause job losses?
2. Having minimized costs of overheads, people and occupancy, what might senior managers focus on next?
3. How might teleworking affect the relationship between employee and employer? What could be the possible upsides and downsides?
4. How might delayering of organizations affect their ability to innovate?

4.6 Managing technology

Technology development

Before the industrial revolution and the growth of the large organization important discoveries, such as in metal working and milling, may have come about by chance. People of independent means pursued life-long interests which gradually advanced understanding and occasionally led to a new exploitable technology. Several people worked independently, but simultaneously, on the steam engine, yet it is Stephenson's first locomotive, the Rocket, in 1818 that we remember. Accidental or random discoveries of important new knowledge such as Alexander Fleming's discovery of antibiotic behaviour are now very much the exception. In the main, discoveries and the innovations resulting from them are not random processes. Scientific and engineering know-how are usually deliberately focused on a problem in response to societal pressures or needs (Ayres, 1991). This is certainly the case today when business and government research funding is clearly targeted on specific social, industrial or agricultural problems, for example.

Yet we should not expect technological progress to be in simple proportion to the amount of R&D invested. Barriers exist to advances which can prove particularly troublesome to overcome. Nuclear fission reactors were developed soon after the first fission (atom) bomb was exploded in 1945. The controlled nuclear fusion reactor once thought to be imminent after the invention of the fusion H-bomb in the early 1950s is still thought to be at least several decades ahead (Ayres, 1991, p. 32).

The state of related and supporting technologies also affects the rate of progress in an area. Consider, for instance, the growth in computerized travel booking systems and the increase in demand for air travel. This simple example shows how progress in one area can accelerate progress in another. Recently motor manufacturers have used advances in electronics to produce engine management systems to help maximize fuel economy. Catalysts are now commonly used to detoxify exhaust gases. But we may consider that the limits of efficiency and cleanliness from the internal combustion engine are being approached. Breakthroughs in vehicle technology await possible advances in fuel systems or radically new engine designs. Arguably, advances to automotive engines have held back the development of alternative drive units like electric motors.

Thus significant technological breakthroughs are not random happenings, nor are they purely dependent upon the amount of research and development by firms and nations. Ayres (1991, p. 41) suggests that important innovations occur in clusters after a scientific breakthrough that opens up new territories for process and product development. Researchers can be imagined pushing on a particular door until it begins to open. They may need to push for years, even decades, until the breakthrough emerges. If this simple vision of the technical environment is representative, then it raises some important questions for managers of research dependent organizations. How do we determine how much money to invest in an area? What is the best organization structure to get results? What collaborative or cooperative research is needed? How do we measure progress with particular research projects? When should we stop supporting a project?

The clustering of innovations was one of five causes of innovation identified by Rothwell and Wisseman (1991). They noted the connections between social, economic and technological developments as follows:

1. *The need for technological change.* Simply stated this says that technologies are developed when there is a need for them, for example the development of RADAR in the late 1930s.
2. *Innovation clusters.* Very often, major inventions are not single advances, but rely upon clusters of related technologies to make them work. There may be a time-lag between one breakthrough and a breakthrough in an important related area.
3. *Social resistance.* Resistance to change is well known and it varies between nations and between age groups. America is associated with entrepreneurship and risk taking and is open to change. Countries in Eastern Europe are not associated with such a spirit of invention. Satellite TV receiver dishes were prohibited in Iran to stop the spread of Western ideas and images (Temourian, 1995).
4. *Driving forces.* In addition to technical capability (such as expertise, finance, organization) dogged perseverance is needed to see projects through to marketable ends, such as new processes or products. The very short time between President Kennedy's announcement of a space programme and Neil Armstrong's lunar walk testifies to a national driving force.
5. *Social objectives.* At a point in time a society will have objectives for its development. These objectives in turn influence the direction of technology development. Volvo's pioneering work with semi-autonomous work teams in the 1970s may well reflect a general Scandinavian preference for group decision making.

Rothwell and Wisseman (1991) argue that there is a reciprocal relationship between technology and culture; technology follows culture and culture follows technology. Both statements seem to be true.

Integrating technology in the firm

When business environments were mostly stable and the rate of technological progress was slow, technology could be integrated into production processes with minimum disruption to an organization. That said, adopting new technology has never been easy. Think of the English Luddite movement of 1811–13 where organized gangs smashed machinery in cotton mills in a reaction to the threat posed to jobs, in a time of general economic depression.

Environments are no longer stable, they are turbulent, dynamic arenas.

While technology to some organizations can still be small, incremental improvements to tools and equipment, it increasingly involves complex interactions between people and information-based systems. Complex systems like this cannot easily be integrated into organizations. In technology-intensive sectors, managers can no longer devise a strategy and a structure for an organization and then seek technologies to make the strategy work. Advanced technologies need careful management if they are to make maximum contribution to organizations. They should not be seen as obedient servants to their masters. Technology choice needs to evolve at the same time as decisions are made about strategy and structure, not afterwards (Parthasarthy and Sethi, 1992). This is illustrated in the mini-case below.

Managing technology

Scandinavian Airlines Systems (SAS) was a profitable airline throughout the 1960s and 1970s. But in 1979–81 SAS reported a small loss equivalent to about 0.6 per cent of turnover. The company was fundamentally sound, however, as revenues still exceeded operating costs. The accounting losses were made after adjusting for depreciation.

The problem was largely caused by the climate and culture that existed within the organization. Over the years SAS had invested in new routes and new aeroplanes and the prevailing internal culture was of a technology-driven company with rigorous operating procedures in both technical and customer domains. This preoccupation with technical issues had focused SAS away from the customer and had spawned a middle management bureaucracy to maintain it.

A new chief executive appointed in 1981 recognized these problems and set about a transformational change process in which the customer took centre-stage and technology was seen, properly, as the servant not the master of the company.

Adapted from Ghoshal, S., 'Scandinavian Airlines Systems (SAS) in 1988'. In B. Dewit and R. Meyer (eds) *Strategy: Process, Content, Context – An International Perspective*, West Publishing, 1994.

The organization of research and development

There are several ways of organizing successful R&D. The simplest approach is to manage in-house facilities under the control of an R&D director. This is the traditional approach and gives full control over projects. Sensitive information is relatively secure. Problems with this approach have surfaced given the trend towards shorter product life cycles and expanding legislation covering products, working conditions and the environment. It can be slow and introverted. To accelerate idea generation and development, organizations actively seek collaborative projects, joint-ventures and acquisitions to supplement in-house research.

R&D staff can attend industry events, designed to bring together people with similar problems and interests. Partnerships thus formed are effective ways of developing skills and acquiring knowledge. Growing concerns about water and effluent qualities led Yorkshire Water to set up a partnership with the University of Manchester Institute of Science and Technology (UMIST) to develop an on-line biosensor to monitor the toxicity of water. Further development of the sensor is underway with the electronics firm Siemens. Once installed, biosensors will allow faster detection and response to pollution incidents. Zeneca, a pharmaceuticals and agrochemical company formed from the ICI demerger, developed a new antibiotic with Sumitomo Pharmaceuticals of Japan. In an effort to keep ahead of so many emerging technologies organizations seek collaboration or sometimes take over another organization to gain access to their R&D know-how.

Organizations enter formal alliances to manage the transfer of technology between them. Rolls-Royce and Westinghouse Power Generators of the United States formed an alliance to cover the joint development of turbine technology and power plant. Rolls-Royce agreed to transfer aero-engine technology for incorporation in Westinghouse's industrial turbines for power generation (Tighe, 1995).

Managing technology – collaboration

Leading nations agreed through the Montreal Protocol to end the production of harmful chlorofluorocarbons (CFCs) by the end of 1995. CFCs are thought to interact with ozone in the upper atmosphere causing a depletion in the ozone layer which protects us from the extremes of the sun's radiation.

CFC producers were already seeking replacements for CFCs following research that pointed to their harmful ecological role. To accelerate commercialization of alternatives the chemicals group ICI and pharmaceutical company Glaxo signed a joint venture. Under the venture, Glaxo provided funds to build a new plant to produce CFC alternatives on one of ICI's sites and took all the production for use in its inhalable asthma drugs. ICI earned a 'generous management fee' reflecting the value of its proprietary technology.

ICI held about a third of the world market for CFC replacements and was determined to 'capitalize on its technology as the market expands'. Expansion was assured by the Montreal Protocol and the continuing need for industrial grade CFC replacements for use in factories as well as purer pharmaceutical grades.

Source: 'ICI & Glaxo join forces to replace CFCs'. *The Times*, 16 January 1995.

When large-scale development takes place, for example building a major industrial complex, the client, possibly a government department, may want a turnkey project, that is, where contractors supply and install all the necessary technology. In turnkey projects, one supplier might be unable to provide all the expertise needed and so alliances with other organizations are essential to win contracts and for project completion. Alliances could also be necessary to begin trading with a particular country. For example, a company with no experience of trading with a country might need to form an alliance with another company already established in that country.

In response to constant competitive pressures an organization may look to acquire another and by combining the two R&D departments create a more effective R&D unit. Glaxo, which spent about £850 million on R&D in 1994, acquired Wellcome which spent around £350 million. One outcome of the new company was job losses among scientists. Here, a predator company, Glaxo, sought and identified a takeover target, Wellcome.

Managing technology – the risks

The market for soap powders is aggressively fought over by two companies in particular: Unilever, the Anglo-Dutch group, and Procter & Gamble. In an effort to boost sales of its Persil brand, Unilever spent over £250 million developing and launching a new formulation containing a manganese-based accelerator.

A new Persil Power brand was launched along with claims that it would remove the most 'stubborn' stains. Arch-rival Procter & Gamble quickly attacked the new brand alleging that it damaged fabrics. Several months later the new brand was withdrawn from the market.

In February 1995, Unilever's chairman admitted that the Persil Power brand was defective. It had been introduced to the market without being fully tested. On top of the £200 million development and launch costs, Unilever also suffered £57 million in write-offs.

Source: 'Persil Power tears £57 million hole in Unilever profit'. *The Times*, 22 February 1995.

In contrast, occasionally an organization comes unstuck in a product area. This happened to Boots Pharmaceuticals in 1993 when clinical trials of their heart drug Manoplax indicated that people taking it had a higher chance of returning to hospital or dying than people not taking it. Boots' drug portfolio was small by comparison to other pharmaceutical companies and the failure of Manoplax, which had attracted hopes of boosting Boots into a more dominant market position, was instrumental in bringing about the division's sell-off. Boots Pharmaceutical division was later sold to the German chemical company BASF. This suited BASF since Boots' portfolio was largely in the United Kingdom, the United States and Commonwealth countries. BASF was mostly focused on continental Europe (Jackson, 1993).

QUESTIONS

1. How might scientists and engineers differ from unskilled and semi-skilled employees in their attitudes to work, their managers and to their organizations?

2. How might the interpersonal skills of scientists and engineers differ from non-scientific employees?

CONCLUSION

Technology can no longer be a concern solely of scientists and engineers. The days of scientists pushing their concepts sequentially through development, production and into markets have gone. Technology management today involves working with suppliers and early adopters of products and processes to learn from each other. Although scientists and engineers will continue to work at the leading edge of technological development, managers must understand how emerging technologies could affect their organization so that the organization responds to threats and opportunities in the best way. There are grounds for thinking that information technologies will affect organizations, society and even entire economies in a revolutionary way. Managing technology into the organization is a skill that must be acquired. This calls for a sound understanding of the benefits technology can offer and of the people management issues created inside the organization.

SUMMARY OF MAIN POINTS

This chapter introduces the technological environment in which organizations operate. We have sought to identify key areas of technology as it applies to business organizations. Specifically:

- Technology evolves, usually in a series of small incremental steps but occasionally in large jumps.
- We are experiencing such a jump in information-based technologies at present.
- Information technologies are having revolutionary impacts upon some types of organization and there are grounds for predicting major shocks to social, political and economic enviroments.
- For optimum performance, organizations need to find the best fit between technology available to them, the socioeconomic environment and their choice of strategy.

- Where technology is a factor in determining organizational performance (there are many organizations and sectors where it is not a factor) it must be seen as central to organizational decision making.
- Wealth creation through the exploitation of information superhighways is an important aim for developed nations.
- Technology should not be seen as something to put in place when 'big decisions' about a firm's strategy and structure have already been made. Technology choice is now a part of those big decisions.

References

Adcock, H., Helms, M. and Jih, W.-J.K. (1993) 'Information technology: can it provide a sustainable competitive strategy?', *Information Strategy – The Executives Journal*, vol. 9, no. 3, pp. 10–15.

Ayres, R.U. (1991) 'Barriers and breakthroughs: an expanding frontiers model of the technology industry life cycle', in G. Rosseger (ed.) *Management of Technological Change*, Elsevier Science, Oxford.

Berry, M.M.J. and Taggart, J.H. (1994) 'Managing technology and innovation: a review', *R&D Management*, vol. 24, no. 4, pp. 341–53.

Burns, T. and Stalker, G. (1961) *The Management of Innovation*, Tavistock, London.

Campbell, M. (1993) 'The employment effects of new technology and organizational change: an empirical study', *New Technology Work and Employment*, vol. 8, no. 2, pp. 135–40.

Clark, J. (1984) 'Food, drink and tobacco', in K. Guy (ed.) *Trends and Employment, 1 Basic Consumer Goods*, Gower, Aldershot, Hants.

Clark, J. (1985) 'Chemicals', in J. Clark (ed.) *Technological Trends and Employment, 2 Basic Process Industries*, Gower, Aldershot, Hants.

Coffey, P. (1995) 'How the risks of IT failure are making business re-assess IT strategies', *Unpublished Combined Honours Dissertation*, Nene College.

Coleman, D.C. and MacLeod, C. (1986) 'Attitudes to new techniques: British businessmen', *Economic History Review*, vol. 39, no. 4, pp. 588–611.

Cookson, C. (1995) 'Breakthrough in mixing the molecules', *Financial Times Survey*, Chemical Industry, 27 October, p. 1.

Cooper, C.L. and Payne, R. (1990) *Causes, Coping and Consequences of Stress at Work*, John Wiley, Chichester.

Courtenay, A. (1995) 'Oracle points to the masters of technology', *The Sunday Times*, 29 October, Section 6, p. 10.

Dussauge, P., Hart, S. and Ramanantsoa, B. (1994) *Strategic Technology Management*, John Wiley, Chichester.

Edgerton, D.E.H. (1987) 'Science and technology in British business history', *Business History*, vol. 29, no. 4, pp. 84–103.

Foster, G. (1993) 'The Innovation Imperative', *Management Today*, April, pp. 60–3.

Freeman, C. (1982) *The Economics of Industrial Innovation*, Frances Pinter, London.

Galbraith, J.K. (1967) *The New Industrial State*, Penguin Books, Harmondsworth.

Gillespie, D.F. and Mileti, D.S. (1977) 'Technology and the study of organizations: an overview and appraisal', *Academy of Management Review Symposium: Organizations and Technology*, vol. 4, no. 1, pp. 7-16.

Gooding, C. (1995) 'Boosting sales with the information warehouse', *Financial Times*, 1 March, Supplement p. 15.

Greiner, L.E. (1972) 'Evolution and revolution as organizations grow', *Harvard Business Review*, July, pp. 37–46.

Gray, B. (1995) 'MoD issues GEC-Marconi ultimatum on deal', *Financial Times*, 6 April, p. 10.

Guy, K. (1984) 'Footwear', in K. Guy (ed.) *Technological Trends and Employment, 1 Basic Consumer Goods*, Gower, Aldershot, Hants.

Guy, K. (1985) in J. Clark (ed.) *Technological Trends and Employment, 2 Basic Process Industries*, Gower, Aldershot, Hants.

Hughes, K.L. (1995) 'Stress at work – is there a link to IT Strategy?', *Unpublished Combined Honours Dissertation*, Nene College.

Jackson, T. (1993) 'Boots withdraws heart drug after 2 year study', *Financial Times*, 20 July.

Johnson, G. (1993) 'A strategy for change at KPMG', in G. Johnson and K. Scholes, *Exploring Corporate Strategy*, Prentice Hall, Hemel Hempstead.

Lazonick, W. (1981) 'Competition, specialisation and industrial decline', *Journal of Economic History*, vol. 41, no. 1, pp. 31–8.

Lazonick, W. (1983) 'Industrial organization and technological change: the decline of the British cotton industry', *Business History Review*, vol. 57, no. 2, pp. 195–236.

Matzner, E. and Wagner, M. (eds) (1990) *The Employment Impact of New Technology*, Gower, Avebury.

Monck, C.S.P., Porter, R.B., Quintas, P., Storey, D.J. with Wynarczyk, P. (1990) *Science Parks and the Growth of High Technology Firms*, Routledge, London.

Parthasarthy, R. and Sethi, S.P. (1992) 'The impact of flexible automation on business strategy and organizational structure', *Academy of Management Review*, vol. 17, no. 1, pp. 86–111.

Porter, M.E. (1979) 'How competitive forces shape strategy', *Harvard Business Review*, March–April.

Porter, M.E. and Miller, V.E. (1985) 'How information gives you competitive advantage', *Harvard Business Review*, July–August, pp. 149–60.

Rassam, C. (1993) 'Science in crisis', *Management Today*, June, pp. 60–3.

Rothwell, R. (1992) 'Successful industrial innovation: critical factors for the 1990s', *R&D Management*, vol. 22, no. 3, pp. 221–39.

Rothwell, R. and Wisseman, H. (1991) 'Technology, culture and public policy', in G. Rosseger (ed.) *Management of Technological Change*, Elsevier Science, Oxford.

Shiman, D.R. (1991) 'Managerial efficiency and technological decline in Britain 1860–1914', *Business and Economic History*, no. 20, pp. 89–98.

Simons, G.L. (1986) *Management Guide to Office Automation*, National Computing Centre.

Small, I. and Swann, P. (1993) 'R&D performance of UK companies', *Business Strategy Review*, vol. 4, no. 3, pp. 41–51.

Souder, W.M. (1991) 'Organizing for modern technology and innovation. A review and synthesis', in G. Rosseger (ed.) *Management of Technological Change*, Elsevier Science, Oxford.

Temourian, H. (1995) 'Iran bans Baywatch with purge on Satan's dishes', *The Sunday Times*, 23 April, p. 18.

Tighe, C. (1995) 'A productive marriage', *Financial Times*, Survey of Power Generation Equipment, 11, 16 May.

Yamazaki, H. (1988) 'The development of large enterprises in Japan: an analysis of the top 50 enterprises in the Profit Ranking Table (1929–1984)', *Japanese Yearbook on Business History*, no. 5, pp. 12–55.

CHAPTER 5

THE SOCIAL AND DEMOGRAPHIC ENVIRONMENT

Ian Brooks and Jamie Weatherston

 LEARNING OUTCOMES

On completion of this chapter you should be able to:

- understand the complex and dynamic nature of social, cultural and demographic forces;
- appreciate that organizations operate in a cultural context;
- understand that national cultural differences influence managerial and organizational activity and have consequences for the organization–environment relationship;
- interpret key population statistics and diagrammatic representations (e.g. population pyramids);
- appreciate some of the prime differences in demographic characteristics at local, regional, national and international scales;
- recognize the characteristics of an ageing population and assess the prime influences on organizations of this trend;
- appreciate the influences upon organizations and geo-political areas of population migration;
- discuss some of the political, social and economic consequences of demographic changes;
- recognize characteristics of, and trends in, a number of key social forces (such as the family, crime and health) and assess their impact on organization;
- assess recent changes in the role and significance of the trade union movement in the United Kingdom and European developments and alternatives.

5.1 The social environment

Introduction

Organizations operate in a dynamic and multifaceted social environment. They experience a complex interactive relationship with a social community or society. Figure 5.1 illustrates a diverse array of social phenomena which individually and collectively both shape, and are shaped by, society.

Figure 5.2 illustrates the broad two-way relationship between organizations and society, that is the social community in which organizations operate. This relationship takes place within a local, national and regional cultural context. Each societal force will not exert the same influence over all organizations. For example, a society's changing health expectations may have little direct relevance for a consumer electronics company yet will assume great importance for many food manufacturers.

This chapter will investigate demographic (population) issues at a local, national and international scale and assess their influence upon organizations. We will then take a closer look at a number of critical social phenomena and identify many of the key consequences of social dynamism for commercial and other organizations. Issues such as crime, health, the family and the changing face of organized labour will be considered. However, the chapter opens with a discussion of national culture which, it is argued, influences all organizational and environmental activity.

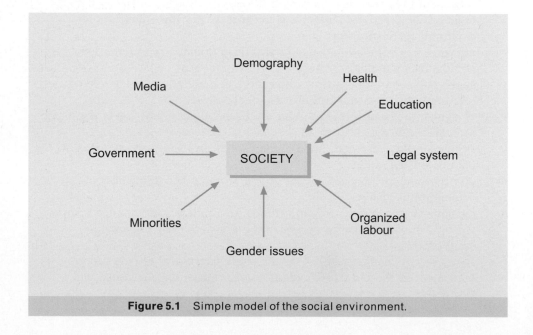

Figure 5.1   Simple model of the social environment.

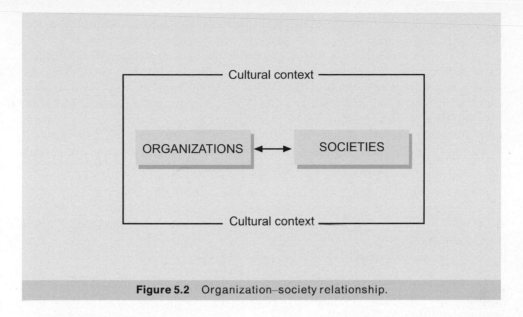

Figure 5.2 Organization–society relationship.

5.2 National culture

Organizations interact with the social community within a cultural context. As such, culture itself acts as a pervasive force influencing all organizations, whatever their nature and sphere of operations. Considerable research has focused on the influence of national (Hofstede, 1983; Adler, 1991), regional and organization cultures (Sathe 1983; Peters and Waterman, 1982; Deal and Kennedy 1982) and their influence on the organization/environment relationship. Argenti (1974) suggests that there is a need to understand the dominant values of society. With this in mind we will explore the work of key researchers in that field as their findings have a bearing on international business activity.

Culture refers to the collectively held values, beliefs, attitudes, assumptions and behaviours of a group. The most deep-rooted element of culture is the set of values held by the group. Such values may manifest themselves in particular beliefs and attitudes and also in people's behaviour. Often surface behaviour is 'driven' by a much deeper belief, for example in the difference between right and wrong, which is itself a product of national cultural conditioning. What is considered to be right or wrong differs between cultures. For example, people of a particular country may cherish their personal right to freedom of speech, while another culture may feel that such a right should be subordinate to the best interests of society as a whole. The United States of America typifies the former category while the Singaporean culture adopts a more societal orientation.

Culture is shared; however, that is not to say that everyone in a particular culture thinks and acts in the same way. Individual differences are significant.

When describing cultures we look for 'typical' values, beliefs and attitudes and 'norms' of behaviours.

Many countries have a distinct national culture; nevertheless, subcultures exist within many countries. For example, in the United Kingdom there are certain regional groups, such as the Welsh and the Scottish, who possess some cultural characteristics which partly differentiate them from the English. There are also differences between the regions in England. Similarly, there are significant, and politically critical, differences between the French- and English-speaking Canadians. Additionally, different subcultures exist based on other criteria, such as:

- social class;
- gender;
- age;
- religion;
- occupational group.

As a consequence all organizations operate within a complex, often multi-tiered, cultural context. Figure 5.3 illustrates some of the features which contribute to the national cultural environment.

The assumption of cultural convergence dominated business, organizational and management studies up to and including the 1960s. The convergence hypothesis argues that management is a universal phenomenon, and that 'good practice', which usually emanated from the USA or Europe, could and should be applied throughout the world. Theodore Levitt (1983) argued that national

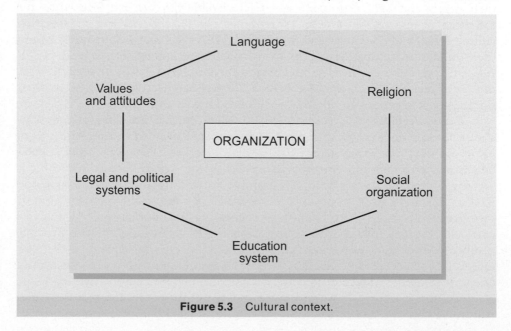

Figure 5.3   Cultural context.

cultures were converging such that culture was becoming an unimportant variable for business to consider. However, in recent decades, and especially since the 1980s, considerable attention has been paid to cultural differences between nations and there is growing acceptance that 'good' managerial practices may be those which best fit and are in keeping with a particular culture. Additionally, differences between countries have been increasingly recognized such that the 'divergence hypothesis' is now given considerable credence. Supranational organizations like the European Union, which was founded on the convergence belief, have had to recognize significant national differences. It is now more widely accepted that national differences are here to stay and that they pose crucial management problems, particularly for multinational, global or multicultural organizations.

National culture is important politically, sociologically and psychologically. Hofstede (1983) argues that 'nations are political units, rooted in history, with their own ... forms of government, legal systems, educational systems ...'. Nationality is also symbolic to citizens who derive part of their identity from it. These national differences are very real to people. Our thinking is conditioned by national culture through the mechanism of the family, our education and the workplace, our friendship groups and the media.

Culture is dynamic and continually evolving; however, fundamental change in cultural values is rather slow. Behaviours may change more rapidly and transparently. Nevertheless, for most observers within any country cultural changes can be noted. For example, most citizens of the United Kingdom recognize that societal norms, values, attitudes and behaviours slowly changed throughout the 1980s such that they are now quite different in many respects to those found in the 1970s. Culture continues to change such that organizations have to be sensitive to new and growing social values, such as concern for the natural environment, or more specifically, for animal welfare.

We will now look at the work of Geert Hofstede who has identified work-related values in 50 world countries on four dimensions. Although methodologically some of the findings may, in detail, be questionable, what they do show is significant and crucial differences between countries. These differences have important implications for all organizations that operate in, have dealings with, or employ people from more than one country. Hofstede (1983) found that cultures differ according to the degree people exhibit:

- individualistic or collective tendencies;
- large or small power distances between one another;
- strong or weak uncertainty avoidance tendencies;
- masculine versus feminine characteristics.

People in the USA, Australia and Great Britain, for example, are shown by Hofstede (1983) to value individualism while many Latin American and Asian countries value collectivism – that is, they possess a group or societal orientation. Knowledge of this may influence an organization's marketing practices and advertising focus, for example. It may influence people's motivation to work and how they decide to utilize their leisure time.

In many countries a large power-distance exists between workers and management or between social classes. Again this is true of many Latin American and Asian countries and France. In France management tends to be highly stratified and considerable deference is expected by superiors. In Scandinavian countries, and in Israel, Australia and Great Britain, for example, power distances are smaller.

Countries also differ in their cultural ability to cope with uncertainty. As uncertainties create anxiety, some cultures attempt to organize everything carefully in order to reduce uncertainty of outcome. Hence in Germany, Japan and France, for example, trains run on time and organization and detail are considered highly important whereas in Scandinavia, Great Britain, Singapore and Hong Kong, for example, Hofstede (1983) argues people are more accepting of uncertainties (and trains are often late!). In a business environment context this may mean that countries with high uncertainty avoidance (e.g. France, Germany, Japan) may undertake more environmental scanning in an attempt to gather information which may reduce uncertainty and facilitate organizational planning.

Some cultures make a clear and strong distinction between the nature and role of men and women. In Scandinavia and Holland men and women experience similar values, beliefs and attitudes. Additionally, 'macho' behaviours are less common than in Australia, Ireland, much of Latin America, the USA and Great Britain.

It is crucial that each of these cultural dimensions are appreciated by managers within multinational, multi-ethnic and global organizations. There are many cases of American and European companies, for example, who have failed to 'acclimatize' to cultural conditions in other countries and suffered financial losses as a consequence.

Ronen and Shenkar (1985) built upon Hofstede's work and identified clusters of countries based on certain cultural commonalities, such as religion and language. Some of these groups are illustrated in Table 5.1. It is interesting to note that member countries of the European Union (shown in italics in Table 5.1) fall into five separate cultural groups (nine were identified in total). It is not surprising that there are differences in perception and in substance between EU members' national governments.

Adler (1991) suggests that cultures vary in the extent to which people adopt particular problem-solving styles. People may perceive problems in the business environment quite differently depending on their cultural orientation. They may also gather data and manage solutions to those problems quite differently. She identifies two types of culture (or personality), that is 'problem-solving' and 'situation acceptance' cultures. Problem-solving cultures, which dominate in the United Kingdom and USA, will identify numerous issues as problems which need to be solved by gathering facts, changing people, making decisions and generally acting decisively and with authority, whereas situation acceptance cultures, more

TABLE 5.1   Groupings of national cultures (after Ronen and Shenkar, 1985)

Anglo	Australia, Canada, New Zealand, *Ireland*, South Africa, USA, *United Kingdom*.
Far Eastern	Malaysia, Hong Kong, Singapore, Philippines, South Vietnam, Indonesia, Thailand, Taiwan.
Nordic	*Sweden, Denmark*, Norway, *Finland*.
Latin-European	*France, Belgium, Italy, Portugal, Spain*.
Near Eastern	Turkey, Iran, *Greece*.
Germanic	*Germany*, Switzerland, *Austria*.

common in Latin and Asian countries, will accept many issues rather than attempt to change them. They may, for example, see certain environmental factors as given. They tend to gather ideas and perceptions rather than just hard facts. Decisions tend to be made slowly and only after consultation.

The field of cross-cultural or intercultural management is now blossoming as the relevance of national culture to the success of business ventures is increasingly being recognized.

QUESTIONS

1.   How might national culture influence organizational activity?

2.   Explore the ways in which global companies might adapt their marketing effort to better 'fit' a national culture. Use Hofstede's dimensions as a guide.

5.3 Demographic forces

Introduction

Demography is the study of human populations. It is often a prime area of focus for those undertaking courses in geography and some other social sciences. Our concern here is the particular insight organizations can gain from analysing population dynamics. Consequently, this section will illustrate how demographic forces can pose both opportunities and threats to all types of commercial, not-for-profit and public enterprise. It takes a closer look at various critical population characteristics, at a variety of geographical scales, and assesses how changes are likely to influence organizations both now and in the future.

Firstly, however, we will explore some demographic characteristics and patterns at a variety of geo-political scales.

Population structure and life expectancy: a small-scale comparison

We are all aware from personal experiences that the age/sex structure of any given population varies between one place and another. Eastbourne, a sleepy town on the south coast of England, is a favourite destination for retired people who seek an attractive environment away from the bustle of city life. On or near retirement, many people sell their homes in London or elsewhere and buy a retirement home in the quieter more picturesque environment of the south coast. This outward migration from urban areas such as London has been common for at least 50 years. It has led to an increase in the numbers of older people in towns such as Eastbourne. Hence, such favourite retirement destinations have a skewed population structure with large numbers of older residents.

This pattern is often compounded by the fact that few seaside resorts have many worth-while employment prospects for the young. Consequently there is often a net outward migration of younger age groups (e.g. 16–30 year olds) seeking employment. This loss of young people, some with small children, further increases the average age of the population.

Eastbourne has a top-heavy population structure with less than average numbers of people in the younger age groups and more than normal proportions of older people. This is illustrated by the simple graph (Figure 5.4) which compares Eastbourne with Kettering, a small town in Northamptonshire in the Midlands of England. In terms of size alone the two towns are similar, with Eastbourne having a population of 85 200 (1991, i.e. the last full census date) and Kettering 76 150 (1991). Further observation, however, reveals significant differences in the age/sex make-up of the populations of the two towns. Over 40 per cent of Kettering's population is under 30 years of age. The comparable figure in Eastbourne is just 30 per cent. However, it is in the older age groups where the differences are most

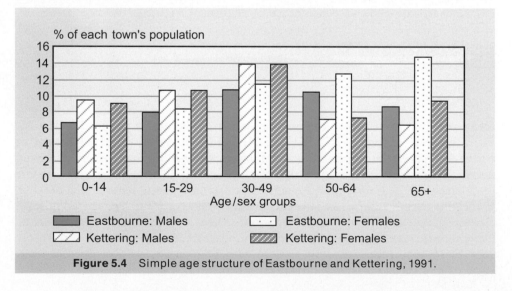

Figure 5.4   Simple age structure of Eastbourne and Kettering, 1991.

TABLE 5.2 Life expectancy in selected countries

Country/region	Life expectancy in years at birth (1990)	
	Males	Females
Sub-Saharan Africa	49	52
Asia Pacific	60	63
United Kingdom	72	78
OECD average	72	78
USA	72	79
France	72	80
Holland	74	80
Sweden	74	80
Norway	74	80
Japan	75	81

pronounced. In excess of 45 per cent of people in Eastbourne are over 50 years of age compared to just 31 per cent in Kettering. Eastbourne has nearly 13 per cent of its population over the age of 75 compared to a national average of less than 7 per cent.

The relatively small proportion of young male adults in Eastbourne would suggest that employment opportunities in Eastbourne were largely in service activities and other roles more popular with females. Another factor which further distorts population structure and accounts for differences between the two towns is the male/female ratio. Table 5.2 shows the average life expectancy at birth in a selection of countries and regions from around the world.

Women, being physiologically more resilient (alas, the authors are male), live longer. This pattern is more or less universal. It accounts for the considerable imbalance in the male/female ratio in both Eastbourne and Kettering among the older age groups. The imbalance becomes increasingly apparent with age as approximately two out of every three people over 75 years of age are female while less than 20 per cent of over 90 year olds are male. Table 5.2 also indicates the differences in life expectancy that exist on a global scale. Such differences, although not normally as acute, also occur within many countries, for example between different social classes or occupational groups.

Population structure: European Union comparisons

Variations in population structure are not confined to the small-scale examples discussed above. Differences in structure become even more apparent on a global scale. However, two particular contrasts are worthy of analysis here. Firstly, we will look at the current difference between two European Union countries – Denmark and the Republic of Ireland – before analysing the predicted changes in population structure in the whole of the European Union to the year 2020. The consequences of these changes, which will have important and far-reaching implications for business and government in the EU, will be discussed later.

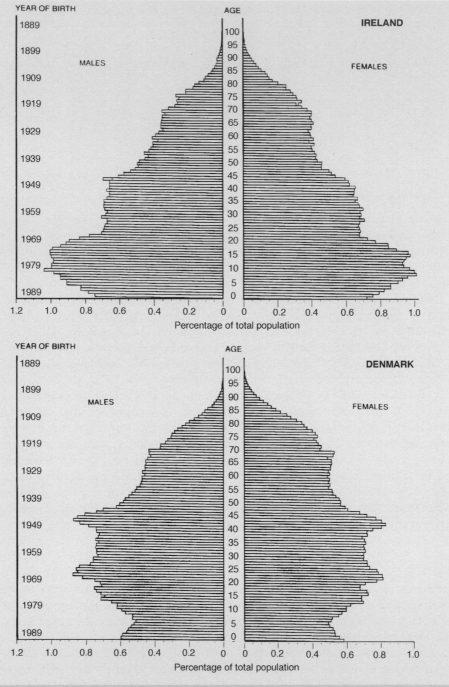

Figure 5.5   Age structure pyramids: Ireland and Denmark.

The Republic of Ireland and Denmark have been selected as they illustrate different structures. In population terms, both countries are dwarfed by many of their European partners. Denmark's population, showing virtually zero growth in recent years, was 5 135 000 in 1990 making it a little larger than the Republic of Ireland with 3 507 000 in the same year. In many ways Denmark's population structure – its age/sex make-up – resembles that of the United Kingdom and Germany, while Ireland's is unique in the EU.

Figure 5.5 comprises two population pyramids. The pyramids show the proportion of each country's population in each five-year age group starting at the base with the 0–4 year olds. Females are shown on the right-hand side and males on the left. It is interesting to compare the two countries.

Ireland has a larger proportion of its population in the younger age groups and fewer older people when compared to Denmark. This is in part a result of differing fertility rates (the number of babies born per 1000 women per year) between the two countries. To put it simply, Irish families tend to be larger than those in Denmark. More precisely the average birth rates for the two countries between 1985 and 1990 were:

- Ireland 18.1
- Denmark 10.7
- Therefore, birth rate in Ireland is 69 per cent higher than in Denmark.

Birth rate represents an annual figure indicating the number of live births in a country for every 1000 of its population. It is a useful, although a little crude, comparative measure.

Another cause of the different population structures between the two countries is the relative life expectancy of their people, with the figure for Denmark being a little higher than that of Ireland. However, a third and more pervasive reason for the observed differences exists. Ireland, unlike its Scandinavian partner, has for well over a century 'suffered' from a mass exodus of its people. Despite its high natural increase in population, outward migration has been on such a scale that the total population of Ireland has barely grown over the last 150 years. Traditionally, the majority of migrants have been young adults, many of whom never return on a permanent basis. The particular economic, political and social issues surrounding migration are discussed below, although many of the consequences for organizations and governments may become apparent to the reader.

Note also the effects, particularly towards the top of the pyramids, of the difference in life expectancy between males and females. In both countries the imbalance becomes apparent in the older age groups despite the fact that 'nature' attempts to correct this by ensuring that for every 100 female babies approximately 105 males are born.

In conclusion, it is clear that even among two closely allied countries population differences are significant. These demographic and related social differences have a profound influence on organizations and governments in the two countries.

Demographic dynamism and ageing

In addition to geographical differences within the European Union, significant changes take place over time. Figure 5.6 shows the change in structure predicted within the EU between 1990 and the year 2020 (estimate). In many ways the pattern indicated resembles that when comparing the current structure of Denmark and Ireland. However, what is clear is that the EU's population is ageing. There is a decreasing proportion of young people and a growing number of old, especially very old (over the age of 80 years of age).

The trend illustrated in Figure 5.6 has been apparent for many years in the United Kingdom, Germany and Denmark, for example, but it is now the southern European countries, particularly Greece, Italy, Spain and Portugal, where the rate of ageing is most rapid as birth rates have plummeted during the last two decades.

Many of the commercial and governmental implications of ageing are discussed below; however, the demographic consequences, for Europe in particular, are interesting. We have listed three demographic 'facts' in this respect:

1.   Europeans currently account for almost 10 per cent of the world's population whereas by the year 2050 they will be less than 3 per cent.
2.   The number of over-65s in Europe will outstrip the number of children under 15 by the year 2020.
3.   In order to replace or maintain a population each woman of child-bearing age needs to produce about 2.1 children – in Europe currently the figure is closer to 1.7, while in Germany the rate is about 1.3.

The dependency ratio, that is, the proportion of working age population to dependent population, will also vary significantly through time. Figure 5.7 indicates the ratio of working age population (15–64 year olds) in Germany, Japan and the United Kingdom, to over 65 year olds. As can be seen, the dependency ratio is set to deteriorate rapidly over the next 40 years, especially so in Germany where by the year 2040 there will be just two 15–64 year olds for every person over 65 years old. This 'switch' from young to old has important policy, social and organizational implications.

There are a number of contributory reasons for this changing structural pattern. Life expectancy has been gradually increasing and fertility rates slowly decreasing over the last 50 years in Europe. However, birth rates in particular are not stable but rather fluctuate in unpredictable cycles. They are influenced by a variety of short-term factors such as the state of a national economy and government family policies and by longer term socioeconomic trends. The estimated figures for the year 2020 reveal a pattern that is almost bound to occur although the detail may vary a little. Life expectancy figures will continue to creep upwards rather slowly while fertility rates will be unlikely to increase significantly.

Clearly, assuming zero migration, it would be necessary for each female on average to have two children, and for these to survive to child-bearing age, for a country's population to remain stable, i.e. the replacement rate. Average annual

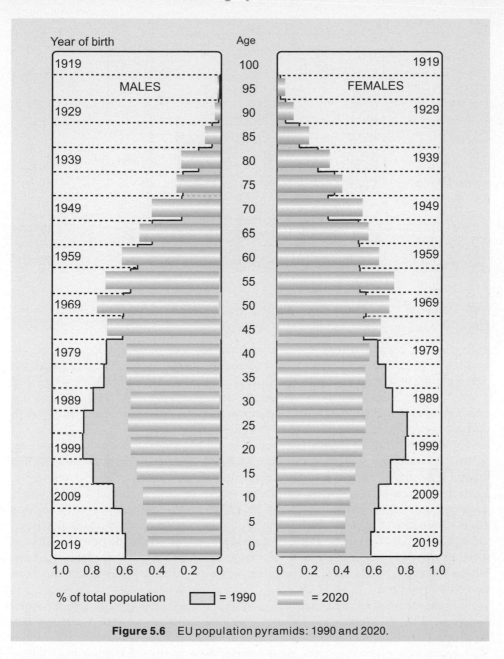

Figure 5.6 EU population pyramids: 1990 and 2020.

fertility rates in many European countries, notably Germany, are often below that necessary to merely maintain population stability. Yet Germany's population continues to grow, a fact which in no small measure has in recent years been due to net inward migration.

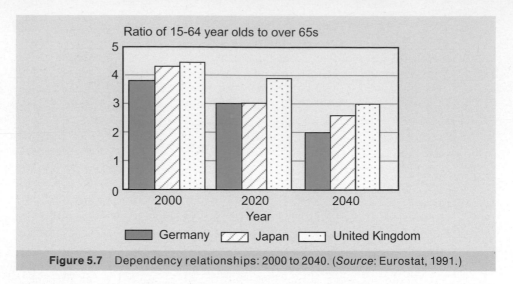

Figure 5.7 Dependency relationships: 2000 to 2040. (*Source*: Eurostat, 1991.)

International migration: the cases of Germany and the Republic of Ireland

Migration of people across national boundaries has been a burning issue of political, social and economic debate for many centuries. It has facilitated the demographic and economic growth of many nations and the decline of some. For example, mass migration to the USA, Canada, Australia and New Zealand has enabled those so-called 'new world' countries to enjoy enormous economic growth and prosperity, particularly in the twentieth century.

Mobility of labour is vital for the successful functioning of economic activity. With structural and geographical changes in industry it is essential that skilled labour is prepared to move to find opportunities in other regions or countries. Without such mobility, either within countries or across national boundaries, economic growth would undoubtedly be stifled in the more prosperous regions while conditions of high unemployment would be further exacerbated in declining areas. In the EU, for example, rates of unemployment vary significantly between different regions. In some parts of Germany and Scandinavia there has long been labour shortages, while in many peripheral regions of Europe unemployment rates exceed 15 per cent.

However, issues that are of economic importance often ignore social concerns. The problems involved in migration tend to be rather acute when considered at the international level, that is involving cross-national migration. The remainder of this section takes a brief look at two EU countries where international migration is a major concern, for quite different reasons.

As outlined above, the Republic of Ireland has long experienced significant outward migration. The United Kingdom is the main beneficiary of these migrants although many Irish live and work all over the world. It is said that there are more

Irish in New York (USA) than there are in Ireland. This is true if those of Irish descent are included. In fact it is believed that there are 44 million Americans of Irish descent, that is, ten times the population of Ireland! The horrific potato famine in 1845/46 was a significant spur to migration, primarily to the 'New World' (USA, Australia) and the United Kingdom. Ireland experienced a large decline in population size as a result of this first major wave of migration.

Unfortunately for Ireland many of those leaving the country today are young, fit adults, often skilled, ambitious and willing to work hard. Such migrants have been an asset in England where the construction industry in particular has long benefited by having such a flexible workforce. One country's gain is another's loss.

Ireland has a disproportionate school age population when compared to its EU counterparts. As stated above, birth rates are high and family sizes tend to be large. However, once educated, many Irish are keen to succeed and see the opportunities offered overseas as substantial. The Irish government have, particularly in recent decades, invested a great deal in terms of education and health expenditure on its young people, many of whom emigrate, often permanently. Figure 5.8 compares birth, death and migration rates in Ireland, Germany, Denmark and the United Kingdom. Of particular interest is the migration rate of each country. Ireland, in 1991, had an outward migration rate of 47 indicating that for every 1000 people in the country 47 emigrated – almost 5 per cent of the entire population each year. So, despite a sizeable birth rate (the highest in the EU) Ireland's population in 1991 declined by about 0.6 per cent. Meanwhile Germany's population growth only remained positive due to a net inward migration of almost half a million people.

Economically, the prosperous German economy has encouraged high levels of immigration and has benefited from an influx of predominantly low-cost labour from Turkey and, more recently, Eastern European countries. However, socially

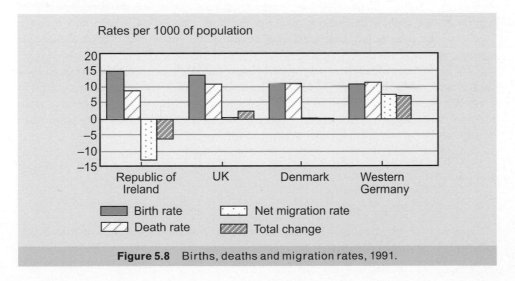

Figure 5.8 Births, deaths and migration rates, 1991.

and politically all is not rosy. Many migrants in Germany have been subjected to sometimes horrific racial attacks, prejudice is rife and large-scale political unrest is simmering. The extreme right in Germany have made little secret of their feelings towards foreign migrants, leading to scenes somewhat frightening to outside observers and the majority of German citizens.

Many migrants face other social and economic difficulties. Some find themselves 'ghettoized', frequently in low-cost, poorly maintained housing. Education standards are often below average for the host country and employment prospects poor. So, whereas a fluid mobility of labour across national boundaries facilitates economic growth and restructuring, it is not without social, economic and political consequences.

Migration patterns within the European Union

Paul White (1993) notes that in addition to the more predictable movements of migrant populations within the EU over the past decade there has been a number of unforeseen developments. These include:

- the political transformation of Eastern Europe and consequent increases in immigration from former Communist countries, e.g. from the former East Germany to the West;
- massive Third World migration into Italy and, to a lesser extent, Spain;
- a rapid decline in fertility rates among many established minority groups within the EU (e.g. the West Indian population in England) and above national fertility rates for other minority groups (e.g. the Indian, Pakistani and Bangladeshi populations in the United Kingdom);
- a reduction in internal mobility rates of EU migrant populations.

It is highly likely that the coming decade will see further significant migration into Western Europe, principally from the Third World and Eastern Europe, while the size of many existing minority groups will also depend on their specific fertility rates.

The pattern of internal migration within the EU has been characterized by a high degree of polarization. There has, for many years, been large-scale migration from the Republic of Ireland to the United Kingdom. Increasing numbers of Irish are now migrating to Germany and other EU countries. Other major migrations in recent years from the peripheral areas include:

- from Portugal to France (about one million Portuguese live in France);
- from Italy to France;
- from Italy to Germany;
- from Spain to France.

Lebon (1990) has classified EU countries according to their status in intra-Union exchanges: (1) countries of departure – Ireland, Italy, Portugal, Greece and Spain; (2) countries of reception – Luxembourg, France, Germany, Belgium and the United Kingdom; and (3) countries with balanced exchanges – Holland and Denmark. In broad terms it seems likely that these patterns will prevail for the foreseeable future. The extent to which new patterns are likely to develop is largely unknown for there remain many obstacles to migration. Whereas legally EU citizens are more or less free to work in any community, country mobility is hampered by problems of language, lack of job-related skills, housing, information and prejudice.

Deurbanization: the case of the United Kingdom

Another migration trend of particular interest is the movement of people within any Western industrialized country away from large urban areas. In the United Kingdom, this trend reverses an almost unidirectional and consistent pattern of urbanization since the Industrial Revolution. Figure 5.9 quantifies such movements of people away from Merseyside and London and into such places as Surrey and Sussex (East and West).

Although both have small natural increases (measured as the difference between birth rate and death rate) the populations of both Merseyside and Greater London are declining. Many people, especially the more affluent and those mature in years, are deserting the large urban areas in significant numbers. Hence during the 1980s London's natural population growth of about 206 000 needs to be compared with a net migration loss of 218 000. It was Inner London in particular which suffered the greatest loss. A demographic consequence of this migration is that the population structure of these two large cities is more youthful than the national average. The majority of inward migrants tends to be young adults, while more mature citizens often seek the relative tranquillity and security of suburban and rural environments.

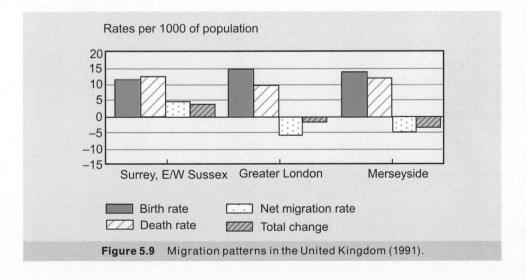

Figure 5.9   Migration patterns in the United Kingdom (1991).

Surrey, East and West Sussex – three counties to the south of London – comprise a mixture of smaller urban areas, villages and rural and coastal landscapes. The counties are prime commuting grounds for London and relatively attractive places to live. Figure 5.9 shows that despite a negative natural increase in population (largely because many young people with young families migrate to London and elsewhere) the southern counties 'benefit' from a significant influx of migrants.

This pattern of migration contributes to unique problems in both the receiving localities and the cities of origin. Increased congestion, environmental problems, high house prices and urban sprawl are but a few of the issues facing southern counties. Meanwhile major urban areas continue to suffer from poor housing and education, declining services, increasing crime and general social and economic hardship. The very old, the unskilled and certain ethic minority groups are less likely to find migration to the southern 'affluent' counties an option. This contributes to increasing inner city difficulties, such as high unemployment, crime and deprivation, for organizations and governments. Additionally, migration of this kind tends to create a divided society; divided economically, socially and geographically.

The global pattern of population growth

The demographic features discussed above comprise a selection of the interesting and relevant demographic patterns emerging in Europe. On a global scale, population growth and distribution add additional complexity to the organizational environment. Population growth remains a prime concern. At current rates of growth world population will double in about 36 years. It has more than doubled in the last 36 years. At this rate of growth, by the year 3000 there would be 2000 people piled on every square metre of the earth's surface!

Population growth in the developing world averages about 2.5 per cent per year. When compared to the minimal growth in Europe it is clear that global population distribution is shifting towards, for example, South-East Asia and away from Western powers. Despite the efforts of many Asian governments to curb their population growth this pattern continues. However, some countries recognize the economic and political benefits of a growing population. In fact the Malaysian government plans to increase its indigenous Malay population rapidly. In the United Arab Emirates (UAE) indigenous population growth is encouraged in attempts to increase the proportion of 'local' to expatriate workers, making the country relatively less dependent on overseas personnel. Figure 5.10 shows some of the disparities of world population growth.

There is little doubt that the continued population growth in China and South-East Asia acts as a spur to economic growth. This is in part due to the need to maintain and improve living standards in such countries which in turn 'demands' that governments strive for economic growth. South-East Asian countries are fighting poverty through industrialization and development; a

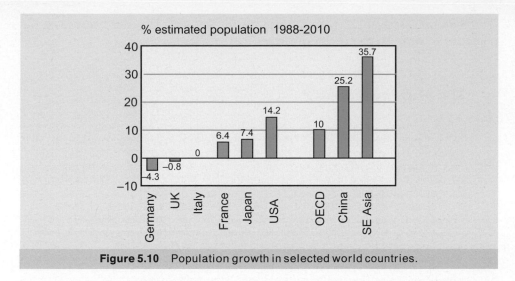

Figure 5.10 Population growth in selected world countries.

consequence of economic growth is a small decline in the rate of population growth. However, with relatively large numbers of young people, labour supplies are assured and increasing prosperity leads in turn to increases in demand for goods and services and ensures an ever vibrant economy. In economic growth terms, South-East Asia has far outstripped both North America and Europe over the last 10 years and looks set to continue this trend.

It is a thought-provoking fact that both the total income and population of Europe comprise an ever-declining proportion of global totals. The changing global patterns of economic development, growth of new power blocs and the prospects for Europe are discussed in Chapter 3.

5.4 Population dynamics: consequences for organizations and governments

Introduction

For many organizations, demographic trends and issues are of little apparent concern. This may be a short-sighted view, although it is true to say that for some organizations there is a very tenuous link between changes in population patterns and their well-being. However, at the local, national and continental level of government the changes discussed above are highly significant. So, too, are they for many commercial organizations who, for example, employ a large labour force, sell their goods or services to age-specific segments, or are considering relocation or growth. Population provides organizations with one of their most important resources, labour, and also the markets for their goods and services.

The mini-case study below, based on the brewing industry, illustrates the relevance of demography as an important market consideration.

The brewing industry

Brewers, such as Bass and Carlsberg-Tetley, depend for a significant proportion of their beer sales on the 18–25-year-old, predominantly male, age group. An average European male in his 20s consumes 70 per cent more beer than one in his 40s. With an ageing population brewers in the United Kingdom, for example, have had to rely on consumption from other age groups and sales of many other products and services to compensate for the relative decline in this age-specific consumption group. Hence there has been an increase in the sale of food in pubs, catering for more mature adults and families, while brewers have diversified into the broader entertainment business (e.g. hotels, gambling, recreation facilities). This is in no small way because of demographic changes, although more general societal change has contributed.

Figure 5.11 shows the decline in beer sales in the United Kingdom between 1988 and 1993 and the number of people in the 18–25-year age group for the same time period. The correlation between the two trends is clear. Consequently, companies with large investments in brewing facilities have shown considerable concern in recent decades at the decline in the number of people within their prime target populations. An ageing population bodes poorly for such companies. There is now considerable over-capacity in the United Kingdom brewing industry.

Most European brewers face similar problems. In Germany, for example, which has the highest beer consumption per capita in Europe, it is estimated that the decline in the male population in their 20s may be as much as 38 per cent between 1987 and the year 2000. The equivalent figure for the United Kingdom is 20 per cent.

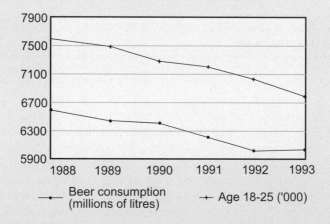

Figure 5.11   Declining beer consumption and youthful population.

Demographic restructuring: commercial implications

Ageing, or demographic restructuring, has many implications for commercial, non-profit-making and public sector organizations. Restructuring may alter patterns of consumption, production, employment, savings, investment and innovation.

Many goods and services are targeted at specific age/sex segments of a population. The brewing industry is just one example of this. In the last 15 years there has been a rapid growth in the financial services sector, for example, with many companies offering numerous 'products' aimed at the retirement/ redundancy market. Life assurance, pension funds and single sum (e.g. a redundancy payment) products have flourished. This has been sustained by the progressive growth in both the numbers and affluence of middle-aged and old-aged people in the United Kingdom. The mini-case below illustrates how one successful company has turned demographic ageing into an environmental opportunity.

Saga holidays

In the mid-1950s entrepreneur Sidney De Haan decided to offer cheap holidays to retired people in off-peak times. He took advantage of the low prices offered by hoteliers who were only too willing to see their poor occupancy rates rise. Less than 40 years on, the Saga group, with a turnover in excess of £130 million, offers holidays, financial services and magazines to the over-50s. Saga recognized that the special needs of older customers represented a market opportunity.

Retired people have grown progressively wealthier and Saga now offers holidays trekking in the Himalayas and round the world cruises costing up to £30 000 per head. They have expanded in the lucrative US market. They have also developed their 'product' portfolio to include financial services, such as insurance broking. They can negotiate many preferential rates for their low-risk customers. Older people tend not to drive great distances, hence reducing the probability of being involved in a car accident. They also spend more of their time in their houses so reducing the opportunity for burglars to strike.

About a half of Saga's 750 staff employed in Folkestone, Kent, now work on the financial services side of the business. What is more, they find their business is virtually recession proof as a decline in a national economic cycle has little influence on the income of retired people. What is damaging, however, is a decline in interest rates which does adversely influence the incomes of their clients.

Manufacturers and retailers of children's clothing and other infant products have had to operate in an increasingly competitive marketplace as birth rates across Europe have been depressed since the late 1960s. Sales of baby foods in Europe's largest market, Germany, did not rise in volume terms between 1983 and 1993.

However, the pattern of fertility decline is not consistent as birth rates fluctuate over time adding further complexity and uncertainty to organizational players in these market segments.

It is evident that people currently in their 40s and 50s expect a different lifestyle from earlier generations. Those who grew up in the 1950s, 1960s and 1970s, without the experience of war and rationing, have different cultural values and lifestyle expectations than those of their parents. These people are seen by marketing departments as a prime target group for leisure products.

Most Western countries have an ageing population and demand has gradually switched in relative terms away from products and services for the young and towards catering for more mature tastes. The tourist industry has seen a steady and unrelenting growth in business from middle-aged and older people, often in search of day trip and short break travel and hotel-based vacations. Airlines and other carriers frequently offer off-peak special concessions to the elderly in order to attract this increasingly affluent and 'adventurous' market segment.

There has been a large increase in the number of registered nursing and retirement homes catering for the older citizen. Similarly, numerous building companies, such as McCarthy & Stone, have flourished constructing specially designed retirement homes and sheltered accommodation. Many elderly people, often single widows or widowers, sell their home after the family has left and seek the more manageable and safe environment offered by sheltered accommodation. With the depression in house prices since 1989, such moves have been more difficult; however, the demand for this type of housing looks set to increase significantly in the next decade.

Changes in population structure will not only affect market demand but will also influence labour availability and other, less tangible, aspects of society. Compared to previous decades, there are now far fewer young people in the 16–25 age group who require employment. In many respects this is not, for the time being at least, a serious problem. In fact considering the larger than average unemployment rates among young people, even many of those with degree level qualifications, it may in fact be a blessing in disguise. Figure 5.12 shows the unemployment rate by age categories for Northampton, a rather typical small city in the United Kingdom. The main features indicated reflect the national pattern. Of course, if conditions of near full employment do re-emerge, labour shortages may result. However, it is more likely that problems of skill shortages will be more acute.

It is often argued that younger populations are more willing to embrace technological and social change while the tendency towards ageing may reduce workforce flexibility and dynamism. Additionally, it is traditionally believed that the young have greater geographical and occupational mobility, qualities which many argue contribute to workforce flexibility.

The decline in the number of young workers has led many organizations to adjust their recruitment and staffing policies. For example, the Tesco supermarket

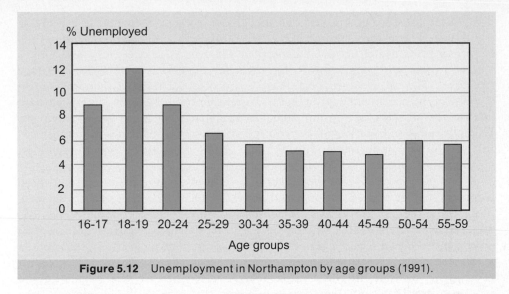

Figure 5.12 Unemployment in Northampton by age groups (1991).

chain and B&Q DIY stores have actively encouraged women with families and other more mature personnel to re-enter the workforce. It is moves such as this which have led to the large rise in the number of part-time jobs in the 1990s. Women returners are seen by many employers to offer a broader array of skills and experience than many school leavers. The Midland Bank is renowned for its policy of encouraging women to return to work after a career break. This, in part at least, is recognition of the fact that there are fewer suitable young people to fill such posts.

Although the recession of the late 1980s and early 1990s created a large body of unemployed labour for companies to draw upon, many stable or growing organizations have made every effort to retain their skilled and experienced workforce rather than rely on a shrinking number of young people from whom to select (and train) to fill available posts.

An ageing population: societal issues

An ageing population creates many issues for governments and society to address. Some have argued from an intuitive, as opposed to a 'scientific', basis that, as average age increases, society and its cultures will more readily take on board the concerns and attitudes of the old as opposed to the young. There is little evidence that this is the case, although it is worthy of debate. It is difficult to assess whether the United Kingdom has become, for example, more past-oriented, security-conscious, wise or reflective – characteristics one might associate with more mature people. The authors are of the rather cynical opinion that the United Kingdom has always been past-oriented, at least in our lifetimes, and not particularly reflective or overflowing with wisdom, especially when it comes to major economic and social policy decisions!

There are further implications for society and governments of an ageing population. Pierre-Jean Thumerelle (1993) argues that 'ageing populations will become a profound structural handicap in the twenty-first century and only a marked revival in reproduction is likely to alter the course of this particular age structure'. The nature of this 'handicap' is multifaceted. Firstly, there may be an increase in the dependency ratio, that is, larger numbers of people (mainly elderly) outside the working age group who are supported by those in employment. Secondly, pension benefits will be required in increasing quantities to support this enlarged group and, finally, health care and other social benefits will be increasingly demanded as population continues to age.

It is quite possible that the universal benefit of a state pension in the United Kingdom may be phased out or scaled down for all but the really needy. In New Zealand the right to universal state pension, whatever one's economic status, has been removed. Hence those who have significant alternative sources of income in retirement receive a reduced benefit even though they may have fully contributed to this during their working lives. Certainly, one contributory reason for the recent government decision in the United Kingdom to increase the female age of retirement from 60 to 65 years old, in line with that of men, is recognition of the enormous cost implications of realigning male and female retirement ages at, say, 60 or even 63 years of age.

All major political parties in the United Kingdom are considering the implications of the changing population structure for both the scale and nature of social benefits to come. The growing burden of pensions has been apparent for some time. Between 1960 and 1985, the period of greatest ageing, expenditure on old age pensions increased by 85 per cent in real terms in the four largest EU countries combined (Italy, Germany, France, United Kingdom). It now stands at about 12 per cent of the gross domestic product (GDP) of these countries. This upward trend is continuing, although not at quite the same pace.

The retirement/pension entitlement age may still be increased in the future; however, paradoxically, many companies across Europe are encouraging older employees to take early retirement. A great deal clearly depends on the state of the EU economy and the ability of individual nations to pay the increasing price of retirement pensions. Again, it is no coincidence that the basic state pension in the United Kingdom has merely been tied to the Retail Price Index (a measure of inflation) since 1979 despite the fact that average real earnings have risen by more than 50 per cent above the RPI since that time. Relative to average salaries in the United Kingdom, state pensions have declined significantly since 1979.

The problem of ageing is also acute for a number of key government services, notably the National Health Service (in the United Kingdom) and other hospital and health organizations across the world. In simple terms, the elderly, being more prone to illness, impose considerably greater costs on the NHS than any other age group. More complicated and expensive medical techniques have become available to prolong human life and improve the quality of that life. It is a rather thought-provoking fact that an average over-75 year old accounts for as much health and social service expenditure as 10 adults in the 20–60 age group. It is also worthy of note that it is this same age category, that is, the over-75 year olds, which has increased in numbers significantly in the United Kingdom and in other developed world countries in recent years.

It is estimated that there will be a further increase of over 20 per cent in the numbers of 'very old' (over 75 years) between 1990 and 2020 in the United Kingdom. Most EU countries had, by 1990, over 6 per cent of their population aged over 75. In Germany, the EU nation with the most rapid natural decline in population, it is estimated that the under-15s will represent just 12 per cent of the country's population in the first decade of the twenty-first century – just half that of the over-64s.

Of course it must be stressed at this juncture that most citizens in the United Kingdom have made weekly contributions to the NHS, through taxation and National Insurance. It is also a recognized and strongly supported belief that society has an unconditional obligation to provide quality medical care to all its citizens. It could be argued that the standard and sincerity with which that care is provided, irrespective of cost, acts as a barometer of the state of advance of society. With increasing advocacy in many EU countries of market forces and individual responsibility, the problem of an ageing population is one which warrants considerable debate within organizations and governments in order to address the inevitable issues and problems that lie ahead.

It is also worthy of note that rising life expectancy is a desirable state. However, if combined with continuing low levels of fertility, the elderly population of the EU by the middle of the next century will comprise as much as one-third of the total. By such time it is likely that these people will be more affluent, better educated, and housed and both able and willing to contribute to the rich fabric of society. It is far from proven that the old will be a 'burden' from either a fiscal or sociological perspective. We, both, hope to be among them!

QUESTIONS

1. Discuss some of the consequences of an ageing population for European countries under the following headings:
(a) product/service marketing
(b) employment
(c) savings and investment
(d) international competitiveness
(e) social welfare and pensions provision
(f) national culture.

2. What are the political and social consequences of migration into and around the European Union?

5.5 Social dynamics and their consequences for organizations

Introduction

In this section we will look more closely at some of the other social issues highlighted in Figure 5.1. Given or inherent within the simple model of the social environment are such elements as health, crime, the family and the changing face of organized labour. It is these four issues which we will now explore.

Changing health expectations: business consequences

Health concerns have been high on most people's agendas for a number of years. It is evident that health consciousness, for many, is not a passing fad, but rather is stimulating a change in lifestyle. It is having an impact in many communities and across major business sectors.

The tobacco story

The tobacco industry has been the subject of considerable debate for many years. It is widely accepted that there are life-threatening consequences for those who smoke. Increasing research evidence also shows links between secondary or passive smoking and smoking-related diseases.

The market for tobacco products in the four major European markets, that is France, Germany, Italy, and the United Kingdom, which in 1993 accounted for two-thirds of the European market, declined by around 4 per cent annually, in value, between 1993 and 1996. This overall decline is not reflected across the whole European cigarette market. Disquiet is being expressed, in some quarters, at the rise in smoking among young women in many countries and increases in cigarette consumption in Eastern Europe. The reaction of European Union legislators to tobacco advertising is also a major source of uncertainty to the industry. Some countries are in favour of a total ban on tobacco advertising.

The situation in the United States is particularly worrying for the industry. In 1977, Americans smoked 617 billion cigarettes; by 1993 it was down to 485 billion. In 1993 the US Environmental Protection Agency (EPA) blamed passive smoking for an estimated 3000 lung cancer deaths a year. In response, President Clinton proposed a quadrupling of cigarette taxes, from 23 cents to US$1 per pack, to help pay for his proposed health care programme. The American Food and Drug Administration (FDA) has asked Congress whether it should ban cigarettes or regulate them as a drug. In the summer of 1995 limits on the advertising, sale and distribution of cigarettes do not seem to be far off. President Clinton aims to cut teenage smoking by 50 per cent over 7 years. Legal action against the tobacco industry is becoming more aggressive, particularly in the United States. A group of airline stewardesses are currently seeking $5 billion in damages for being forced to inhale the smoke of passengers.

In response to this, and other threats, many tobacco companies have diversified from tobacco. British American Tobacco's (BAT) 'tobacco turnover' is only half of its business activity. It is currently expanding further into the financial services sector. Another response from the tobacco industry has been to target specific groups more clearly in their advertising campaigns. Targeting of different geographic areas has also been a tactic with companies gearing up for sales pushes in other continents, for example Africa, where increasing industrialization together with higher disposable incomes may create an extended market.

The mini-case study above illustrates how growing health consciousness may influence the fortunes of a major global industry.

A similar problem to that experienced by the tobacco business may be unfolding in the brewing and meat industries. Health concerns and changing social attitudes to drinking alcohol have meant that of the four main European Union alcohol-consuming countries (Germany, France, United Kingdom, Italy), only Germany showed a significant rise in beer consumption between 1989 and 1993 (refer to Table 5.3). This provides little solace for the major European brewers, particularly as the German market is dominated by home producers with very little penetration of foreign brands. Moves have been made by some UK brewers to diversify from their reliance on the sale of beer. Scottish and Newcastle, for example, now have interests in the wider leisure sector including hotels and holiday complexes.

The trend in meat consumption indicated a small decline between 1988 to 1993 in the four major markets combined, with the United Kingdom showing the largest decline of over 8 per cent. The future prospect for this industry is not much brighter, although forecasts for 1993 to 1997 are for consumption to remain unchanged. Health scares regarding the consumption of chicken and beef, the animal welfare debate and the popularity of a vegetarian diet, contributed to a fall in consumption of meat between 1988 and 1993. The uncertainty over the cattle-infecting disease bovine spongiform encephalopathy (BSE) may serve to further emphasize the risks associated with the consumption of meat in the minds of some consumers. Although these health scares are of primary concern to farmers, the

TABLE 5.3   Beer consumption (in million litres)

Year	1988	1989	1990	1991	1992	1993
France	2 186	2 284	2 334	2 284	2 294	2 273
Germany	10 681	10 751	10 821	11 390	11 493	12 302
Italy	1 324	1 252	1 324	1 298	1 272	1 278
UK	6 555	6 465	6 445	6 160	6 005	6 020
Sub total	20 746	20 752	20 924	21 132	21 006	21 873

effects of the changing pattern of consumption are likely to spill over into the meat-processing industry.

Health care professionals all over the world are becoming increasingly strident in their calls to protect the health of the population. The British government launched the Health of the Nation initiative in 1995, which focuses largely on targets for reducing illnesses which, in part, are caused by poor diet, smoking and other self-inflicted causes. Also, in 1995, UK dentists called for a 10 per cent tax on sweets in a move to protect children's teeth from decay. The voice

The fat story

A multi-million pound industry has been built around hydrogenated fats partly because they are perceived to be healthier and partly due to the economic appeal of their longer shelf life. Hydrogenated fats are made solid or semi-solid by mixing them with fragments of nickel or copper and bombarding them with hydrogen atoms. The process of hydrogenation creates man-made substances known as *trans*-fatty acids.

Increasingly hydrogenated fats have replaced animal and non-animal fats as a staple part of many diets in spreads and as a constituent of many processed foods. The main source of *trans*-fats is in spreads but also in meat pies, pastries, biscuits, bread, cakes and breakfast cereal. The fast food industry now uses heavily hydrogenated oils, containing 25 per cent to 35 per cent *trans*-fats, for deep frying.

New evidence now suggests that there is a correlation between the use and consumption of *trans*-fatty acids and the rise in coronary heart disease and that vegetable fats are best consumed in their natural unhydrogenated form. Hydrogenated fats are not the only cause of coronary heart disease, but they may be a strong contributor.

Trans-fats are said to raise the low-density lipoprotein (LDL) or bad cholesterol and at the same time lower the high-density lipoprotein (HDL) or good cholesterol thus presenting a 'double whammy'.

A major concern is the consumption of *trans*-fats by children and women, though consumption by men is also a problem. Work carried out in Europe indicates that women who consume high amounts of *trans*-fats in their diet seem to have lower birth weight children.

It is unlikely that consumers will know how many grams of *trans*-fats are in the products they purchase. Food processors, too, are more likely to increase the content of *trans*-fatty acids, rather than raise the levels of saturated fat, which have to be shown on food labels. Clearly, it is very difficult for consumers to make informed decisions on consumption of *trans*-fats when they are given so little information.

Adopted from: Willett, W.C. and Ascherio, A. (1994) 'Trans fatty acids: are the effects only marginal?', *American Journal of Public Health*, vol. 84, no. 5, pp. 722–44 and the Radio 4 Food Programme, April 1994.

of professionals is being heard, increasingly, in the media as they strive to bring health issues to the attention of the public. This media coverage will increase public awareness and give more power to pressure groups like ASH (Action against Smoking and Health). This is likely to further encourage governments to take action to limit the more undesirable health problems.

It is important that firms are aware of likely health-related issues concerning their products before they are communicated (or mis-communicated) to the public, so that responses can be coordinated and action taken to protect profits. The mini-case above illustrates a potential problem for margarine manufacturers.

The changing health agenda has had a number of positive results and provided opportunities for business. Individuals have been encouraged to change to a 'healthier' lifestyle. A bonus for firms should be a healthier workforce and reduced absenteeism. Food producers have responded to the health campaign and created profitable market niches. Low fat spreads, lean cuisine menus and natural foods have attracted a following because of their perceived health qualities. Sales of fruit and pasta increased substantially between 1988 and 1995. Many leisure activities, including aerobics and gardening, have also benefited from increased participation. Sales at UK garden centres managed to buck the downward retail trend in the recession of the early 1990s, rising by 30 per cent to over £1 billion. The plethora of new health clubs and gyms is evidence of a dynamic and burgeoning market in that sector.

As people have become more health conscious, the demand for sporting facilities has increased. It has been recognized that facilities are required by older age groups, in response to the changing demographic patterns. The general rise in life expectancy and a healthier older population has had a large impact throughout the business world.

The family: changing patterns

The role and structure of the traditional family has undergone substantial change over the last 20 years. There has been a significant increase in the number of private households in Europe (see Table 5.4). This trend is evident across Europe except in Ireland and Germany where emigration and the low birth rate, respectively, have caused a shift against the European trend. The increasing participation of women in the workforce and the rise in the number of one-parent and one-person households has also added to this changing picture. As a consequence, business has had to respond to the needs of this, now diverse, market.

This fundamental change in the structure of society has had enormous consequences for business. One of the results of the change can be seen in the retail sector where there has been an increase in demand for convenience products; for example, a number of companies have promoted easy-to-cook ranges and 'one-person' products. Shops have also had to respond to changes in shopping habits. The change, in 1994, to allow shops to open for up to six hours on Sunday was

TABLE 5.4   Number of private households

Year	1988	1989	1990	1991	1992	1993
France	21 305	21 482	21 542	21 614	21 736	21 883
Germany	33 821	34 477	35 170	34 570	34 510	34 186
Italy	18 081	18 113	18 174	19 766	20 306	21 472
UK	21 050	21 145	21 196	21 198	21 290	21 337
Holland	5 935	6 026	6 069	6 112	6 185	6 230
Ireland	875	874	873	869	869	867
Euro total	141 471	142 652	143 930	145 262	146 264	147 592

brought about by pressure from the stores, prompted by consumers pushing for more flexible opening times. Supermarkets are likely to go even further and provide 24-hour opening at some outlets. Even the United Kingdom's most profitable retailer, Marks & Spencer, which was opposed to breaking the law on Sunday opening, is likely to fall into line with rivals.

Marketing and selling to different types of households represents a task that is very different to satisfying the needs of the typical nuclear family of popular mythology. It is also clear that the change is not consistent throughout Europe, which brings problems for firms as they struggle to cope with the disparate needs of Europe's 350 million consumers.

The change in working patterns and family structure has other consequences for organizations. Child care facilities are of great importance to working and single parents. A large number of child care centres have been established which has created a need for government to regulate this activity. A commitment to universal nursery school places for 3 and 4 year olds may become a campaign platform for many political parties as they seek to win votes from the growing numbers for whom child care and pre-school education are important concerns. Because of the cost of child care facilities, more pressure may be put on businesses to provide facilities attached to the workplace. This will inevitably increase costs for organizations. Additionally, there is pressure on government to make child care costs tax deductable.

New job opportunities and patterns of employment are also bringing a change to traditional family roles with greater employment of women in part-time, semi-skilled and professional jobs. From 1971 to 1994 the number of jobs for part-time employees increased by 2.6 million; the proportion of employees in part-time jobs now stands at 9.7 million, 38 per cent of the workforce. The United Kingdom has a far higher proportion of part-time jobs than its main European Union competitors. About 86 per cent of part-time employees are women and more than half of these are over 40 years of age. Almost 75 per cent of part-timers prefer this mode of employment (Naylor, 1994). There has been a further decline of traditional full-time male occupations. The regions that traditionally relied on the old staple industries like heavy engineering, ship building and the iron and steel industry, such as the north-east of England, have seen a continued demise of jobs in these traditional sectors. A further decline in male-dominated engineering jobs has been forecast by trade unions.

The projected rise in the labour force between 1994 and 2006 will be accounted for solely by women (Ellison, 1994). There is even some evidence, from the Equal Opportunities Commission, to suggest that men are being discriminated against when applying for certain jobs. Employers are keen to employ women on a part-time basis, originally partly because part-time workers have fewer employment rights, but also because they are cheaper to employ and traditionally are non-unionized. As a result, employment patterns within households have changed.

Heidensohn (1991) suggests that the quite dramatic change that continues to affect family life and gender roles may have an impact on crime. She points out that a growing number of children are being raised in one-parent households, often poorly housed in the worst areas. It seems that these children may be more likely to be 'pushed' into criminal activity.

Rising crime: myth or reality?

Crime is a constant feature of every modern society and is a product of that society. As such changing social conditions will affect the incidence of crime. United Kingdom government statistics show that crime increased throughout the 1980s and into the 1990s. Although the rate of increase has declined, and most recently reported crime figures have actually fallen, it is likely that the numbers of crimes committed will continue to increase. Of equal importance to government and the business community is people's perception and fear of crime, even though they are unlikely to be direct victims of serious crime.

The authorities in Florida have become particularly aware of the twin problems of crime and people's fear of crime following a number of high profile incidents involving tourists in 1992 and 1993. The number of visitors to Florida subsequently showed a decline, even though the chance of being involved in such an incident was extremely slim. It is very important for the economy of the state to make sure that tourism is not affected adversely in the long run by the bad publicity following these episodes; and it is of equal concern to holiday companies who generate substantial sales from this important holiday destination.

Unemployment is thought by many academics to be linked to crime (Svindoff and McElroy, 1984; Farrington et al., 1986), so the rising unemployment experienced in the European Union may be a contributory factor to higher levels of crime evident in some countries. Unemployment is likely to stay at historically high levels throughout the Western world.

Drug abuse has also been linked with crime, unemployment and social deprivation. The easy availability of crack cocaine and so-called designer drugs, which are highly addictive and extremely profitable, is highlighted as a major contributory factor to the upsurge in crime in the United States and a number of European countries, including the United Kingdom.

The continuation of old forms of crime, such as the hidden economy, which has been described as 'the illicit buying and selling of cheap, usually stolen goods among ordinary people in honest jobs' is likely to continue and to expand, particularly with the introduction of new and improved consumer durables. The scope of the hidden economy has also increased from its traditional roots. An issue of great concern is the counterfeiting of substandard manufactured goods, such as brake pads, whose failure can have serious consequences for the consumer. Added to this is the effect that these failures can have on the reputation of the company whose name the product bears.

The hidden economy can be stimulated by the actions of the legislative authorities. In Canada the hidden economy accounts for over 50 per cent of spirits consumed (Gibbens, 1995). This is in response to the high level of taxes levied by the Canadian government. The differences between tax and VAT rates among European Union members has led to the growth of large amounts of 'smuggling' across national borders. The situation is problematic for UK drink retailers, especially off-licences in the southern part of the country. From here access to the Continent is relatively easy and the large amount of cigarettes and alcohol coming through the Channel ports has affected profits. This has led to demands for the UK government to reduce excise duties on alcohol and tabacco in line with other EU countries.

The farming community is not immune to this form of crime. The European Union milk quota system may be contributing, unintentionally, to the establishment of an under-cover milk market. Farmers who produce milk over their quota have to pay a levy of 29p per litre, so encouraging them to sell the extra production illegally. It is estimated that 50 000 animals are smuggled from Northern Ireland into the Republic of Ireland each year in order to defraud the EU and take advantage of lucrative Common Agricultural Policy (CAP) subsidies.

The 9th United Nations Congress on the Prevention of Crime and the Treatment of Offenders (Cairo, May 1995), identified computer crime as a major concern. Wasik (1991) suggests that total losses as a direct consequence of computer misuse vary greatly. He points to a 1986 Home Office study which suggests that commercial fraud amounts to about £1 billion a year, although only part of this was computer-related. In this study, 45 per cent of respondents identified computer fraud as a growing concern. Many organizations view the official figures on computer fraud with scepticism, believing they are an underestimate. A 1995 study of 1200 American companies by the management consultants Ernst & Young confirms the growing problems of computer crime. Over half the companies in their survey had suffered financial losses related to computer security. The theft of computers and computer parts, rather than the theft of information, seems to be a problem for small business in particular. It is estimated that computer theft in the United Kingdom more than doubled from 1992 to 1994 and is now worth over £175 million a year.

No one is exempt from the risks associated with computer crime. Bloombecker (1986) and the National Center for Computer Crime Data in the United States describe victims as commercial users, banks, telecommunications authorities, government, individuals, computer companies, retail firms and universities. As with any activity there can be positive effects as market niches can be created that offer business opportunities. The number of corporate investigation agencies, like Kroll Associates in the United States, has mushroomed in the past 20 years largely in response to the growing menace of computer-related crime.

Virtual reality shops, and the creation of Broadband Malls (a term coined by Goldman Sachs), a virtual shopping centre, may be the ultimate response from retailers as they attempt to provide for ever-changing customer needs. Single parents, working parents and the elderly will all be able to shop at their convenience at the virtual store. Congestion and parking problems could be a thing of the past. Stores will benefit from reduced crime. The long-term implications of this type of development could be profound (Cane, 1995). Nevertheless, even the Internet is open to substantial criminal activity.

The changing face of organized labour

For many European countries the three decades after the Second World War seemed to herald a move towards industrial democracy. In Sweden, for example, trade unionists have, since the 1970s, taken seats as members on company boards and were able to bargain with management over strategic decisions.

Nevertheless, in the United Kingdom in particular, the position of trade unions in the 1990s has radically changed since the late 1970s. The harsh economic climate of the 1980s and 1990s checked the rise in union membership and density (the percentage of employees who belong to a union). Not all countries fared badly: in Scandinavia, Germany and Belgium union membership was maintained (Clarke and Bamber, 1994). Italy and France saw sharp falls in membership. In the United Kingdom it is evident, since 1979, that trade union power and membership has been significantly reduced. Table 5.5 illustrates that membership fell from 13.3 million in 1979 to 9.0 million in 1992.

In the United Kingdom trade union density, too, has shown significant change. The proportion of employees who were union members fell from 39 per cent in 1989 to 33 per cent in 1994 (see Table 5.6).

Kavanagh (1987) argues that

> the government's legislation on industrial relations and trade unions has taken hold. Here is an area where the balance of advantage has changed since 1979 (the election of a Conservative government), from union to employers and managers and from the consultative role granted to the unions to one in which they are virtually ignored by the government.

The main legislation which brought this about was the 1980, 1982, 1988 and 1990 Employment Acts, and the 1984 Trade Union Act.

Marsh (1991) outlines the six major elements of this legislation.

1.   The blanket immunity enjoyed by unions, as distinct from unionists, was removed by the Employment Act 1982.

TABLE 5.5 Union membership and number of unions in the United Kingdom, 1974–92

Year	Total membership (millions)	Number of unions	% change in membership	Cumulative change in membership (millions)
1974	11.8	507	+2.7	
1975	12.2	501	+3.6	+0.4
1976	12.4	473	+3.0	+0.2
1977	12.8	481	+3.7	+0.4
1978	13.1	462	+2.1	+0.3
1979	13.3	453	+1.3	+0.2
1980	12.9	438	−2.6	−0.4
1981	12.1	414	−6.5	−0.8
1982	11.6	408	−4.2	−0.5
1983	11.2	394	−3.1	−0.4
1984	11.0	375	−2.2	−0.2
1985	10.8	370	−1.6	−0.2
1986	10.5	335	−2.6	−0.3
1987	10.5	330	−0.6	N/C
1988	10.4	315	−0.9	−0.1
1989	10.2	309	−2.1	−0.2
1990	9.9	287	−2.1	−0.3
1991	9.5	275	−3.6	−0.4
1992	9.0	268	−5.6	−0.5

Source: Adapted from Department of Employment and Labour Force Survey, 1994.

2.   The definition of a legitimate trade dispute has been successively narrowed so as to reduce the immunities enjoyed by unionists and unions.
3.   The legal basis of the closed shop was initially restricted by the 1980 and 1982 Employment Acts and subsequently removed in the Employment Acts of 1988 and 1990.
4.   Under the Trade Union Act 1984 unions are required to hold secret ballots

TABLE 5.6 Trade union density (percentage)

Year	1989	1990	1991	1992	1993	1994
All employees	39	38	37	36	35	33
Men	44	43	42	39	38	36
Women	33	32	32	32	31	30
Full time	44	43	42	40	39	38
Part time	22	22	22	22	22	21
Manufacturing	41	40	38	35	34	34
Service	37	37	37	35	35	33

Source: Adapted from Labour Force Survey, 1994.

for the election of officers. Unions are also required, under this act, to conduct political fund ballots.

5.   The Employment Act of 1988 gives individual unionists a series of rights *vis-à-vis* their unions.
6.   The 1990 Act makes unions responsible for their members' unofficial action, unless the unions repudiate the strike, or make it official, after a ballot.

None of this legislation has any positive benefits for trade unions. It has been suggested by Freeman and Pelletier (1990) that the vast bulk of the observed 1980s decline in union density in the United Kingdom is due to the changed legal environment for industrial relations. Metcalfe (1990) argues that the decline in union membership is the result of an interaction of five factors: the macroeconomic environment; the composition of jobs and the workforce, including the relative decline in manufacturing industry; the policy of the state; the attitudes and conduct of employers; and the stance taken by employers. Social attitudes towards trade unions have also altered in the United Kingdom.

There is no agreement between academics on the causes of the lessening of trade union power; however, it is clear that the Thatcher government of the 1980s was intent on curbing union power to remove this perceived constraint upon the operation of the market. The industrial relations environment in which organizations operate was transformed within just 11 years. Other changes are now forthcoming as we approach the millennium. Pressure from the European Union, together with the implications of the Social Charter, should a new government support these measures, will undoubtedly contribute to further change.

There have been concerns within the EU about the United Kingdom gaining 'unfair' competitive advantage through 'social dumping' – a consequence of Britain's decision to opt out of the Social Charter of the Maastricht Treaty and so undercut workers' rights and thus create a lower cost environment for companies. This was highlighted by Hoover's decision in 1995 to shift some of its production from France to Scotland. Hoover was determined to take advantage of the lower costs that production in Scotland will involve, prompting protest from France.

In a number of European countries social plans are being introduced which govern the relations between employers and employees. In France, Spain, Portugal, Greece, Italy, the Netherlands and Germany regulations are in place that give government or workers an effective veto over redundancies. Works councils operate in some countries. In Germany and Belgium, for example, the councils have the right to be consulted over closures and redundancies. There is only one European-Union-wide redundancy rule in operation. This requires worker representatives to be given 90 days' notice and proper consultation over large-scale redundancies. However, an EU directive on workers' councils is pending, which may force the United Kingdom to introduce them despite opposition from the Confederation of British Industry (CBI) and the government.

The differences in industrial relations between countries make it difficult for multinational corporations to operate. Evidence suggests, however, that international investment may seek out those European countries where union legislation is most severe and imposed social costs on employers are minimal. There are other approaches to employee–employer relations and many companies have made great progress towards developing a more sensitive and creative relationship. The mini-case below illustrates one such case.

Scania Production Angers S.A., France

Built on the river Loire in northern France, Angers is the location for Scania's large new truck assembly plant. Scania, a Swedish company, manufactures heavy goods vehicles. Trucks from this plant are distributed across France, Spain and Italy.

Within the plant there are just four levels or grades of personnel from the chief executive to the individual operatives. The senior management team is mainly from Sweden, apart that is from Bernard Proux the French human resource manager. The vast majority of the working people within the factory are grouped into clusters. Currently (1996) there are 12 clusters each with between 20 and 25 staff. These clusters concentrate on building a significant part of the trucks, for example the cab. Each cluster has one manager. In addition to a part of the production line, clusters are also responsible for budgetary control, quality, routine maintenance of machinery and even the tidiness of the shop floor. Considerable responsibility and accountability is thus devolved to the cluster managers and ultimately to the team.

The cluster managers negotiate, individually, the salaries of all personnel within their team. The manager holds an annual performance review with each worker in his cluster. Discussion covers such topics as training needs, performance since last review and salary negotiations. The human resource management (HRM) department issues broad guidelines for such negotiations.

Members of each cluster work cooperatively with their colleagues. Morale appears to be high. Workers are given ample training opportunities and the resultant multi-skilling is rewarded through salary enhancements. Absenteeism in the plant is considerably below the national average at just 2 per cent and labour turnover is virtually non-existent.

The ideas encompassed within this system are in part unique. They reflect innovative Swedish thinking. The Swedish are renowned for their desire to build consensus in the workplace and for their liberal, non-hierarchical approach to social organization generally.

This cultural force clearly influences organizational activity in Angers, where traditionally (rather like the United Kingdom) a more adversarial relationship between workers and management existed and where mutual antagonism was rife. As a result, collectivization of labour was a natural mechanism to combat the power of the employer.

QUESTIONS

1. What are the consequences for the tobacco industry of the changing public perception of their products?

2. What is the response from the tobacco industry to these changes?

3. How may the use of *trans*-fats in the fast food industry affect consumers?

4. What could the industry and consumers do in response to the *trans*-fats problem?

5. Utilizing resources in your library and elsewhere, establish what may be the consequences for business and other organizations of the United Kingdom accepting the Social Chapter of the Maastricht Treaty.

CONCLUSION

This chapter has explored some key aspects of the social environment. Although we could not hope to cover in detail the vast and complex issues which exist within the social community, and which influence organizational activity, we have attempted to explore a number of crucial areas. Some of the issues raised are further explored in the final chapter of this book.

SUMMARY OF MAIN POINTS

This chapter has focused on the social environment. More specifically it has looked at three broad aspects of that environment, that is, national culture, demographic restructuring and various social changes. The main points made are:

- Organizations interact with society and operate within a cultural context.
- National culture varies considerably between countries on a number of key dimensions, each of which fundamentally influences an organization's interaction with its environment.
- Population structure, life expectancy, birth rates and migration patterns vary both from place to place and through time, creating a dynamic demographic environment in which organizations operate.
- Population structures, and ageing in particular, have crucial implications for patterns of consumption, production, employment, savings and investment and for government and society as a whole.
- Changing health expectations have important implications for food and other manufactures.

- The traditional family structure, in the United Kingdom in particular, is rapidly changing with social implications and consequences for patterns of consumption and employment.
- Crime of many types, such as theft, white collar fraud, computer fraud and black market trading, appears to be increasing in most Western countries.
- The power of trade unions, particularly in the United Kingdom, has been significantly reduced since the early 1980s.

References

Adler, N.J. (1991) *International Dimensions of Organizational Behaviour* (2nd edn), PWS, Kent.

Allison, G.T. (1971) *Essence of Decision: Explaining the Cuban Missile Crisis*, Little Brown, Boston, p. 168.

Argenti, J. (1974) *Systematic Corporate Planning*, Nelson, London.

Bloombecker, J.J. (1986) 'Computer crime, computer security, computer ethics', *Statistical Report of the National Center for Computer Crime Data, Los Angeles*, NCCD.

Cane, A. (1995) *Financial Times*, 20 February.

Clarke, O. and Bamber, G.J. (1994) 'Changing management and industrial relations in Europe: converging towards an enterprise focus?', *International Journal of Human Resource Management*, vol. 5, no. 3, September.

Deal, T.E. and Kennedy, A.A. (1982) *Corporate Culture*, Addison-Wesley.

Ellison, R. (1994) 'British labour force projections: 1994 to 2006', *Employment Gazette*, April.

Farrington, D., Gallagher, B., Morley, L., St. Ledger, R.J. and West, D.J. (1986) 'Unemployment, school leaving and crime', *British Journal of Criminology*, vol. 26, no. 4.

Freeman, R. and Pelletier, J. (1990) 'The impact of industrial relations legislation on British union density', *British Journal of Industrial Relations*, vol. 28.

Gibbens, R. (1995) *Financial Times*, 15 June.

Heidensohn, M. (1991) *Crime and Society: Sociology for a Changing World*, Macmillan, Basingstoke.

Hofstede, G. (1983) 'The cultural relativity of organizational practices and theories', *Journal of International Business Studies*, Fall.

Kavanagh, D. (1987) *Thatcherism and British Politics*, OUP, Oxford.

Lebon, A. (1990) 'Ressortissants communautaires et etrangers des pays tiers dans l'Europe des Douze', *Revue Européenne des Migrations Internationales*, vol. 6.

Levitt, T. (1983) 'The globalisation of markets', *Harvard Business Review*, May–June.

Marsh, D. (1991) *Trade Unions in Britain: Union Power and the Thatcher Legacy*, Macmillan, Basingstoke.

Metcalfe, D. (1990) 'Union presence and labour productivity in British manufacturing industry. A reply to Nolan and Marginson', *British Journal of Industrial Relations*, vol. 28.

Mintzberg, H. (1983) *Power in and around Organizations*, Prentice Hall, London.

Naylor, K. (1994) 'Part-time working in Great Britain – an historical analysis', *Employment Gazette*, December.

Peters, T.J. and Waterman, R.H. (1982) *In Search of Excellence*, Harper and Row.

Ronen, S. and Shenkar, O. (1985) 'Clustering countries on attitudinal dimensions: a review and synthesis', *Academy of Management Review*, July, pp. 445–54.

Sathe, V. (1983) 'Implications of corporate culture: a manager's guide to action, *Organizational Dynamics*, Autumn.

Svindoff, M. and McElroy, J. (1984) *Employment and Crime New York*, Vera Institute of Justice.

Thumerelle, P.-J. (1993) 'Age and sex structures', in D. Noin and Woods, R. (eds) *The Changing Population of Europe*, Blackwell, pp. 76–81.

Wasik, M. (1991) *Crime and the Computer*, Clarendon Press, Oxford.

Wedderburn, Lord (1986) *The Worker and the Law*, Pelican, London.

White, P. (1993) 'Ethnic minority communities in Europe', in D. Noin and Woods, R. (eds) *The Changing Population of Europe*, Blackwell, pp. 206–25.

CHAPTER 6
THE ECOLOGICAL ENVIRONMENT
Alistair Sutton and Jamie Weatherston

 LEARNING OUTCOMES

On completion of this chapter you should be able to:

- understand some serious ecological concerns affecting the earth;
- appreciate the basic economic arguments which underlie the operation of the marketplace (including the law of demand and supply and the concept of externalities) and which underpin any analysis of how business organizations are able to pollute the environment;
- outline the range of actions which can be taken by governments to monitor and regulate the output of pollutants from economic activity;
- appreciate the range of organizational responses to ecological issues in general and to environmental legislation in particular;
- recognize the impact of economic activity, and of different regulatory regimes, on consumers and appreciate the extent of consumer power in respect of ecological issues;
- set the above outcomes in the context of actions taken at global, national and local scales.

6.1 Introduction

We are all aware of a range of environmental problems facing the planet. In this chapter we look at some of the most serious ecological concerns and the extent of their impact, investigate the economic arguments which help us analyse how organizations are able to pollute the environment and explore the range of actions which can be taken by governments to monitor and regulate the output of pollutants from economic activity. Over recent years the basis of much regulation of business activity which has adverse environmental effects has been via market-based mechanisms. Therefore, the introductory part of this chapter examines the economic arguments which underpin the operation of market-based economies. The areas covered include the laws of demand and supply and the price mechanism. This section also has a wider purpose: it links to the coverage competition in Chapter 2, as demand theory underpins much of the work related to market structure. (Readers will note that this section features general, rather than environment-related, examples to explain the ideas.)

The chapter moves on to consider externalities and different approaches to regulation. These sections build upon the foregoing section on the operation of the marketplace. We end the chapter by examining the different approaches adopted by organizations towards environmental issues, discussing the impact of these upon consumers and noting the extent of consumer power in respect of ecological issues. This analysis is set in the context of actions taken at a global, national and local scale.

Environmental pollution has an impact on a number of areas which affect us all. In order to assess the nature of this impact we need to distinguish between renewable and non-renewable resources. Renewable resources can be replaced, but non-renewable resources when used are lost for ever. There has been considerable concern about the effects of acid rain, loss of biodiversity, sea pollution and depletion of natural resources, like tropical rainforests and the destruction of the ozone layer. Over the last 15 years a number of scientists have expressed serious concern for the future of the planet as a result of global warming. This warming is thought to result from the greenhouse effect, itself a product of excessive carbon dioxide (CO_2) emissions. It is interesting to pursue some of the interrelationships which contribute to this complex problem.

The greenhouse effect has contributed to the increase in the earth's temperature by 0.5° Celsius during the twentieth century. This increase in temperature has caused a rise in sea level of at least 10 cm (Radford, 1990). It has been predicted that, at current rates of increase, sea levels could rise by another 50 cm by the year 2100. This would have a serious impact on coastlines, particularly those in East Anglia, Holland, Egypt, India and Bangladesh, as well as imperilling many small, low-lying islands such as the Maldives in the Indian Ocean and the Marshall Islands in the Pacific Ocean (Brown, 1995). Effects would clearly be felt in communities near the coast and have severe consequences for agricultural areas such as the Ganges Delta in India, an area already prone to flooding.

Without naturally occurring greenhouse gases like carbon dioxide, methane, nitrous oxide and water vapour, human life would not exist. However, industrial development has necessitated the burning of significant amounts of coal, oil and methane and the felling of more and more forests. This has contributed to the increase in global temperatures. Carbon dioxide has been blamed for 56 per cent of the greenhouse effect (Radford, 1990). We have also created chlorofluorocarbon (CFC) gases which are being steadily banned due to their adverse effects on the earth's protective ozone layer. The CFC gases are also thought to contribute to 23 per cent of the greenhouse effect (Radford, 1990).

Whatever one's view of the seriousness of the problems of global warming and destruction of the ozone layer, it is clear that environmental problems result from economic activity. The growth of business activity is often at the expense of the environment.

The balance of power between business organizations, particularly large multinationals, on the one hand, and individuals and environmental groups on the other, is grossly unequal. Government, therefore, needs to take action to control the potentially polluting activities of organizations. Regulation proceeds, essentially, from a knowledge of how markets operate. It is therefore appropriate to examine the theory of demand and supply and of externalities in order to appreciate the debate on environmental regulation and the role of government intervention.

For the global economy to become ecologically sustainable, it may be necessary to organize business and industry along ecologically sound principles. This will require the transformation of corporations, their products, production systems and management practices (Shrivastava, 1995). Radical change is necessary if lasting solutions are to be found. Government, business and individuals all have a part to play to achieve sustainable societies (Hamel and Prahalad, 1994). In this chapter we will explore the role and activities of each of these actors and their effect, both positive and negative, on the environment.

6.2 The impact of the marketplace on the environment: an economic perspective

Introduction

The two extremes of economic management, the command economy and the free market (discussed in Chapter 2), are not evident in their entirety within any country. The recent past has seen the demise of command economies all over the world, for example in Poland, the Czech Republic, Bulgaria and the former Soviet Union. Market forces have been allowed to become more active in these economies to alleviate the worst excesses of state control.

Hong Kong resembles, but falls somewhat short of, a pure market economy. Within all Western-style market economies government has to influence the allocation of goods and services. It does this for a number of reasons:

- to moderate the trade cycle by demand management and supply-side policies to promote such things as employment, investment and direct structural change (see Chapters 3 and 7);
- to restrain unfair use of economic power by, for example, monopolies (see Chapter 2);

- to correct inequalities through the redistribution of wealth via taxation or regional policy to support industry (see Chapters 3 and 7);
- to manage price levels, employment, balance of payments and growth rate in accordance with social objectives (see Chapter 3);
- to provide public goods, such as defence, law and order, roads and parks; such things are socially desirable, but unprofitable, and it is generally not possible to directly charge for them;
- of specific relevance to the subject of this chapter, to remove socially undesirable consequences of commercial activity. The private profit motive does not always ensure that public wealth will be maximized; it can create environmental problems, such as pollution and resource depletion.

Society has to find a way of resolving the primary economic issues of what to produce, and how and for whom to produce it. In many economies we have seen that these questions are now, more commonly, being answered by market forces (see Chapter 2). In this chapter we will explore the problems that industrial activity causes to the environment. However, in order to understand how market forces can result in environmental problems and to appreciate the viability of potential solutions it is necessary to understand the foundations of the market system, that is the concepts of demand and supply.

The theory of demand

By 'demand' we mean demand backed by money, or effective demand. We are concerned with the quantity of a commodity which will be demanded at a given price over a certain period of time. For most goods (normal goods) the quantity demanded will rise as price falls, even if this increase in consumption leads to an increase in pollution or environmental damage. A lower price will mean that more will be purchased; at a higher price less will be purchased. This is the law of downward sloping demand. For any commodity it is possible to use market data to construct a demand schedule, showing how many units of the commodity would be demanded at various prices (refer to Table 6.1 which shows a fictitious schedule for CDs).

Using the coordinates from the demand schedule we can construct the demand curve as shown in Figure 6.1.

TABLE 6.1   Demand schedule for compact discs

Price/unit (£)	Quantity demanded per week (000s)
13	80
12	130
11	200
10	260
9	300

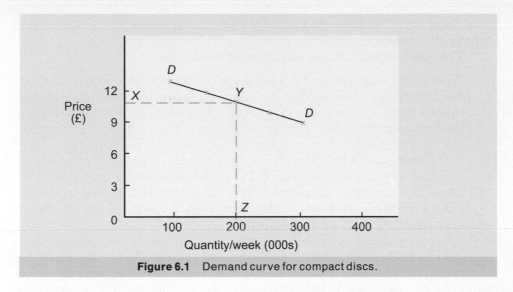

Figure 6.1   Demand curve for compact discs.

The demand curve tells us the quantities which would be demanded at each price. From the area of the rectangle $OXYZ$ we can calculate the total revenue at the given price, as the area of the rectangle is equal to price multiplied by quantity ($P \times Q$). As price (P_x) changes there will be extensions or contractions of demand (changes in the quantity demanded) as shown in Figure 6.2.

As price decreases from £12 to £11, demand extends along the demand curve to 200 000 units. The opposite effect is evident, as can be seen from Figure 6.2; as price rises there is a contraction of demand. In this example we see the effect of a

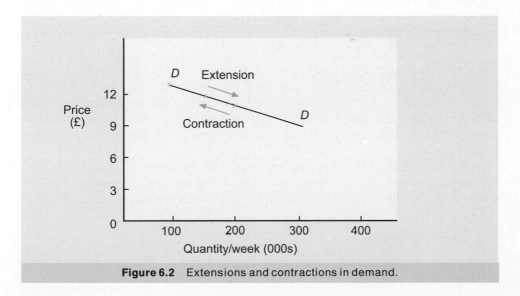

Figure 6.2   Extensions and contractions in demand.

price change only. However, it is not only price that determines or influences the demand for a product.

The other determinants or conditions of demand are:

1. *Price of other related goods* (P_r). Changes in the price of other goods will affect the demand for CDs, whether the goods are substitutes, like pre-recorded cassette tapes, or complements, such as CD players. Substitute goods are competitively demanded. If the price of cassette tapes rises then demand for that product will fall. Some consumers will switch to the substitute product; in this case demand for CDs will rise. Complementary goods, in comparison, are jointly demanded: if the price of CD players falls, for example, then more people will buy them and demand for CDs will also rise. Demand for CDs trebled between 1988 and 1993, largely as a result of the increased affordability of compact disc players.

2. *Income* (Y). A rise in income will result in more goods demanded at each price. A fall in income will obviously have the reverse effect. However, in the case of inferior goods a rise in income will result in a fall in demand.

3. *Taste* (T). A change in taste or fashion (perhaps influenced by advertising) will alter the demand for that product. Popular new artists in the music industry have often achieved staggering success for a relatively short period of time. Artists such as the Osmonds, Wham, and Bros have also all suffered from the fickle desires of the young consumer.

4. *Other factors* (Z). These include: changes in the weather or seasons, the availability of credit and changes in population size or structure.

Demand for a good can be influenced by all of these factors. We can express this by the demand function:

$$D_x = f(P_x, P_r, Y, T, Z)$$

If any one of these determinants of demand changes then the demand curve will shift to the right or the left. For example, in a spell of hot weather (a change of Z in the equation) demand for ice-cream will increase and the demand curve moves to the right. As cold weather returns, less ice-cream will be demanded so the demand curve will move to the left (refer to Figure 6.3). Note that we need to qualify this by stating that we expect this to happen *ceteris paribus* – other things being equal.

To summarize, it is important to distinguish between movement ALONG the demand curve, due to change in price of a good, and movements OF the demand curve, due to change in one of the other determinants of demand.

The theory of supply

The market for goods and services is determined not only by demand. The demand which consumers express through their willingness to buy, needs to be

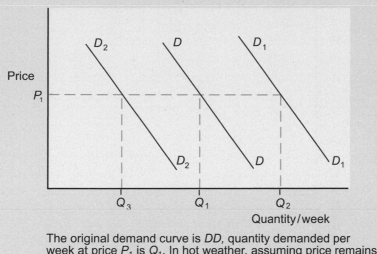

The original demand curve is *DD,* quantity demanded per week at price P_1 is Q_1. In hot weather, assuming price remains fixed, *DD* shifts to the right D_1D_1, quantity demanded rises to Q_2. When temperatures drop demand shifts the other way to D_2D_2 and quantity demanded falls to Q_3.

Figure 6.3 Changes in the demand for ice-cream.

met by the willingness of producers to supply a good. Supply is the propensity of producers to sell the commodity at a given price.

More goods will be supplied at a higher, rather than at a lower, price. This law of the upward-sloping supply curve can be explained by the aim of producers to maximize their income (profit maximization). From the fictitious supply schedule for CDs, as shown in Table 6.2, we can construct a supply curve (Figure 6.4). This illustrates the quantities which would be supplied at each price.

As price changes there will be extensions or contractions along the supply curve (changes in the quantity supplied). For example, if the price of CDs moves from £11 to £10 the quantity supplied falls from 200 000 units to 145 000 units per week, as shown in Figure 6.5.

The supply curve may be shifted by changes in the conditions or

TABLE 6.2   Supply schedule for compact discs

Price/unit (£)	Quantity supplied per week (000s)
13	350
12	280
11	200
10	145
9	45

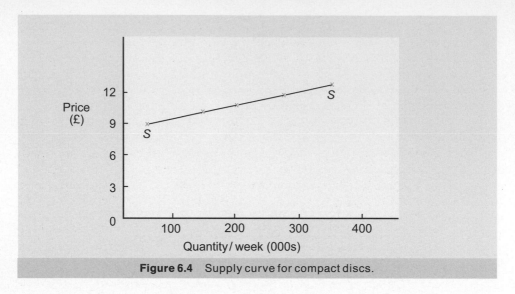

Figure 6.4   Supply curve for compact discs.

determinants of supply resulting in increases or decreases in the quantity of goods
made available. Other determinants are:

1.   *The objectives of the firm* (B). A firm aiming to achieve maximum profits will
      have a different level of output from one which is aiming to maximize sales.
2.   *The price of certain other goods* (P_g). Where goods are jointly supplied, they
      are said to be complements in production, like beef and leather; a decrease in
      the price of one good will lead to a decrease in the quantity of the other good
      which will be supplied. If the price of beef falls then farmers are less likely to

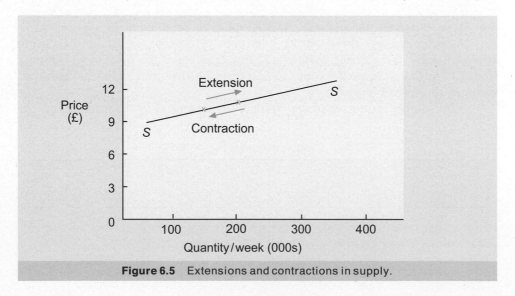

Figure 6.5   Extensions and contractions in supply.

supply it to the market. This occurred during the BSE scare in 1996, discussed in Chapter 7. The result may be a reduction in the supply of leather. Goods that are substitutes, such as housing land and agricultural land, are said to be competitively supplied: an increase in the price of land used for housing will lead to a decrease in the quantity of agricultural land as farmers seek to obtain planning permission.

3.   *Price of the factors of production* (P_f). Changes in costs of labour, in the form of higher wages, have meant that Siemens of Germany has reduced its manufacturing capabilities in Germany and relocated production elsewhere, notably Tyneside in the United Kingdom. This will increase the supply of products from the United Kingdom and reduce the supply coming from Germany. Other costs, such as raw materials and the cost of capital, are also important to companies and influence their output decisions.

4.   *The state of technology* (T). Part of the success of United Kingdom industry in the 1980s and 1990s has been achieved through introducing new technology which reduced costs and made firms more competitive.

5.   *Other factors* (Z). Although this heading acts as a 'catch all' it is important in its own right. Changes in government practices with regard to taxation, subsidies or regional policies have a substantial impact which will be discussed below.

Supply of a good can be influenced by all of these factors. We can express this by the supply function:

$$S_x = f(P_x, B, P_g, P_f, T, Z)$$

The rules that apply to the demand curve also apply here. If there is a change in one of the conditions influencing supply, assuming price is held constant (*ceteris paribus*), then this will change the supply of a product. For example, a business organization may seek to improve its competitive position by increasing its market share. This is a change in the objective of the organization (B). As a result the supply curve will move to the right because the firm has increased its output. The reverse situation will also be true (refer to Figure 6.6).

To summarize, it is important to distinguish between movement ALONG a supply curve, due to change in price of a good, and movements OF the supply curve, due to change in one of the other determinants of supply.

Price determination

Market price is determined by the price at which consumers are willing to buy and producers willing to sell. This is called the equilibrium price. The corresponding quantity is called the equilibrium quantity. The point of intersection is called the equilibrium point in the market (refer to Figure 6.7).

Economists use the term equilibrium to describe a state in which internal forces, or variables, are in balance and there is no tendency to change.

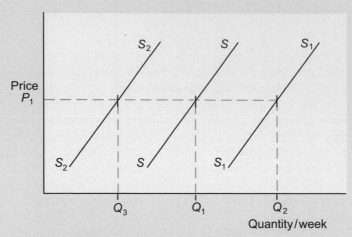

The original supply curve is *SS*, quantity supplied at price P_1 is Q_1. As output rises, assuming price remains fixed, *SS* shifts to the right S_1S_1, quantity supplied rises to Q_2. If the firms cuts back supply shifts the other way to S_2S_2 and quantity supplied falls to Q_3.

Figure 6.6   Firm increases its output.

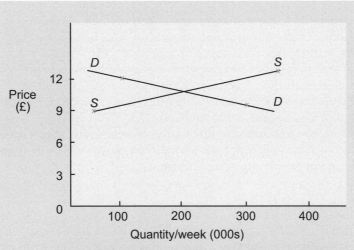

The equilibrium price is £11 and equilibrium quantity is 200 000 per week: at any other price there would be excess demand or supply.

Figure 6.7   Market price of compact discs.

(a) Changes in EITHER demand or supply have predictable effects on BOTH price and quantity.

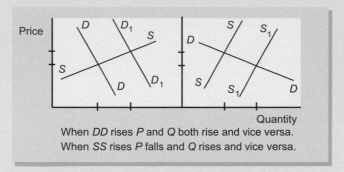

When *DD* rises *P* and *Q* both rise and vice versa.
When *SS* rises *P* falls and *Q* rises and vice versa.

(b) Changes in BOTH demand and supply have predictable effects on EITHER price or quantity

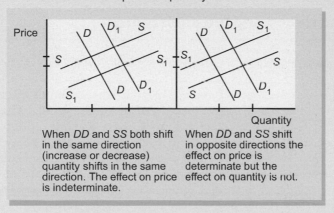

When *DD* and *SS* both shift in the same direction (increase or decrease) quantity shifts in the same direction. The effect on price is indeterminate.

When *DD* and *SS* shift in opposite directions the effect on price is determinate but the effect on quantity is not.

Figure 6.8   Effect on market equilibrium of changes in demand and supply.

If there are changes in demand (*DD* moves) and changes in supply (*SS* moves), then both market price and quantity will change. The extent of the changes depends on the price-elasticity of supply and elasticity of demand, that is, the extent to which demand and supply are sensitive to changes in price. The direction of changes in price and quantity are summarized in Figure 6.8.

 QUESTIONS

1.   What do you understand by the 'price mechanism'? What are its virtues and weaknesses?

2.   What are the advantages and disadvantages of a free market economy?

3.   Why does the typical demand curve slope down from left to right? Are there any exceptions to this rule or law?

4.   Distinguish, with the help of graphs, between extensions of demand and increases in demand.

5.   Explain how the decline in petrol consumption in the four main European markets between 1991 and 1993 corresponded with a sharp decline in the number of new car registrations in those years.

6.   With the help of graphs, indicate how to distinguish between extensions of supply and increases in supply.

7.   The phenomenon of ring-road building in the UK has increased the price of the 'fenced-off' land and decreased the amount of agricultural land available. Explain this statement with reference to complementary goods.

6.3 Market forces and the environment

Introduction

When every person's standard of living is maximized, market forces can be said to be an efficient mechanism for the allocation of resources. In this case the market can operate free from any regulatory control. This scenario is unrealistic; it is unlikely that a market can ever achieve such an allocation and so be completely free from intervention. The release of CFCs from, for example, aerosol containers, was thought to be having a serious impact on the ozone layer (see above). Resources, in this case, were not being allocated efficiently. Ultimately, the market acted to reduce the impact by the widespread adoption of less-polluting propellants, but only after consumer and political pressure (e.g. the Montreal Protocol). Even so, many refrigeration systems and car air-conditioning units still use CFCs. This example shows that, although the market may act to reduce the harmful impact that it has on the environment, it is often in response to stakeholder pressure, discussed later in the chapter, and frequently an incomplete response. Finally, governments had to play a role in reducing the use of CFCs; on 1 January 1995 the production and import of CFCs was banned in the European Union.

It is probable that market forces will not bring about the best or optimum allocation of resources. It is beyond the scope of this chapter to look in detail at all aspects of the failure of markets, but it is vital for us to assess how this failure can result in damage to the environment. Pollution is the result of economic activity. An organization producing chemicals may discharge waste into the river causing fish to die. In this case the producer, while undertaking its normal business, has harmed third parties such as the marine life and fishermen. It has created an external cost known as an externality (Lipsey and Harbury, 1992); in this case, a negative externality. Positive externalities are created when there is an external benefit from economic activity.

Organizations do not, generally, fully consider the wider social costs or benefits of their business activities. For example, a company may skimp on the provision of anti-pollution controls if the cost of those controls is greater than the effluent charges likely to be imposed on it for emitting waste.

It is not only in market systems that high levels of pollution have been experienced. The former communist states have also suffered. In east-central Europe considerable pollution may be the result of four decades of central planning by Communist parties, which failed to adhere to declared priorities for sound environmental management; instead, there was serious ecological damage of the sort previously attributed only to Western capitalist regimes (Carter and Turnock, 1993).

A business organization can argue that it is not in its economic interest to invest more than it can save in anti-pollution systems. In this case 'private costs' are of uppermost concern to the organization. This may lead to higher levels of noxious emissions into the environment.

Figure 6.9 shows the demand curve DD for a product x (DD also represents the benefits consumers attach to their consumption, what economists call the marginal private benefit (MPB)). SS is the supply curve, which corresponds to the marginal private cost (MPC). This only takes account of the private costs of production, ignoring the wider social costs, like pollution, that may be caused by the activity of the organization. In this case the market price for good x is P and the quantity is Q.

However, if the organization were to take stock of all of the costs involved in its activities it would have to include external costs, that is, the cost to society of the

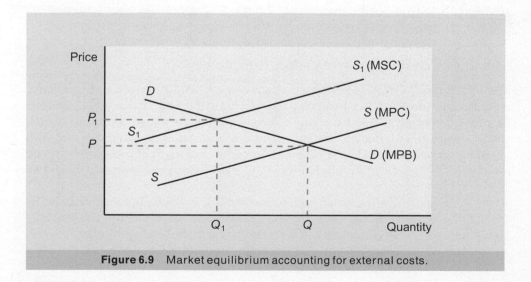

Figure 6.9   Market equilibrium accounting for external costs.

pollution caused. Adding external cost to private cost shifts the supply curve or MPC curve to the left (to S_1S_1). Price would rise from P to P_1, and quantity demanded would fall from Q to Q_1. The resulting lower output should reduce the amount of pollution entering the environment. This new level of output is the socially efficient level of output with no welfare loss to society.

It is clear that negative and positive externalities arise in specific circumstances. Companies do affect individuals and vice versa. We can examine this situation under four main headings:

- actions by companies which affect other companies;
- actions by companies which affect individuals;
- actions by individuals which affect companies;
- actions by individuals which affect other individuals.

Actions by companies which affect other companies

It is best to illustrate this with an example. Industrial waste from production processes can enter the sea and so affect the ability of commercial fishermen to catch fish. The gradual pollution of Japan's inland sea, between Honshu and Shikoku, in the 1950s and 1960s severely damaged fish stocks. A similar situation can be seen in the North Sea and in many of Europe's rivers. In these cases private costs have predominated as it is not in the economic interests of those industries producing the waste to reduce pollution caused by their activities. In all these cases a negative externality has arisen.

Positive externalities can be of great benefit. The success of some football clubs, such as Newcastle United, has enhanced business activity in their region. With over 35 000 spectators for every home game the knock-on effect on shops and pubs in Newcastle is substantial. The 'feel good' factor is also felt by supporters, who, as employees, may even bring benefits to their employing organizations.

Actions by companies which affect individuals

Companies can affect individuals in many ways. Pollution of water used for recreational purposes has become a big issue. In the United Kingdom, Surfers Against Sewerage (SAS) have held a long-standing campaign to encourage the water companies to upgrade treatment plants in order that the latter can deal with both bacteria and water-borne viruses. Because of the length of time surfers spend in the water they seem to be more prone to viral infections, probably caused by sewerage discharge.

A dramatic illustration of producers affecting individuals was illustrated by the Union Carbide disaster in Bhopal, India in 1984, when methyl isocyanate, a poisonous gas, was released from the plant causing 2600 deaths and many adverse long-term consequences for the surrounding community.

Alternatively, Merck, the American pharmaceutical company, are committed both to the advancement of medical science and to the service of humanity; they see the latter as a logical extension of their mission (Collins and Porras, 1993). Even BT's 'it's good to talk' advertising had a positive impact during the rail strikes in the summer of 1995, by encouraging teleconferencing and reducing the number of car journeys.

Actions by individuals which affect companies

The example of traffic congestion illustrates how individuals do not consider their full impact on road conditions. The private cost of motoring is only gauged in terms of the cost of running the car. However, the resulting congestion increases transportation costs for firms and has direct repercussions on the price of goods in the shops.

A further example involving the actions of individuals, though not strictly speaking an externality, was the 1995 European demonstrations, particularly in the United Kingdom, against the transportation of live animals. This had a negative impact on the activity of livestock farmers and ferry companies.

There is a clear positive benefit to industry of a better trained and more highly qualified workforce. However, it is increasingly difficult for organizations, particularly in times of recession, to fund in-house training. This training gap is now being filled by individuals taking the initiative for their own training. Over 30 per cent of 18 year olds are now enrolled on higher education courses. Through undertaking training and extending their education, often at their own expense, these students should provide a well-trained workforce for business organizations.

Actions by individuals which affect other individuals

There are further, potentially serious, social costs which result from current levels of private motoring. Concerns have long been raised about problems to health from exhaust emissions. This is clearly an example of a negative externality where the activity of individuals affects other individuals. On the other hand, a positive externality was created in 1994/95 by the National Health Service in the United Kingdom when it immunized young school children against measles. Not only are those that have been immunized protected from the disease, but others in the wider community, who have not received the treatment, also benefit as there will be less carriers of the disease overall. The statistical likelihood of contracting measles is now reduced. In this case the social benefits of the programme exceed the private benefit to the individual.

Summary

Negative externalities are a direct consequence of economic activity. If private producers exclude the costs imposed on other people from their output calculations they will produce more of the good than is socially desirable. The direct result will be negative externalities, as outlined earlier, and a welfare loss to society. It has been suggested that it is in the economic interests of individuals and companies to accept the consequences of these externalities. This view, which encourages negative externalities, may be blinkered. Short-term benefits of having more and cheaper products to consume may not be in the wider long-term interests of the community and the environment. However, organizations are often encouraged to take this short-term view by their shareholders as they strive for greater returns. An equally important view may be that some pollution is socially optimal because of the enormous cost of reducing many types of pollution to zero.

Having considered the difference between the private and social optimum output, we now need to examine the role of the government.

QUESTIONS

1.   What do you understand by the word 'externality'?

2.   Give examples of both positive and negative externalities. Into which of the four categories used in the text do your examples fall?

6.4 Intervention measures available to limit externalities

Introduction

This section first examines the possibility of resolving environmental disputes through bargaining on the part of those involved. For a variety of reasons this is unfeasible and, so, the role of the government in initiating a number of intervention measures is critical. A key consideration in deciding upon the appropriate type and timing of intervention is the cost to the government and the firms involved. In this section we discuss four areas of government-sponsored intervention: taxes and charges; marketable permits; grants or subsidies; and regulation and anti-monopoly legislation.

Governments do not have to let all negative externalities persist. They can intervene in the market by a range of means, including adopting policies that use, or improve, the price mechanism (discussed above), or by employing extra-market policies. Government activity in this area is governed by the 'polluter pays' principle. This principle proceeds from the notion that the environment has a monetary value and that damage to it should be paid for. The principle entails forcing producers to internalize costs – that is, to pay for their pollution. The landfill tax, discussed under the next heading, is an example of this. Organizations will usually try to pass on their increased costs to the consumer. Some consumers will then refuse to pay the increased price and consumption of the good will fall. As was noted earlier in the chapter, this will reduce the level of externalities, for example pollution, and result in a more socially efficient level of production. (See Figure 6.10, p. 217.)

Unless firms are forced to pay for the environmental damage they cause there will be a disincentive for them to develop or install new, more environmentally friendly equipment, because the costs of so doing would be likely to make their prices uncompetitive. The United Kingdom shoe industry, for example, has a dilemma regarding the harmful effects that can result from the extensive use of adhesives in the manufacture of shoes. The excessive cost of pollution control equipment will increase costs overall and, perhaps, result in an inability to compete with cheaper, less environmentally conscious, overseas competitors. Taking no action may mean that stricter legislation will be imposed on the industry.

Promotion of bargaining

If it is possible to identify the legal rights of the parties involved then bargaining may be a viable alternative. For example, a business organization may be willing to compensate a sailing club that owns a stretch of water if the latter accepts a certain amount of pollution. In return the organization will save money on its waste treatment.

Three problems with the use of bargaining are evident. Firstly, it is difficult to establish the legal rights involved; secondly, it would be impossible to list everyone who is affected by noxious emissions from a particular factory for the purpose of compensation; and, thirdly, the costs to an organization of administering such a system, even if agreements were reached, would be enormous. Because of this, and other problems, this method is unlikely to be successful. As the market finds it very difficult to respond to the problem, many argue that there is a need for government intervention.

Taxes and charges

The tax mechanism can be used to impose extra costs on both producers and consumers. The increasing problems caused by road congestion present governments with a range of options, for example increasing the duty on petrol. Imposing duty at a rate higher than inflation, such as the 5 per cent (in addition to the Retail Price Index) per year increases to which the United Kingdom government has committed itself, should increase the private cost of motoring and result in less car journeys. This, in turn, should produce wider health benefits and reduced congestion to all road users. However, the Royal Commission on Environmental Pollution in its October 1994 report made many proposals, including a recommendation that the price of fuel should be doubled by increasing duties at the rate of 9 per cent per year for 10 years. Other proposals included the halving of road building and increased investment in public transport. These proposals have been put 'on ice'. The government feels that such measures would have little impact on the number of car journeys and that stronger action needs to be taken in respect of such issues as car parking, pedestrianization and road pricing. Some approaches to this issue are discussed in the mini-case below.

Tackling road congestion head on

In the United Kingdom the Confederation of British Industry has estimated that the cost to industry alone of traffic delays is £15 billion a year. This excludes adverse health and environmental effects.

The problem of road congestion has been tackled in Europe by pedestrianization of city centres and the provision of more public transport. In Singapore car-buying permits are necessary before anyone can purchase a car. Additionally, high import duties, which increase the purchase price of a car, high road tax and road pricing in the central business district, all serve to reduce demand for cars. Allied to this is a very efficient public transport system.

In the USA, government programmes have been set up to assist people with finding suitable car-share arrangements; in Washington the ride finders network has reduced the number of car journeys by over 2500 daily since 1993. Los Angeles even has special lanes for cars carrying more than one person.

An article published in *The Economist* entitled 'Roads policy: bumper to bumper to . . .' (1 April 1995) sets out some of the rationale for a system of tolls. It states,

> As road traffic grows, so do the indirect costs it inflicts on everyone, motorist and non-motorist alike. In London, for example, congestion causes more air pollution today than existed before the Clean Air Act banned the burning of coal in 1956. Consumers pay for gas, electricity and water. Rail fares include a return on the capital costs of the track. It is difficult to see, at least in terms of economic rationality and equity, why drivers should not pay for road use if some way can be found to charge them for it.

Other countries have used a variety of means of electronic tolling of cars; the methods are getting increasingly 'high-tech'. According to another article published in *The Economist* entitled 'Pay as you go' (1 April 1995) more than half of the vehicles entering Oslo pay electronically via an electronic tagging system of vehicles. Singapore is apparently in the final stages of testing a system capable of debiting prepaid smart-cards mounted in vehicles moving at up to 80 mph.

A firm could be forced to pay an indirect tax, such as the carbon taxes imposed by the Danish and Swedish governments, on each unit of its polluting emissions. The effect of the tax is to increase the costs of production for manufacturers and reduce the output of pollutants (see Figure 6.10). The Swedish environment minister indicated that tax is 'one of the few efficient tools for reducing CO_2 emissions because when it comes to economy and industry, this task requires the market's own tools' (Boulton, 1995).

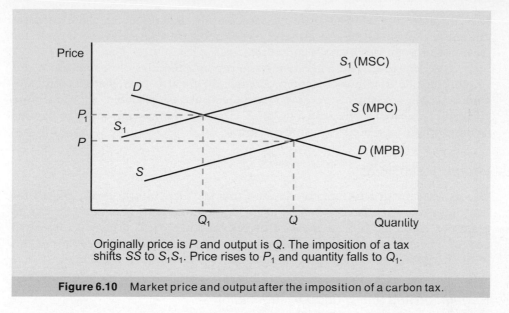

Originally price is *P* and output is *Q*. The imposition of a tax shifts *SS* to S_1S_1. Price rises to P_1 and quantity falls to Q_1.

Figure 6.10   Market price and output after the imposition of a carbon tax.

In the United Kingdom a new tax on waste going to landfill sites is planned for introduction in October 1996. The tax will be levied at £2.00 per tonne for inactive waste and £7.00 per tonne for other wastes (Croner Guide, 1996). The scheme is designed to encourage greater use of incineration, recycling or waste minimization in the first place. Currently about 70 per cent of UK waste goes to landfill. These proposals are designed to reduce this percentage to 50 per cent by the year 2015 (Lascelles, 1995).

If a tax reflects the full external environmental cost then the externality has been fully internalized. This is a very big 'if', since the issue is whether the tax can ever accurately reflect the external cost. The aim is to impose a tax that will result in the socially efficient level of output. In such situations firms have a choice: they can continue to pollute and pay for it or invest in anti-pollution measures which will, in the short term, reduce their tax liability and, possibly, save them money and/or offer competitive advantages in the long term.

Marketable permits

Under the marketable permit system an authority issues a fixed quantity of permits giving authorization to discharge a certain level of waste. These permits are freely tradable. Under this system a market for discharge permits is established. Organizations which find the cost of pollution control to be relatively low are in a position to sell their rights for a fee. This fee will be above the cost of the pollution control that they would have had to undertake. Other firms who find the cost of pollution control to be high are in a position to buy rights to discharge, as long as the cost is below the cost of the pollution control measures they would otherwise have to undertake. Having such a market means that resources are used more efficiently to control the overall level of pollution. It also raises the income for government to tackle environmental problems.

In America clean air legislation sets a cap on emissions of nitrous oxide and sulphur dioxide from power stations. Companies are also given annual permits to emit a certain amount of the gases. These permits are tradable, allowing those companies prepared to invest in long-term 'clean-up' measures to sell their permits to those whose emissions exceed their permit.

Grants or subsidies

Grants are provided to farmers via the Common Agricultural Policy (CAP) for land improvement schemes that enhance the environment. However, the use of grants or subsidies flies in the face of the 'polluter pays' principle (discussed above). These would be provided to polluters as an incentive to reduce the amount of discharge and encourage environmentally friendly forms of behaviour.

Regulation and anti-monopoly legislation

A common method of intervening in the market to force organizations to address negative externalities is by regulation, usually by imposing a set of legal obligations upon organizations. Regulations are commonly used to impose external costs on producers. Regulations can take many forms which include (Lee, 1994):

- prohibiting the abstraction, use or disposal of particular substances, products and processes which are considered to be environmentally damaging;
- setting maximum limits for the abstraction of particular natural resources;
- setting maximum limits for discharges of pollutants to air, water or land;
- prescribing the technology which may be used for particular processes of production or the materials which may be used in particular processes;
- establishing ambient quality standards.

Regulations are used because they are easier than other types of intervention to administer. Taxation of, for example, CO_2 discharge into the atmosphere requires sophisticated and costly monitoring. Regulations may not require this level of monitoring as spot checks may be enough. Through regulation, such as the placing of a legal maximum on the amount of pollution that a business organization can produce, an organization could be prohibited from producing more than the socially efficient level of output.

Alternatively, regulations can be applied to change the way goods are produced in order to reduce the amount of pollution. In the United Kingdom, for example, the Environment Act 1995 makes producers responsible for ensuring that certain types of products are recyclable, for example milk bottles and newsprint. Although the amount of materials which are recycled in the United Kingdom is increasing, other European countries are much better placed. Recycling rates in

Germany and Denmark are around 80 per cent. In Germany, for example, household waste is sorted by householders into separate containers to facilitate recycling.

However, regulations do cause problems. Firstly, because they are often uniformly applied across industries they may not represent the most cost-efficient means of reducing pollution. There is no incentive to improve performance beyond compliance with the regulation. It has been suggested that trying to make industry cleaner, by applying tighter standards, may protect old, dirty technology already in place and discourage cleaner innovation. Secondly, in order to identify the socially efficient level of output government needs to know the value of the damage that the pollution causes; an almost impossible task.

Regulations, however, may also be able to promote business activity. Opportunities will flourish in the waste clean-up industry, giving export opportunities as other countries adopt similar regulations that tend to minimize waste. Porter (1990) argued that environmental regulations can create new jobs. It is possible that the imposition of strict regulations can actually improve the ability of a firm to compete. Stringent standards for product performance, product safety, and environmental impact can stimulate companies to improve quality, upgrade technology and provide features that respond to consumer and social demands. Easing standards, however tempting, is counter-productive (Porter, 1990). Environmental standards can also act as a barrier to entry (see Chapter 2): the car manufacturers which already fitted catalytic converters on cars for sale in the United States lobbied in favour of their adoption in the European market.

Although counter-intuitive, organizations that are based in countries with substantial regulations, such as Sweden, may be in a position to gain competitive advantage over organizations operating under a more lax regime. As legislation changes and converges throughout Europe and the world, those organizations which have worked under the strictest regimes will have a distinct competitive advantage. Scania, the multinational truck manufacturer, has used the strict legal environment in Sweden to compete successfully in the truck industry (refer to the Scania case in this book, p. 194). The advantage to the early movers is most likely to arise from (Murray and Fahy, 1994):

- positive consumer perceptions and attitudes which become attached to companies and their brands;
- the accumulated experience of dealing with new materials, technologies and processes; and
- the ownership of proprietary design, recovery and recycling technologies and processes.

It may be difficult for organizations that are left behind to catch up.

Anti-monopoly legislation may be necessary to prevent the abuse of monopoly power which could include infringement of environmental regulations. Firms may be taken into public ownership and their output controlled to take into account both public and private costs. How ineffective this may be can be judged by reference to the high levels of pollution in the former Soviet Union. One of the key foundations of environmental policies adopted by the Conservative government in the United Kingdom from 1979 was that effective regulation did not require legal ownership of industries.

QUESTION

Outline up to five responses to controlling pollution and congestion resulting from excessive use of the road network in the United Kingdom.

6.5 Government regulation at different geo-political scales

The marketplace is overseen by government at various geo-political scales, from international to local. Increasingly, much of the development of policy relating to environmental issues is taking place at global and regional scales. Nation states, which will have participated in the formulation of policy, will then often have to give domestic effect to such things as international treaties or European directives via legislation and appropriate executive action. Various global and regional institutions monitor activities in different nation states.

Regulation at global/regional level

At the global level regulation is primarily concerned with nation states agreeing to environmental protection initiatives via international summit meetings. As a result, treaties are being signed which set standards, such as that at the Rio Earth Summit in 1992. Treaties such as these might, perhaps, be thought to have a somewhat distant effect on individual business organizations. However, the International Treaty on Ozone Depleting Substances, or 'Montreal Protocol', which, for example, established a schedule for the phased withdrawal and elimination of CFCs by the year 2010, can be seen to have a direct impact on producers and users of those gases.

Often progress at this global scale is slow. At the Berlin Conference on climate change, in March 1995, it became evident that little progress had been made towards reaching the targets agreed at the 1992 Earth Summit in respect of reducing the output of 'greenhouse' gases. At Berlin the tensions between rich and poor countries provided an interesting focus for the issue of trade-offs between environmental protection and economic growth.

At this global level the chief guiding concept is 'sustainable development'. This involves assuring that, for the sake of generations to come, the amount and quality of what has been called 'natural capital' – for example, atmosphere, water, tropical rainforest and biodiversity – is not reduced by economic development.

From the early 1980s onwards a range of key reports from institutions, such as the World Commission for Environment and Development and the World Bank, made pleas for integrating environmental considerations into policy making on economic development. The traditional and underlying assumption is that environmental regulation impedes growth.

We turn now to the regional scale to discuss the role of the European Union in respect of environmental regulation. The signatories to the Treaty of Rome (1957), which created the EEC, were not particularly concerned with environmental issues. This oversight was rectified by the Single European Act (SEA) 1987 which adopted the specific environmental objectives in article 130R, namely:

- to preserve, protect and improve the quality of the environment;
- to contribute towards protecting human health;
- to ensure a prudent and rational utilization of natural resources.

These objectives were extended by the Treaty of European Union (1992) (the so-called Maastricht Treaty) to include:

- sustainable and non-inflationary growth respecting the environment;
- promotion of measures to help resolve global environmental problems.

The European Commission, through Directorate General DG XI, is responsible for the environment. DG XI takes the role of initiating and implementing European Union policies on the environment. EU policy intentions are set out in its Environmental Action Programme. To date there have been five such programmes, the first from 1973 to 1976 and the fifth from 1993 to 2000. EU policy has, over the years, changed in its scope. In the past, European environmental initiatives tended to be reactive and based on regulation; they are now becoming more market-driven and voluntary. The 'polluter pays' principle, discussed above, is now at the centre of much EU legislation.

It has also been recognized, by the fifth programme, that legislation is a toothless beast without compliance, so there is now increased emphasis on the enforcement of existing legislation.

Towards the end of 1993 it was agreed that a long-planned European Environment Agency should be set up in Copenhagen, Denmark. One of the Agency's major tasks is to set up a European Information and Observation Network to provide objective, reliable and comparable scientific and technical information at a European level. The aim is to provide data to enable the European Union to 'take the steps necessary to protect the environment as well as to assess the results of their actions' (CEC, 1994).

It is expected that the European Environment Agency will work with other EU bodies, together with organizations with a broader international brief such as the Organization for Economic Cooperation and Development (OECD) and the United Nations Environment Programme (UNEP) (CEC, 1994).

Before moving on to discuss the impact of regional activity on nation states it is useful to note another example of the interaction of the two areas discussed under the present heading: global and regional activity. At the Berlin Conference, discussed above, the ambassadors of the Alliance of Low Lying States (AOSIS) sought to persuade the European Union to agree to stiffer targets in respect of CO_2 emissions than had been agreed at Rio, arguing that, 'a rise in sea levels of 10–30 cm by 2030, which is the corollary of a rise in the earth's temperature of 0.3° C every 10 years, would result in the disappearance of whole islands' (EIU, 1995). The EU's Environment Council refused to agree to this and confirmed the intention to stabilize emissions at 1990 levels by the year 2000.

At Berlin, it was decided that existing efforts to combat climate change were inadequate and that 1997 should be set as the deadline for negotiations on further legally binding measures. Developing countries refused to accept any responsibility for reducing emissions and the European Union failed in its aim of achieving agreement to a protocol with specific targets and timetables (EIU, 1995).

As we turn to consider regulation at a national level, it is important to note that for each European Union member the objectives of its environmental laws are increasingly determined by the Union, 'while the mechanisms through which these objectives are to be reached are determined nationally' (Welford and Gouldson, 1993).

Regulation at national level

In the United Kingdom, the task of central government in regulating health and environmental issues or providing support for organizations is largely carried out through the Department of the Environment (DoE). Support is also provided by other ministries, such as the Department of Trade and Industry whose Business Link scheme provides advice on environmental issues for small firms in particular.

Before an organization can be granted authorization to make emissions from any 'prescribed processes' under Part 1 of the Environmental Protection Act 1990 (EPA), the process must satisfy a test known as BATNEEC ('best available technique not entailing excessive cost'). There is considerable debate – which is beyond the scope of this chapter – about the interpretation of each element of the principle. However, Welford and Gouldson (1993) note that organizations which have developed self-regulation schemes such as BS 7750 (discussed below), 'will be at a considerable advantage when gathering the information and applying the criteria of BATNEEC'.

Additionally, part A of the EPA subjects the most polluting processes to an 'integrated' scheme of pollution control. Here, control is integrated in the sense that the impact of an organization's emissions to air, water or land must be treated in a holistic way, in order to achieve what is known as the 'best practicable environmental option'.

Enforcement notices may be served if an organization is in breach of the terms of its authorization to emit. More serious risks which cannot be dealt with in this way will result in the issue of a prohibition notice, which can force the closure of a facility until an organization complies with its authorization.

The Environment Agency is a key body in respect of such enforcement issues in the United Kingdom. It came into existence in April 1996. Part 1 of the Environment Act 1995 established this body for England and Wales, which combines all the functions previously undertaken by HM Inspectorate of Pollution, the National Rivers Authority and the waste regulation authorities under one umbrella. The Act establishes that the principal aim of the agency is, subject to costs, to protect or enhance the environment as a whole and make a contribution towards attaining sustainable development.

If a business organization produces waste it has a duty of care in respect of that waste under the EPA 1990. Managers in such businesses need to be aware that breach of this duty of care can lead to fines and prison sentences in addition to civil liability for causing damage to environmental or human health by waste. (Legal issues are looked at in more detail in Chapter 7.) Welford and Gouldson (1993) say, 'The increased use of financial instruments, such as regulatory charges, landfill levies (and) fines ... are all manifestations of the "polluter pays" principle.' This principle was discussed above in the section on intervention measures. We turn now to examine regulation at the local level.

Regulation at local level

In the United Kingdom, local authority (LA) environmental health departments have the responsibility for regulating food hygiene, health and safety (together with the Health and Safety Executive (HSE)), pest control and air and noise pollution. Local authorities are also responsible for planning, licensing and trading standards.

Clearly the issue of planning controls is a crucial one in terms of more localized environmental issues. In England and Wales a series of Town and Country Planning regulations between 1990 and 1994 gave effect to a European directive on Environmental Impact Assessment which required member states 'to ensure that before consent is given to projects likely to have significant environmental effects they should be made subject to an assessment of the effects' (Croner Guide, 1996). The regulations require developers to produce an 'environmental impact statement' to help the planning authority make a decision.

The Environment Act 1995 set up an improved network of centres for monitoring air quality; by the end of 1996 there were expected to be 36 such locations in the United Kingdom. This local authority responsibility is the only area not incorporated into the work of the Environment Agency, discussed above. The European Union is also emphasizing local regulation in its current Environmental Action Programme.

In the United Kingdom, the city of Leicester was the first to receive the designation 'Environment City'. The city council's experience of this project suggests that the greatest progress at this local scale results from local authorities developing links with community groups and both local charitable and business organizations. A number of local businesses, including the brewers Everards, are reported to have made savings as a result of 'waste minimization' reviews encouraged by the project (Gosling, 1996).

In summary, it is true to say that progress at the global level in taking ecological regulatory action is often slow. However, since most serious ecological concerns tend not to be confined within particular geographical boundaries the ability to make progress at this global level is critical to the effective tackling of many of the earth's ecological problems. Action at regional, national or local levels often stems from these wider global initiatives.

 ## QUESTIONS

1.   What do you understand by the 'polluter pays' principle?

2.   What does the concept of 'sustainable development' imply?

3.   Give an example of a national regulation that has evolved from a global initiative. Trace the progress of this issue in terms of time scale and geo-political scale.

6.6 Organizational agendas

Introduction

During the 1980s a short-hand reference to environmentally concerned organiza-tions, and consumers, was use of the word 'Green'. 'Green' organizations, such as the Body Shop, had a positive and proactive stance towards environmental issues. Kleiner (1991) identified three key components of green companies. They will:

- have developed a mechanism for placing a monetary value on the complete life cycle of a range of alternative product/packaging proposals; such 'cradle to the grave accounting' will assist in the development of products and limit environmental impact;
- record and publish environmental data, possibly thereby averting environmental disasters and improving community relations as a result;
- be committed to reducing waste at source, for example via some form of TQM (total quality management) programme.

All firms may be liable to cause environmental problems and disasters as a direct result of their activities. A 1992 survey by the Loss Prevention Council (LPC) identified a large number of problem industries, for example agriculture, food, metal processing, paint, tanning and textiles.

Obviously, the scope and scale of environmental problems and disasters will vary enormously. Exxon faced a $2000 million (£1.3 billion) clean-up operation and fines of a similar amount, resulting from an oil spillage, when the tanker the *Exxon Valdez* ran aground in March 1989. This caused oil contamination to about 4000 km of Alaskan coastline, killing substantial numbers of wild creatures including at least 32 000 birds and millions of fish. However, Cannon (1994) has estimated that loss of market share, disruptions to supplies, compliance with new regulations and the effect on share price cost the company a further substantial sum between $8000 and $15 000 million (£5.2–9.7 billion).

In addition to the fines and clean-up costs, the bad publicity surrounding such events can also have serious effects on the reputation of an organization; rebuilding consumer confidence in such cases may prove very difficult.

Given the nature of the business environment facing them, it is clear that organizations throughout the world have the choice of a wide range of environmental agendas.

Environmental stances adopted by organizations

In much of our coverage of factors in the business environment we have often noted that organizations perceive changes as posing threats or creating opportunities, depending upon their unique 'perceptual filters'. Research has revealed that a wide range of theoretical positions may be adopted by organizations. Roome (1992) sets out a continuum of five possible environmental options for organizations:

- non-compliance;
- compliance;
- compliance plus;
- commercial and environmental excellence;
- leading edge.

The first three options, 'non-compliance', 'compliance' and 'compliance plus', may be taken by businesses whose primary reference point is legislation. An organization that adopts a non-compliance position may, because of lack of resources or managerial inertia, be unable to satisfy legal requirements. Some may make a policy decision not to comply with the regulations in order to secure lower costs. The 'compliance' standpoint is clearly reactive in its nature and may tend to focus efforts upon the action required to satisfy the BATNEEC standard discussed above. This represents a minimal response. These two stances are essentially reactive. In these circumstances, it is possible that a company may fall behind competitors who are developing products to meet the changing conditions.

The third option is 'compliance plus' where there is more evidence of a proactive stance towards legal standards. Such an organization might aim to integrate an environmental management system into the context of its overall business strategy via a standard such as BS 7750 (discussed below).

Roome's (1992) two remaining options tend not to apply to a large number of businesses. A business focused on 'commercial and environmental excellence' would ensure that its core corporate and managerial values always take account of environmental management issues; while 'leading edge' businesses set the standard for a particular industry through the adoption of 'state of the art' environmental management systems.

More proactive stances, as displayed by the final two of Roome's options, can be illustrated by the systems adopted by Shanks & McEwan, a major UK waste management company. The company integrates the management of environmental issues throughout all areas of the organization. Key elements of its approach are:

- a corporate environment policy;
- the use of the quality management standard BS 5750 for quality assurance;
- the setting up of an 'independent' advisory board;
- the use of regular audits and assessments.

A proactive stance may require substantial amounts of initial capital investment and put an organization at a cost disadvantage in relation to more reactive competitors. However, there are a number of cases of organizations who justify investment, in, for example, waste minimization schemes, as making hard-headed, if long-term, business sense. The increasing cost of landfill dumping may cause more organizations to make such decisions. One such organization is 3M (see mini-case below).

3M

Some companies have put in place ecological strategies that seek to eliminate emissions, effluents and accidents through preventative action and continuous improvement at every step of the production process (Shrivastava, 1994). This preventative approach is more efficient than controlling discharges at 'end-of-pipe', which involves pollution control to purify air or water before they leave the plant. End-of-pipe control is often viewed by companies as cheaper than pollution prevention. However, there is an argument that an effective pollution prevention strategy is cheaper in the long run. One company that has taken the longer-term view is the multinational 3M (Minnesota Mining and Manufacturing Company).

3M has a diversified portfolio of businesses, based largely on its expertise in substrates, coatings and adhesives. It has a strong reputation for product innovation, for example 'Post-it' notes. 3M develops product lines around a series of small, discrete, freestanding products. The company forms new venture units comprising small, semi-autonomous teams, led by a product champion to develop its new products.

One of the key tasks of this team is to minimize pollution from the first phase of product development. 3M's 'Pollution Prevention Pays' (3P) programme is designed to cut pollution at source. The programme is in four stages:

- Product reformulation. Here the issue is whether products can be made using fewer raw materials or less toxic materials.

- Process modification. In order to cut down on waste.
- Equipment redesign.
- Resource recovery. Can waste be salvaged, reused or sold?

Each project undertaken by the 3P programme must meet four criteria:

- eliminate or reduce pollution;
- save energy or material and resources;
- demonstrate technological innovation;
- save money.

As a direct result of the programme, waste per unit of output fell, though the reduction was not enough to satisfy the company. In 1989 3M introduced Pollution Prevention Plus (3P+), committing itself to stricter environmental controls and increased R&D expenditure.

The importance of the organization's environmental context

Much of the continuum developed by Roome (1992) revolves around environmental legislation. Azzone and Bertele (1994) suggest that decisions on positioning a company in the context of ecological factors has to be linked with a broader environmental context. They outline five such contexts which relate either to national context or to the situation prevailing in certain product/service markets:

1. *Stable context*. Here there may be either slow changes or no changes in environmental legislation. There may be a lack of public perception of environmental issues or an almost complete lack of consumer power. Organizations in these circumstances will find it easy to ignore legislation and adopt a non-compliance stance. This could be the case in developing countries of South America or the former Eastern bloc nations.

2. *Reactive context*. Here environmental problems are known by small groups; consumer interest is limited and legislation evolves slowly. In this context, organizations can take a compliance stance responding only slowly when the pressures build up. Many United Kingdom firms have opted for this approach to dealing with environmental problems.

3. *Anticipative context*. Here the public are more aware and have the ability to move issues onto the political agenda. It is more difficult for firms to influence the political process. Legislation and regulations become more demanding and organizations need to develop a compliance-plus strategy, anticipating changes and using technological developments to ensure that new standards can be met. The regulatory regime in the European Union and the United States is increasingly encouraging this approach.

4. *Proactive context*. Here not only is legislation at the heart of environmental change, but 'green' consumers also have a major impact. Commercial and environmental excellence is vital to compete in this environment, which tends to exist in niches.

TABLE 6.3 Organizational implications of environmental stance

	The context				
	Stable	Reactive	Anticipatory	Proactive	Creative
Environmental problems	None	Problems addressed when defined	Anticipates new legislation	Examines opportunities for products and company	Searches for new technology
Activities involved					
• R&D	No	No	Yes	Yes	Yes
• Production/ logistics	Limited	Yes	Yes	Yes	Yes
• Marketing/sales	No	No	No	Yes	Yes
• External relations	No	Limited	Yes	Yes	Yes
• Legal	No	Limited	Yes	Yes	Yes
• Finance	No	No	No	No	Yes
• Environmental department	No	No	Usually	Usually	Usually
• Top management	No	No	Sometimes	Yes	Yes

Source: Reprinted from *Long Range Planning*, Vol. 27, No. 6, Azzone, G. and Bertele, U., 'Exploiting green strategies for competitive advantage', pp. 69–81. Copyright (1994), with kind permission from Elsevier Science Ltd, The Boulevard, Langford Lane, Kidlington OX5 1GB, UK.

5.   *Creative context.* Here public opinion is extremely aware of environmental problems and there is a lack of accepted technological solutions to problems. One of the problems facing the car industry is that of exhaust emissions, a problem to which a number of solutions have been suggested. A leading edge company will be at the forefront of the technological push for the optimal solution.

It is necessary for firms to establish an organizational response to the environmental context in which they find themselves. Table 6.3 illustrates the increased level of activity which an organization has to undertake as its environmental context moves from stable, at one end of the continuum, to creative at the other. It is important to recognize the substantial costs that will be incurred by an organization as it moves from one stance to another.

A further influence on an organization's environmental stance will be its perception of its stakeholders and the relative power which each possesses.

The influence of stakeholder power

Of issue is the extent to which an organization is prepared to take account of its stakeholders to limit the externalities referred to above. Stakeholders are groups or

individuals who have a stake in, or an expectation of, the organization's performance (refer to Chapter 1). Argenti (1980) identifies three categories of stakeholder:

- those internal to the enterprise, such as employees, management and
  shareholders;
- those immediately external to the enterprise, for example suppliers and
  customers;
- other external stakeholders, such as the community.

Expectations and aspirations of stakeholder groups differ. Shareholders are
major stakeholders. Short-term benefits to shareholders are often given priority
over other interests. It is often a legal requirement for firms to maintain
shareholder value at the expense of other stakeholder requirements and wider
social costs. Shareholders aim to maximize the return from their investment
through higher dividends or a better capital return from the sale of shares that have
increased in value. For shareholders to achieve their required returns the firm
must perform well. This requirement frequently conflicts with adoption of more
socially oriented policies.

A 1992 survey by the University of Westminster, commissioned by the Co-
op Bank, into managerial attitudes to business ethics in the conduct of business,
employee relations, social conscience and the environment was published in
January 1993. The survey, based upon 645 managers, of whom 480 were senior
managers or professionals, showed some ambivalence in respect of green issues.
Although awareness of the issues was high, managers often lacked the motivation
to take specific action. Ninety per cent said business should pay for causing
environmental damage, but 57 per cent believed that whether or not a company has
a recycling policy is a minor issue. Nevertheless, 32 per cent of those surveyed
advocated a ban on products which consume the world's scarce resources. The
survey also suggested that the closer executives were to responsibility for company
profit, the more they seemed prepared to act against the best interests of the
environment. However, only 7 per cent would back selling weapons to oppressive
regimes or exporting pesticides banned in the United Kingdom, while around
three-quarters would firmly avoid such practices.

The expectations of the local community may substantially differ from that
of firms. Social aims may include the provision of more jobs, the improvement of
local amenities and minimum pollution. There may be a conflict of interests in this
situation. A major problem for the external stakeholders, such as the local
community, is that they have insufficient power to influence company strategy
because of their fragmented nature. Ansoff (1984) suggested that the dominant
coalition, those in positions of power such as the board of directors, usually bias
strategy towards their own preferred course of action (see survey above). In this
way senior management can initiate strategies to support shareholders' wishes
which may be to the detriment of the environment and the local community. It
would be unusual for external stakeholders to be part of the dominant coalition, so
their influence is rarely felt.

Welford and Gouldson (1993) develop a model of stakeholder pressure in respect of environmental performance which adds three significant elements to those outlined by Argenti (above). They include the impact on the organization of pressure groups, media and insurers. The mini-case below, entitled 'Shock for Shell', illustrates the impact which pressure groups and media can have in mobilizing consumer action and public opinion.

Shock for Shell

Shell is Europe's largest company. Its 1994 net profit was over £4 billion on sales of £62 billion. The company is Anglo-Dutch – 40 per cent British owned and 60 per cent Dutch.

In early June 1995 Shell had planned to dispose of the life-expired Brent Spar oil storage buoy in the deep water of the Atlantic Ocean. This intended action gained the full agreement of the British government, following three years of talks. On 20 June 1995 the plan was abandoned, despite the fact that Shell, the British government and a number of marine biologists still believed deep-water disposal to be a better environmental option than on-shore dismantling. The buoy contained some oil and sludge and some heavy metals and radioactive salts, although the amount of these substances has been the subject of a variety of reports. Later, in September 1995, Greenpeace admitted that their original estimates on the quantity of these substances had been incorrect; they overstated the amount of pollutants by a large factor.

What factors had brought about this publicly embarrassing reversal? Shell were keen to downplay the effects of the direct-action campaign mounted by Greenpeace (which had included landing people on the buoy). However, it is clear that the latter's action was significant in mobilizing public opinion. As a result of boycotts, called by the German Green party, Shell are thought to have lost around 70 per cent of trade at some petrol stations and hundreds of millions of pounds in revenue. Additionally, the German government put considerable pressure on Shell to reverse their decision.

A number of commentators felt this was a significant development as the company was compelled to take account of a wider range of stakeholder interests in pursuit of their business. There was some anger concerning whether the British government and Shell were flouting the 'polluter pays' principle – a key plank of the government's environmental policy.

The reaction of Greenpeace to Shell's eventual decision was predictably ecstatic. In *The Economist* of 24 June 1995, a spokesperson was quoted as proclaiming it as 'A victory for common sense and a victory for the environment'. Both Swedish and German environment ministers expressed satisfaction at the outcome. Predictably the British government was furious. Shell's 'U-turn' came only a day after Prime Minister, John Major, had given strong backing to deep-water disposal. The government had argued that sea dumping was within the guidelines set by the International Maritime Organization, the United Nations agency which oversees sea pollution.

A Friends of the Earth spokesperson said, 'Everyone should be heartened that the consumer can force industry and governments to take responsibility' (*The Guardian*, 21 June 1995). In the future it will be interesting to see the extent to which the general public will continue to fund environmental pressure groups, such as Greenpeace, Friends of the Earth and the Worldwide Fund for Nature. For the present, anyway, it seems that their high-publicity campaigns will continue to have a significant effect in mobilizing public opinion.

As a result of this débâcle there will be an effect on Shell's image as an environmentally friendly company. A spokesperson from Shell thought that it might take years to repair their reputation. For a company known to thoroughly evaluate all possible occurrences in its business environment, a number of commentators found it surprising that Shell did not seem to have taken sufficient account of the impact that a mobilized consumer opinion, in key northern European countries, might have.

Some believe that the bureaucratic structure of Shell, and its devolved decision making under its matrix structure, made it slow to appreciate the overall scale of consumer protests and, therefore, slow to act. In March 1995 announcements had been made of the loss of over 1000 jobs at their Hague and London headquarters. The long-established matrix organizational structure was thought to be on the verge of being dismantled, following a scheme proposed by the management consultants McKinsey, in favour of a structure which would streamline decision making and eliminate layers of bureaucracy world wide.

At the time of writing the redundant platform is anchored in a Norwegian fiord, at a cost of £20 000 a month, while the company considers 200 different suggestions for its disposal. These include conversion into an off-shore tax-free casino or a floating lighthouse. The company has said it now prefers land disposal but feels it needs to be given some assistance. A spokesman, quoted in an article on 12 October 1995 in *The Guardian*, stressed that it would now be a year before a decision is taken in respect of the buoy and that the decision will be based on 'sound science, reason and careful balance of environment, safety, health, technology and cost'.

We must be careful not to suggest that all shareholders are short-term investment opportunists seeking a return at any cost. A brief examination of a range of company annual reports, like those of ICI, suggests that shareholder expectations, in respect of a company's environmental record, may be increasing. There is evidence, also, of the increasing popularity of 'Green' investment funds.

Hart and Owen (1992) identify the Caird Group, a company operating in the waste disposal industry, and RPS Group, a small environmental consultancy, as notable examples of innovators in terms of 'green reporting' in their annual reports. It is thought that around 25 per cent of UK company annual reports make some sort of environmental disclosure (Maddox, 1995). This may be partly in response to pressure groups, which have sought to purchase shares, to gain access to annual general meetings and be in a formal forum to put over their views.

Firms with some of the 'greenest' credentials tend to be engaged in self-regulation schemes of one type or another. Clearly, such firms are in the categories of 'compliance plus', or beyond, in Roome's (1992) classifications.

Self-regulation

Self-regulation schemes are having a considerable impact at global, European and national levels. Organizations involved in such schemes will, at a minimum, fall into Roome's 'compliance plus' category (discussed above) – if not one of the two most proactive categories.

At the global scale there is an extensive range of such self-regulation schemes sponsored by the International Chamber of Commerce (ICC) and the International Organization for Standardization (ISO), among others. The ICC's 'Business charter for sustainable development', for example, outlines a range of actions to integrate the management of environmental issues with the general policies and activities of organizations.

An example of self-regulation at a European level, however, is the system sponsored by the European Petroleum Industry Association (EUROPIA) and the voluntary eco-audits. In the United Kingdom significant examples include the British Standards Institution (BSI) and the Confederation of British Industry Environment Business Forum, which involves in excess of 200 organizations, such as Biffa Waste Services, BP Chemicals, British Nuclear Fuels, ICI and Nottingham Business School.

These self-regulation schemes require organizations to 'sign up' to regimes which typically involve making information available to the public, principally via an environmental policy statement, together with clear targets and objectives needed to meet the policy. In such schemes, considerable stress is placed on plans to achieve continual improvements and of integrating environmental issues with those concerns of general management. Environmental audits and further statements on the progress made in respect of environmental objectives, tend to be the final pieces of the jigsaw. The concept of environmental audit, in particular, requires organizations to monitor and collect detailed information in order to judge whether improvement has been achieved.

The British Standards Institution (BSI) is a leader, in the United Kingdom, in the development of company self-regulation. The British Standard for Environmental Management BS 7750 built upon BS 5750, the quality management standard. BS 7750 attempts to guide a company in the formation, management and execution of an environmental policy and system. The standard has been achieved by a number of companies, for example Vauxhall Cars at their Ellesmere Port plant. The British Standard was influential in developing both the International Standard ISO 9000 and the European Eco-management and Audit Scheme (EMAS) implemented in May 1995. Indeed, in January 1996 the European Commission decided that organizations certified under BS 7750 would not need to undergo separate assessment for EMAS registration. Both standards aim to help organizations establish environmental management systems that require regular third-party audits of plants and the reporting of environmental performance data. Although EMAS registration is voluntary, future customers might place considerable pressure on supplier organizations to 'sign up', as was the case with BS 5750. BS 7750 will also form the yardstick for the globally applicable ISO 14001 to be published in 1996.

To summarize, it is evident that there are many non-legally binding reasons why organizations need to be aware of their impact on the natural environment and, perhaps, to take action to improve the situation. The sort of environmental agenda which an organization adopts will be influenced by both its environmental context and the extent of the stakeholders' power and interest.

QUESTIONS

1. Conduct a search of recent press articles on environmental concerns. Can you find examples of organizations which fit each of Roome's (1992) categories?

2. Comment on Shell's actions in the 'Shock for Shell' case. In what ways do you think Shell's structure might have had a bearing on its actions in respect of the Brent Spar?

3. What do you believe will be the effect of increased numbers of single-issue campaigners like Greenpeace on (a) governments and (b) business organizations?

4. Using Table 1.1 as an example, complete a power/interest matrix for all of Shell's stakeholders.

5. What benefits might accrue to an organization from the adoption of such an approach as BS 7750?

6. How has the Shell 'story' developed since the time discussed in the case?

6.7 The position of the consumer

Consumers are becoming more environmentally conscious, according to Gallup International's 1992 Environmental Opinion Survey. A clear majority of consumers in the most advanced countries say they are willing to sacrifice some economic growth for environmental protection. It is difficult to be precise in the use of the term 'green consumer'. The characteristics of 'green' consumers have been summarized by Elkington and Hailes (1988). These consumers will avoid products likely to:

• endanger health;

- cause significant environmental damage or consume a disproportionate amount of energy during manufacture, use or disposal;
- cause unnecessary waste;
- use materials from threatened species or environments;
- involve unnecessary use of, or cruelty to, animals or adversely affect other countries – particularly those in the developing world.

Clearly consumers can only act in a 'green' way if they possess reliable information about the relative effects of a range of products on the environment. In Britain, towards the end of the 1980s, the ability of consumers to respond in an environmentally sound manner was much enhanced by best-selling guides like *The Green Consumer Guide* by Elkington and Hailes (1988), although information was still patchy.

Azzone and Bertele (1994) suggest that as eco-labels with third-party certification are developed, such as the Blue Angel in Germany, 'green' qualities of products will become more obvious and 'green' consumers will become more important. It is easier for Germans to adopt 'green' purchasing habits because they have a comprehensive system of eco-labelling. This provides them with better quality information about products and the effects which their production, use or disposal might have on the environment.

The real test for 'green' consumerism is whether consumers will pay premium prices for environmentally friendly products. A Mintel survey in December 1994 showed an 11 per cent decline in the numbers of British people expressing worries about such issues between 1990 and 1994. During recessionary times as the early 1990s, it is to be expected that consumers will be less prepared to pay premium prices for such goods. This has been compounded by consumer scepticism about the quality of many products for which 'green' claims have been made.

There is a lack of published data comparing the 'greenness' of consumers between countries. One of the few examples is the 1992 *Eurobarometer* which suggests that 46 per cent of a sample of consumers from 12 member states were prepared to buy an environmentally friendly product, even if it was more expensive. The pattern of response was not uniform throughout the European Union. For example, 75 per cent of former West German consumers were 'green' compared to 53 per cent of consumers in former East Germany.

It is interesting to examine the collective power which consumers can exert in respect of ecological issues. As was noted above, at the end of the 1980s and in the absence of any legislation, consumer boycotts of aerosols led to a reduction in their demand. In a short time the new industry standard product became a nominally 'environmentally friendly' one.

During the 1980s and early 1990s Greenpeace mounted many successful campaigns. These included the threat of a poster campaign to gain concessions from car companies regarding catalytic converters. They also lobbied shoe companies concerning the use of kangaroo hide in the manufacture of sports shoes.

The 'Shock for Shell' mini-case, above, illustrates the way in which international consumer action can be stimulated by the well-orchestrated campaign of an environmental pressure group.

In the concluding chapter of this book we discuss the attractions of single-issue protests for young people and its impact, in the United Kingdom, on their 'disconnectedness' from the parliamentary political process. Individuals have increasingly campaigned against government road-building plans, such as that for an extension of the M3 at Twyford Down in Hampshire, England, which is now open. However, road protests in the United Kingdom are currently ongoing in respect of the A30 outside Exeter, the M66 outside Manchester and the Newbury bypass.

In the United Kingdom we have grown accustomed to violence attending road-building and live-animal export protests. However, an event in Nigeria shocked the world in November 1995. The military government of Nigeria executed Ken Saro-Wiwa and eight other environmental activists on, what was believed by many international governments to be, questionable evidence and an unfair trial. Saro-Wiwa had encouraged his fellow Ogoni people to protest about the effects upon their lands of 30 years of oil exploitation by Shell Oil. This provoked further consumer backlashes against Shell, similar to those experienced during the Brent Spar incident. Body Shop founder, Anita Roddick, promised to pressurize Shell's shareholders to reform the company and banned the use of Shell products by her staff at work. The Body Shop, like the Co-op Bank (see mini-case below), believe that 'good ethics' will pay in the long term (these two companies could be described as being good performers), and a number of American studies have tended to confirm this.

Transnational and multinational organizations are key players in respect of the trade-off between business growth and concern for the environment. These organizations have a large stake in economic development in less developed countries (LDCs). Just like the Ogoni people, many communities in such countries as India and Mexico have campaigned against the activities of Western companies. Often, it has been argued, these companies have exploited the less stringent environmental controls of many LDCs as those countries strive for economic development. Is this an example of organizations trying to shirk their environmental responsibilities?

There is some suggestion that consumer power is also starting to be influential in respect of products made using child labour. Adverse publicity has caused the Levi Strauss company to amend their sourcing arrangements and for retailers of rugs, like Ikea, to seek assurances about the circumstances of manufacture. Perhaps there is a shift to 'ethical consumption' as the next step from 'green consumption'.

As can be seen from the mini-case below, the Co-op Bank is an organization which is very clearly stating its ethical principles.

Co-op Bank

The Co-op Bank was established more than 120 years ago. For the year to January 1995 record pre-tax profits of £27.5 million were achieved, an increase of 55 per cent on the previous year.

Part of this recent success can be attributed to its public stance on a range of ethical issues. In 1992 the Co-op Bank published a 12-point ethical policy statement which included statements to the effect that it will not do business:

- with any regime or organization which oppresses the human spirit; takes away the rights of individuals or manufactures any instrument of torture;
- which involves the manufacture or sale of arms to countries with oppressive regimes;
- which speculates against the pound sterling;
- which enables drug trafficking or tax evasion to take place;
- with tobacco manufacturing firms;
- with firms which experiment on animals for cosmetics;
- which involves 'exploitative' factory farming or the production of animal fur; and
- which involves blood sports.

The policy statement also states that the bank will actively seek out business compatible with this ethical position and that it will encourage its existing customers to take a proactive environmental stance. Terry Thomas, managing director of the bank, said: 'We say to all concerned people: If you're our kind of people, we're your kind of bank.'

The Co-op Bank conducted a detailed survey of customer attitudes which revealed that 84.2 per cent of those asked said it was a good idea for the bank to have a clear ethical policy. The types of activity identified in the policy statement had struck some significant chords with their customers.

It was the bank's view, expressed in a press release of April 1995, that its advertising campaign, highlighting the strongly ethical stance which it had developed, had led to growth in both business and personal banking sectors. Its average deposit base increased by 19 per cent in the year to January 1995, with many charities and voluntary organizations contributing significantly to this increase by opening new accounts.

Source: Press releases supplied by the Co-op Bank and *Ethical Attitudes, How Upright is British Business?*, Co-op Bank.

To summarize, it is clear that individual consumers have limited influence either upon the environmental stance of organizations or upon government policy in this regard. However, there is increasing evidence to suggest that consumers can, when mobilized by environmental pressure groups, have considerable influence upon organizations, most particularly via the threat of a mass product boycott.

CONCLUSION

Since it is often difficult to confine ecological problems within individual countries it is becoming increasingly apparent that 'world solutions' need to be sought. There is also an increasing recognition that in order to address ecological problems it is no longer possible for environmental campaigners and businesses to snipe at each other from entrenched positions. Both sides are recognizing the importance of agreeing trade-offs between economic development, which is important in terms of providing people with the means to live, and environmental protection, which seeks to ensure that the natural environment is used sensibly. The essence of this 'trade-off' is encapsulated in the principle of 'sustainable development' – the notion that we need to protect the natural environment for the sake of the generations of people which will follow us on the earth.

SUMMARY OF MAIN POINTS

In this chapter we have identified some of the issues that are important to the well-being of the planet and models that enable us to compare the different stances of organizations with respect to ecological issues. The main points are:

- The earth is facing a number of serious environmental issues, including the greenhouse effect.
- The operation of the market is based upon the law of supply and demand.
- The concept of externalities describes the situation where an organization has not fully internalized its costs; most polluting emissions are, therefore, seen as negative externalities.
- Governments can use a range of actions to monitor and regulate the output of pollutants from economic activity, including taxes and charges; marketable permits; grants or subsidies; and regulation and anti-monopoly legislation.

- Progress at the global level in ecological regulation action is often slow since it operates via a series of International Summit meetings, such as that at Rio in 1992. However, since most serious ecological concerns tend not to be confined within geo-political boundaries, the ability to make progress at this global level is critical to the effective tackling of many ecological problems.
- The viewpoints which organizations can adopt in respect of ecological regulation range from non-compliance and compliance, through to some more proactive stances and culminate in the use of state-of-the-art processes by what have been called 'leading edge' organizations.
- The ecological viewpoint adopted by an organization is likely to be strongly influenced by the nature of its business environment and by its perceptions of the interest and power of stakeholders.
- The extent of individual consumer power in respect of ecological issues is clearly weak. However, there is an increase in single-issue action taken by environmental pressure groups which is capable of having a serious effect on how organizations view their stakeholders.

References

Ansoff, I. (1984) *Implementing Strategic Management*, Prentice Hall, Englewood Cliffs, New Jersey.

Argenti, J. (1980) *Practical Corporate Planning*, Allen & Unwin, London.

Azzone, G. and Bertele, U. (1994) 'Exploiting green strategies for competitive advantage', *Long Range Planning*, vol. 27, no. 6, pp. 69–81.

Boulton, L. (1995) 'Higher carbon tax heats up debate', *Financial Times*, 14 June, p. 20.

Brown, P. (1995) 'Global warming summit at risk', *The Guardian*, 25 March.

Cannon, T. (1994) *Corporate Responsibility, a Textbook on Business Ethics, Governance, Environment: Roles and Responsibilities*, Pitman, London.

Carter, F.W. and Turnock, D. (1993) *Environmental Problems in Eastern Europe*, Routledge, London.

Collins, J.C. and Porras, J.I. (1993) *Built to Last*, Century, London.

CEC (1994) *Background Report: The European Environment Agency*, ISEC/B6/94, 11 February, Commission of European Communities, London.

Croner Guide (1996) *Environmental Management*, Croner Publications.

EIU (1995) *European Trends, Key Issues and Developments for Business*, EIU Regional Monitor, 2nd quarter, pp. 8–54.

Elkington, J. and Hailes, J. (1988) *The Green Consumer Guide*, Victor Gollancz, London.

Gosling, P. (1996) 'Cleaner investor in Leicester', *Financial Times*, 10 March.

Hamel, G. and Prahalad, C.K. (1994) *Competing for the Future*, Harvard Business School Press, Boston.

Hart, G. and Owen, D. (1992) 'Current trends in the reporting of green issues in annual reports of United Kingdom companies', in D. Owen (ed.) *Green Accounting, Accountancy and the Challenges of the Nineties*, Chapman & Hall, London.

Kleiner, A. (1991) 'What does it mean to be green', *Harvard Business Review*, July–August.

Lascelles, D. (1995) 'Time to take charge of waste', *Financial Times*, 17 May, p. 6.

Lee, N. (1994) In M. Artis and N. Lee (eds) *The Economics of the European Union*, OUP, Oxford.

Lipsey, R.G. and Harbury, C. (1992) *First Principles of Economics*, Weidenfeld and Nicolson, London.

Loss Prevention Council (1992) *Pollutant Industries Report*, SHE 8.

Maddox, B. (1995) 'Green light turns amber', *Financial Times*, 21 June.

Murray, J.A. and Fahy, J. (1994) In N. Nugent and R. O'Donnell (eds) *The European Business Environment*, Macmillan, London.

Porter, M.E. (1990) 'The competitive advantage of nations', *Harvard Business Review*, March–April.

Radford, T. (1990) 'The greatest threat in the world', *Education Guardian*, 6 November.

Roome, N. (1992) 'Developing environmental management systems', *Business Strategy and the Environment*, Spring, part 1.

Shrivastava, P. (1994) *Strategic Management: Concepts and Practises*, South-Western, Cincinnati.

Shrivastava, P. (1995) 'Environmental technologies and competitive advantage', *Strategic Management Journal*, vol. 16, pp. 183–200.

Welford, R. and Gouldson, A. (1993) *Environmental Management & Business Strategy*, Pitman, London.

CHAPTER 7

THE POLITICAL AND LEGAL ENVIRONMENT

Alistair Sutton and Jamie Weatherston

 LEARNING OUTCOMES

On completion of this chapter you should be able to:

- identify political activity at global/regional, national and local levels;
- outline the roles of key European Union institutions and the implications of European Union developments for organizations;
- understand the framework in which both United Kingdom and European decisions on regional aid issues are made;
- outline the workings of the United Kingdom constitution, including the role of Parliament, Cabinet, the Civil Service and the Judiciary;
- outline the role of the media in the context of the political and legal environment and understand United Kingdom regulatory issues;
- outline the main sources of law and the court system in the United Kingdom;
- correctly use legal terminology applying to different ways of classifying law in England and Wales and Scotland.

7.1 Introduction

The main aim of this chapter is to examine political institutions and developments at a range of geo-political levels: global/regional, national and local. We distinguish between each level to ensure that readers are aware of the bodies which exist and appreciate the basic role of these bodies within a specific context. Readers should, however, be aware that the processes involved in making any decisions, particularly ones at global/regional levels, are very complex and sometimes the rational institutional approach we adopt as a framework for this chapter may not fully reflect the extent of 'horse-trading' involved in policy and decision making.

The regional level of decision making, in particular, has a significant impact on organizations. The European Union is so important to business activity throughout the world that we will explore its background, its institutions, the processes and mechanisms by which policies and decisions are made and examine its impact on business. One aspect of this is the support offered by the European Union and national governments to industry and regions.

Readers should be aware that although the title of the chapter includes the word 'legal', this element is not treated as extensively as the political area. The discussion of specific legal considerations relating to the legal system of England and Wales concentrates upon outlining the sources of law, the nature of the court system and the ways in which law may be classified. This will help the reader develop the vocabulary necessary to understand the areas of legal debate within the book as a whole and to appreciate the impact which legislation may have upon business organizations. It is not the intention of the chapter to provide a comprehensive coverage of all the law which may affect organizations. Readers requiring details of laws which apply to business may refer to Owens (1995), or, if they have access to a law library, to the original statutes or law reports. An Internet site concentrating on United Kingdom law is available at http://www.gold.net/ifl/ which offers the reader an extensive range of up-to-date sources ranging from Commercial Law, Employment Law, Environment Law and European Law to Criminal Law & Practice and Legal History. Readers should be aware that the law of Scotland is somewhat different to that which applies in England and Wales, particularly in respect of criminal law, the law of property and constitutional and administrative law. Readers requiring more details of Scottish law are advised to consult the following Internet site: http://www.link.org/SCOT2.HTM.

We consider it appropriate to combine both the legal and political elements in one chapter because they interlink in our discussion of issues connected with democratic institutions. This discussion covers a range of areas such as bills of rights, the concept of separation of powers, the role of the judiciary, the issue of parliamentary lobbying and the standards of conduct expected of members of Parliament (MPs). These areas require a fusion of the legal and political elements to provide a rounded discussion.

7.2 The impact of political decisions at different geo-political scales

Decisions which affect business organizations are made at all geo-political levels. The oil shocks of the 1970s brought about by the supra-national OPEC cartel and the entry of the United Kingdom into the European Community in 1973, for example, both had profound consequences for many organizations.

Competition policy is determined by the European Commission and national governments (refer to Chapter 2) but is also monitored by local authorities through, for example, trading standards departments. Political decisions, such as those on social policy, the control of pollution and support for technology, each of which is examined in other chapters of the book, all have an impact on business activities.

The business environment is liable to change as a result of a radical political shock, a gradual shift, or indeed, a combination of the two. The BSE (bovine spongiform encephalopathy) scare which dominated UK news in March/April 1996 illustrates such a combination. The case which came to a head in March 1996 had been 'simmering' since 1987. The impact on the beef livestock and meat processing industry was, initially, fairly limited. In 1989 the government introduced a number of measures to limit the amount of bovine offal entering the food chain. The impact on farmers, at this stage, was minimal; they were still able to sell their cattle. Slaughter-houses could easily recover the extra cost of separating offal and processors were virtually unaffected. However, in March 1996 scientific evidence was published which suggested a probable link between BSE and the human form of the disease, Creutzfeldt-Jakob Disease (CJD). A new strain of this disease had recently been thought to be the cause of death of two teenagers and four dairy farmers. This brought a swift response from the United Kingdom's European Union partners, who, contrary to the provisions of the Treaty of Rome (1957), unilaterally banned the import of British beef. This decision was soon ratified by the agriculture ministers, with the exception of the United Kingdom. The impact on the industry was immediate and extensive, with plant closures and job losses.

Organizations will perceive political change differently; some may feel threatened, others may see the changes as offering business opportunities. While many cattle farmers felt very threatened by the developments in relation to BSE, discussed above, we might find that the effect of the scare upon producers of vegetarian foods was somewhat different. It is evident that decisions and actions made at the higher geo-political scales can have an impact on organizations, both large and small. This is the context of our analysis of the political environment. The analysis will concentrate on three geo-political scales: global, national and local. This is followed by discussion of one of the most significant regional scales, that is, the European Union.

Global scale

In this section readers will recognize that the changing international scene, with its powerful interests, has an enormous impact on the operating activities of many organizations. However, readers should not view the relationship between politics and business organizations as a 'one-way street'. Business is not that weak that it always has to pander to its political masters. Many multinational companies, for example, have considerable ability to influence the political decision-making processes. The possibility of inward investment, by companies, is a great attraction to all governments. The creation of new jobs in Europe, and particularly the United Kingdom, by Japanese, Taiwanese and Korean multinationals has led governments to provide significant grants in many cases and to reduce obstacles to such investments, for example by relaxing planning regulations.

Political changes are also likely to create opportunities or present threats to organizations. In this section we consider a number of such changes, and look, in general terms, at their impact upon business.

The collapse of communist systems in the former Soviet Union, and throughout the world, and the establishment of fledgling market economies is bringing about the demise of some organizations as it offers opportunities to others. The whole European axis seems to be undergoing an eastward shift; this will be even more evident when other former communist countries, such as Poland, the Czech Republic and Slovakia, become members of the European Union. Such countries are increasingly recognized as being 'central European'. Perhaps this factor, allied with the isolationist stance of the present UK government, may have the effect of marginalizing the United Kingdom, and make it more difficult for UK businesses to participate fully in the Single European Market (SEM). The United Kingdom government's declared distrust of European integration is well known. Its propensity to opt out of significant parts of European legislation, such as the Social Charter, and its overtly nationalistic stance may make the situation more difficult for UK companies. The government insists, however, that it is helping industry by taking a tough European stance.

The so-called 'peace dividend' has had an adverse impact on organizations in many fields, not least defence contractors. Weapons manufacturers, military-vehicle suppliers and ship builders have all lost orders, or closed down, because of the decline in demand from the armed forces. Swan Hunter, ship builders on Tyneside, were unable to secure enough orders from the civilian market to replace their traditional Royal Navy orders, and were forced to close, temporarily, in 1994. This was despite the fact that they had actively sought new markets, particularly in the Far East. Other organizations have grabbed opportunities to invest heavily in the former communist states. Volkswagen have secured ownership of Skoda of the Czech Republic, extending their ability to access a growing market. East Germany has presented enormous opportunities to business and has succeeded in attracting substantial funds as efforts to rebuild its crumbling infrastructure continue.

The opening of communist China too, has had a two-fold effect. Firstly, foreign companies have been allowed access to the mainland, particularly in the special economic zones. The reduced labour costs enjoyed by the incomers, mostly multinational corporations (MNCs), have enabled them to become more competitive on a world scale. In the recession of the early and mid-1980s, which largely affected the manufacturing sector, a substantial number of job losses in the United Kingdom were a result of MNCs transferring capacity to cheaper newly industrialized countries (NICs) (see the case study on the South-East Asian 'tigers', p. 399). Secondly, competitors of China and the NICs have found themselves unable to compete with the cost advantages enjoyed by these 'transplants'.

This has led to redundancies or even closure of factories. The British shoe industry, which is still relatively labour-dependent, has suffered because of cheaper Chinese competition. Even Japanese companies have had to face the reality of this harsh new climate as they struggle to compete with the 'tigers' (South Korea, Taiwan, Hong Kong and Singapore) and the 'new tigers' (China, Indonesia, Malaysia and Thailand). Around the world traditional 'job for life' employment philosophies are gradually being replaced by a range of more flexible approaches (discussed in Chapter 9) which are more suited to a changing world scene.

Organizations are increasingly operating in a diverse range of countries. A number of factors are relevant when making decisions about the countries in which to locate any business activity. Clearly, certain countries, particularly developing ones, may be attractive because they are sources of important natural resources and lower labour costs. It is, however, also important to assess the stability of the political, financial, social and cultural systems when evaluating a potential base in a given country. Organizations will place high priorities on peace and political stability. Inward investment into Northern Ireland in the first year since the 1994 ceasefire increased substantially. Derry benefited from the establishment of American computer company, Stream International. A Ecu 300 million initiative to support peace was approved in July 1995 to promote social inclusion and industrial regeneration (CEC, 1995a). It is not only Northern Ireland that benefited from the peace dividend. Growth in the Republic of Ireland is forecast at 7 per cent for 1995/96 (Ham, 1995), though this forecast may not be achieved due to the precarious nature of the peace process. In other instances political decisions have forced companies to miss potential investment opportunities. American companies were left behind in the early rush to invest in Vietnam because relations between the two governments had remained frozen since the end of the Vietnam War. It was only much later, in 1994, that American companies were given the green light to enter a potentially fast-growing market.

The international agenda is increasingly being set by international protocols. For example, a joint venture by Glaxo and ICI, in response to the Montreal Protocol (see Chapter 6), aims to establish a strong world position in the market for chlorofluorocarbon replacements (see Chapter 4).

If companies export, or have production facilities, outside their home base, action by foreign governments may present both opportunities and threats. These include the following possibilities:

- governments may nationalize an organization and may freeze assets or curtail overseas sales contracts;
- exchange controls may be imposed which can reduce the amount of money organizations can draw out of profit-making overseas subsidiaries;
- the privatization of former nationalized industries presents opportunities for investment and trade; the willingness of some American utilities to buy out regional electricity companies in the United Kingdom must suggest a reasonable profit potential to the acquirer (see Chapter 2); and

- import barriers may be raised or lowered, making an organization's product or service more or less competitive in a foreign market.

Import barriers may be:

- quotas which limit the number of Japanese cars entering the European Union;
- tariffs paid to the government; and,
- technical requirements that a product must be of a particular standard, for example, or it must not contain certain substances. (Vehicle exhaust emission standards in the United States is such a case. These standards have placed an added cost on manufacturers exporting to the American market.)

Even non-commercial organizations are increasingly having to face up to economic issues. It is interesting, in the light of this, to examine the work of the United Nations (see mini-case below).

The United Nations

The United Nations (UN) was established in June 1945, following the Second World War. The stated aims of the 50 members included putting an end to 'the scourge of war' and reaffirming the rights of both individuals and nations.

The UN has two main bodies: a General Assembly, which is essentially a 'talk-shop' for all nations, and the Security Council. All key decisions are taken by the Security Council which has only five permanent members at present (the United States, China, Russia, France and the United Kingdom) each with a veto on all decisions. It has been argued that the representativeness of the Security Council might be improved by the addition of other countries, such as Japan, Germany, India, Brazil and even Nigeria.

The work of the UN has tended to be of two types. Firstly, it has a *peace-keeping* role; it claims to have negotiated numerous peace settlements that have ended regional conflicts in countries such as Cyprus, El Salvador and Cambodia as well as having played significant roles in Afghanistan in 1989 and in the Iran–Iraq war of 1990. Secondly, the UN has a *humanitarian* role, which includes emergency relief, helping refugees and monitoring elections.

Since the inception of the UN the 'scourge of war' has not disappeared, although it can be said that the threat of world war has diminished with the end of the Cold War. There is, however, an increasing number of localized conflicts around the world. Indeed, the number of UN peace-keeping missions more than doubled between 1990 and 1995. Forty per cent of UN income goes on peace-keeping and emergency aid.

Recent events in Rwanda, Bosnia and Somalia have damaged the reputation of the United Nations. In Rwanda UN peace-keepers were criticized for standing by while tens of thousands of people were killed by the government and its supporters. The need for the UN to act through its member states can make it difficult to mobilize enough troops sufficiently quickly in such emergencies.

The UN's humanitarian work, carried out by the World Health Organization (WHO), UNICEF, the Food and Agricultural Organization and others, has often been judged valuable. However, such organizations have also been accused of inefficiency.

The conflict in Bosnia in 1995 focused much world attention on the role of the UN. The UN-sanctioned NATO (North Atlantic Treaty Organization) air-strikes on the Bosnian Serbs in August and September 1995 marked a significant move, in the UN's peace-keeping role, from its traditional 'policing by consent' approach to a more aggressive role which involves the taking of sides ('peace enforcement').

It has always been difficult for the UN to carry out its mandate. In June 1995, however, it was reported that the UN was so short of money that it would have to stop most of its reimbursements to member states in respect of peace-keeping activity. This was at a critical time as a rapid-reaction force made up of British, French and Dutch troops was about to be sent to Bosnia to reinforce its peace-keeping mission there. In October the UN was owed £2.2 bn ($3.3 bn @ £1=$1.5) by the member states, including £0.93 bn ($1.4 bn) by the United States of America. In America the Republican-dominated Congress stressed the need for the UN to reduce bureaucracy, become more efficient and reassess the extent of its peace-keeping role.

Many think the UN should concentrate on peace-keeping and not get involved in peace-enforcement. The current secretary general of the UN, Dr Boutros Boutros-Ghali, has suggested an agenda based on a fusion of the peace-keeping and humanitarian roles. The financial crisis currently afflicting the UN is sure to prompt a reassessment of the organization's aims in the light of the range of activities which member states are prepared to fund!

At this global scale a large range of interactions takes place, involving such groupings as supranational bodies, governments, multinational companies and international pressure groups. The activities of these groups will often result in new law or policy being formulated, which will have implications for business organizations. Some of the political pressures which manifest themselves at the national and local scale will have their origins at this global scale.

National scale

Commentators, for example Ohmae (1995), claim that given the increasing globalization of markets, nation states are of diminishing importance. He argues that, 'Nation states are no longer meaningful units in which to think about economic activity. In a borderless world they consign things to the wrong level of aggregation.' Ohmae (1995) lists a number of what he calls 'natural economic zones', which do not recognize geographical or political boundaries. These include northern Italy, Hong Kong and southern China, and Singapore and its neighbouring Indonesian islands.

Ohmae (1995) also draws attention to the fact that some previously important nations, for example the Soviet Union and Czechoslovakia, no longer exist. They have been broken apart to form the Commonwealth of Independent States (CIS) and the Czech and Slovak Republics respectively. In other countries, such as Germany and Spain, powers are to be transferred from the centre to local levels. This reduces the influence of national government. Such pressures also exist in the United Kingdom, with proposals for the devolution of power to elected representative bodies in Scotland and Wales and, possibly, Northern Ireland.

However, in most cases nation states possess considerable autonomy and the capacity to 'do things differently'. For example, the extent of government intervention in the economy varies enormously between countries. In Hong Kong public spending is as little as 16 per cent of gross domestic product whereas the comparable figure is 33 per cent in America, 42 per cent in the United Kingdom and 68 per cent in Sweden (refer to Chapter 8). Even when a government is trying to maintain a 'hands off approach' its actions can have an impact on an industrial sector. For example, the 1995 UK budget for the 1996/97 tax year reduced duty on spirits by 27p a bottle and froze duty on beer and wine. In December 1995 the Minister of Health announced a rise in the government's recommended healthy consumption limit for alcoholic drinks from 21 to 28 units per week for men and from 14 to 21 for women. Both announcements were a boost to the drinks industry.

The political systems adopted by each country also vary as a result of independent evolution over hundreds of years. It is important to recognize that the local political system will have an important impact on the operation of business in a given nation state.

Not all countries have democratic systems; a number of military governments exist, such as in Iraq and Nigeria. However, there are still considerable differences between systems which share democratic governments. The 'proportional representation' system in Italy has, for example, created a much more volatile environment for business than the 'first past the post' system in the United Kingdom. Italy has had a succession of unstable coalition governments for most of the post-1945 period. In the United Kingdom, 651 Members of Parliament (MPs) are elected to serve in the House of Commons. The United Kingdom's voting system invariably brings to power a party with a majority in the House of Commons. This majority will usually allow it to govern for a full five-year term.

Other European countries offer different approaches. Germany uses a system of proportional representation. A party must poll 5 per cent of the vote to gain representation in the federal and state parliaments. France, in contrast, has a directly elected President and polling takes place every seven years. The President appoints a Prime Minister whose task is to oversee day-to-day government. Elections for the National Assembly are every five years.

The impact of government: the United Kingdom case

A brief analysis of the United Kingdom can be used to illustrate the impact which the party of government has on business organizations; the influence of this on the public sector is explored in Chapter 8. In the United Kingdom the leader of the largest party is, normally, appointed as Prime Minister. A Conservative party Prime Minister chooses MPs to serve in the Cabinet as heads of the various ministries, whereas in the Labour party MPs are elected to the Cabinet. The Cabinet makes policy which is debated in the House of Commons and the House of Lords. Changes in policy often require legislation and much of the work of both Houses is in reviewing and debating the contents of new Bills. Given that the members of the House of Lords are not elected their ability to delay the passage of legislation is limited by the Parliament Acts. Policy is implemented administratively by civil servants and quangos. Bills become Acts of Parliament or statutes when given the Royal Assent. Every year a large number of new Acts are added to the statute books.

Government policy in respect of media regulation, for example, is to be seen in the Broadcasting Bill, published in December 1995. This bill followed a detailed set of proposals published in May 1995. The ownership of the two main forms of media (national newspapers and television channels) poses questions to government concerning the need to preserve a diversity of opinion in the media. This bill also provides an interesting insight into the effect that legislation can have on particular organizations.

In May 1995, Rupert Murdoch, chief executive of the News Corporation, which owns The *Sun*, *The Times* and the *News of the World* (37 per cent of the newspaper market), spoke out strongly against the government's original proposals which included restricting companies to 10 per cent of total *national media*. However, Mr Murdoch was much happier following publication of the Bill, since the overall ownership limit had been amended to 15 per cent of the total *television audience*, despite the fact that News International will be prevented from controlling any ITV companies since it possesses more than 20 per cent of total *national newspaper circulation*.

In April 1996 the Labour party proposed amendments to the Bill. These would increase the proportion of national newspaper sales, above which a company is barred from controlling terrestrial television companies, to 25 per cent. The impact of such a move would certainly enable the other main player in the newspaper market, the Mirror Group, to develop into the area of terrestrial television (Harding, 1996). This issue of policy is an unusual scenario, since it features the Conservative party arguing for more regulation and the Labour party arguing for less.

In 1979 the election of a Conservative government, with a good working majority under the premiership of Margaret Thatcher, proved to be a significant political milestone. Traditional economic thinking, based on the Keynesian approach to controlling the economy, was replaced by a 'monetarist' philosophy. The Keynesian approach rests on the assumption that the economy is inherently unstable and in need of active government intervention, largely through fiscal policy, to control demand in the economy. It is believed that the level of activity in the economy could be controlled, business cycles smoothed out, eliminating peaks and troughs, and unemployment limited. However, the orthodox Keynesian model was unable to deliver a strong economy. The 1960s and 1970s saw increasingly high levels of unemployment and inflation which could not be explained by Keynesian theory or solved using traditional demand management policies. Keynesian theory was open to criticism, especially by the monetarists. The monetarist approach, in contrast, regards the economy as inherently stable and advises that fiscal policy has no role in regulating the economy and that, in fact, fiscal policy can actually exacerbate business downswings. Monetarists argue that firm control of money supply will not affect the business cycle and that policy should be targeted at the supply side of the economy. The mini-case below takes a closer look at supply-side economic measures.

Supply-side measures

The goal of supply-side policy is to remove barriers which prevent or deter organizations and individuals from adapting quickly to changing demand and changes in production and, therefore, to increase efficiency and promote economic growth and employment. The Conservative governments, from 1979, have introduced a number of measures aimed at improving the supply side and giving organizations flexibility. These are discussed below.

Taxation

Prime Minister Thatcher suggested that 'if people find too big a chunk of their pay taken away in tax they won't work so hard'. Measures have been introduced to ensure that people were better off in work: direct taxes such as income tax have been reduced to be replaced by indirect taxes such as VAT; thresholds above which people start paying tax have been raised and unemployment benefit is now taxed. Companies, particularly small- and medium-sized enterprises, have also benefited from reductions in, for example, corporation tax.

The labour market

The government have introduced a number of training schemes designed to promote work skills, e.g. the Youth Training Scheme. Whether these schemes have been successful is open to debate. Certainly the United Kingdom is still some way behind competitor nations, for example Germany, in the provision of quality training. Other measures have attempted to safeguard the interests of individuals in the workplace and restrict trade unions (see Chapter 5). These measures aim to create a more flexible labour market and reduce unemployment.

Deregulation

Deregulation is the process of dismantling regulations governing the activities of business organizations. Deregulation has opened many other markets to greater competition and aims to make consumers better off by increasing competition. For example, the telecommunications sector was opened up so that Mercury communications could use BT's cable infrastructure to carry calls. Other sectors that were deregulated include road haulage, national buses and the capital market (see Chapter 8).

The capital market and financial sector

This is the market to which companies and the government turn when they need medium- and long-term funds. A whole range of controls have been abolished in the capital market. Foreign exchange controls were abolished in 1979; hire purchase controls in 1982; deregulation, the 'Big Bang', increased competition in the stock market in 1986, especially from foreign securities houses; the Financial Services Act 1986 and the Building Societies Act 1986 allowed non-banking financial institutions to provide services previously closed to them. These changes are seen as a way of encouraging competition and, therefore, improving the competitiveness of UK businesses.

Privatization

Privatization usually implies the transfer of assets from the public to private sector. The aims of privatization are: to introduce competition into previously monopoly-controlled public sectors and increase efficiency; to increase the extent of share ownership and to reduce government borrowing by raising revenue (see Chapter 8).

While we may support or oppose political decisions, depending on our political leaning, some important changes affecting managers and consumers have been made in the years since 1979. These will have a lasting effect on business. The change of emphasis and thinking in the 'corridors of power' has had some influence on the values and assumptions held by managers. In turn, this has affected the way managers consider customers, employees and other groups with an interest in their organization (the stakeholders). In essence, the role of government intervention in the economy has been reduced and the importance of self-reliance emphasized. This important theme is further developed in the two remaining chapters.

Local scale

In the United Kingdom, as in many other countries, local authorities are run by elected councillors whose powers are laid down by Parliament. They provide services and have regulatory responsibilities. Local government provision in the United Kingdom has traditionally been organized into a series of tiers involving county and district councils. A Local Government Commission was set up in 1992 to investigate the structure of local government. Since then it has created 38 new 'unitary' (single level) authorities, by merging former county and borough councils. In December 1995 the Commission recommended unitary status for a further group of 8: Blackburn, Blackpool, Halton, Warrington, Peterborough, the

Wrekin, Thurrock and a new Medway Towns authority, with a view to implementation in April 1997. As a result of the work of this Commission it seems to be the government's view that metropolitan areas, and some large towns, are best served by unitary authorities, with the multi-tiered system applying beyond the boundaries of the metropolitan areas. Such changes may simplify the dealings of many organizations with local government, as there will only be one body with which to deal in a unitary authority. In the long term, efficiency gains may result in a lower business rate.

Some disquiet has been raised regarding the trend towards centralization by the government of the United Kingdom and the use of non-elected bodies to administer policy, for example quangos. It is argued that excessive centralization has resulted in many local initiatives being stifled. Some feel that the fact that quangos now do much of the work previously carried out by local councils has raised a serious question about democratic accountability. Members of quangos do not need to seek election, or re-election, as local councillors do. It is paradoxical that many organizations, for example grant-maintained schools, NHS trusts and Civil Service agencies, are managed at the lowest local level but funded and controlled at the highest, that is, by central government (in these cases by the Department for Education and Employment, the Department of Health and the Treasury).

If we accept that the political system in the United Kingdom has become increasingly centralized then it should not surprise us that many consider the system has little to offer them. In Chapter 9 we examine the 'disconnectedness' of many young people in the United Kingdom from the established political system.

We can illustrate the effect of European, national and local political decisions by reference to a particular sector (see the mini-case below). It is evident that legislation at each geo-political level has an effect on the housing market.

The housing market

Many regulations that govern the way houses are bought and sold have changed substantially. The change to the metric system, to come into line with other European nations, has meant that all records have had to be altered to meet the new regulations, at a considerable expense to companies.

Estate agents have to be careful how a property is described: no personal opinions are allowed, only facts. The owner's signature must be obtained to verify the details; there is no room for the once infamous estate agents' jargon! Due care must be taken when room dimensions are taken and stated, instruments must be checked weekly. Agents have been found liable in many cases. In one case an agent had to pay to extend a swimming pool by 6 feet because of an inaccurate measurement stated in their sales literature. Legislation also requires no more than one sale board per house and specifies a maximum size for the board.

Since January 1995 all organizations have had to disclose the commission they receive and the running costs of life policies that they sell. The Life Assurance and Unit Trust Regulatory Organization (LAUTRO) also requires regular updating and training for all staff selling financial products. Because of the expense involved in carrying out this activity many estate agents and other institutions, e.g. the Cheltenham and Gloucester Building Society, have stopped offering the service.

Advertisements are checked by the Trading Standards Office for accuracy and to ensure that prices do not differ from those displayed in office windows.

In this section we have noted the impact of decision making at three different geo-political scales on business: the supranational level, by central government and by a more locally accountable means. In moving on to look at the European Union, we will examine a major area in this debate.

QUESTIONS

1. Outline key political developments which are likely to have implications for UK organizations. What are some of the specific implications for UK organizations?

2. In the light of disquiet about the position of the United Nations has any international consensus emerged, since 1996, regarding its role? What are the outstanding differences of opinion?

3. What trends are discernible in respect of the tension between nation states and demands that government should be more locally responsive?

4. Using the housing market mini-case identify the geo-political level that gave rise to each piece of legislation that affected that market.

5. Debate the advantages and drawbacks of various electoral systems such as 'first past the post' and 'proportional representation'.

7.3 The European Union

Introduction

The European Coal and Steel Community (ECSC) was established by the Treaty of Paris in 1951 between Belgium, the Federal Republic of Germany (West Germany) France, Italy, Luxembourg and the Netherlands. Its aim was to establish a unified market which could prosper from reduced barriers to trade. In 1957 the Treaty of Rome, signed by the six countries, created the European

Economic Community (EEC) and the European Atomic Energy Community (Euratom). The Treaty extended economic ties by creating a customs union and common market. These three communities came together to establish the European Community (EC) in 1965. The first enlargement was in 1973 when Denmark, Ireland and the United Kingdom became members. Greece joined in 1981, followed in 1986 by Portugal and Spain.

The signing of the agreement on the European Economic Area in May 1992 created the world's biggest free trade area. Austria, Finland, Norway, Iceland and Sweden joined the European Community 12 and established an integrated economic entity with a 372 million population and enormous opportunities for trade and commerce. In 1995 Austria, Finland and Sweden became full members of the European Union.

The most recent expansion of the European Union should bring substantial benefits. The three new members, Austria, Sweden and Finland, have a higher GDP per person than the European Union average and low inflation rates (Eurostat, 1994). As a result, the budget will rise as Austria and Sweden become net contributors. This should assist the poorer regions. (For other effects of enlargement see Chapter 3.)

The Community has evolved largely through amendments to the original treaties, notably via the Single European Act (SEA) 1987 and the Treaty of European Union (TEU) 1992, more commonly known as the Maastricht Treaty.

The SEA changed decision-making procedures within the Community. Prior to its adoption decisions had to be agreed by a unanimous vote; this condition was replaced by the ability to adopt decisions subject to a qualified majority, clearing the way for speedier decision making within the Community.

The SEA also required that the Single European Market (SEM) should be in place by the end of 1992. Its objectives were to improve the environment for business by providing for the free movement of labour, capital, goods and services within the Community and facilitate closer cooperation between countries on a range of other matters. It was anticipated that the benefits would include increased growth, higher employment, lower prices and wider choice for consumers.

The adoption of the SEM represented a vital supply-side initiative, as pioneered internally within the United Kingdom, which enhanced the ability of European business to compete in world markets. Action to reduce the non-tariff barriers that governments introduced partly to protect home industries, was an important supply-side strategy of the SEA. The most important non-tariff barriers are identified in Table 7.1.

Following the creation of the SEM it was envisaged that businesses would have unrestricted access to the European market and face lower costs and economies of scale. The UK industries that were thought likely to gain from the SEM are indicated in Table 7.2. However, a more open market also brings with it increased competition.

When the TEU came into force on 1 November 1993 the European Union came into being. The European Union comprises the European Community, a

TABLE 7.1   The most important barriers to trade
Range of ranks: 1 (most important) to 8 (least important)

Barriers	West Germany	France	Italy	UK	EU-12
National standards and regulations	1	1	4	1	2
Government procurement	8	7/8	2	4	8
Administrative	2	2	1	2	1
Physical frontier delays and costs	4	4	3	3	3
Differences in VAI	5/6	3	7	8	6/7
Regulations on freight transport	5/6	5	8	5	6/7
Restrictions in capital market	7	7/8	5	7	5
Community law	3	6	6	6	4

Source: Adapted from Paolo Cechini, *The European Challenge*, Wildwood House, 1988.

Common Foreign and Security Policy, and a common approach to Justice and Home Affairs: the so-called three-pillar structure (Thomson, 1995).

The TEU was the focus for much internal disagreement in both the Conservative and Labour parties in the United Kingdom, and debate in Denmark and France where it was only ratified following referenda.

Perhaps the most contentious issue in the TEU, as far as the UK government was concerned, was the 'Social Charter'. The government felt that the costs to business would result in substantial job losses. The idea of applying regulations to the labour market is totally contrary to the supply-side approach that the government has adopted since 1979 (see earlier). The 'Social Charter' includes minimum requirements on:

TABLE 7.2   Impact of 1992 on UK industrial sectors

Probable gainers	Possible gainers
• Some electrical engineering sectors • Pharmaceuticals • Food and drink • Precision and medical equipment • Insurance • Airlines	• Banking • Office and data processing equipment • Aerospace • Road transportation • Telecommunications services

Source: *Lloyds Bank Economic Bulletin*, No. 121, 1989.

- health and safety;
- consultation between management and employees;
- working conditions; and
- equality between men and women regarding job opportunities and treatment at work.

The government said that the maximum 48-hour working week (excluding overtime) in the 'Social Charter' would reduce the competitiveness of the UK in the global marketplace. Nine of the 15 member countries already had such a maximum (or a figure below it); only the United Kingdom, Denmark and the Irish Republic set no limit on the working week.

By opting out of this part of the Treaty the government hoped that the low-cost environment it created within the Community would prove attractive to inward investment. It is evident, however, that a number of multinational companies that operate throughout Europe have adopted the requirements of the 'Social Charter' for their UK plants.

The 'Social Charter' was only included as a protocol annexed to the Treaty, as a result of the opposition by the UK government. The Treaty was ratified by the UK Parliament in 1993, though the United Kingdom (and Denmark) secured an opt-out clause on significant parts of the Treaty such as the section on economic and monetary union.

The European Union has created a number of key supranational bodies. The four most important such bodies are:

- the European Commission;
- the Council of Ministers (the Council of European Union);
- the European Court of Justice; and
- the European Parliament.

Other bodies may have a lower profile, but play an important role in economic life. These are examined in Table 7.3 and include:

- the European Investment Bank;
- the Economic and Social Committee;
- the Committee of the Regions;
- the European Environment Agency;
- the European Monetary Institute;
- the Court of Auditors.

While we will take the opportunity to examine each of these briefly, readers should be aware that many more such bodies, each with a specific role, do exist, for example the European Training Foundation and the Agency for Health and Safety at Work. Information about all these is available from the Commission of the European Communities.

TABLE 7.3   European Union institutions

The European Investment Bank
Based in Luxembourg, the EIB is a non-profit-making, independent institution established by the Treaty of Rome. It obtains finance from member states and raises funds on international money markets to provide long-term loans and guarantees for priority investment projects, particularly in the less-developed regions.

The Economic and Social Committee (ECOSOC)
Made up of representatives of various interests, including trade unions, employers and consumer associations. It is consulted on legislation and can draft opinions on matters of concern, though its influence is limited.

The Committee of the Regions
Created by the TEU, its role, to some extent, overlaps that of the ECOSOC. It is a consultative institution which represents local and regional authorities. It is consulted by the Council or Commission on issues affecting the regions.

The European Environment Agency
Established in 1990 to achieve the aims of environmental protection and improvement. The agency publishes a report on the state of the environment every three years. Certain areas of work are given priority, such as air quality, water quality, waste management, land use and natural resources (CEC, 1994(a) and (b)). The work of the Agency is discussed in more detail in Chapter 6.

The European Monetary Institute (EMI)
Established in 1994 following the TEU. Its role is to help establish the conditions necessary for EMU. The main objectives are the coordination of monetary policy, development of the Euro and preparation for the European System of Central Banks (CEC, 1994b). The EMI will eventually be replaced by the European Central Bank.

The Court of Auditors
Established in 1975. It was introduced to improve efficiency of resource-use and identify corruption. It monitors the EU budget, examines accounts and oversees budgets. It produces an annual report.

Source: Commission of the European Communities (1994) *The Institutions of the Community*, Background Report, ISEC/B7/94, London, CEC.

Source: CEC (1994b).

The European Commission

The Commission consists of 20 members (commissioners), appointed, by national governments, to a specific portfolio for a period of five years (renewable). The Brussels-based Commission is the civil service of the European Union. The main role of the Commission is to make proposals about future policy in consultation with the Council of Ministers (for an example refer to Chapter 2 on competition policy). Other functions include:

- acting as guardian of the treaties;
- mediating between governments to secure agreement on legislation;
- managing the technical details and day-to-day policing of agreed policy, for example the Common Fisheries Policy, and ensuring compliance by governments, companies and individuals;

- representing the European Union in negotiations, for instance within the World Trade Organization (WTO), formerly GATT, and defending collective interests.

The Commission is divided into 23 Directorates General, through which it issues directives to member nations on many matters. National legislation must be enacted to turn these directives into national law. The Commission ensures compliance by member states with the rules of the European Union. For example, the External Affairs Commissioner, Mr van den Broek, expressed worries in April 1995 that the balance of power in the 15-member European Union needed to be readdressed. He suggested that decisions about the common foreign and security policy (referred to above) had tended to be dominated by France, Germany and the United Kingdom at the expense of the smaller EU countries and the newcomers, Austria, Finland and Sweden (Barber, 1995). He made it clear that the large member states would have to pay the price through a dilution of the national veto, more qualified majority voting and an enhanced role for the European Parliament to assure democratic accountability.

The Commission also oversees the day-to-day running of the European Union and allocates funds for social and regional policy.

The Council of Ministers (the Council of the European Union)

The Council of Ministers was renamed the Council of the European Union following the TEU. This is the main decision-making body of the European Union; it makes law by adopting proposals from the Commission. It consists of ministers of member states. Each government appoints a representative to each of the councils. For example, the UK Minister of Agriculture, Fisheries and Food (MAFF) sits on the Council of Agriculture Ministers. This Council deals with agricultural matters, notably the Common Agricultural Policy (CAP) and the Common Fisheries Policy and, in 1995, the BSE problem (discussed above). Other ministries are also represented at the Council of Ministers. Much of the work of the Council is undertaken by the Committee of Permanent Representatives (COREPOR) which screens proposals before passing them on to the Council. The presidency of the Council is held by each member country in turn and lasts for six months. It is the role of the president to chair the meeting of the Council. The Council take some decisions by a unanimous vote. In many key areas, such as foreign policy, immigration, aspects of employment law, taxation, national education and policy, the United Kingdom still has an effective veto (CEC, 1994a).

However, more decisions are now being taken by qualified majority voting following the provisions laid down in the SEA and the TEU. This has significantly increased the speed of decision making in the Council.

The Council of Ministers should not be confused with the European Council which meets twice a year. This is a forum for the heads of government of member countries which is important in the strategic development of the European Union;

its proposals are passed on to the Council of Ministers for transposition into law. The Madrid meeting in December 1995, for example, affirmed that a single currency, the Euro, would be launched in 1999 and the Maastricht timetable for European Monetary Union (EMU) would be followed. The final decision on which countries are eligible to join will be made in the Spring of 1998.

The European Court of Justice

The European Court of Justice (ECJ), based in Luxembourg, is concerned with the application and interpretation of EU law. It follows directives and regulations and through its judgements ensures the compliance of member states. It interprets legislation and European treaties. The ECJ consists of 16 judges (one from each member state), one nominee and six advocates-general. Cases can be brought to the court by individuals, companies and governments as well as by the Commission. Member states are bound by the Court's rulings. It is likely that organizations and individuals will increasingly feel the effects of the judgments of the Court. A subsidiary court, the Court of First Instance, was established by the SEA to deal with certain cases, particularly those brought by companies. The mini-case below shows how the Court is influencing a multi-million pound business.

The Bosman case

The Bosman case, in September 1995, demonstrated the impact that the European Court of Justice (ECJ) can have. Jean-Marc Bosman is a Belgium soccer player who was prevented from moving from his club at the end of his contract. He sought to apply the concept of freedom of movement (as enshrined in the TEU) to himself and, as a result, to other soccer players. Under the Belgian transfer system players who are at the end of their contract can be sold by their clubs. If they do not accept a move they may have to accept more unfavourable terms of employment on their new contract. This was unacceptable to the Advocate-General. He found that a player could move at the end of a contract with no transfer fee to be paid. Subsequently, in December 1995, the full court ratified this opinion.

Article 48 of the Treaty of Rome 'prohibits a football club from demanding or receiving payment . . . when one of its players whose contract has expired is engaged by another club'. The case could have wide ramifications for clubs in the United Kingdom, though the transfer system is by no means as restrictive as in other parts of Europe. The small clubs may be unable to generate income from the sale of players as they have in the past because transfer fees will not be payable. Some clubs may have to go part-time and others may close. A substantial amount of the balance sheet value of big clubs is in players and the likely fall in transfer fees will affect this position. The case could present top players with the opportunity to negotiate higher salaries, as some money, previously used to pay transfer fees, could be diverted into their pockets.

It is not only football clubs which may be affected. Other sports, such as handball in Germany, basketball and ice hockey and more traditional businesses in the Community are likely to be affected by the result. At this stage the long-term impact of the Bosman case is unclear. However, it does provide a good illustration of how the European treaties can, through the courts, give rise to individual rights which can, in turn, have effects on business in the European Union.

The European Parliament

Since 1979, the European Parliament has been directly elected by member states on a five-year mandate. It is located in Strasbourg, where it meets for 12 week-long sessions each year, and Brussels where additional plenary sessions are held. Following the 1995 enlargement of the European Union the number of MEPs rose from 567 to 626, with 87 from the United Kingdom. The Parliament is a consultative institution whose powers have gradually been extended, principally by the SEA 1987 and the TEU 1992. It retains control over the EU budget and must ratify proposals made by the Commission and the Council of Ministers. It has the power to amend or reject legislation and dismiss the Commission.

Legislative procedures

The procedure for drafting legislation was put in place by the SEA 1987. The new procedure represents a democratization of the legislative procedure, as can be seen in Figure 7.1. Under the former system decisions were taken by the council with very little recourse to the European Parliament.

All the bodies of the European Union, particularly the four main ones outlined earlier in this chapter, have the power to influence the day-to-day activities of all European business organizations. It is in response to this that numerous lobby groups have been set up, principally to influence the Commission. Not only do the groups try to manoeuvre their interests to the top of the agenda and keep their own members informed, they also provide valuable information to the Commission. The business lobby can be divided into two main groups:

- national trade and business groups (the so-called Euro-groups); and
- large companies that often keep their own 'in house' lobbying unit.

Policy making, therefore, relies on a huge network of contacts and upon the effectiveness of each lobby group in getting its case heard. It is still the case that national interests are promoted through these groups. In some cases UK companies have yet to develop effective lobbying practices – perhaps to their detriment. As the European Parliament becomes more directly involved in the legislative process, it is likely that it too will become a target for the lobby groups.

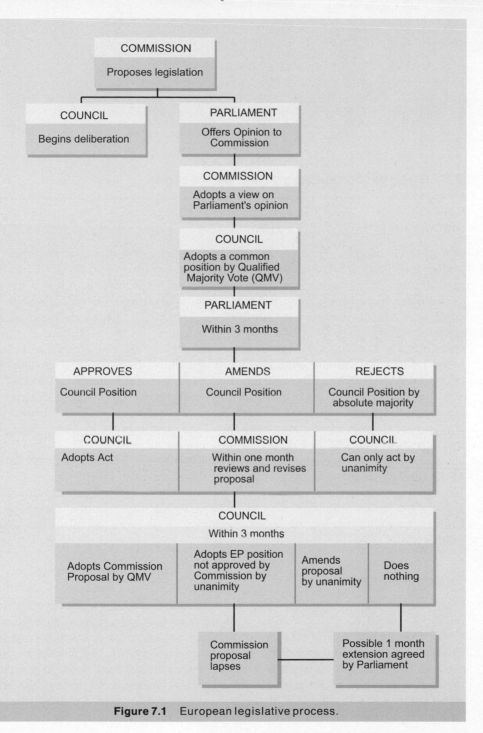

Figure 7.1   European legislative process.

7.4 Support for industry and the regions

Introduction

One of the main roles that a government has to play is that of a customer through public spending on infrastructure, such as roads, railways and hospitals. Public expenditure supports a significant amount of economic activity. Cuts in government expenditure are likely to have a significant adverse impact on employees and businesses that supply those sectors. The problems faced by the construction sector in the 1990s may be due, in part, to the downturn in capital investment by the United Kingdom government. However, not all companies have to be limited by national boundaries and, therefore, by individual government decisions. MNCs do not rely solely on their home base for business opportunities. When one government, such as that in the United Kingdom, makes a decision to cut expenditure it is important for such companies to look elsewhere for business. Key projects, such as the construction of the new airport in Hong Kong or infrastructure building in Europe, provide opportunities for MNCs from many countries to bid for business and gain valuable contracts. The international nature of the market has never been more evident. More recently, projects in the United Kingdom have been financed by the private sector, such as the Channel tunnel, the £28 billion water industry investment programme and the new Severn road bridge. It may be that private sector investment in projects will offset the loss of public works.

Regional policy

One way in which government can support industry is through selective regional policy. Regional policy is often used to support political rather than economic aims. Governments in many countries have intervened to correct regional imbalances and unemployment differentials by taking work to the workers, and have gained electoral support as a result. Industry support is made available through a number of schemes. Since 1979 UK regional-aid policy has been significantly revised. The aim of the policy is to reduce regional imbalances in employment opportunities and to encourage the development of indigenous potential within the Assisted Areas on a stable, long-term basis (HM Government, 1992). Gradually, the system has been made much more selective. Aid is apportioned on more of a 'need' basis, rather than automatically as it tended to be in the past. The thrust of the policy has moved away from manufacturing and towards the service sector. The free-market, enterprise culture fostered by successive administrations in the United Kingdom between 1979 and the present day, has also been applied to regional aid.

The new regional aid map, effective from August 1993, has a two-tier system of assisted areas in addition to Northern Ireland (see Figure 7.2) as under the previous scheme:

- development areas;
- intermediate areas; and
- Northern Ireland.

Areas are defined as being in need of aid if economic conditions, particularly employment, are below a notional national average. The 1993 configuration sees a shift of aid away from the north to the south of Britain. This was in response to the substantially higher levels of unemployment suffered by southern areas in the recession of the early 1990s. The two main types of grant available are Regional Enterprise Grants and Regional Selective Assistance.

Regional Enterprise Grants are discretionary and available, particularly, to help small- and medium-sized enterprises (SMEs) in the start-up phase and to facilitate their growth (refer to case study on SMEs, p. 406). Two types of assistance are available under this scheme, that is regional investment grants and regional innovation grants.

Regional Selective Assistance, also discretionary, is available to any organization in a designated area. The grants are made available to top up private sector investment in a project. Organizations must demonstrate that the project makes a contribution to the local and national economy.

The Business Link scheme is the latest government initiative aimed at providing assistance to industry. This scheme is targeted at the SME sector and has a 1995/96 pump-priming budget of £38.5 million. Business Link offers a wide range of services. A further £50 million is available in 1995/96 for services delivered through Business Links, including Personal Business Advisers, specialist Innovation and Technology, Design and Export Counsellors, and the Diagnostic and Consultancy Service.

The impact of government does not stop there. Further funding is available through:

- the Urban Programme, to support urban regeneration; and
- Enterprise Zones, which offer allowances and a simplified planning regime.

There is also a growing desire in the European Union to develop an integrated regional policy, through the Committee of the Regions, to overcome disparities between the rich and poor regions of the Union. This is more important

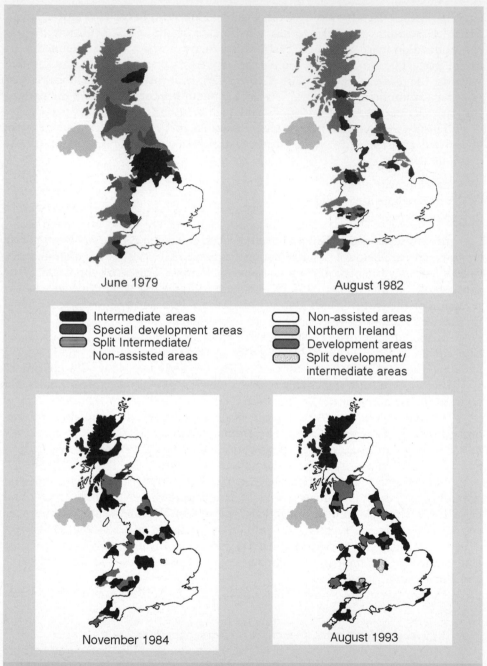

June 1979

August 1982

- Intermediate areas
- Special development areas
- Split Intermediate/
  Non-assisted areas
- Non-assisted areas
- Northern Ireland
- Development areas
- Split development/
  intermediate areas

November 1984

August 1993

Figure 7.2 The regional aid map of the United Kingdom. (*Source*: Martin, R. (1993) *Regional Studies*, **27/8**, pp. 797–805. Reproduced with permission: Carfax Publishing Company, Abingdon, Oxfordshire OX14 3UE.

now because of the restructuring effects accompanying SEM and EMU. Forty manufacturing industries and a number of key service sectors are thought likely to be affected by SEM (CEC, 1990). The Maastricht Treaty sets out its goal:

> To promote its overall harmonious development, the Community shall develop and pursue its action leading to the strengthening of its economic and social cohesion. In particular the Community shall aim at reducing disparities between the various regions and backwardness of the least favoured regions, including rural areas. (Council of Ministers, 1992)

Areas eligible for assistance have been established under a set of five objectives. These 'objective regions' represent, for the first time, a European Union map of regional aid. Eighty per cent of structural funds are being allocated to Objective 1 regions; the dominant share will go to Italy, Spain, Greece and Portugal. In the United Kingdom only Northern Ireland, Merseyside and the Highlands and Islands of Scotland come under the Objective 1 banner. However, a number of regions are classified as Objective 2 and, overall, the United Kingdom will be the fifth-largest recipient of funds in the European Union. Table 7.4 shows the priority objectives of the structural funds.

There are three separate funds:

- the European Social Fund is targeted at training and reducing labour market discrimination;
- the European Regional Development Fund is designed to support infrastructure and development projects, mostly through grants; and

TABLE 7.4   Assistance available and funds responsible

Priority objectives	Funds available
Objective 1: Development and structural adjustment for regions lagging behind	ERDF, FSF, EAGGF
Objective 2: To support regions affected by industrial decline	ERDF, ESF
Objective 3: To combat long-term unemployment (over 1 year) and help young people and other excluded persons into the labour market	ESF
Objective 4: To help in training of personnel and adjustment to industrial change	ESF
Object 5: The promotion of rural development	
(a) To speed up adjustment of agriculture to changes in the Common Agricultural Policy	EAGGF, FIFG (Financial Instrument for Fisheries Guidance)
(b) To support development and new industry in rural areas	ERDF, ESF, EAGGF

Source: Adapted from the European Commission, 1993.

- the European Agricultural Guidance and Guarantee Fund provides investment for farming and for stimulating the non-farm sector of the rural economy.

Further Community initiatives have been designed to support specific projects and industries. Science and Technology for Regional Innovation and Development in Europe (STRIDE) provides funds for a range of technology initiatives in less-favoured regions. In December 1995 the RECHAR II programme announced a Ecu 27.8 million package to help regenerate industry in former coal-mining areas in the West Midlands. Its three main themes focused on business development and diversification, local community development and environmental improvement (CEC, 1995b)

Aid, as we have seen, is available to business on a discretionary basis, from both national and European sources. The availability of aid could be a decisive factor in a business organization's location or expansion decisions. It is clearly a big incentive to an organization if it is to receive substantial funds to facilitate a project.

QUESTIONS

1. Support from the government comes in various guises and is open to extensive modification. What current government policy initiatives are in place to support business?

2. Identify two companies that have benefited from support initiatives. How has that intervention helped their business activity?

7.5 Democratic systems of government

Constitutions and the role of the legislative, judicial and administrative functions of government

This section considers the formal basis of democratic systems of government and looks at the legislative (law making), judicial (law applying) and the executive or administrative functions which play crucial, complementary roles within such systems of government.

British parliamentary democracy has been influential as a model of democratic government in, for example, Germany and Malaysia. However, it is ironic that the United Kingdom is the only Western European country without either a bill of rights or domestic legislation which gives its citizens the ability to seek redress, in its own courts, for breaches of the European Convention on Human Rights. The Convention includes such human rights as the right to life, freedom from torture or slavery and freedoms of thought and expression.

Indeed, certain groups in the United Kingdom, notably Charter 88, have argued for the need for a written constitution, or 'bill of rights', to legally enshrine certain fundamental rights of citizens. It has been argued that a bill of rights is essential on the basis that the United Kingdom's record before the European Court of Human Rights in Strasbourg is one of the 'worst records of any of the 35 signatories to the European Convention' (*The Economist*, 1995) with 37 cases decided against it. There have been causes for concern in many areas, such as telephone tapping, birching, immigration rules, homosexuality and the ruling that the killing of the IRA terrorists on Gibraltar in 1988 was unlawful.

The United States of America has a written constitution and a clear 'separation of powers' in that the legislative, judicial and administrative functions are kept distinct. It is often thought that such checks and balances are important for the effective operation of a democracy. One of the hallmarks of a totalitarian regime is thought to be the lack of a clear separation of the judicial function from the legislative and executive functions.

The United Kingdom, however, is not completely fastidious in ensuring that there is a rigid separation of powers. The Lord Chancellor, for example, is a member of all three afore-mentioned groupings: being a member of the Cabinet (the executive), sitting in the House of Lords (the legislature) and being in charge of all the judges (the judiciary). In the United Kingdom, the province of each of the three groups is ever-changing. The role of the judiciary, for example, within the constitution has increasingly come to the fore in recent years. The number of cases of 'judicial review' of administrative actions increased to nearly 3000 in 1994, including the judgment that the government had misused £234 million of foreign aid by tying it to a construction contract for the Pergau Dam in Malaysia in 1993. The pressure group, the World Development Movement, successfully challenged the then Home Secretary, Douglas Hurd, in the Pergau Dam case. This case gives an indication of the increasing number of pressure groups who might be able to establish an interest in a government executive decision. It is evident that this kind of intervention may have a wide impact on specific organizations and business in general. Following the Pergau Dam affair the Malaysian Prime Minister, Dr Mahathir Mohammed, banned United Kingdom companies from bidding for work with the Malaysian government, because of accusations, mainly in the UK press, of bribery of Malaysian officials by UK government and business. This was at a time of enormous spending on infrastructure projects, such as the new international airport outside Kuala Lumpur.

The increased willingness on the part of the judiciary to review administrative decisions, particularly those made by ministers, indicates that the interrelationships between the legislative, judicial and administrative functions in the United Kingdom are in a state of flux. Many would argue that the willingness of judges to develop the law of judicial review shows that although the United Kingdom does not have a written constitution there are sufficient 'checks and balances' to offer redress to citizens and companies. It has also been suggested that judges would not have shown such willingness to extend the boundaries of judicial review if Parliament had proved to be a more effective vehicle for keeping the activities of the administrative branch of government in check.

Judges are also seen to be suitable persons to conduct independent reviews, such as those relating to standards in public life (the Nolan Committee) and the issue of 'Arms to Iraq' (the Scott Inquiry). Clearly, the role of judges would be much enhanced in the United Kingdom if the government chose either to make the European Convention of Human Rights of direct domestic effect or to legislate for a bill of rights.

The increased centralization of government in the United Kingdom, implied above, has made Parliament somewhat vulnerable to lobbying activity by individual pressure groups (see Chapter 6) and professional lobbyists, on behalf of sectional interests. The recent higher profile given to these professional lobbyists and their ties with MPs has been linked to various scandal stories in Parliament, for example the 'cash-for-questions' 'scandals' relating first to Graham Riddick MP and David Tredinnick MP in July 1994 and then to Neil Hamilton MP and Tim Smith MP in October 1994. Such was the level of concern in 1994 that the Prime Minister set up a Commission chaired by Lord Nolan which reported on the activities of MPs in July 1995 (see mini-case below). The United Kingdom is not the only country where politicians have been brought into disrepute: the situation is not unknown in Europe. In Italy, for example, many politicians, including two former prime ministers, have come under scrutiny because of their close links with business and the Mafia. This type of relationship between politicians and business people has been the subject of debate in many countries, not least in Japan, which has seen the resignation of a prime minister because of bribery allegations. In a 1993 case the chairman of Shimizu, one of Japan's leading construction companies, was alleged to have bribed an official in the hope of winning a share of a large public works project in the Ibaraki prefecture (Thomson, 1993).

The Nolan inquiry into standards in public life

The UK Prime Minister, John Major, set up the Nolan inquiry into standards in public life towards the end of 1994. At this time the conduct of certain MPs in accepting cash for asking questions in the House of Commons was receiving considerable adverse publicity.

The inquiry comprised a permanent standing committee. In respect of the conduct of MPs the inquiry took evidence from a range of groups including ministers, public servants, experts, academics and pressure groups.

The committee recommended that:

1. A Parliamentary Commissioner for Standards should be appointed to investigate complaints, complemented by a disciplinary panel of MPs whose hearings would be in public.
2. MPs should not work for lobbying firms and must disclose details of any other parliamentary services performed.

3.   The long-established Register of Members' Interests should be made clearer and updated electronically.

4.   Both MPs and ministers should be given new Codes of Conduct. Ex-ministers should wait three months before taking a job outside Parliament and all appointments should be vetted by the committee which currently deals with such matters for civil servants. Where there appeared to be a conflict of interest a delay of up to two years could be advised.

5.   A new Public Appointments Commissioner should be appointed to oversee the fairness of appointments to quangos.

Subsequently, the Prime Minister referred the issue of implementation of the report to a special Select Committee of the House of Commons. This committee recommended that a Parliamentary Commissioner for Standards be set up, but voted against disclosure of paid consultancies, typically said to be worth around £20 000, on the basis that, among other arguments, disclosure would involve unwarranted intrusions into MPs' personal privacy.

However, in November 1995 the full House of Commons rejected, by a substantial majority, the recommendation of the select committee.

MPs voted to:

- appoint a Parliamentary Commissioner for Standards;
- ban paid advocacy by all MPs, including the tabling of questions, motions and amendments to legislation, and restrict the right of MPs to speak in debates on behalf of outside paid interests;
- require MPs to disclose their earnings from consultancy work arising from their parliamentary role and to register details of all contracts with the Parliamentary Commissioner from March 1996;
- approve a code of conduct.

In summary, one of the key features of a democratic system of government is the ability of the judicial, legislative and administrative functions to operate in a reasonably autonomous way so as to be able to provide a system of 'checks and balances'. In the United Kingdom we have noted the willingness of judges to develop the concept of judicial review, perhaps to compensate for the lack of a written constitution.

QUESTIONS

1.   What do you understand by the doctrine of the 'separation of powers'? Discuss the doctrine in the context of a range of countries with which you are familiar.

2.   Research the arguments for and against a bill of rights for the United Kingdom.

7.6 Classifying laws

As we noted in the introduction to this chapter the main purpose of this section is to develop a basic vocabulary which is necessary to understand the range of types of law. Laws may be classified in a large number of ways. Each main classification used below has a number of subclassifications.

We start by examining international law. This can be subdivided into two subclassifications: public and private international law. Public international law is the law regulating the relationships between nation states. It is also concerned with international bodies like the United Nations (discussed above). The Rio Convention in 1992, discussed in Chapter 6, is an example of this type of international law.

Private international law, sometimes known as the 'conflict of laws', concerns jurisdictional questions in cases where disputes arise between individuals or organizations based in different nation states. Clearly, the growth of multinational and transnational corporations and the increasingly global nature of economic activity means that questions about which courts have jurisdiction and which country's laws apply to a particular dispute may arise more frequently than in the past. However, such issues are normally resolved by the contracting parties, in advance of any dispute, via a standard contractual term.

All nation states will then have some *public* laws and *private* laws. Public law is made up of a number of branches, and includes: constitutional laws concerning the relationships of the different organs of government; criminal law setting out offences against the state; administrative laws which concern administrative actions taken by ministers and officials; EU law and laws involving the state itself, such as those on citizenship and immigration. There is then a huge range of *private* laws which are designed to regulate the behaviour of individuals and groups in areas which are not criminal. Private law offers ways of obtaining redress for individuals or organizations with grievances in areas such as the law of property, contract and consumer law, company and partnership law, the law of torts (for example, civil wrongs like negligence) and the laws of succession and trusts.

In April 1996 the Court of Appeal ruled that Turner & Newell (T&N), the motor components and engineering group, was liable to pay out damages in two cases where adults had contracted mesothelioma (an asbestos-related illness) as a result of playing, as children, near to a factory which used to be owned by the group. The High Court had awarded £115 000 in the cases after hearing evidence that children often used to play 'snowballs' with the asbestos dust in the 1930s. The basis of T&N's liability in this, as in all negligence cases, was that the company had broken a duty of care which they owed to those living nearby (and not just those working in the factory). The Court of Appeal confirmed the High Court decision.

For consumers who suffer product-related injuries a key question will be whether or not a contractual relationship exists. Contractual liability on retailers, for example, will often be 'strict', which means that the consumer does not need to prove fault on the part of the retailer. This situation is discussed in more detail below. However, if there is no such relationship then there may be a need to prove negligence (a very costly and time-consuming procedure) except in cases where a claim can be made under the Consumer Protection Act 1987. To succeed under this Act the injured party must be able to show that the injury (or property damage) was caused by a defective product and, on this basis, they may be able, subject to certain conditions, to obtain damages from the producer of the product.

It is important to understand that the different classifications of law, particularly the distinction between criminal and civil law, involve distinct sets of terminology and are largely dealt with in different courts. It is also important to note that words like 'prosecute' and 'guilt' are used only in respect of the criminal law and that the civil law equivalent terms are to 'sue' and to be found 'liable'.

Since many business transactions involve the provision of goods or services in exchange for money then the notion of a contract underpins a lot of commercial activity. Increasing trends towards privatization and the outsourcing of certain services, mean that it is important for managers to have a grasp of basic contract law. One of the key questions relates to the point in time at which a contract comes into existence. This is a crucial matter since it is at this point that one party's failure to comply with its part of the bargain can result in the other party being able to sue for a remedy: either rescission of the contract, that is treating the contract as over, *and damages* for breaches of contractual 'conditions', or for *damages only* in cases of breaches of 'warranties' (less serious contractual terms).

If an organization is involved in providing products or services to other organizations or to individuals it is important that the implications of a wide range of Acts of Parliament are understood. Relevant Acts in this context are:

- the Consumer Credit Act 1974;
- the Unfair Terms Contract Act 1977;
- the Sale of Goods Act 1979;
- the Supply of Goods and Services Act 1982;
- the Sales and Supply of Goods Act 1994.

Detailed consideration of this legislation is beyond the scope of this book. However, it is important to understand that such Acts include many instances where Parliament has deemed it necessary to intervene in freely negotiated contractual relationships between individual consumers and businesses by giving the former some 'extra' rights.

The method of intervention most often used in the United Kingdom is the use of an 'implied-term' such as the implied condition of 'satisfactory quality' in respect of goods sold 'in the course of a business', as implied by section 14(2) of the Sale of Goods Act 1979 (as amended by the Sale and Supply of Goods Act 1994). Supermarkets, for example, must offer a consumer who has bought goods which are not of 'satisfactory quality' a remedy under section 14 of the Act. Such implied terms operate irrespective of what was agreed between the parties themselves at the time the contract was made. The economic rationale for such interventions is to redress particularly glaring inequalities of bargaining power.

As can be seen from the dates of the above-mentioned Acts the high point of this legislative intervention in the United Kingdom was in the 1970s. The torch of consumer protection now seems to have passed to the European Union, as instanced by the directive on Unfair Terms in Consumer Contracts (93/13 EEC OJ 95, 21 April 1993). The directive was put into effect in the United Kingdom via the Unfair Terms in Consumer Contracts Regulations 1994. These regulations, which came into effect on 1 July 1995, apply a general concept of 'fairness' to terms in contracts for the supply of goods and services, excluding certain contracts such as contracts of employment, which have 'not been individually negotiated' (Regulation 3(1)). The Regulations are, therefore, targeted at standard-form contracts where the consumer has had no opportunity to influence the terms of the contract. Regulation 4(1) states that an unfair term is one which,

> contrary to the requirement of good faith causes a significant imbalance in the parties' rights and obligations arising under the contract, to the detriment of the consumer.

Here, again, we can note that inequality of bargaining power is the basis for intervention.

As far as organizations are concerned, the areas of relevant criminal law are areas of serious wrong-doing such as theft or fraud; and more minor breaches of 'regulatory' criminal offences, such as false descriptions or misleading prices in respect of goods or services. Although breaches of some criminal offences may be minor in terms of legal scale, organizations need to be aware that the publicity resulting from breaches of the criminal law tends to be rather wider than that arising from civil law liability.

To summarize, we have noted that it is important to understand how laws may be classified, in order that appropriate vocabulary may be used to frame any discussion of the impact of particular laws – for example, civil or criminal – upon organizations. As noted in the introduction to this chapter, the aim is not to provide a comprehensive discussion of all the areas of law likely to affect organizations. Students requiring detailed coverage of particular areas of law are referred to the sources listed in the introduction to this chapter.

 ## QUESTION

Find some newspaper reports of legal cases which feature significant impacts on business organizations. Identify and classify the particular laws referred to in the reports.

7.7 Sources of law and the court system in England and Wales

The expression 'sources of law' is usually taken to mean the different sorts of law used to solve a legal problem. There are two principal sources of present-day law: statutes, and decisions taken by judges (case law).

Statutes

Statutes, or Acts of Parliament, are, constitutionally speaking, the supreme source of law in England and Wales. Thus, Parliament can, by an Act, make any law it sees fit without any legal limitation. Under the afore-mentioned doctrine of separation of powers judges cannot question the legality of any statute and their only latitude in interpreting an Act exists where there is ambiguity.

Parliament is supreme, but it can authorize others to pass 'delegated legislation', for example local authority by-laws. European law is logically an extension of this idea of delegated legislation, as it is under the European Communities Act (ECA) 1972 that the English courts will take note of European law and, where a conflict exists, will enforce it in preference to any other. Thus, in theory, Parliament remains supreme because the ECA *could* be repealed. In practice, however, a considerable amount of legal sovereignty has been surrendered to the European Union. It is precisely the prospect of further ceding of sovereignty that caused considerable internal dissension within the Conservative party in the United Kingdom in 1995. This precipitated the resignation of Prime Minister, John Major, as leader of the party and the re-election contest. He succeeded in becoming re-elected and the dissension seemed, at least in media reports, to die down. The government defeat in the House of Commons by two votes, on a Labour party fisheries amendment in December 1995, showed that the debate was still far from resolution.

Decisions taken by judges

Judicial decisions form case law. Nowadays, much case law involves interpretation of statutes passed by Parliament. However, cases such as that relating to Turner & Newell (T&N), discussed above (p. 270), are based upon long-established 'common law' principles. Although the T&N case was not treated as a 'test case' the decision clearly opens up the possibility of a range of such claims against the company. In recent years T&N has had to make substantial provisions to meet a range of compensation claims, particularly in the United States of America.

It is often difficult to be clear about the law in a range of areas, particularly where competing rights are being asserted. A court decision represents a definitive judgment on the law as it applies to a given situation.

By virtue of the doctrine of 'judicial precedent' judges are bound to follow rules of law established in previous court decisions. Detailed rules exist to establish the circumstances in which a judge will be bound but they are too specialized for consideration in the present text.

The court system

The English court system strongly reflects the distinction between civil and criminal law (discussed above). Normally, small civil law claims are brought in the County Court; larger civil claims, like that involving T&N, are processed in the High Court. The vast majority of criminal cases in the United Kingdom are dealt with by the Magistrates' Court. Magistrates are only paid expenses, are not legally qualified people and operate, in respect of matters of law, under the guidance of a Clerk who must have considerable legal experience. More serious criminal cases will be heard in the Crown Court, before a judge and jury. There are then two levels of appeal court in the United Kingdom: the Court of Appeal and the House of Lords. Beyond this lies the European Court of Justice (discussed above in section 7.2) for certain types of case.

In summary, we have noted that the two main sources of law are statutes and case law. Government policy is often translated into legislation. This tends to generate further case law in order to obtain definitive applications of complex statutory wording to particular situations. It is beyond the scope of this book to look in detail at case law and statutes. Finally, this section concluded with a very brief summary of the court system in the United Kingdom. Here we emphasized two features of the system: its hierarchical nature and the division into civil and criminal courts.

QUESTIONS

1. What have been the implications for the sovereignty of Parliament of the United Kingdom joining the European Community, as it then was, in 1972?

2. What is the relationship between statute law and case law?

CONCLUSION

It is important for managers in organizations to understand the level (global, regional, national or local) at which different political decisions are taken in order that lobbying can be carried out effectively. If an organization is keen to influence a political decision then it may employ professional lobbyists who understand the detail, for example, of the United Kingdom or European Union political processes. Many organizations are prepared to pay considerable sums of money to achieve such influence, perhaps in the hope of trying to persuade government, for example, to either relax or tighten the applicable regulatory regime depending upon their assessment of their position in the competitive marketplace. The activities of some MPs in the United Kingdom in this regard were instrumental in introducing a much tighter regulatory regime in respect of their behaviour.

Clearly, most organizations will want to ensure that appropriate staff have a good general idea of the law and of the legal system; it will generally be of considerable benefit to an organization if its staff understand when their actions might have legal/regulatory implications. Nevertheless, most organizations will retain solicitors and barristers to give them advice on specific legal disputes.

SUMMARY OF MAIN POINTS

This chapter has examined a range of political issues and outlined a number of key areas of legal terminology important to the context of the book as a whole. The main points made are that:

- Political change can occur at all three levels which we have identified: global/regional, national and local.
- At the global scale there is a huge diversity of interactions which will cascade downwards to the lower geo-political levels and affect the activities of a substantial number of organizations.
- There needs to be awareness by organizations, who wish to compete across a range of countries, that the interests of those countries may, on occasions, conflict with their own goals. As a result they must be prepared to respond flexibly when local political factors demand.
- Organizations can, and do, take action to influence political decisions at all political levels, for example via lobbying. In this way they can seek to neutralize political threats posed by political change or enhance their business opportunities.
- A diverse media is an important feature of a democratic political system and this has influenced regulatory approaches in the United Kingdom.
- The roles of key European Union institutions need to be understood in order that organizations can understand the implications of developments at this level.
- Organizations can obtain considerable benefit from domestic and European regional aid schemes.
- In the United Kingdom the relationship between the judicial, legislative and administrative functions is in a state of flux. Here it is important for

citizens and organizations to be aware of the possibility of bringing a claim for judicial review of certain administrative decisions.

- It is important to recognize the different classifications of United Kingdom law in order that appropriate legal terminology may be used.

- One of the key areas of civil law for organizations is the range of statutes which regulate contractual activity.

- The rationale for legislative intervention in freely negotiated contacts between businesses and consumers is often an attempt to make up for a lack of bargaining power on the part of the consumer.

- In the United Kingdom, although Parliament is the supreme law-making body, case law is often required in order that judges can clarify the meaning and application of particular statutes.

- The distinction between the criminal and civil law is critical to understanding the legal system of England and Wales; the distinction is reflected, particularly, in the court structure.

References

Barber, L. (1995) ' "Hi-jack" of EU foreign policy condemned', *Financial Times*, 19 April.

CEC (1990) 'The impact of the internal market by industrial sector', *European Economy Special Edition*, Commission of the European Communities, Luxembourg.

CEC (1994a) 'Your Ministers decide on Europe', *Factsheet*, Commission of the European Communities, London.

CEC (1994b) 'The institutions of the Community', *Background Report*, ISEC/B7/94, Commission of the European Communities, London.

CEC (1995a) 'Aid for Northern Ireland', *The Week in Europe*, WE/29/95, Commission of the European Communities, London.

CEC (1995b) 'Financial boost for the West Midlands', *The Week in Europe*, WE/43/95, Commission of the European Communities, London.

Council of Ministers (1992) *Treaty of European Union*, Council of Ministers, Brussels.

The Economist (1995) 'Why Britain needs a bill of rights', 21 October.

Ham, P. (1995) 'Peace profits Emerald Isle', *Sunday Times*, 29 October.

Harding, J. (1996) 'Broadcast plan is news to some Labour MPs', *Financial Times*, 17 April.

HM Government (1992) 'Regional policy: review of the assisted areas', *Consultative Paper*, Department of Trade and Industry, HMSO, London.

Martin, R. (1993) *Regional Studies*, **27/8**, pp. 797–805.

Ohmae, K. (1995) 'Putting global logic first', *Harvard Business Review*, January–February.

Owens, K. (1995) *Law for Business Studies Students*, Cavendish Publishing, London.

Thomson, I. (1995) Editorial, *European Information Association*, January, pp. 5–20.

Thomson, R. (1993) 'Corporate bribe structure starts to crack', *Financial Times*, 23 September.

CHAPTER 8

THE PUBLIC SECTOR ENVIRONMENT

Ian Brooks

 LEARNING OUTCOMES

On completion of this chapter you should be able to:

- appreciate the rationale for the existence of public sector organizations;
- examine the changing political agendas and objectives which influence public sector activity;
- understand the wider business environmental forces acting upon public sector organizations;
- appreciate the scale and scope of privatization, market testing and competitive tendering within public sector organizations;
- understand the structural and managerial changes that have occurred within the public sector;
- appreciate the unique characteristics of the public sector environment;
- appreciate the nature of the drivers and resistors of organizational change within the public sector.

8.1 Dynamism in the public sector

Introduction

Both the scale of the public sector and the rate of change within its environment make it a valuable, but often neglected, field of study. This chapter takes a closer look at the legal, social, economic and technological forces which influence the public sector. Emphasis is placed on the political arena where most pressure for change originates. Public sector organizations conduct government business, are largely funded from the public purse and are usually accountable to government at some level. As the vast majority of funding and support for most public sector organizations is provided from taxation, it is the duty of government to ensure that proper care is taken when dispensing these resources. Hence, government at local, national and international levels has a pervasive and powerful influence over public sector bodies, particularly in their role as legislators and resource providers. Consequently, we pay particular attention to the role of government within this chapter. A theme of environmental change or dynamism, together with ever-increasing complexity and uncertainty, prevails throughout this chapter which largely, but not exclusively, focuses upon the United Kingdom. The environmental changes are themselves part of a global transformation in the nature of public sector organizations. The chapter also illustrates how the private sector environment is increasingly influencing public sector activity.

This introductory section aims to explain why publicly owned organizations exist. Attention will then be focused on the political influences on the public sector, firstly, by analysing the changes that have taken place in political agendas in recent decades. The chapter will then focus on the broader aspects of the public sector business environment and, in so doing, embrace technological, ecological and social concerns operating on a global scale. We then take a closer look at privatization and the contracting-out of services. Finally we concentrate upon the structural and managerial changes which have evolved since the early 1980s.

In most countries the public sector is a major employer and service provider. It also accounts for a significant proportion of gross domestic product. For example, in 1995 the British government expenditure was about 42 per cent of GDP. In 1979 almost 7.5 million people were employed within the public sector in the United Kingdom, although this figure had fallen to about 5.5 million by 1995. Nevertheless, the public sector far outweighed any branch of industry in scale and importance.

Given the global context in which all organizations now operate it is not surprising that the nature of the public sector and its business environment have fundamentally changed in recent decades. This has created a state of flux where many organizations have changed ownership from public to private sector and others have been so transformed as to be virtually unrecognizable. There is little doubt that the complex array of political, social and economic objectives of governments over the last two decades have created enormous pressures for change within publicly owned organizations creating a state of near permanent tension between different interest groups. So radical are the changes that the term 'new public sector' is in common usage in the United Kingdom.

Somewhat flippantly we can illustrate the changes that have occurred in the past two decades within the mixed economy by rewriting a quote from Brown and Jackson (1992) which aimed to demonstrate the importance of the public sector. It reads,

> most of us in the United Kingdom were born in public sector hospitals, are tended by public sector doctors, were educated in public sector schools,

colleges and universities, play in public sector parks, are protected by the public sector, will end up in a public sector hospital when we are old and will be buried in public sector graveyards.

This cradle-to-grave philosophy is fast waning, such that the above statement could, in the not too distant future, read,

> most of us in the United Kingdom were born in quasi-independent NHS Trusts where many of our mothers rented a private room, were tended by GP fundholding doctors and paid full market rate prescription charges, were educated in private or grant-maintained schools and private or quasi-independent universities as no-grant, fee-paying 'customers', play in poorly maintained public parks or lavish privately operated adventure parks, are protected by private security firms and public sector police forces supported by privately run support services, will end up not receiving state pensions, will be nursed in private nursing homes and will be cremated and buried on EU 'Sct-Aside' farming land or other privatized graveyards by our dependants.

The scope and pace of change in the public sector and of the role of government since 1980 has been both dramatic and rapid when compared to virtually any period in the United Kingdom's history.

The market system, public goods and change

It can be argued that the existence of the public sector is due to the failure of the free market system to provide all the services required by the general public and by government. However, both the scope and scale of the public sector in any country is in part the result of prevailing political ideologies, or those that have been prevalent in the past. A multitude of other factors also influence both the level of government involvement in the economy and the scale of public expenditure. However, there is no indisputable law of economics which argues that the public sector should, for example, operate the full range of services that it did in the United Kingdom in 1980, or for that matter, that it does today. Neither is there, at any time, a 'correct' or indisputable level of government expenditure.

There are a certain, strictly limited, number of services which most politicians, academics and the general public agree should be conducted by the government or at least under its tight scrutiny. Relatively uncontroversial examples include the judiciary, the police and the armed services – although, as we will discover, some non-core 'support' roles for these services have already been subjected to market testing and private operation. However, there are a large and growing number of activities which are the subject of considerable public debate in many countries regarding the most appropriate form of ownership and operation.

Many politicians and some academics believe that private markets are capable of providing some services that are more usually regarded as 'public goods'. These include health care (supported by private insurance) and education (backed with means-tested education vouchers). Others argue that this would lead to a multi-tiered system and a restriction of access to high-quality services for a significant section of the community. They further argue that the indirect benefits of a healthy and well-educated population are shared by all such that the costs should also be shared. Additionally, objectors to the idea of a market economy argue that the conditions necessary for perfect competition rarely, if ever, exist. Critics also suggest that competition in the provision of many public services, such as health care, is morally unacceptable and practically unworkable.

However, there is widespread recognition that in many circumstances the market is a sound and appropriate mechanism for the allocation of scare resources (refer to arguments in Chapter 2). As such the marketplace, via the price system, allocates goods and services to individuals and organizations. It is increasingly being recognized in many countries, since the collapse of communism in Eastern Europe, that the marketplace is the most efficient system of allocation of many, but not all, goods and services. Although the market economy is far from faultless, the alternatives are not necessarily guaranteed to be more efficient or effective in servicing the needs of society or individuals.

The trend towards a mixed economy, where economic activity is shared via both public and private ownership, proceeded apace in the developed industrialized world with the introduction and growth of government services throughout the nineteenth and twentieth centuries. The scope of government activity in most countries grew to include responsibility for education, health and other services and, as in the United Kingdom from 1945 to 1975, for many industrial organizations, e.g. the steel, gas, railways and water supply businesses. As this chapter will reveal, there has been a partial reversal of this trend since 1980 with the market economy once again becoming more dominant. Hence many outputs previously classified as 'public goods' are now provided by privately owned profit-making companies.

Political ideology and economic circumstances: the roots of change in the United Kingdom

It is without doubt the political environment which is of first and foremost importance to public sector organizations. Although we cannot easily disaggregate each environmental force, this brief section will focus upon the power of political ideology to shape public opinion and public organizations. The changes outlined within this chapter stand as testimony to the powerful influencing role of government. Of course economic, social and technological forces, which are discussed below, inform and otherwise influence government policy. However, government and political activity 'filter' these forces and impose constraints or afford opportunities to the public services. In short, governments draw up the agenda for change within the public sector.

This section takes a closer look at political changes which have occurred since the mid-1970s in the United Kingdom. Although it is often said that the arrival of the Thatcher government in 1979 signalled major political change, the origins of the transformation that was to occur stem from earlier developments. From the Second World War (1939–45) there existed a broad consensus in British politics which favoured the development of the role of the state in the economy. A mixed economy, with many industries in state control, was considered the norm. This consensus ensured that annual government expenditure on the NHS, education and the Civil Service increased steadily, funded by economic growth, made possible by full employment. However, the 1970s saw a period of recession, high inflation and increasing unemployment. Many academics and politicians began to realize that the growth of spending on the public sector, which included large publicly owned industries, would have to be reduced. In 1976 the British Labour government was forced to seek a sizeable loan from the International Monetary Fund (IMF) – a condition of which was to further control public expenditure. Unfortunately for them this coincided with a steady increase in the demand for public services. By the mid-1970s United Kingdom government expenditure amounted to about 45 per cent of GDP.

The 1970s also saw an acceleration in the decline of Britain's traditional industries, a sharp rise in the price of crude oil, strong overseas competition and the United Kingdom's entry into the European Community in 1973. These wider economic and political changes altered 'the ground rules' for Britain and many of its neighbours. No longer was low inflation, steady economic growth and near full employment assured. The economic and social changes in the 1970s coincided with the rise of the New Right and a political ideology which, although not new, became increasingly appealing to middle- and working-class voters. This ideology emphasized individual choice and endeavour and advocated a reduction of the role of government in the economy and the lives of individuals. Margaret Thatcher was a prime proponent of the new ideal. Although the Heath government of the early 1970s toyed with change and the Callaghan administration, which followed, started the process under the direction of the International Monetary Fund (IMF), it was the Thatcher reign from 1979 that effectively broke the post-war consensus and sought a fundamental change in the role of the state.

Thatcher exhibited a thinly disguised hostility towards the public sector with which she associated bureaucracy, waste and inefficiency. She promoted the role of the free market and freedom of choice. No longer were lame duck industries to be saved by government interference, despite the social consequences which might ensue. Attention changed from a prime concern for levels of employment to the monetarist agenda comprising a preoccupation with inflation and control of the money supply. The New Right also pushed for reductions in taxation, especially income and corporation tax, so releasing funds for investment and giving the public greater choice over their spending. The 'enterprise culture' became paramount within the political economy of the 1980s. Growth in the number of small and medium enterprises (SMEs), it was widely believed, would lead to national economic prosperity. Keat and Abercrombie (1991) summarize its prime characteristics:

- continual process of privatization;
- deregulation of industries;
- structural reorganization of publicly funded bodies;
- diminution of the culture of dependence, including reduced reliance upon government agencies for support;
- competitive market organization and commercial modes of operation becomes the dominant role model for all organizations (including public sector).

Clearly, these 'environmental' changes have far-reaching consequences for public sector organizations and this new orientation, embracing market values and objectives, ensured that the public sector became something of a problem for the radical Right. The Thatcher government believed that the public sector required both restructuring and cultural change if the ambitious attempt at national turnaround was to be successful. It was assumed that such a radical departure from perceived practice could only come about via government intervention. Major reforms were introduced within public sector organizations. Many of these changes, which aimed to achieve significant productivity gains and 'better value for money', are discussed in this chapter. The term 'value for money', probably more than any, symbolizes government intention to reform the public sector. This term is defined as 'the provision of the right goods and services from the right source, of the right quality, at the right time, delivered to the right place and at the right price' (HMSO, 1993).

In broader evolutionary terms academics have argued that the 1970s, and subsequent years, saw a fundamental change in the way organizations operate. Since the success of Henry Ford in mass producing motor vehicles at a fraction of the cost of many of his competitors, manufacturing and many service organizations broadly followed Ford's doctrines. Hence most tasks were tightly prescribed and mechanistic, management control and centralized planning was crucial and customer choice limited. Post-Fordism (after or following from Henry Ford's mass production culture) has meant that organizations, private and public, have sought new managerial and operational forms, including flatter and leaner structures, greater decentralization, flexibility, teamworking and informality (Hoggett, 1987).

However, new pressures on the public purse have ensured that significant reductions in the scale of government spending have not been realized. Figure 8.1 shows the fluctuations in government expenditure over a decade in the United Kingdom.

Short-term fluctuations in government expenditure in the United Kingdom are clearly related to the fortunes of the economy, that is, they are cyclical. In times of relative boom, such as the late 1980s, expenditure (as a percentage of GDP) declined as a result of reductions in unemployment and other social welfare claims.

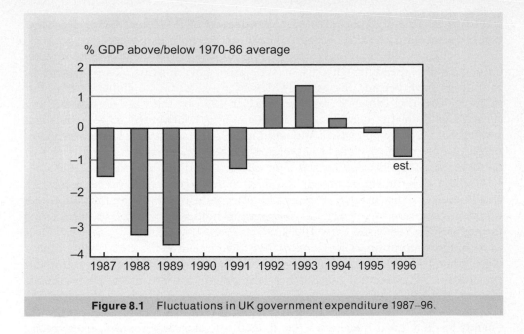

% GDP above/below 1970-86 average

Figure 8.1   Fluctuations in UK government expenditure 1987–96.

Additionally, tax revenues rise as the economy booms. In the longer term, structural cycles occur as a result of, for example, changing demand for old age pensions, child support and education. The United Kingdom is certainly not alone in experiencing continued pressure on the public purse as public spending in most OECD countries shows signs of considerable in-built momentum. It is proving very difficult to achieve real decreases despite the efforts of many governments.

Table 8.1 indicates the relative stability in government expenditure (as a proportion of total GDP) in the United Kingdom over the last three decades. There is, however, a significant difference in government expenditure between

TABLE 8.1   Government expenditure as a percentage of GNP

	1970–86 average	1987–93 average	1994	1995 (est.)	1996 (est.)
Belgium	54.2	55.9	56.0	54.9	54.0
Denmark	50.5	58.4	62.5	60.1	58.7
France	45.4	51.7	55.5	54.3	53.3
Italy	41.3	52.6	54.8	53.6	52.4
Holland	53.1	56.5	55.9	53.2	51.3
United Kingdom	42.3	40.9	42.6	42.1	41.4
EU (excl. Greece and Portugal)	**44.2**	**48.4**	**51.0**	**50.2**	**49.1**
USA	33.6	37.0	36.5	36.6	37.0
Japan	28.6	32.3	33.4	33.9	43.3

Source: European Economy Supplement B, December 1994.

countries in the EU. This is, in part, a reflection of both the historical context within each country and the broad political objectives of its government.

Changing macroeconomic conditions in the 1970s and 1980s directly influenced the spending patterns of successive governments. These economic conditions have become increasingly driven by external or global forces. For example, post-war affluence was threatened in 1973 by the Arab–Israeli war and consequent dramatic increases in oil prices. This contributed to recession and consequent high unemployment and rapid inflation. It also threatened government public sector spending plans. Maintaining a sizeable annual increase in levels of public expenditure became increasingly difficult, and indeed less desirable after 1979 when government acted out the Thatcherite agenda. However, Table 8.1 clearly indicates that many European and other industrialized countries allowed a significant increase in government spending in both proportional and real terms throughout the 1980s and early 1990s.

In more recent times the Conservative government in the mid-1990s suffered repeated and sizeable budget deficits necessitating the strict control of government expenditure. This control was further stimulated by a strong desire to reduce income and other forms of taxation by an unpopular government facing the prospects of a General Election. In late 1995, for example, many local authority schools in the United Kingdom were obliged to make some redundancies among their teaching staff. It was also reported that approaching one half of all primary age children were taught in classes with over 30 pupils. Hence, as a result of the recessionary period of the early 1990s and government objectives and policy, schools in the United Kingdom suffered rigid and sometimes stifling budgetary constraint. Many political commentators argue that the NHS has been similarly affected.

There is a wider issue raised by these events. Although it is difficult to be specific, many public sector organizations experience a funding climate which is perceived at least to be related to the popularity of government and its need to court public support. Awarding a popular public service an additional tranche of funding, or indeed denying public sector organizations funds in order to reduce taxation, are tactics often considered by government. This is particularly the case when a General Election is approaching. Governments are frequently accused of manipulating public sector organizations in order to achieve party political objectives. Although many such accusations are undoubtedly unfounded the Conservative government openly discussed in 1995 the need for spending and tax cuts in order to 'win back disenchanted voters'. However, to be fair to that government, reductions in taxation were a long-term objective outlined in their manifesto.

In conclusion, it is true to say that from reducing the role of government in the economy an increase in the 'incidence' of taxation and levels of public expenditure (in real terms) occurred between 1979 and 1996, that is, following some 16 years of Conservative party rule. However, when compared with many of its EU and OECD neighbours the United Kingdom government has resisted large-scale increases in public expenditure.

The wider public sector 'business' environment

The political forces outlined above are themselves driven by powerful economic, social and technological changes within the global arena. Wider environmental changes inform political agendas and mould ideologies. However, the mechanism of influence between the wider environment and political activity is two-way as government decisions profoundly influence other environmental forces. For example, whereas changing social needs creates dynamism to which government and public organizations have to respond, those same social changes are, in part, the result of government policy and behaviour. For example, the income level of people in the poorest 10 per cent of United Kingdom society actually declined between 1979 and 1995. This has resulted from a lack of political will to address the problems faced by this sector of society through more progressive taxation or welfare policies. In turn the relative poverty of this group has contributed to many social problems such as urban deprivation, long-term unemployment, crime and drug abuse. As a result government and public sector organizations are faced with a social environment which is, in part, a consequence of their previous activity. Figure 8.2 illustrates some of the environmental influences on government and public sector organizations, together with the two-way nature of some of these relationships.

Prevailing and evolving competitive, economic and social conditions and information technologies are stimulating and facilitating moves towards further decentralization, desegregation and competition among current, or previously publicly owned, organizations. Emphasis on efficiency and effectiveness, customer orientation and performance management are partly a result of more fundamental and widespread global change.

Forces within the business environment impinge upon and otherwise

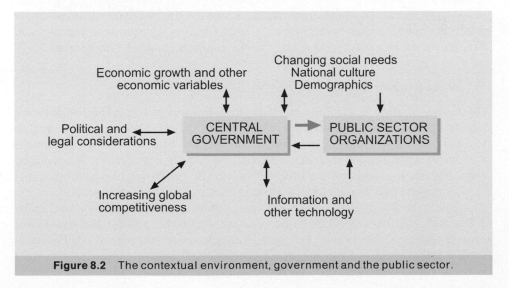

Figure 8.2 The contextual environment, government and the public sector.

influence public sector organizations every bit as much as they do commercial companies. Technological change, for example, is not discriminatory. It does not merely influence private companies. Information systems have transformed the work undertaken by many United Kingdom Civil Service agencies, while societal changes profoundly influence the objectives of public organizations. For example, demographic changes (see Chapter 5) have been a powerful influencing force upon many public sector organizations in the United Kingdom and elsewhere. For example, the NHS is facing a steady increase in demand for its services due partly to the rapidly ageing nature of Britain's population. Older people tend to require more health care provision than their younger counterparts. This ageing population, combined with high levels of unemployment since the 1970s, have created an ever-increasing burden on the state's social services. National culture is also changing with the development of a more sophisticated, assertive and less subservient populous (Isaac-Henry *et al.*, 1993). Consumers today are demanding better quality service and proven value for money. These changes create added pressure on all service providers.

Information technology, telecommunications and automation have influenced both private and public organizations significantly in recent decades. The pace of change has become more rapid during the 1990s as information has increasingly become recognized as a vital tool for strategic planning, budgetary control and devolution of authority. For many public organizations the intro-duction of new technology has been problematic. Lack of expertise, individual resistance to change and poor technology management have often been cited as reasons for the failure or under-achievement of information and other technologies in some organizations. Process technology which may enhance or replace tradi-tional manual operations, and may lead to a reduced need for labour, is making inroads in many respects yet progress has been fraught with difficulties.

Many of the environmental forces discussed in previous chapters apply equally to public sector organizations so that there is no reason to repeat them here. However, you are urged to refer to the relevant chapters and sections.

Private and public sector environmental contrasts

There are important 'environmental' characteristics within which the public sector operates which, by and large, are alien to the private sector. This is highly pertinent when considering the degree of public accountability government organizations are obliged to assume. Each Civil Service department, for example, is accountable to a government minister and to the general public who both vote for government and provide funds, via taxation, to run the public services.

The extent and significance of public, political and professional account-ability within a typical NHS Trust hospital wields far greater influence over management practice than it does in a similarly sized commercial organization. Table 8.2 illustrates this by comparing two organizations, one public, the other a private company, in Kettering, a town in Northamptonshire (United Kingdom).

TABLE 8.2   A comparison of the public, political and professional accountabilities of a private and a public organization

External forces	Kettering General Hospital NHS Trust	Weetabix PLC (Burton Latimer, Kettering)
From the general public	• KGH NHS Trust serves the local community, providing accident and emergency and a wide range of services • Funded from taxation • Activities frequently reported in the local press; keen community interest in its future • Employs 2400 people • Incineration and disposal of toxic and other wastes • Traffic flows in the vicinity of the hospital (now bypassed)	• Emissions from the manufacturing plant have been the subject of some concern by local inhabitants • It employs local labour • Access to a public footpath which runs through the grounds of the plant was restricted
From government or its agents	• Accountable to and influenced by the Ministry of Health • Regional Health Authority • Funding bodies (including fund-holding GPs) • Environmental health controls and planning legislation (local government)	• Local planning legislation and control, e.g. planning permission for expansion turned down necessitating building in nearby Corby • Environmental health controls (local government)
From professional bodies	• Influence and control of standards and members' activities from numerous union and professional associations, including the BMA, Royal College of Nursing, UNISON who aim to direct, monitor and influence practice within the hospital	• Some relatively minor union influence; some employees are members of professional associations

QUESTIONS

1. What are 'public goods'? Why is there considerable disagreement concerning the correct level of public sector activity in the economy?

2. Undertake research using primary sources, the media and other secondary sources of data into the effects of information technology on specific public sector organizations.

3. Having read Chapter 5 on the social and demographic environment, summarize the potential effects of the United Kingdom's changing demographics on the activities of the public sector.

4. Identify the fundamental drivers of public sector change.

8.2 Privatization and deregulation

Introduction

Perhaps the most radical and transparent indication of government intention to 'change the face of the public sector' is privatization. The global phenomenon of privatization has involved the transfer of ownership from public to private operation of literally millions of jobs and billions of pounds of assets across the world. The change of ownership has, in many cases, proven to be a major spur to change within the organizations affected. This is in part due to a range of new and evolving environmental opportunities and constraints facing the privatized companies. Many, although by no means all, have faced renewed competitive pressures which were largely alien to the old publicly owned entities. This is certainly the case for British Airways which now successfully competes on the world stage, while in the United Kingdom the regional water companies enjoy virtual monopolies in their core business.

The management agenda within the privatized companies has been transformed. Parker (1993) argues that privatization 'implies a rematching of the organization to its external environment to achieve "strategic fit"'. Under state control industries are protected from many environmental forces, notably competition, which arguably makes them slow to change. Privatization and deregulation often requires management to utilize greater innovation and creativity and rely less on bureaucracy and the protection afforded by rules and procedures. Parker (1993) argues that the internal environment of privatized companies needs to change in order to cope with the challenges faced from the dynamic external business environment. These changes are often far reaching. Changes introduced within privatized companies include:

- restructuring, often involving 'downsizing' or 'rightsizing' (reducing the numbers employed), and delayering (reducing the number of levels in the organizational structure);
- alteration to human resource management policies and procedures including a reduction in the power and role of trade unions in pay negotiations;
- an emphasis on 'leadership' and extension of management accountability;
- changes in the product/markets and geographical emphasis including attempts at globalization;
- a transformation in business objectives.

Although privatization was not invented in the United Kingdom it was the Conservative government of the 1980s and 1990s that led the way. This section focuses on the privatization process in the United Kingdom and illustrates the unfolding events in the former Czechoslovakia via a mini-case. It also briefly reviews regulation and deregulation issues. There are many sound and in-depth analyses of the privatization process in the United Kingdom and elsewhere should the reader wish to go beyond this brief coverage.

Privatization: aims, criticisms and the future

Privatization has stimulated considerable debate concerning the wisdom and success of both the process and its outcome. It is a debate which will continue for many years throughout the world. The initial aims of the privatization programme themselves are a matter of some dispute in the United Kingdom. In broad terms, privatization has been a central policy tool to combat what successive governments through the 1980s and 1990s have seen as economic failure of state activity. More specifically, government aims include a desire to:

- reduce the scope and scale of the public sector;
- seek an increase in efficiency by introducing competition;
- reduce public sector financial commitment and associated borrowing requirement;
- provide proceeds from the sale of state-owned organizations to fund tax cuts;
- facilitate a reduction in the power of trade unions and professions;
- widen share ownership;
- encourage enterprise and customer choice, improve quality of provision, and reduce dependence on the state.

Criticism of the privatization programme has been widespread and often fierce. Nevertheless, no mainstream political party in the United Kingdom has plans to renationalize large tracks of industry. Many of the problems created by privatization continue to emerge as events unfold and knock-on effects take their toll. For example, the closure of many British coal mines, and subsequent decimation of the coal-mining industry, has been linked with the privatization of the electricity companies. Freed from the obligation to purchase British Coal to fire thermal power stations, newly privatized electricity generators are increasingly switching to natural gas and imported coal as alternative sources of power. Another longer-term implication of privatization has been the political and social storm resulting from the sometimes massive salary and bonuses many directors and chief executives have awarded themselves. Although not particularly significant in a competitive sense, or when compared to many of the more fundamental criticisms levelled at the process, it has contributed to a change of public opinion away from further privatization programmes.

The prime criticisms of the privatization programme are varied. Many of the previously nationalized corporations were effectively state monopolies. Privatization of these does not in itself produce or increase competition. Consequently, there are a number of privately owned and operated companies which now enjoy monopolistic market conditions and which are regulated by government or its appointed bodies. The regional water and electricity companies in particular, and British Gas and BT to an extent, operate in restricted markets and hence enjoy some of the benefits of restricted competition. However, the act of privatization does not guarantee improvements in performance. Not all privatized companies have achieved productivity improvements (Parker and Martin, 1993).

Until the stock market crash in October 1987 the general public developed a distorted view of share ownership, seeing share subscription in the newly privatized companies as resulting in instant gain. For example, those subscribing to British Airways shares when they were first floated enjoyed an instant 36 per cent premium on their investment. Additionally, this also indicated that government had underpriced many companies upon flotation so 'selling the country's silver off on the cheap'. A more accurate estimate of the demand for shares would have led to substantial additional revenues earned by government which might have financed additional services or tax cuts. Again, it was British Airways which best illustrated this point as it was oversubscribed 36 times while BT was oversubscribed nine times and British Gas four times. Criticism was often levelled at governments in the 1980s and early 1990s for using the once-in-a-lifetime revenue from privatization to fund spending or to reduce taxation rather than to invest it in improvements in national infrastructure such as the rail, road network or housing stock.

Many privatized companies, such as BT, have shed thousands of employees, so contributing to national unemployment and increasing the demands upon the welfare state. Additionally, with the loss of the old nationalized corporations, government is no longer in a position to use such organizations as tools of social, economic and regional policy. Finally, the cost of underwriting the multiple share issues in the 1980s was estimated at £325 million while the advertising campaign to facilitate the sale of British Gas alone amounted to £21 million. The estimated total cost to date of selling the state-owned enterprises is in excess of £700 million.

Privatization and other public sector structural changes led to over 650 000 jobs being transferred to private ownership between 1980 and 1996. Although privatization looks set to continue as long as the Conservative party forms the government, the scope for further privatization is now somewhat restricted as the most suitable candidates are already in private hands. Few straightforward businesses remain in the public sector. The Post Office and the BBC, together with a number of local authority airports and transport companies, could eventually be candidates for privatization.

Privatization in the Czech and Slovak republics

As in Britain the origins of privatization in Czechoslovakia lie in political realignment following the perceived failure of state industry. But in the independent Czech and Slovak republics the change is of a different scale involving 'turnaround management' across the entire economy. In the mid-1980s around 97 per cent of the countries' value added came from the state sector. In 1989 61 per cent of its exports flowed through COMECON; by 1991 COMECON was disbanded and trade with the former communist states had collapsed.

Privatization is taking place by many routes, namely by return of property to those dispossessed under communism; by direct sale through auctions and tenders to domestic citizens; through a voucher scheme under which citizens purchase from the state, at nominal cost, vouchers to buy shares in privatized firms; and by sale to, or joint ventures with, foreign investors of which a prominent example is the Volkswagen investment in Skoda. By the end of 1992 over 31 000 small businesses, mainly shops and workshops, had been sold, largely by auction, under the October 1990 Small Privatization Act. By mid-1992, 67 per cent of shares in over 1400 state companies had been sold through the voucher method and 171 firms had been completely privatized under the Large Privatization Act of 1991.

Business has been privatized with the minimum of reconstruction. The speed of the desired privatization, driven by the political need to dismantle state control quickly following the fall of the communist government, has ruled out the low-risk strategies adopted in the United Kingdom. Consequently, failures among privatized businesses are predicted and indeed are desirable to remove some of the economic distortions introduced by state planning. This means that some investors will be disappointed. For overseas companies investment is high risk. At the same time the republics need foreign investment including involvement in joint ventures and strategic partnerships.

The privatization programme has involved the management of transformational change. There are interest groups from within and outside the businesses which oppose change. The programme also requires management with a knowledge of how to succeed in competitive markets, something often lacking among incumbent administrators working according to central plans. Too many Czech and Slovak companies have suffered from low motivation at work and high absenteeism and have produced low-quality products which have sold in Western markets on price alone. Low prices alongside low productivity have led to inadequate surpluses for reinvestment.

Abridged: Parker (1993).

Conversely the planned privatization of the Post Office was delayed in 1994 due to a combination of public opposition and dissent from within the parliamentary Conservative party. Whether that privatization proceeds is mere speculation. It will depend upon the political 'complexion' of the Party in government and ultimately, upon the will of the people. Sizeable privatization programmes are now well underway in most European countries. In France the scale and scope of this programme is likely to match that of the United Kingdom's in the past decade and a half. A global trend, which started before the collapse of communism in Europe, has freed whole tranches of industry from direct government control. The long-term consequences of this transformation are as yet unknown.

Regulating privatized monopolies

The United Kingdom government have maintained some control over the more monopolistic privatized companies who might otherwise abuse their position. This

TABLE 8.3   Privatized companies and their regulators

Privatized company	Official regulator
BT	Office of Telecommunications (OFTEL)
Severn-Trent Water	Office of Water Regulation (OFWAT)
Northern Electric	Office of Electricity Regulation (OFFER)
British Gas	Office of Gas Regulation (OFGAS)

has largely been achieved within a regulatory framework and the appointment of official watchdog bodies. Table 8.3 lists some of the regulators in the United Kingdom.

However, the work of regulation is not without its critics. Many investors in the privatized utilities criticize the inconsistencies and uncertainties caused by the current regulatory system, while consumer groups and elements within the Labour and Liberal Democratic parties argue that regulation is not always sufficiently robust, nor conducted in the best interests of the public. It is a debate which is certain to continue as many public utilities are 'natural monopolies' which require some form of regulation or control if the interests of the general public, the nation and the consumer are to be upheld.

Deregulation

Governments through the ages have established a regulatory framework for many industries. Often the result of years of separate and well-meaning pieces of regulation, these frameworks sometimes restrict that industry from growing and competing on the world stage. It has been a central tenant of Conservative government policy since 1979 to deregulate many industries to, as they see it, free them from unnecessary and unhelpful constraint. Hand in hand with deregulation, moves to ensure consumer protection, often in the form of new regulation, have taken place.

By way of example, in the 1980s the market for spectacles was largely deregulated. This resulted in greater competition and a reduction in prices to the consumer. It also led to the levying of a charge for eye tests, leading many to forgo such 'treatment'. There has been an increase in the numbers diagnosed with eye diseases in the United Kingdom during the past decade. Bus services, outside London, have largely been deregulated leading to further competition and the growth of major transport operators. Public transport deregulation has led to the proliferation of bus services on some routes and total absence of regular services on others. As companies are largely responsive to market demand this has led to a reduction in service for those living in rural areas. The financial services industry has benefited from significant deregulation enabling a multitude of organizations to compete in the growing pensions, insurance and other financial services markets. Government has also tightened or further regulated some sectors and industries as circumstances change. This is also true of the financial services industry where spurious new 'products' and means of marketing them have often led to renewed pressure to regulate. Although the vast majority of the organizations which have benefited from deregulation fall within the private sector, their new-found freedoms stem from political and economic influence and the direct hand of government.

However, many politicians and consumers argue that insufficient regulation exists in certain fields (such as financial services). The issue of regulation and deregulation is the subject of considerable political debate (refer to Chapter 7 for further details).

QUESTIONS

1.   Conduct research into the privatization process involving one company in the United Kingdom or elsewhere. Summarize the political, social, economic and other arguments given both in favour and against the privatization. Which do you think was the more persuasive argument? What do you think now?

2.   What do you think are some of the potential long-term issues facing many previously privatized companies? What problems might governments and the general consuming public face following the privatization of an industry?

3.   To what extent do the regulators of privatized industries help compensate for the lack of competitiveness facing those industries? What are some of the inherent complexities facing the role of regulation?

4.   Study the quality press and other secondary sources and write a mini-case study on the privatization process in one country (e.g. Malaysia, France, Germany, Russia). Structure the case so that you comment on the scale and scope of privatization, its pitfalls and problems, the likely benefits and the long-term aims and consequences of the programme. Focus on the 'new' business environment facing privatized companies.

8.3 Changing the face of public sector organizations

An equally powerful yet less controversial mechanism for changing the delivery of services is taking the place of the privatization process. The NHS, state schools and large parts of the Civil Service and local government are being continually subjected to further market or competitive pressures. There have been three broad thrusts in government policy in this regard. Firstly, compulsory competitive tendering and market testing of many local and national government services has taken place. Secondly, fundamental structural changes have been thrust upon the

Civil Service and NHS in particular, but also the education service. Finally, the private finance initiative launched by Norman Lamont, then Chancellor of the Exchequer, in 1992 which had attracted just £500 million of private money for public projects in the first two years of operation, aims to promote private/public sector partnerships. The relative failure of this initiative is in large measure due to uncertainty about rates of return. However, the scope for private/public partnership in both developing and operating 'public' projects suggests that this approach may achieve greater success in the future. A £150 million computer system to store National Insurance records will be the first project of its kind to be funded through the 1992 initiative.

Exposing government services to competitive forces

This section focuses on the measures taken by government at national and local levels in the United Kingdom to expose many of its services to competitive conditions. As a result of competitive tendering there has been a vast increase in contracted-out work, that is, services and goods supplied to public 'customers' by private or voluntary organizations. In such cases public authorities such as Northampton County Council still hold the responsibility, for example, for refuse collection, but their direct employees do not necessarily deliver the service. Contracting out is very common in certain fields such as refuse collection and disposal. It is clear that government departments and agencies, as well as local authorities, NHS Trusts and educational services, have been encouraged by their political masters to follow industrial trends and contract out non-core business. In 1985 the Ministry of Agriculture Fisheries and Food (MAFF) broke new ground by market testing the fisheries aerial surveillance service. However, compulsory and voluntary competitive tendering had been used extensively prior to this date as a mechanism for encouraging both competition and 'privatization'. Many of the successful organizations tendering for the right to operate public services have been private profit-making companies.

Government have argued that market testing holds many advantages. It is thought that competition helps ensure value for money while a focus on performance outputs will produce clear standards, an improved quality of service and an explicit customer/supplier relationship. Additionally, it is believed that market testing enables both external and in-house bidders to be more innovative in their field while monitoring contracts and service level agreements focuses on outputs, objectives and targets in order to improve efficiency and effectiveness. Naturally, these claims are the subject of considerable ongoing debate.

As the scope for further wholesale privatization had waned by the mid-1990s the scale of market testing and competitive tendering had grown to encompass areas hitherto considered 'safe' within both local and national government. At local government level political and media attention has focused upon a number of 'flagship' authorities which have embraced central government objectives with vigour. Notable among these during the 1980s and early 1990s have been

Wandsworth and Westminster, in London. Both councils reduced council tax to a fraction of that charged in some other London boroughs and claimed that lean and skilful management, including the contracting out of many roles and a reduction in 'non-essential' services, accounted for huge financial savings. Certainly, council taxes in these authorities were much lower in the early 1990s yet the case has naturally raised a number of critical issues of relevance to local government across the country, not least accusations of favouritism. For example, central government, an active and vociferous supporter of Wandsworth council, have been accused of awarding the council sizeable tranches of grant monies and of showing 'favouritism' in other regards. Westminster Council was able to set one of the lowest council tax levels in England in 1994–95 (i.e. £245 for Band D properties) which represented a £50 reduction on the previous year. Critics argue that a combination of poor services and central government favouritism made this possible, although the council was at the forefront of extending competitive tendering into hitherto 'sacred' areas such as nursery education. Dame Shirley Porter, the figurehead of this flagship council, was no stranger to financial, political and legal controversy during her eight years as leader facing various accusations including fraud and 'gerrymandering'.

At the national level, market testing and competitive tendering has increasingly broadened its scope throughout the 1990s with few government departments exempt from its influence. Many 'support' functions which can be differentiated from the core business of a department have been identified for such 'privatization'. For example, the armed forces fleet of 95 000 support vehicles is being targeted for private operation. A pilot scheme was established in 1995 which aimed to place non-combat Land Rovers, trucks, vans and cars under private management. The vehicles will be owned and often maintained within the private sector and leased or rented back to the Ministry of Defence. The *Competing for Quality* White Paper (HMSO, 1991) emphasized the role of public service managers in buying services on behalf of the citizen as opposed to automatically providing them internally. It aimed to move a minimum of £2300 million, or about 10 per cent of MoD expenditure, into the private sector by the year 2000. Other MoD services to be market-tested include:

- *Royal Navy*: operation of the tug and tanker fleet;
- *Army*: provision of logistics information to the quartermaster;
- *RAF*: engineering support for the Hawk jet trainers and the operation of training aircraft.

These and many private business incursions into the Civil Service will undoubtedly result in a reduction in staff requirements. Naturally, trade unions and employee associations have grave reservations concerning competitive tendering and market testing. Not only do they fear job losses but also a reduction in the quality of services offered. Following proposals in late 1994 to allow private companies to compete with Inland Revenue staff in the collation of potentially sensitive financial information on individuals and companies, concern was expressed about potential lapses in confidentiality. The Inland Revenue Staff Federation fear that such information may be used for other, non-legitimate purposes by a less than scrupulous private operator. Similar concerns have been expressed over the Prison Service's plans to shortlist 12 'suitable' prisons for market testing. The BBC is also engaged in the process of market testing for some of its services.

In many cases, however, there has not been a great deal of interest shown by suitable private companies who wish to operate government services. Additionally, a department's own tender is often, financially, the most attractive, such that the service remains in public hands. In many cases, however, internal bids have been discouraged or even forbidden. Almost three-quarters of the first £1.1 billion of directly contracted-out Civil Service work was awarded to private sector operators while in-house bids were not allowed. Where in-house bids were acknowledged, over half of the market tests were won by the public servants. Similarly, estimates of the actual financial savings made by contracting out services vary significantly. Some not uncontroversial government data has indicated that the policy is proving to be a growing success in financial terms. The government claimed that a saving of 23 per cent was made on that first £1.1 billion of contracted-out services which involved a reduction of 14 500 Civil Service jobs with just over 12 000 transferring to the private sector.

Public sector reform in New Zealand

The concept of the 'New Public Management' was warmly embraced by the Labour government in New Zealand (1984–90). They brought in dramatic changes to both the organization and management of the state sector. The aim was to improve efficiency and accountability. The government has:

- commercialized many of the functions performed by public organizations;
- separated commercial and non-commercial operations;
- transferred trading activities to private operation;
- moved away from national pay bargaining to decentralized/enterprise-based systems;
- introduced accountability systems for chief executives which include fixed-term contracts, performance-related pay and annual performance reviews.

There has been a great deal of contracting out of public services and the sale of many public assets, although widespread privatization has not occurred.

The mini-case above briefly shows how the Labour government in New Zealand has tackled the growing problem of government expenditure and reform.

Consumerism: charters and league tables

Another mechanism government have employed to encourage both public accountability and quality improvement is a variety of quality charters, publicly disclosed quality standards and measurements of performance. These charters set service standards which individuals might rightfully expect. They have, by and large, been imposed on public sector organizations. Hence, in the United Kingdom, we have the Citizen's Charter, the Patient's Charter, and school and hospital league tables where individual units are 'benchmarked' against each other.

The Education Reform Act of 1988 gave parents the right to send their children to the school of their choice. Schools were obliged to provide information, including examination performance league tables to facilitate that choice. It is now possible to obtain a list of schools within each local authority ranked according to the level of achievement of their pupils in external examinations. What is more, each authority is ranked for its overall performance (Table 8.4).

Like so many of the public sector 'reforms' introduced since 1980, charters and league tables have been a source of bitter dispute between organizational managers, trade unions, government and other interest groups. League tables of performance, such as that shown in Table 8.4, invite the public to compare organizations or, in this case, local authorities. Those who have been responsible for the introduction and dissemination of such 'performance' measures argue that they serve to inform the general public, and to indirectly improve the quality of services. Many public sector organizations, such as individual schools, feel that league tables disguise a whole host of relevant and critical information which parents should be aware of when making a decision about choice of school. They also argue that such figures can be thoroughly misleading, especially if taken at face value. For example, let us assume two schools, one located in the Isles of Scilly and another in Southwark (refer to Table 8.4). School league tables will measure the GCSE and GCE 'A'-level results and truancy rates of both sets of students and probably indicate that the Scilly Isles school fared best. What the tables do not show is the 'value added' to students by their whole school experience; nor do they measure things such as artistic or creative development or the sporting excellence of students. They do not clearly show how some schools, despite enormous

TABLE 8.4   Extract from schools' league tables by local authority (ranked 1 to 108)

LEA	GCSE '94	GCSE '93	A-level 1994	Truancy	Social deprivation
Isles of Scilly	1st	1st		1st	1st
Sutton	2nd	3rd	7th	3rd	42nd
Kingston upon Thames	3rd	2nd	30th	10th	38th
Barnet	4th	10th	25th	2nd	79th
West Sussex	5th	5th	52nd	4th	4th
Lambeth	104th	102nd	103rd	100th	107th
Islington	105th	104th	102nd	103rd	104th
Knowsley	106th	108th	99th	97th	89th
Tower Hamlets	107th	106th	97th	106th	106th
Southwark	108th	107th	101st	107th	102nd

Source: Department of Education; Department of the Environment.

difficulties with social deprivation and related problems, are indeed 'successful', while others located in prosperous relatively trouble-free areas may indeed be rather complacent and mediocre. In other words, the 'right' things are not always being measured.

Criticisms of the Patient's Charter, which sets out standards of care for the NHS and invites patients to insist upon such standards being met, has led to a vast increase in the number of complaints about the quality of service. Whereas charters and league tables may introduce a certain amount of competition, and may indirectly encourage some 'quality' improvement, many public organizations, such as the remnants of British Rail and many NHS Trusts, argue that they have insufficient resources to deal with the problems highlighted.

Structural changes in the public sector

The reader would be excused for assuming that there was very little of the public sector remaining after the privatization and contracting-out processes outlined above. However, public sector expenditure still accounts for over 40 per cent of gross domestic product. The NHS alone employs over 1 million of the United Kingdom's total workforce of about 25 million and, as such, is the largest single employer in Europe. Although the public sector has changed it still accounts for a very significant element of Britain's economic activity.

A great number of the changes that have been introduced to the public sector are primarily structural in nature. That is, the organizational structures and reporting relationships have altered significantly. These transformations have, in turn, led to other 'softer' operational changes which have influenced prevailing management style and cultures. We will first focus on these structural changes before looking at management practices.

Structural changes have occurred within the public sector on a grand scale. The Civil Service, NHS and education service have been characterized by a degree of decentralization. Distinct units within these services, such as a hospital or a school, have been encouraged to 'opt out' and become semi-autonomous. In the case of education some secondary and a few primary schools have taken themselves out of local government control and have sought funding directly from the Department for Education and Employment. They have been given additional budgetary responsibilities and freedoms and required 'to stand on their own feet'. Many have thrived under their newly granted powers, released from the constraints and regulations that an additional tier of control may have imposed. However, there have been problems both within some 'opted out' units and for those that remain as 'managed' units. Similarly, the issue of dual or multiple standards has risen to the fore.

The majority of the Civil Service and NHS is now managed within such opted-out units, referred to as 'Agencies' and 'Trusts' respectively. Schools have, by and large, been more reluctant to opt out, preferring instead to work within a local government framework. However, with Local Management of Schools

(LMS) and the Education Reform Act of 1988 they have assumed greater responsibility for budgetary and staffing matters than was previously the case.

Public and private sector collaborative partnerships

Considerable political attention has been paid in recent years to the furtherance of private and public sector partnerships. The right wing of the Conservative party have argued for some time that the state ought to have an enabling rather than controlling role. That is, the state should facilitate and cooperate with private organizations in providing public services rather than assuming those services should be offered exclusively within a public framework. This basic ideology has been taken on board by the other major political parties. However, the Conservative governments through the 1980s and 1990s have had only limited success in operationalizing this belief. More Left Wing proponents see such partnerships as an opportunity for local governments to concretize their influential role within the community. The growth and acceptance of such partnerships would begin to recast the prime role of the state as that of 'an enabler' as opposed to 'a provider'.

QUESTIONS

1. What are the objectives of competitive tendering and market testing for (a) the public sector organization concerned and (b) the government of the day? Assemble evidence to debate whether these objectives are being met.

2. What is the purpose of School League Tables? Outline some of the key contentious issues concerning their use. How might such league tables improve, or otherwise change, managerial and professional activities within schools?

3. How might some of the structural changes discussed within this chapter influence managerial processes and the quality of services?

4. Utilizing library and/or primary sources, explore the future possibilities for private/public sector partnership.

8.4 The consequences of environmental change: managerialism

Private managerial practices and public objectives

During the 1980s and 1990s governments have been concerned to develop within the public sector a 'businesslike' approach to management which draws upon private sector practice. Largely spurred on by the efforts of a number of policy advisers such as Griffiths (NHS, 1983) the view prevailed that core managerial roles and skills should be portable between private and public sectors. It became widely acknowledged that the public sector had a great deal to learn from private organizational practice (not, notably, the other way round).

Public sector organizations have imported a succession of management techniques strongly associated with notions of good practice in the private sector. These include devolved budgetary control, total quality management (TQM), business process re-engineering (BPR), teambuilding and benchmarking. Many ideas are associated with notable management gurus, best-selling texts and local interpretations of 'the enterprise culture'. In general, attempts at adoption of such initiatives reveal a strong desire among key managers to mimic good practice elsewhere, yet often insufficient consideration is given to the suitability of the model to the specific public sector organizational context.

Many administrators, managers and notably 'professionals' within the public service have resisted moves in this direction as they view them as inappropriate to their roles. Practices which are suitable for commercial profit-oriented companies are not, they argue, easily transferred to public service nor is their adoption entirely desirable. The objectives of the public service differ sufficiently from those of private firms, it is argued, to ensure that transferability of styles, skills and practices is often inapplicable.

The public sector has long assumed distinctive goals from those of most private firms, such as the 'pursuit of equity, justice and fairness, accountability and the enhancement of citizenship' (Isaac-Henry *et al.*, 1993). In other words, it can, and often is, argued that the fundamental values of public sector managers and organizational objectives differ from those of the private sector. Differences in values encourage a divergence in managerial behaviour such that 'the private sector' model of management fails to 'fit' many public organizations. McKevitt and Lawson (1994) have identified both a private and public sector model which is abbreviated and simplified in Table 8.5.

Many practitioners and academics argue that private sector managerial models are inadequate as a basis of management in the public sector. The distinctive conditions within the public sector, such as the greater role of collective

TABLE 8.5   Private and public sector management

Private sector model	Public sector model
• Individual choice	• Collective choice
• Demand and price	• Need for resources
• Closure (in private domain)	• Openness (public domain)
• Market	• Need
• Search for market satisfaction	• Search for justice
• Competition	• Collective action

Source: After McKevitt and Lawson (1994).

choice, citizenship and issues of need and justice, are not as apparent in the private sector. Fundamental differences exist with regard to the role of the marketplace. Even NHS quasi-markets remain heavily regulated and, far from wanting to stimulate demand, most public organizations are required to ration the service they offer.

Traditionally, public sector employees are seen as motivated by public service ideals and driven by a desire to serve the public and the country, as opposed to the business or oneself. However, 'public choice theory' suggests that public officials are motivated, among other things, by budget-maximizing goals – that is, they seek to increase their power and status by increasing their departmental budgets. Nevertheless, the public sector administrative culture embraces meritocracy and acts as a guarantor of probity. The rise of entrepreneurial and enterprise-oriented management is seen as a threat to such values.

Partly as a consequence of the differences between private and public sector objectives and roles, researchers and policy makers have sought new insight concerning the appropriate form for management in the new public sector. Much attention is now focused upon the difference between the two sectors as opposed to their similarities. The following section briefly investigates this issue further.

New public management

Increased attention has been focused on the concept of the 'New Public Management' both in the United Kingdom and internationally (Ferlie *et al.*, 1994). This has created pressures upon managers to change inherited roles and behaviours. These changes have had political implications as the power of managers in many public services, not least the NHS, has been in the ascendancy, while that of 'professional' groups is, in relative terms, in decline. Many public sector arenas, previously dominated by professional groups, have been brought within political and 'managerial' control. For example, more exhaustive forms of auditing and inspection have been introduced within Higher Education both in relation to the 'quality' of teaching and research. The outcome of such audit and monitoring influences future funding arrangements. In the NHS even the powerful stakeholder group comprising doctors and consultants are seen to be losing ground to the new management. For example, Ferlie *et al.* (1994) suggest that many contracts in the new style quasi-market within the NHS are now signed off by managers as opposed to consultants. Consequently, public sector managers, in relative terms at least, can be seen to have gained as a result of change, while professionals have by and large become less powerful.

Ferlie *et al.* (1994) suggest four 'variants' or management models in evidence during the last two decades (Table 8.6).

In reality many of the themes and indicators which portray each model are present in different public organizations at different times. It is not the case that one variant was universally dominant for a brief period before the next took precedence.

TABLE 8.6　Four 'new public sector' management models (after Ferlie *et al.*, 1994)

Themes and indicators
Variant 1 Value for money; efficiency improvement; market-line mechanisms; greater competition; strong general management spine; external audits
Variant 2 Organizational downsizing; search for flexibility; greater customer orientation; increased decentralization of strategic and budgetary control; increased contracting out
Variant 3 Emphasis on organizational development and organization learning (bottom-up); organizational cultural change; vision; leadership (top-down)
Variant 4 Concern with quality; 'value driven'; empowerment

Private sector practices, if it is possible to precisely define what they are, have made inroads within public service organizations. Decentralization and devolved budgetary control are now more common practices within the public sector. Progress was, however, slow at first partly due to a lack of clarity in the objectives of various change initiatives. In the early years of Margaret Thatcher's government the prime concern was with efficiency; a war on waste was declared. Rather than attempt to radically alter the culture of public service the Thatcher government established the Efficiency Unit, fronted by Derek Raynor, in 1980. Its primary aim was to secure efficiency savings and better value for money. The work of this unit made little impact. Consequently, it was followed by the development of a Management Information System for Ministers (MINIS) which provided government ministers with more financial and other information about their departments. It aimed, as did the Financial Management Initiative in 1982, to further decentralize budgetary and management responsibility within the Civil Service. These measures were attempts to devolve management responsibility and to encourage the development of managerial skills and awareness at lower levels than had hitherto been the case.

Change was initially slow to take root; however, the development of Civil Service agencies and structural changes within the NHS and education services has hastened the speed of reform. 'Managerialism' has now infiltrated most public service organizations although it is enjoying mixed fortunes in terms of both public and employee perceptions and when evaluated against measurable organizational outcomes. Although the subject of dispute, many academics, public sector managers and informed members of the public would argue that the changes have held many advantages, which include:

- a reduction in bureaucracy, which has enabled organizations to respond more rapidly to environmental changes;

- increased flexibility and the development of a customer orientation, which have improved the quality of service offered (at the same time customers have become more vociferous in their complaints and more demanding generally of the public sector);
- improvements in efficiency and effectiveness as a result of clearer organizational and individual objectives and greater accountability.

The British Civil Service

This section discusses the nature of structural and managerial changes within the Civil Service since the late 1980s. It illustrates the strong and pervasive influence upon the public sector of its political masters.

In 1987 the 'Next Steps' report commissioned by the government showed how little in the way of real financial and management responsibility was devolved down the line within the Civil Service (HMSO, 1987). This was despite the Financial Management Initiative of 1982. The report revealed that decentralized budgetary control had not been introduced in many departments, and where it had, budget centre managers were invariably members of the senior management team. Decision making resided in the centre of departments or with senior management, and problems that demanded resolution were all too often delegated upwards. The Treasury remained meddlesome and the conservative and cautious culture continued to prevail. The report recommended a real devolution of power over budgets, manpower, pay, hiring and firing to executive agencies in areas of activity embracing the 95 per cent of the Civil Service involved in the delivery of services. The structural changes suggested have largely been achieved and currently (1996) Civil Service executive functions are conducted by over 100 agencies employing 350 000 civil servants. Agencies range in scale from the Social Security Benefits Agency, an organization employing 65 000 civil servants, to the Wilton Park Conference Centre in Sussex with 30 employees. It is believed that a further 60 candidates for agency status have been identified covering around 90 000 civil servants.

The dawning of agency status in the Civil Service signalled what was probably the most radical departure from current practice the Civil Service had known in the twentieth century. Agency status, although some way short of privatization, gives each executive unit opportunities to develop a structure, system, style and culture which suits its environment. A Civil Service Agency represents a newly created identity for an organization, or part of a previously larger unit, which manages a set of predetermined government functions, such as administering the Common Agricultural Policy of the European Union. Thus government functions are parcelled off into manageable units of similar operations. Each agency is responsible to its parent department or directly to a minister of the government. The Treasury closely monitors running costs. Agencies are required to set a framework, tailored to the job to be done, which specifies policies, objectives, the results required, the resources available and their indicators of performance. Clearly, government in the United Kingdom has attempted to encourage a degree of self-determination, especially among agencies with income earning capabilities. Many agencies have 'trading fund status'. By enabling them to actively market and deliver their services widely, this increases their capacity to supplement running costs by income generation. Some agency functions have been the subject of 'market testing' to assess the feasibility of conducting these activities within the private sector. However, it is widely believed that agency status is the first step towards privatization.

The Intervention Board Executive Agency

The Intervention Board was established as a government department in 1972. It administers the market regulation and production support measures of the European Union Common Agricultural Policy (CAP) within the United Kingdom. This role involves the licensing of imports and exports, the payment of subsidies and the collection of levies together with the buying, storage and sale of agricultural products. It became a government agency on 1 April 1990.

The Agency employs just over 1000 staff and has a turnover in excess of £2.5 billion. On becoming an agency the Intervention Board established a corporate plan inclusive of a mission statement, strategic and financial objectives and performance targets. Additionally, the Chief Executive is responsible for developing a policy and resources document detailing the Agency's aims, responsibilities and delegated authorities, which was issued to all staff. The Agency aims to achieve 2 per cent efficiency savings annually, against a Treasury demand of 1.5 per cent. Its customers are the food and agricultural industries. It has been making efforts recently to improve both the service it gives its customers and its own corporate image. The Agency now has a customer care policy and publishes a booklet endorsing its services under the 'Citizen's Charter'.

There are nine levels of hierarchy within the Agency, that is, from grade 3 (Chief Executive) to Administrative Assistants. The 'clerical factories', those parts of the Agency where claims are processed, are largely staffed by administrative officers and assistants and their first line supervisors, executive officers. In many ways, the change of identity and external structure has had little effect on internal structures and work organization. The strong Civil Service organizational culture largely remains intact (Brooks and Bate, 1994).

Change within the Civil Service has involved major structural realignment and attempts at fundamental change to managerial practices. However, the ultimate aim is to transform the organizational culture of the Civil Service and to make it more responsive to customers, less bureaucratic and more effective, that is to achieve better value for money. Many critics argue that levels of both efficiency and effectiveness within the current Civil Service are already high and that further change would adversely affect service quality. As if to symbolize continued government determination to slim down and change public service organizations, significant internal changes were announced in late 1994 to the Treasury which lies at the very heart of the Civil Service. Senior posts were to be reduced (from 99 to 72); a proposed internal restructuring will remove two departments; areas of existing business are to be transferred to other Civil Service agencies or the private sector; and the Treasury is to specialize on overall financial strategy.

Numerous other Civil Service agencies and departments are experiencing competitive tendering and market testing which will, ultimately, involve the transfer of many services to private sector operators. This illustrates the depth of change that has occurred within the very bastion of British public service. However, whether a radical change in managerial and organizational behaviour has taken place within all agencies is a matter of some debate (Brooks and Bate, 1994). Undoubtedly some have enjoyed their new-found freedoms while others have proved less determined to 'go their own way'.

A more recent attempt at Civil Service reform comes in the shape of the *The Civil Service Continuity and Change* (HMSO, 1994) proposals. The White Paper sets out the government's plans for building on the previous reforms aimed at improving efficiency, effectiveness and quality. The paper expresses the continuing need to separate policy making and service provision, embodied within the Next Steps initiative and the Citizen's Charter, and for further delegation of management responsibility by developing appropriate management structures, flexible pay systems and by further developing staff. Civil Service agencies are encouraged to apply key management techniques such as priority-based cost management, benchmarking and process re-engineering. Further strategic contracting out, privatization and market testing are encouraged in the White Paper (HMSO, 1994).

One of the case studies at the end of this book (p. 343) is based on the NHS in the United Kingdom. It explores in more detail the environmental characteristics and managerial issues facing the NHS. However, the following mini-case on Hong Kong illustrates the global nature of concern surrounding an all-important element of public provision – that is, health care. It looks at one province's attempt to come to terms with change. It explores the dynamic political and environmental influences which act upon the health care system in Hong Kong and outlines the responses that the system has made to these external changes and pressures.

The Hospital Authority of Hong Kong

For many years prior to the commissioning of a consultant report on the public hospital system in Hong Kong the government had become concerned about the rising cost of providing medical services and the increasing community expectation of the service. Other concerns focused on the perceived lack of flexibility and management competence within the health care system. It was with little surprise that the consultants recommended establishing a statutory hospital authority, structural changes within hospitals, measures to reduce overcrowding in hospitals, new staffing and management structures and further cost control and recovery measures.

A Provisional Health Authority was established and reported that the future hospital management structure should 'ensure staff serve the patients in a more efficient and effective manner'. In 1991 a new Hospital Authority took control of all public hospitals.

The Hospital Authority aimed to integrate government hospitals into a single system and to provide uniform terms and conditions of employment for its staff. It was also charged with encouraging further public participation in the operation of the public hospital system and thus inviting direct accountability to the public. In addition to the structural changes, the reforms hoped to achieve a 'cultural transformation' in public medical care, replacing a culture centred on the values of professionalism, specialization and hierarchical management with a patient-centred approach emphasizing empowerment of staff, teamwork, continuous improvement of service quality and overall organizational effectiveness. By 1994 the Hospital Authority had developed a mission statement, corporate plan, business plans and had articulated its corporate values.

The environment

The Authority is funded almost exclusively by government and had an operating budget of approximately £1.4 billion in 1995/96, which represented about 10 per cent of government's recurrent expenditure.

Prior to the establishment of the Hospital Authority decision making was centralized. It is argued that this led to the hospital system becoming out of step with its environment. This was particularly significant in areas of non-medical technology and hospital management practices. Critics suggest that clinical decisions were often made without consideration of the financial implications and service development was led by medical professionals. Services were criticized for not being customer oriented. This was politically unacceptable.

The Hospital Authority is responsible for identifying the future medical needs of the population of Hong Kong. Estimates are based upon information such as population growth and distribution, including the recognition of a rapidly ageing population structure, and other health indices. It is estimated that as many as 50 per cent of Hong Kong residents aged over 65 years have some form of chronic disease and 20 per cent some form of disability. The identification of gaps in service provision, often created by changes within the external environment, is an important dimension of the Authority's work. For example, currently there are few resources focused on the growing adolescent problem of drug abuse and suicide.

With increasing affluence in Hong Kong, better education and improvements in communication, there is greater awareness of the benefits health care can offer and increased customer expectations. A more informed public in a changing socio-political environment results in the emergence of demands to be involved in the decision-making process. This necessitates information sharing and the invitation to active input from political and non-political groups.

The changing social structure in the province has had an effect on the care for the elderly who are becoming increasingly institutionalized due to a process of extended family breakdown. Although common in the West this is a relatively new phenomenon in South-East Asia.

Public sector change: drivers and resistors

Environmental and organizational change is a theme that has run throughout this chapter. The 'business' environment facing public sector organizations is in a state of flux largely, although not exclusively, due to changes in political ideologies and agendas. No public organization is immune from change yet internal resistance is rife. There are within most organizations, not least publicly owned entities, both active and passive forces which encourage a state of stability and which serve to reduce the potency of the forces for change. Hence a dynamic balance exists between the forces which promote change and those that favour stability. Both sets of pressures comprise a combination of external environmental and internal organizational forces.

Lewin (1951) encompassed such tensions within a force-field model. He argues that the two sets of forces 'push' against each other. If the forces for change, the 'drivers', are more pervasive and powerful than the 'resistors' then change will occur. Conversely, if resisting forces are more powerful they may well scupper the intensions of change agents. Hence an intense, continuous and highly political process of change and stability is unfolding within the public sector. Figure 8.3 shows the force-field model.

We have extracted from this chapter and other sources just some of the forces for change and stability in the public sector (Table 8.7). These are not ranked according to their potency. Nor is this an exhaustive list. The forces encouraging change are largely, but not exclusively, external to public sector organizations. These have been outlined within this chapter. Factors encouraging stability and other resisting forces are largely internal to public organizations.

Although the causal relationships between many of the factors are not shown in the force-field model (e.g. is the 'New Right ideology' a cause or contributory factor in encouraging 'managerialism'?) it does indicate the complexity of the tensions that exist. It is also curious that some items, such as public accountability, can act as both a force encouraging change and reform and a pressure to guard against the flux and uncertainty which change often involves. This model could just as easily be applied to any single organization or government department.

Just how much real change has occurred within the public sector over the past two decades is, like so many aspects of public policy, hotly disputed. There

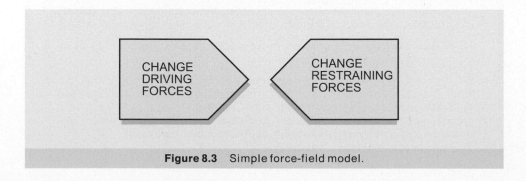

Figure 8.3 Simple force-field model.

TABLE 8.7   Conflicting forces for change and stability within the public sector

Forces for change	Forces for stability
New 'Right' ideology	Organizational cultures: accepted practices and behaviours; taken-for-granted beliefs concerning how activities should be conducted; attitudes to colleagues, members of the public and politicians; fundamental public service values
Margaret Thatcher and continuous Conservative government	
Only moderate economic growth	
High levels of unemployment	Hierarchical organizational structures, formal reporting relationships and historically accrued bureaucracy
Increasing resource demands on welfare provision	
Ageing population	Statutory and regulatory, duties and procedures
Cultural change, e.g. increasing community expectation, power of the media, consumerism	Employee organizations, e.g. trade unions (UNISON), BMA and other individual or group vested interests
Technological advance, e.g. in medicine and information technology	Lack of 'ownership' of change, i.e. top-down imposed model is usually favoured
Globalization, e.g. restructuring of industry, deregulation, increased competitive forces	Resource constraint
	Individual and group overt and covert resistance
New blood, e.g. management trained/ educated elites, managerialism, benchmarking	Public accountability
Public accountability	

has been significant transfer of activity to private operators and major internal restructuring has altered patterns of responsibility and accountability. Whether organizational culture and workplace behaviour have altered radically within the public sector is far less certain.

QUESTIONS

1.   In what ways do the objectives of private companies differ from those found in the public sector?

2.   What are the key differences in emphasis between the environmental forces acting upon public organizations and those found within the private sector?

3.   How might managerial activities differ between public and private organizations as a result of the differences you have identified above?

4.   Conduct a force-field analysis for any public sector organization using primary and/or secondary sources of information.

5.   Using suitable sources of information, explore the likely future developments concerning the role of the state in the economy. You may wish to do this for the United Kingdom or any other country or group of countries. You will need to consider the strength, politically and otherwise, of each argument and assess for yourself this highly complex but vitally important issue.

CONCLUSION

The reinvention of government activity has proceeded apace during the last decade and a half. This transformation has embraced a desire to focus on results rather than procedures. It is characterized by decentralization, performance measurement, accountability and competition. The range of mechanisms government has employed since 1979 include: privatization; contracting out government and public sector services; quality charters, league tables and published performance targets; performance management and performance-related pay; more effective complaints procedures; tougher and more independent inspectorates and better redress for the citizen when things go wrong.

The number of people employed within the public sector in the United Kingdom declined by a little under 2 million between 1979 and 1995. Much of this decline is due to the privatization and contracting-out processes while general government staffing has shown only a slight decrease. In fact many services, such as the NHS and police, have shown increases since 1979. Despite overall reductions, the United Kingdom public sector still employs about 22 per cent of the total workforce and 30 per cent of all professional workers (e.g. doctors and teachers). These and other issues concerning the role of government are further discussed in Chapter 9.

SUMMARY OF MAIN POINTS

This chapter has focused on public organizations and their 'unique' business environment. The prime points made are:

- Political aspects of the business environment are particularly important for public sector organizations.
- Dynamism and complexity are key characteristics of the public sector business environment.
- Although certain services are always likely to be in public hands, there is little agreement considering the extent of government involvement in the provision of goods and services.
- Political ideologies, economic and social circumstances and global environmental changes all influence public organizations although the government of the day often filters and interprets these external forces.
- Privatization processes are ongoing in many countries and seek to reduce the role of government in the economy and increase commercialization and competition.

- Many government services in the United Kingdom and elsewhere have been exposed to competitive forces by privatization, deregulation, competitive tendering and market testing.
- Benchmarking and other mechanisms aimed at increasing competition and consumer involvement have been developed since the early 1980s.
- There have been major structural changes in the public sector.
- Public/private sector partnerships are in their infancy but likely to be given greater credence in the future.
- Managerial practices within the public sector have been exposed to external change and influence.
- Managerial values and organizational culture, organizational objectives and environmental conditions often vary significantly between private and public sector organizations.
- A dynamic tension exists within the public sector between forces encouraging change and those seeking stability.
- The role government plays in the economy is a major ongoing debate.

References

Brooks, I. and Bate, S.P. (1994) 'The problems of effecting change within the British civil service: a cultural perspective', *British Journal of Management*, 5, no. 3.

Brown, C.V. and Jackson, P.M. (1992) *Public Sector Economics*, Blackwell.

Ferlie, E. *et al.* (1994) 'Characterising the New Public Management', *Paper presented to the BAM Annual Conference,* September 1994.

HMSO (1988) *Improving Management in Government: The Next Steps*, Efficiency Unit, Cabinet Office, London, HMSO.

HMSO (1991) *Competing for Quality*, presented to Parliament by the Chancellor of the Exchequer (Norman Lamont), HM Treasury, London, HMSO.

HMSO (1993) *The Government's Guide to Market Testing: Efficiency Unit*, Office of Public Service and Science, London, HMSO.

HMSO (1994) *The Civil Service Continuity and Change*, presented to Parliament by the Prime Minister, London, HMSO.

Hoggett, P. (1987) 'A farewell to mass production: decentralisation as an emergent private and public sector paradigm', in P. Hoggett & R. Hamblett (eds) *Decentralization and Democracy*, Occasional Paper No. 28, School for Advanced Urban Studies, Bristol University.

Isaac-Henry, K., Painter, C. and Barnes, C. (1993) *Management in the Public Sector: Challenge and Change*, Chapman & Hall.

Keat, R. and Abercrombie, N. (eds) (1991) *Enterprise Culture*, Routledge, London.

Lewin, K. (1951) *Field Theory in Social Science*, Harper & Row, New York.

McKevitt, D. and Lawson, A. (1994) *Public Sector Management: Theory, Critique and Practice*, Sage, London.

NHS (1983) *The Griffiths Report: NHS Management Inquiry*, DHSS, London.

Parker, D. (1993) 'Privatisation and the International Business Environment', *University of Birmingham WPC* 93/15.

Parker, D. and Martin, S. (1993) 'The impact of UK privatisation on labour and total factor productivity', *University of Birmingham Working Paper*.

CHAPTER 9

CHALLENGES AND CHANGES

Ian Brooks and Alistair Sutton

 LEARNING OUTCOMES

On completion of this chapter you should be able to:

- appreciate the main characteristics of the business environment and the prime themes identified within the text;
- understand the move towards greater dynamism, complexity and uncertainty (turbulence) in the business environment of most firms;
- outline the nature of chaotic and turbulent environments and the implications of these for long-term planning;
- understand the motives and characteristics of flexible firms and the advantages and drawbacks of flexible working;
- speculate about the future prospects for organizations, individuals, governments and groups in society as a result of environmental turbulence;
- discuss the influences that the changing business environment, and in particular the trend towards flexible working, has upon individuals and groups in the social community;
- debate the future role of government.

9.1 Introduction

Throughout this text we have consistently suggested that the business environment is ever-changing, often in unpredictable ways. This implies considerable uncertainty for many organizations and can give rise to a near permanent state of internal flux as they attempt to respond to the changes in their environment.

Broadly speaking, greater dynamism, complexity and uncertainty are synonymous with turbulence in the business environment. Such environments demand considerable flexibility on the part of organizations who wish to prosper. However, some evidence suggests that organizations operating in turbulent environments do not necessarily suffer a decline in profitability as the 'costs' of change are not always born by the organization initially influenced by such turbulence. Perrow (1986) argues that problems are often 'externalized' to dependent parts of the wider organizational system, such as employees (who may be made redundant), suppliers (who will lose orders) and other outworkers and persons responsible for non-core activities. This raises critical issues about how we define an organization and where the boundaries lie between an organization, its environment and its stakeholders. The organizational relationship with its 'inner' or 'task' environment is itself undergoing major change and organizational boundaries are increasingly becoming flexible and dynamic.

In this chapter we will outline the consequences for organizations, individuals, groups and governments of environmental and organizational turbulence. This will include analysis of the implications for long-range planning within organizations and of one major organizational response to environmental flux, that is, the growth of the flexible firm and of flexible working. Before this we will look at the nature of change and of chaos theory. Firstly, however, we have identified, by way of a summary or stock take, a number of dynamic environmental issues which have been raised in this book. Critical environmental trends include:

- globalization in manufacturing, and increasingly in service provision, creating international competition and the development of new markets for goods and services;
- increasing emphasis on free market economics, competition and managerialism including the privatization, contracting-out and 'marketization' of public services;
- different economic growth rates around the world, for example rapid growth in the NICs in South-East Asia (average about 8 per cent annual growth), moderate growth in Europe and North America, including the prevalence of long-term unemployment, and economic stagnation or decline in many African countries;
- technological advances in a wide range of fields, including information technology and communications, biotechnology and materials science;
- growth in the power and influence of economic and political unions, such as the European Union, ASEAN and the World Trade Organization;
- the demographic transition typified by declining fertility rates and ever-increasing life expectancy leading to an ageing population in most countries;
- dynamic national and international cultures;
- increasing availability of information;
- changing attitudes towards the family and health and rising crime, including internationally organized felony;
- atmospheric, water, space, land and noise pollution, resource depletion and

other ecological concerns;
- the spread of atomic weapons capability and religious fundamentalism;
- ethnic divisions, such as in Eastern Europe and the old Soviet Union, but also the 'peace dividend';
- increasing debate on the future role of government.

This list provides ample food for thought. Many of the issues raised have crucial implications for governments and organizations, groups and individuals. Collectively, these environmental forces are fundamentally influencing, and being influenced by, patterns of economic growth, employment and investment. They will ensure that organizations are required to be dynamic and that change will be an omnipresent feature of human existence. However, it is not the intention of this book to crystal-ball gaze or to explore, in detail, likely future events.

The nature of the business environment

In Chapter 1 we identified dynamism and complexity as two key factors in the business environment of many organizations. These are the prime characteristics of a turbulent environment. The models discussed there help us to categorize environmental influences (the LE PEST C model) and to devise lists of key organizational opportunities or threats (SWOT analysis). However, Johnson and Scholes (1993) argue that organizations need to understand the nature of their environments before they audit the individual environmental factors. Such an analysis might be expected to help an organization decide upon the sorts of systems which are required to monitor and respond to environmental change. This will then govern the audit stage as it is likely to have a significant influence on the factors which will be identified and upon the way in which each factor will be perceived.

If dynamism and complexity are key factors in analysing the nature of an organization's business environment, it seems reasonable to ask whether there are any academic models which may be of assistance in such a process. Miles (1980) devised a useful series of questions for evaluating the nature of an organization's environment. The suggested process involves mapping an organization's environment using a series of continua, for example from simple to complex and static to dynamic. These are examined by Richardson and Richardson (1992), from which Table 9.1 is adapted.

Richardson and Richardson (1992) say it is likely that an organization which attempts to map itself on these scales will find that 'most positions are likely to be at, or moving towards, the difficult and critical ends of the continuums'. It follows from this assessment that organizational planning cannot be seen as a continuous 'rolling out' of previous plans. If the environmental factors are less predictable then it follows that planning needs to be seen as a more flexible, adaptive and generally more responsive process and one in which the perceptual filters within a firm need to adapt to fit the environmental position of the firm. It is these two key

TABLE 9.1   Assessing the nature of the business environment of an organization

Simple/static end of the continuum	Key questions	Complex/dynamic end of the continuum
Simple	How complex is the environment? That is: How many different external variables impact on the organization?	Complex
Routine	How routine (i.e. established and pre-planned) are organizational interactions with environmental parties?	Non-routine
Unconnected	How interconnected and how remote, initially, are significant organizational variables? Increasingly new technologies may suggest a need to understand links between	Interconnected
Proximate	previously unconnected areas	Remote
Static	How dynamic and how unpredictable are the changes taking place around the organization? This clearly affects the amount of time an organization has to prepare considered responses to environmental	Dynamic
Predictable	changes.	Unpredictable

Source: Adapted from Miles (1980) and Richardson and Richardson (1992).

areas, that is, the planning process and the need for organizational flexibility, which are given considerable attention in the next section. However, during this discussion we should be aware of the impact an organization can have on its environment and the operation of the market by way of its strategic, tactical and operational actions.

In Chapter 6 we referred to a number of events, such as the Bhopal disaster, which had serious impacts on the ecological environment and caused considerable adverse publicity for the organizations involved. Richardson and Richardson (1992) catalogue a range of 'increasingly "commonplace" surprises which threaten today's organizations', such as major global accidents, terrorism, kidnappings, hostile takeovers, sabotage via product tampering, investigative journalism, equipment breakdowns, political upheaval and pressure group activity. We looked at the activity of the pressure group Greenpeace in Chapter 6 and later on in this chapter we examine the reasons why young people might find pressure group politics more attractive than parliamentary politics.

The following are just some of the shock events from an alarmingly large list noted by Richardson and Richardson (1992):

- the Lockerbie aircraft bomb;
- the King's Cross underground fire;
- the Hillsborough football disaster;
- the Challenger space shuttle explosion;

- the capsizing of the *Herald of Free Enterprise*;
- the Chernobyl nuclear plant explosion.

The common characteristics in these events were: a triggering event creating damage inside or outside the organization; large-scale damage to human life and the business environment; large economic costs; and large social costs.

There is a growing field of literature on crisis and shock event management, but consideration of this is outside the scope of a book essentially focused on the environment. Underlying such 'shock events' in the business sphere, however, is the developing body of knowledge about the concept of chaos. James Gleik's (1988) book *Chaos, Making a New Science* offers some fascinating insights into the discoveries about the behaviour of things in the natural world. These include the graphically termed 'butterfly effect' in global weather forecasting; the notion that a butterfly stirring its wings today in one part of the world might transform weather systems next month in another far-off area. Gleik (1988) says that such discoveries have begun to 'change the way business executives make decisions about insurance, the way astronomers look at the solar system, the way political theorists talk about the stresses leading to armed conflict'.

Writers such as Stacey (1993) have looked at the business impact of chaos theory. He notes the tendency in many business cycles towards the sort of 'non-linear feedback loops' observable in the natural world. We will look at this in more detail below.

 QUESTIONS

1. What are the key global trends in the business environment?

2. Which academic models help us audit and classify the various environmental influences on organizations?

3. What 'shock events' have happened since this book was published in 1997?

9.2 Implications for organizations

Whatever their objectives and legal status, organizations have, almost without exception, changed over the last decade. Very many have restructured internally, realigned their business processes to improve customer service, made focused strategic changes to their management control systems, developed their staff, improved their technological positioning and adjusted their product market portfolio. Most of these changes reflect a conscious response to turbulence in the business environment and a deliberate effort to influence that environment. Many organizations have undergone fundamental change because the environment has itself undergone a transformation.

A number of researchers, among them some notable management 'gurus', have attempted to predict the ways in which organizations will change in the next decade and beyond. Such predictions are often based on current trends and collective expectations together with a pinch of 'educated' guesswork. To a large extent it is the changing nature of the business environment that will dictate the nature of these changes and, in turn, the way organizations respond to change will alter the nature of the business environment for all. This section will look firstly at the implications of the changing business environment for long-term planning and will then explore one particular organizational response to environmental turbulence – that is, the growth of the flexible firm and of flexible working.

Implications for long-term planning

Operational plans have always been distinguished from strategic plans on the basis of the time period they cover and the scope and detail they contain. Strategic plans have tended to imply a planning horizon of about five years and to cover the organization as a whole. To be able to plan over this sort of period implies a reasonable level of certainty about the business environment in which the organization operates. However, turbulence in the environment leads to an increasing lack of stability and predictability which, in turn, makes long-term strategic planning hazardous. This has led many writers on strategy to question whether organizations should adopt long-term, centralized approaches to planning. Authors such as Quinn (1978) and Mintzberg (1994) believe that incremental and emergent approaches to the process of strategy formulation should increasingly be considered by organizations. Increased environmental turbulence also suggests that systems of planning which devolve responsibility to individual business units are likely to make organizations more adaptable and responsive to environmental flux.

Stacey (1993) questions many of the underlying assumptions used by firms in the process of long-term planning. He points out that many of these assumptions are based upon a range of quantitatively based analytical techniques. These techniques contribute to an underlying assumption, on the part of some theorists and many managers, that there is a 'best way' to plan. However, as noted above, long-term organizational planning is becoming less and less reliable or valid in today's turbulent environments.

Perhaps we should not over-react; after all Mintzberg (1994) reminds us that each succeeding generation tends to perceive its present situation as more turbulent than its predecessors. He suggests the key factor is whether organizations can learn to think strategically and avoid inappropriately formal processes of planning. He reminds us that 'changes that appear turbulent to organizations that rely heavily on planning may appear normal to, even welcomed by, those that prefer more of a visionary or learning approach. Put more boldly, if you have no vision but only formal plans then every unpredicted change in the environment makes you feel that the sky is falling.'

He also suggests that the perceptual filters, discussed in Chapter 1, may operate differently in different countries. He notes that what was seen as turbulence in the USA was perceived as opportunity in Japan. Turbulence demands an organizational response. One such 'reaction' has been for organizations to attempt to develop far greater flexibility; hence the growth of the concepts of the 'flexible firm' and of 'flexible working'.

Flexible working

Many organizations have responded to turbulent environmental conditions by attempting to become more flexible. This real or perceived need for flexibility is increasingly influencing employment conditions. Within organizations, people are both the most vital resource and the most costly. Traditionally, however, they have been prone to inflexibility and inertia. As a consequence many individual employees and organizations have sought to achieve greater flexibility in employment conditions in recent decades. This section will outline the nature of flexible working and of the flexible firm, discuss some of the trends towards such flexibility and comment upon current and emerging debates in this field. Firstly, however, we will look at some of the assumptions which underscore the actions taken by organizations.

The old 'industrialized' scenario of reliable employment, which allowed families shared times for shopping, travel and leisure, together with patterns of work and retirement within the nuclear family, is metamorphosing into what some have called a 'post-industrial' age. Alvin Toffler (1985), a well-known writer about the future shape of work and of organizations, has termed the present moves towards such a society as a 'super-industrial' age or a 'third wave'. Toffler likens this 'wave' to the Agricultural Revolution (the first wave) and the Industrial Revolution (the second wave). Others have referred to it as post-Fordism; that is, after or following Henry Ford's mass production era.

Key characteristics of this new age are expectations on the part of employers that workers will be very flexible (examined in some detail below) and be able to adapt products and services almost at will to meet the particular needs of customers. The enhanced capabilities of many organizations to customize products and services has been strongly influenced by developments in microprocessor technology and management techniques. Computers enable us to process and communicate data and information extremely rapidly. Advances in tele-communications technology (telephones, faxes, multi-media computers, satellites and the Internet) have delivered significant improvements in the quality of data about life and work throughout the globe. These technologies have been harnessed by organizations who wish to operate in a range of countries throughout the world. Quinn (1992) conceives of intelligent enterprises 'converting intellectual resources into a chain of service outputs and integrating these into a form most useful for certain customers'.

To help you understand the dominant assumptions of this 'third wave' we have included, in the mini-case below, a table adapted from Toffler's 1985 book *The Adaptive Corporation*.

Comparison: industrial and super-industrial assumptions

In *The Adaptive Corporation*, Alvin Toffler (1985) summarizes many of the dominant assumptions of the industrial and super-industrial paradigms in terms of what Theodore Vail might have known or not known. Vail was a key founder of the Bell System, as AT&T (American Telephone & Telegraph Company) used to be known. During the first half of the twentieth century he was responsible for developing much of the culture of that organization.

What Theodore Vail knew	What Theodore Vail did not know
Most men want the same things out of life, that is, economic success, so that the way to motivate them is through economic reward.	Once basic subsistence needs have been met, most men do *not* want the same things out of life. Economic rewards alone are *not* enough to motivate them.
The bigger a company, the better, stronger and more profitable it would be.	There are upper limits to economies of scale, both for a corporation and for governmental organization.
Labour, raw materials and capital, not land, are the primary factors of production.	Information is as important as, perhaps even more important than, land, labour, capital and raw materials.
The production of standardized goods and services is more efficient than one-by-one handcraft production in which each unit of output differs from the next.	We are moving past factory mass production towards a new system of 'handcraft' or 'headcraft' production based on information and super-technology. The final output of this system is no longer millions of identical standardized finished units, but 'customized' goods and services.

Source: Toffler (1985).

A decade after Toffler's work, Bridges (1995) argued that we are 'caught in the flow and ebb of evolution, jobs emerged under one set of conditions and now begin to vanish under another'. He drew an analogy between the present period and a time in the United Kingdom between 1780 and 1830 when riots, arson and killings accompanied a shift from rural land-based jobs to industrial, factory work. Both are periods where two systems overlap and cause us to think again about our underlying assumptions about the nature of work.

He identified some 'new rules' which are still evolving and are becoming operative in some parts of the economy more quickly than in others. The rules are divided into three key points:

1. Everyone's employment is dependent on the organization's performance and, as a result, workers need to continuously prove their worth to the organization and to behave more like an external supplier than a traditional employee.
2. Workers should, therefore, plan for career-long self-development by taking primary responsibility for health insurance and retirement funds and by renegotiating their compensation arrangements with each organization when, and if, organizational needs change.
3. Wise companies will need to work closely with these new-style workers to maximize the benefits for both parties and to bring a range of projects to satisfactory completion.

Having looked at some of the assumptions which underlie recent trends we can now examine the different forms of flexible working which may be found. Firstly, we can identify various types of 'numerical' flexibility, which generally affect employees' hours of work. These include long-standing practices such as overtime, homeworking, shift and part-time work and other increasingly common practices, such as flexitime, teleworking, annual hours and zero-hours contracts, the use of temporary staff and job sharing. A few of these require some further explanation. Zero-hours contracts are similar to temporary work. For example, Burtons, the retail clothes chain, terminated the contracts of 2000 of its staff in the mid-1990s. Some of these people were re-employed on part-time contracts but many others were offered work as and when required by the employer. These 'zero-hours' contracts enable the organization to adjust staff levels in line with customer shopping patterns. Needless to say, most of the employees concerned were less than satisfied with this arrangement as it introduced considerable uncertainty into their working lives. Another market-driven change is apparent in the electricity generating business. One company encourages some employees to engage in 'winter/summer stagger', where they work longer hours in the winter to accommodate demand. Hence people are employed on an annual hours basis.

Homeworking is not new, although the scale of this activity is increasing. However, teleworking goes a step further by connecting home-based employees by use of computer modem to the organization and/or other teleworkers. The availability of communications technology has also led to the 'virtual office' where laptop computers, portable faxes and mobile phones enable people to work in any location. Linked with this is the practice of 'hotdesking' where employees 'touch base' at the office and use whatever work space is available, picking up messages on e-mail. Stanworth and Stanworth (1992) found that the most popular working pattern among teleworkers is a combination of home and office working which helps to overcome the inherent isolation of working from home and increases the feeling of belonging to a team. 'Telecottaging', where a local venue acts as a central point for teleworkers, may be one way of solving this problem. From an ecological perspective greater teleworking, which is particularly commonplace among consultants, computing and sales personnel, may help reduce rush-hour traffic and air pollution.

A second form of flexibility, referred to as 'distancing', is where employees are replaced by subcontractors and employment contracts are replaced by contracts for service. Again this has been commonplace in many industries, such as construction and manufacturing, for many decades. However, the process is increasingly popular in other types of activity including service industries and the public sector.

A third form of flexible working is broadly termed 'functional flexibility'. Although in many organizations strict lines of demarcation exist between jobs, these are seen as offering little flexibility and often prove obstacles to effective teamwork and subsequent productivity gains. Hence multi-skilling is becoming more commonplace, where individuals are trained to undertake a broader array of tasks. The mini-case below illustrates one such attempt at flexibility in an NHS hospital.

Kettering General Hospital NHS Trust: generic working

An objective expressed in the Trust's business plan is to 'produce a multi-skilled workforce' (KGH NHS Trust, 1994, p. 14). The relevant objective states: 'to introduce teams of generic hotel service assistants at ward level so as to improve flexibility and responsiveness to patient needs by combining the role of porters, domestics and catering staff'.

At Kettering Hospital (1995) it is proposed that all domestic and portering staff are to be based at ward level; a relocation which would involve severing many existing formal and informal relationships. Most of the 260 personnel will require additional training in food serving, cleaning and portering skills in order to develop multi-skilled competencies. Staff will then undertake a wider array of tasks and be required to embrace flexibility and teamwork. There may be reduced role certainty. They will need to manage the interface with clinical and other staff groups on the ward. All existing formal status and pay differentials between porters, catering domestics and cleaners will be removed. Some staff will be required to change their shift pattern and the total hours they work within any one week.

It is argued, largely from a managerial perspective, that successful implementation will help to 'provide good value for money' and 'make cost savings'. It will ensure, for the time being at least, competitiveness with external commercial players. The single grade and pay spine will reduce status differentials and simplify the highly complex bonus schemes that had evolved. From an operational point of view it will bring enormous benefits of flexibility and simplify work scheduling. It will serve to even out the workload for porters and improve efficiency by avoiding waiting-for-action time and duplication of effort. Managers believe it will improve worker motivation as people would feel part of a team. They would, it is believed, take a pride in their work at ward level.

In conclusion, the philosophy underpinning the generic worker concept is a familiar one. A multi-skilled, flexible workforce is thought to facilitate operational planning and enhance both the efficiency and effectiveness of service provision. The assumption is that employees benefit from the resultant job enrichment and cooperative teamwork, cost savings are there for the making, via enhanced efficiency, and patient care is improved.

Fourthly, pay flexibility is increasingly commonplace. This may involve the harmonization of terms and conditions, including the removal of artificial barriers between white- and blue-collar workers, such as differences in pension, sick pay and holiday entitlements. This is an approach that the Rover Group, the motor vehicle manufacturer, has used to encourage the development of a teamwork culture. Many organizations have, however, taken a contrasting approach, offering personal non-standard contracts.

Many of these ideas find their ultimate focus in the concept of a 'virtual corporation'. Virtual corporations have been defined by Davidow and Malone (1992) as 'almost edgeless, with permeable and continuously changing interfaces between company, supplier and customers. From inside the firm, the view will be no less amorphous with traditional offices, departments and operating divisions constantly reforming according to need.' Such an organization 'structure' is a clear culmination of a teleworking, information-based, constantly evolving enterprise.

Finally, there are a number of related concepts which include career breaks, paternity and maternity leave, secondments, domestic leave for carers, childcare assistance and school holiday leave. Many of these measures may be considered as 'family friendly' and are intended to help motivate and retain staff.

There is strong evidence to suggest that flexible work practices are on the increase, although less agreement concerning whether this is part of a strategically planned reaction to changing environmental circumstances or the result of short-term economic expedience. The lack of strategic planning of flexibility by organizations has been identified in numerous research exercises.

A major study carried out in 1993 into flexible working in Europe concluded that, although there was an overall trend towards greater use of flexible working patterns, there was considerable variation in practice between countries, sectors and sizes of organization. About 15 per cent of the workforce in the European Union works part time while growth in this respect is most notable in Holland, Germany and the United Kingdom. Non-permanent employment has increased significantly in all European Union countries, as has subcontracting. Watson (1994), using Labour Force Survey data in the United Kingdom, found that 9.7 million people (38 per cent of all employees) were either part time, temporary, self-employed, on a government training scheme or unpaid family workers. This represented an increase of 1 250 000 between 1986 and 1993. Over 80 per cent of all medium and large organizations in the United Kingdom employ some temporary staff. The BBC now offers the majority of new recruits only short- or fixed-term contracts. These contracts are becoming increasingly common for researchers and lecturers in higher and further education.

In the United Kingdom there has also been an increase in the number of men working flexibly, from 18 per cent in 1986 to 27 per cent in 1993, while the proportion of women in this category remained stable and high at 50 per cent. Men in this category were largely self-employed while women were mainly part time or on temporary contracts. Additionally, over 12 per cent, that is 2.6 million people, work flexitime, while 2 million, or 9 per cent of the workforce, have annualized hours (most common in the professions, particularly teaching). Over one million employees work school term-time only while about 200 000 people job-share. For example, the Alliance & Leicester Building Society have offered some employees, who are parents of school-age children (both mothers and fathers), the opportunity to work during term-time only, while Boots, the chemist, have provided more than 50 job-share 'partnerships' in positions from supervisor to pharmacy manager. These family-friendly measures attempt to motivate employees and help parents balance work and family demands. They also facilitate the retention of competent and well-trained staff.

The mini-case below, based on changes within the Metropolitan Board of Works in Melbourne, Australia, illustrates some interesting characteristics of flexible working and organizational change. Largely as a response to changes within its business environment, such as government directives inspired by wider technological and competitive conditions, the organization has undergone a major restructuring. The result is a smaller, leaner, delayered and more flexible company. The organization has moved from a 'mechanistic' to an 'organic' structure (Burns and Stalker, 1961) and from a 'defender' to a 'prospector' strategic orientation (Miles and Snow, 1978) (refer to Chapter 1). It also demonstrates that the boundary between the organization and its 'task' environment is not fixed but is dynamic and flexible.

Melbourne Water

Melbourne Water was formed in 1993 from the long-established Metropolitan Board of Works, a typical government bureaucracy which operated in a protected and stable business environment with guaranteed superannuated employment. Impending privatization has encouraged management to structure the organization along competitive commercial lines as it aims to become a market leader in the Asia Pacific region in the provision of water storage, purification and distribution capabilities. The new structure is shown on the right (Figure 9.1) while the previous hierarchical structure is on the left.

A layer of middle management has disappeared altogether. The executive and senior levels have been combined and supervisors have been reclassed as team leaders. The core workforce is now described as full-time employees and nobody in the organization is considered to have guaranteed life-long employment. All maintenance and construction activities are contracted out. Casual semi-skilled workers are employed as required on a daily basis while skilled casual workers are recruited through specialist agencies. Much of the professional work is conducted by consultants. A number of major suppliers are now considered as partners in the organization as they are required to carry out some of the duties formerly conducted by employees.

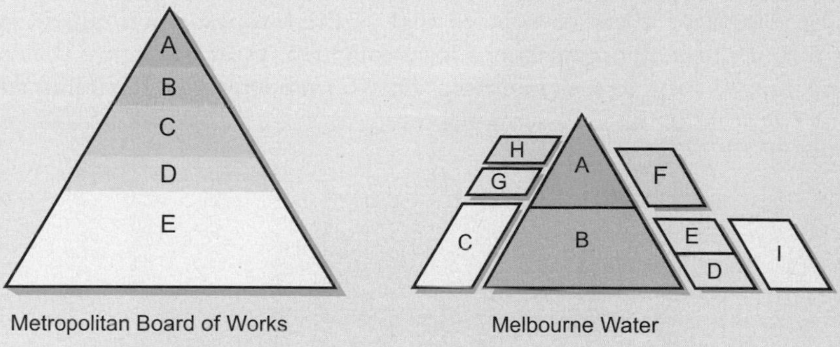

Metropolitan Board of Works   Melbourne Water

ORGANIZATIONAL STRUCTURE

A: Executive management
B: Senior management
C: Middle management
D: Supervisors
E: Permanent employees

A: Management
B: Full-time employees
C: Full-time contractors
D: Casual contractors - semi-skilled
E: Casual contractors - skilled
F: Consultants
G: Suppliers
H: Clients
I: Emergency services

Figure 9.1   Melbourne Water: the flexible firm.

Changes in the external environment, which may have encouraged the moves towards flexible working, have been identified by Cole (1993), Curson (1986), Pollert (1991) and Beardwell and Holden (1994). These factors combined, they argue, ensure that the flexible firm and flexible working will become an increasing reality. Summarized here, they include:

- increased national competition;
- globalization and consequent competitive pressures;
- uncertainty created by market volatility and, in part, a hangover from recessionary periods;
- technological change, particularly in information technology and communications, which facilitates some forms of flexible working;

- investment in new plant requiring new and ever-changing skills;
- a move from Fordism to post-Fordism, from mass production to flexible specialization;
- continued emphasis on costs and budgets and financial stringency in the public sector;
- political influence, particularly in the public sector;
- reductions in trade union power;
- increasing numbers of women and other employee groups 'demanding' alternative employment conditions.

In summary, it has been noted that as the business environment becomes more turbulent many organizations have sought ways of managing change. This has encouraged them to seek increased short-term operational flexibility and more adaptive approaches to long-term planning.

QUESTIONS

1. What are the implications of increased turbulence and chaos in the business environment for the ways in which organizations plan for the future?

2. Referring to the mini-case which compares industrial and super-industrial assumptions, compare and contrast the various arguments and assess the extent to which you feel developed world countries have moved away from the early twentieth-century assumptions. You may find it helpful to discuss organizations with which you are familiar.

3. What broad changes do you think are taking place in the nature of work? Illustrate your answer with examples from the mini-cases 'Kettering General Hospital' and 'Melbourne Water'.

9.3 Implications for individuals

When environmental change demands organizational change, as it almost continuously does, then we as individuals have to respond. It is becoming increasingly uncommon for people to work within a stable environment and undertake similar tasks and responsibilities for any length of time. Individuals are required to change at least as rapidly as the business environment if they are to remain effective. They need to continually develop their capabilities in order to function effectively within changing organizations. As Charles Handy (1989) reminds us, 'standing still is not an option'. We have to develop new skills and behaviours, perhaps more importantly, new attitudes and ways of thinking, as the business environment demands flexibility and the capacity and willingness to seek personal development opportunities.

Moves towards greater flexible working and the growth of the flexible firm are of direct relevance to individuals in the workplace. It is individuals who are being made 'flexible' and it is they who will, or will not, cope with the changes in working patterns outlined above. Handy (1995) identifies the 'portfolio career' which many people experience these days. This is multifaceted and may include holding a number of 'loose' employment contracts, none of which is full time or with just one employer. For example, a management consultant might work on a few short-term projects with a number of organizations, undertake to write a management textbook for a publishing company and work for a university business school as a part-time lecturer. Most individuals have been accustomed to regular '9 to 5', permanent, pensioned employment, such that new developments present personal challenges in balancing work and life patterns.

Increasing numbers of mid- and older-age people are having to adjust to changing employment patterns. The Organization for Economic Cooperation and Development (OECD) calculated that just 33 per cent of the British aged over 55 years were in paid work in 1992. The equivalent figure for France was 27 per cent while for Italy it was just 11 per cent. Redundancy, early retirement opportunities and the lack of employment prospects for those over 50, together with youth unemployment and increasing numbers in higher education, ensure that the vast bulk of the workforce in Western Europe is between 25 and 55 years old. Many people's working life is restricted to just 30 years. In the 1960s the vast majority of young adults started work aged 15 and were expected to retire at 65 (male) or 60 (female); a working life of up to 50 years. For some people changes in this regard have been unwelcome and have led to a reduction in their standard of living. Many have had to adjust their work-life expectations.

There is also a wider social implication for many millions who are not employed. They do not all do nothing! Handy (1995) suggests that there will come a time when no distinction will be drawn 'between full- and part-time work, when retirement will become a purely technical term … and when "overtime" as a concept will seem as outmoded as "servant" does today'. At present, however, it is evident that many people have more time than they know what to do with, while others have far too little time to do what they want. The typical American and British citizen already work longer hours than they did in the 1980s. The average American works 164 hours a year longer then he or she did 20 years ago (equivalent to an extra month a year), concludes Juliet Schor (1992).

A major Labour Force Survey conducted in the United Kingdom in 1995, by the Central Statistical Office (CSO), noted four significant changes in the preceding 10 years. These were:

- a decline in full-time male employment;
- a significant increase in part-time employment for both men and women (refer to Figure 9.2);
- an increase in the numbers of self-employed (refer to Figure 9.2);
- an increase in the number of people with multiple jobs (in 1995 1.28 million people in the United Kingdom had at least two jobs).

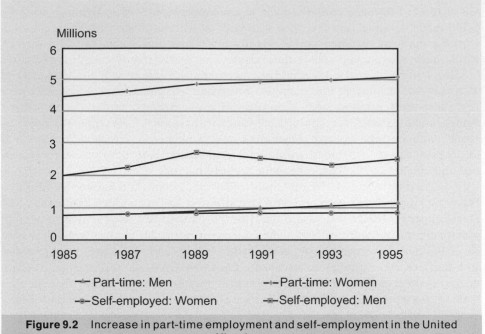

Figure 9.2   Increase in part-time employment and self-employment in the United
Kingdom.

An increasingly 'flexible', self-employed and mobile workforce requires new forms of employment representation. Many trade unions are having to respond by providing different services and making different social responses. Increases in 'flexibility', which may often be forced upon employees, create personal uncertainty and anxiety about the future. Such uncertainties have complex implications. For example, uncertainty is thought to be a contributory factor in the mid-1990s to declining house prices and sluggish retail sales. Another response may be for people to actually save more. This perceived need for savings is, in part, caused by a reduction in the value of state retirement pensions when compared with wages. Unfortunately, many people are in no position to save a large proportion of their income as the poorest groups in the United Kingdom have, since the early 1980s, experienced little if any real growth in income. It appears that uncertainty, and all that it entails, is likely to be a permanent or long-term reality, especially for low- and middle-income groups; this is discussed below within the context of the impact of environmental change on groups in society.

It is not surprising that, in recent times, voters in the United Kingdom should have used local elections as an opportunity to voice protests against these mounting levels of uncertainty. Commenting on some very poor local election results for the Conservative party in June 1995, David Marquand said,

It is voting against the brave new world of the business schools, not just against the Conservative Party; against de-layering, down-sizing, job-shift, performance indicators, short-term contracts ... the buzz words of the eighties have become the boo words of the nineties. 'Flexibility', 'dynamism', 'enterprise', 'competitiveness', 'choice', now send shivers down the nation's collective spine. We know that they are code for harder work for longer hours, with less protection against more powerful bosses.

At the end of this chapter we will examine briefly whether we may be able to reject the medicine referred to by Marquand or whether the globalization of markets and the consequent need to be internationally competitive is an inexorable force.

Of concern for the management of organizations which are undergoing seismic change is the potential for loss of worker motivation and commitment. Stevenson and Moldoveanu (1995) argue that anxious employees will ensure that their curriculum vitaes are kept up to date in case they fall prey to the latest round of re-engineering or restructuring. The authors contrast the mounting uncertainty for ordinary workers with improvements in certainty that senior managers gain from such things as golden parachutes – that is, the certainty of sizeable severance deals should their contracts be rescinded.

Previously predictable life-cycle patterns have, in the last two decades, changed considerably. Handy (1995) refers to the Sigmoid Curve (Figure 9.3) as an analytical model for depicting a person's working life cycle.

He argues that people start life falteringly, then make steady and consistent progress before peaking and enjoying a 'decline' during retirement. However, the time-frame for the Sigmoid Curve, rather like many product life cycles, is now being squeezed. This, he argues, means that people need to develop new options for a 'second', or even third, career during their working lives. Evidence suggests that an increasing number of people switch careers at least once during their working life and undertake a seemingly different occupation (e.g. from executive to management lecturer). Figure 9.3 shows this secondary curve superimposed on the

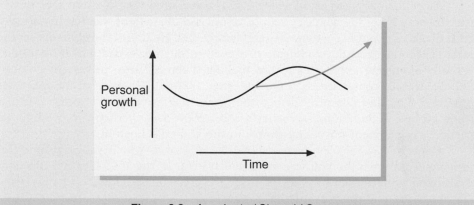

Figure 9.3 An adapted Sigmoid Curve.

Sigmoid Curve, indicating that many people can sustain personal growth by developing a second career.

This discussion has highlighted a trend in society towards greater life and employment uncertainty. For many people flexible working improves choice and freedom while for others it constrains or sidelines them. Unfortunately, as individuals we are powerless to change societal trends or governmental policy. Globalization and technological change conspire to transform our social and working worlds. What we can do is exercise some control over our own patterns of living. The paradox is that fragmentation and flexible working can offer new freedoms for those able to take advantage of them.

QUESTIONS

1. Assess the implications for individual workers of the increased use of flexible working practices by organizations.

2. Contrast your parents' work-life experiences with those of your grand-parents. How do you expect your work-life experiences will differ from those of your parents?

9.4 Implications for groups

In this section we look at the implications of environmental change on a number of groups. Although the focus here is largely on the United Kingdom, similar patterns are to be found elsewhere. We look at the position of certain groups – in particular, under-25 year olds, women and racial minorities – and at the increasing economic vulnerability suffered by many families as a result of the growth of flexible working.

More than 20 years ago Pawley (1974) considered that Western society was withdrawing from 'the whole system of values and obligations that has historically been the basis of public, community and family life'. He was of the opinion that the sorts of technological developments discussed in this book, and which he termed 'socially atomizing appliances', were fuelling a retreat into 'private lives of an unprecedented completeness'. During the 1980s, the then prime minister Margaret Thatcher famously denied that there was a concept of society distinct from groups of individuals. Pawley's assessment has, perhaps, proved to be particularly pertinent for young people in the United Kingdom.

Concern has been expressed about the degree to which young people feel 'disconnected' from the political and social system. In the 1992 General Election, 2.5 million people under 25 years old failed to vote, while around 20 per cent of the 18–25 age group did not even register to vote.

In 1995, DEMOS, an independent think-tank, surveyed a number of people representative of the full spread of age groups. Their aim was to discover the percentage which believed they were not part of 'the system', and who would emigrate if they had the chance, who felt that they did not belong to their neighbourhoods and would not agree that they would generally buy British. The results of the survey show a marked contrast between the attitudes of young and old in society. Over 50 per cent of 18–24 year olds were judged to be 'disconnected' from the British system (based on the measures outlined above), whereas less than 10 per cent of 55–64 year olds felt similarly. The survey showed a steady increase in the sense of belonging as age increased.

Moore (1995) draws attention to the fact that many young people have been attracted by single-issue campaigning on such matters as animal rights and environmental protection. She believes the attraction here is, as mentioned in Chapter 6, that the ethical basis of such campaigns contrasts sharply with the predominantly political atmosphere of parliamentary processes. She argues that, 'while the state has washed its hands of financial responsibility for the young, trapping them into economic dependence on their parents for longer and longer, it has intervened long enough to tell them that many of their leisure activities are illegal. The idea of voting once every four years is no compensation for the lack of say in the rest of their lives.' The use of the phrase 'underwolves' in the title of Moore's article reflects a feeling that increasing proportions of young people are not content to be 'underdogs' and are starting to fight back.

The National Youth Agency, in October 1995, estimated that there were about 10 000 youths in the United Kingdom who failed to attend school after the age of 12 or 13 and who did not work or undergo training. It is thought that in some areas about 10 per cent of 16–18 year olds have no contact with 'official' society at all. Many believe that this 'underclass' will continue to grow, with its attendant effects on crime rates, unless the issue of youth unemployment is tackled.

However, Hutton (1995) has argued that 'unemployment and low pay are no longer the sole measures of inequity and lack of social well-being'. He calls the United Kingdom a '30/30/40 society'. The bottom 30 per cent are the unemployed and economically inactive who are increasingly marginalized in society. The middle 30 per cent are a group he considers to be newly vulnerable to pressures beyond their control as a result of 'the rise of new forms of casualized, temporary and contract forms of employment' discussed above. Hutton (1995) points out that much of the growth in part-time and insecure work has fallen to women, particularly to married women who are balancing work and family commitments. He says,

> 70 per cent of all new part-time jobs are for 16 hours or less, and so do not attract employment protection or any benefits such as holiday or sickness entitlement.[1] ... Such work is becoming essential for family incomes and

---

[1] New (1995) part-time protection regulations have slightly improved employment protection conditions.

women are slowly becoming less content. When the capacity to avoid repossession depends on earnings from an employer who can sack you at will, family stability hangs on a thread.

Further pressures to family life are caused by the fact that two-thirds of British workers now work more than 40-hour weeks and a quarter work more than 50 hours. The available time to engage in social pursuits and community activities is consequently diminished. Even the proposed EU directive on maximum working hours (that is, 48 hours per week except by agreement) will do little to change this as most workers need the overtime payment.

The remaining 40 per cent, in Hutton's (1995) 30/30/40 society, are tenured workers. These, Hutton suggests, have reasonably certain prospects. An increasing number of workers in this group have been termed an 'overclass'. People in this group are highly competitive and ambitious and earn substantial salaries. Parallels have been drawn between this class and the underclass. It has been noted that both groups share an existence outside ordinary society; the overclass being able to insulate themselves from many of society's services by, for example, 'buying into' private health care.

The gap between rich and poor in the United Kingdom has widened in the 1980s and 1990s. A Hay Management Consultant report (1995) indicates that average earnings grew by 92 per cent between 1984 and 1993, while base salaries for senior executives rose by 242 per cent.

We have noted the impact of the growth of temporary and contract forms of work on female employment. According to a 1995 report entitled *Social Focus on Women*, published by the Central Statistical Office (CSO), the proportion of working women increased from 44 per cent in 1971 to 53 per cent in 1994 and is set to increase to 57 per cent by the year 2006. Just over a quarter of all women work full time. In April 1994 a third of women earned a gross weekly wage of £190 or less, compared with just 13 per cent of men. The 1995 Women's Conference in Beijing was a focus for much debate on the role of women in society. It was argued that unpaid women's work is worth $11 000 billion and that 70 per cent of the world's annual global output is unpaid (two-thirds undertaken by women), representing a serious under-valuation of women's work.

Many countries have legislation designed to combat race discrimination in the world of work. However, the difficulties experienced by many racial minorities when it comes to seeking work, known as 'exclusion', have fuelled violent reactions in Belgium and France. This led companies such as Philips, BT, British Petroleum and Société Générale de Belgique to sign the 1995 European Declaration of Businesses against 'exclusion' (Dickson, 1995). Perhaps it is possible to see such initiatives as part of an increasing trend towards firms acknowledging the effects that their activities have on a wider range of societal stakeholders and an acknowledgement of ethical issues and societal responsibilities.

QUESTION

Do you consider the situation for the under 25s, working women, families and for racial minorities has improved or worsened since the early 1980s? Discuss the reasons for your answer.

9.5 Implications for governments

This section explores some of the implications for government of environmental change before focusing on the current debate facing politicians and governments concerning the role of government.

Government at local, national, continental and global levels is a powerful environmental force which influences the business environment of all organizations. However, there is a range of environmental phenomena which are themselves of major concern to governments at various levels. Many of these are listed in the introductory section of this chapter. We will look at just four areas and briefly assess the consequences for governments. These areas are:

- globalization and consequent intense international competition;
- technological advances creating issues which many argue require a coordinated 'strategic' approach;
- the growth of the flexible firm and flexible working;
- conflicting pressures for both a reduced and an extended role for government.

Globalization

Progress towards the globalization of production and trade has been rapid in recent decades. It has been hastened by the successes of the General Agreement on Tariffs and Trade (GATT), now known as the World Trade Organization, by market and political union, and by many genuine attempts on the part of world leaders to reduce 'distance' between nations and communities.

The case study based on the industrialized countries of South-East Asia (see pp. 399–405) indicates that many countries in Asia are experiencing very rapid economic growth, while Europe and North America are making slower progress. Some areas in the world actually experience negative 'growth'. Nevertheless, we have witnessed, in the last decade, a large increase in global income and in levels of international trade in both goods and services. Many protective barriers have been removed or reduced, such that competition between nations and companies is, by and large, more fierce than in previous decades.

It is now important for companies and governments to consider the level of national and regional competitiveness. Undoubtedly, some countries enjoy political, social, technological and economic advantages which encourage multinational, transnational or truly global companies to invest in them. A number of organizations and researchers attempt to calculate national competitiveness and produce 'league tables'. They consider such things as average wages rates, workforce skills and capabilities, income and corporation tax rates and the degree of political stability.

Many individuals, groups and organizations in most countries argue that government should play a major part in attempting to maintain or improve their national competitiveness. By so doing they may facilitate the achievement of comfortable economic growth rates, better and secure employment opportunities and improvements in standards of living. Although most governments actively pursue policies which they believe will enhance the competitiveness of their country and its organizations, there is considerable disagreement on how best to achieve this aim. Some argue for a heavily 'interventionist' policy in which government plays a major role, for example by directly investing in industry, providing training, by building state-of-the-art infrastructure and facilitating international trade. Conversely, other arguments favour a more *laissez-faire* approach, such as is traditionally the case in Hong Kong and, since the 1980s, in the United Kingdom. Broadly, government's role in this scenario is to 'free' private enterprise from many 'constraints', such as high social costs and taxes, and to allow it to compete in free markets. Government does not significantly intervene, for example, to develop national industry or transport policies or to invest directly in industry.

Both broad schools of thought can claim successes. The USA and Hong Kong, for example, have flourished by adopting a predominantly *laissez-faire* approach, while Singapore and Japan have experienced very rapid economic growth in the past 20 years, in part, it is argued, by active government involvement in industrial policy making.

Whatever one's views, it is clear that national and/or regional competitiveness is increasingly becoming an important determinant of the material well-being of a population. Consequently, government has an obligation to its citizens to ensure they share in global successes.

Technological change

Technological change has a significant influence over economic growth. Government, therefore, has a role to play in the development of conditions suitable for technological advances to be made and transformed into economic wealth-creating opportunities. The approach governments adopt will largely depend on their ideological stance, as indicated above. One government may, for example, invest a significant element of revenue collected from taxation into research which might lead to economic wealth-creating opportunities largely for private industry. Another may prefer to allow market mechanisms to dictate research and development spending levels within industry. Clearly, the role of government, although crucial, varies considerably across the world.

It is reported, for example, that in Hong Kong multinational organizations have been invited to invest, irrespective of the technological benefits they might bring to the province. However, the Singaporean government have been somewhat more vigilant and active in encouraging companies who might also bring transferable technological advances to their country.

In addition to creating the 'right' conditions for technological development and diffusion, government also has a regulatory role to perform. This role may involve prohibiting, or otherwise regulating, potentially unethical research and technological development. Many countries are currently debating issues concerning the advances in genetic engineering which have been made in recent years. There are important and far-reaching ethical consequences of many technological advances. Although self-regulation by researchers and professional bodies, for example, is important, many people expect governments to adopt an ideological and regulatory stance in this regard.

Flexible working and the role of government

The role of government in broad employment issues is multifaceted. Beardwell and Holden (1994) argue that government policy needs to reflect the dynamism shown in employment changes. However, there are a number of highly contentious issues associated with flexible working. For example, centre-right government policy in the United Kingdom may favour a reduction in the legal restrictions on the hiring and dismissal of workers, which would most certainly increase flexibility. However, this would have significant, often harmful, consequences for many groups and individuals. Beardwell and Holden (1994) also suggest that government might remove all state intervention in pay setting and further extend the law to curb trade union influence over pay and employment. These measures have been promoted by Conservative governments in the 1980s and 1990s. However, these policies often conflict with European Union legislation, which favours a statutory minimum wage, protection for workers, and takes a more interventionist, less free-market, approach. Additionally, it is possible that a Labour government in the United Kingdom might not support the more focused pursuit of 'flexibility'. Nevertheless, for a decade and a half in the United Kingdom, government departments have promoted greater labour market flexibility, both in White Papers such as *The Challenge for the Nation* (1985) and *People, Jobs and Opportunity* (1992), and in various policy initiatives.

Changes in employment and career patterns have important and far-reaching consequences for pension provision and some welfare payments. The government in the United Kingdom has responded to long-term change by increasing the age of retirement for women to 65 years, to match that for men, and by strongly encouraging employees to take out additional private personal pension provision. With an ageing population and increasing long-term unemployment, government fears the rising burden of pension and welfare demands upon the public purse.

Role of government

There has been a tendency in many countries in the 1980s and 1990s for governments to move away from direct provision of goods and services towards a focus on regulating more and producing less. The range of mechanisms which government in the United Kingdom has employed since 1979 include:

- privatization;
- deregulation;
- contracting out public sector services;
- quality charters, league tables and published performance targets;
- performance management and performance-related pay;
- more effective complaints procedures;
- tougher and more independent inspectorates;
- better redress for the citizen when things go wrong.

The Conservative government in the mid-1990s, and the Labour party in opposition, have both conducted 'fundamental' reviews of current and likely future government expenditure. They have addressed some highly sensitive issues, such as welfare spending, and have identified areas where spending cuts may be made. These reviews are highly controversial and the eventual outcomes for the nation will depend on the 'complexion' of the government(s) in power in the late 1990s and beyond.

A reduction in the role of government will involve significant cuts in public expenditure. However, reining back growth in government expenditure is fraught with difficulties. There is considerable inertia from a series of built-in mechanisms which ensure future government commitment. For example, the rapid growth in higher education, seen as essential if the United Kingdom is to compete in the global economy, has meant that government has had to increase expenditure in this area. The expectation will be for even greater numbers to experience higher education. The criminal justice system has seen rises in the prison population, and consequent increases in government expenditure, throughout the 1990s to date, in part as a result of rising crime rates, but also due to 'get tough' government policies. Governments, especially in the old Western industrialized world, are increasingly concerned about the long-term social and financial costs of unemployment. An ever-ageing population continues to put increased demands upon the NHS and welfare system, necessitating increased government expenditure.

It is estimated that improvements in life-expectancy and medical care, combined with changing demographic factors, will mean that long-term care for the aged in the year 2005 may account for 11 per cent of the gross domestic product (GDP) of the United Kingdom compared to a figure of just 7 per cent for the whole of the NHS in 1995. The government of the United Kingdom currently (1995–96) spends about £87 billion on social security and a further £33 billion on health. Together this amounted to about 38 per cent of government expenditure in 1995–96. Figure 9.4 illustrates government expenditure in 1995–96.

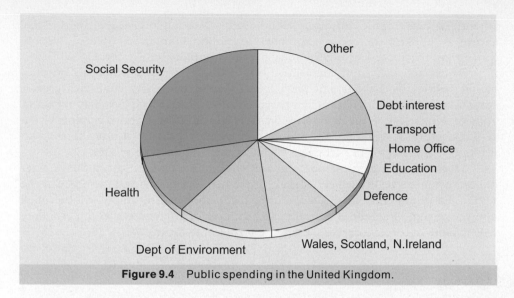

Figure 9.4 Public spending in the United Kingdom.

Despite the 'radical' changes that have occurred within the public sector, such as privatization and compulsory competitive tendering, the fact remains that the burden of taxation and the scale of the public sector have not declined. In large part this is because of the rise in welfare demands, including unemployment benefits, pensions and increases in health care costs.

The problem of potentially spiralling demands upon the public purse is certainly not unique to the United Kingdom. Many European Union countries have experienced alarmingly rapid increases in government expenditure during the past decade. Business leaders, employee representative bodies, Right-Wing think-tanks and politicians frequently call for major reform.

Many, especially those on the right of mainstream politics, argue for a funda-mental rethink of the role of the state. Duncan and Hobson (1995) suggest that

> after a decade and a half of cuts, public expenditure is higher than at any time since the war. The burden of taxation is heavier than it was in 1979. One in every five workers is still employed by the state. There are more officials and regulators and policemen, enforcing more laws and more regulations, than in any previous era.

They outline a controversial thesis concerning the role of government. This may involve substantial and truly radical changes to government social welfare policies and the scaling-down of the role of the state. Measures might include the privatization of the national health and education services, deregulation in all walks of life, rejection of European Union controls, and an end to many state old age pensions, sickness, housing and unemployment benefits. However, because of the enormous hardship – and subsequent outcry – such changes would create, and the potentially catastrophic consequences for society that might ensue, change of this nature is unlikely to occur, especially as public opinion is divided already concerning the success or otherwise of previous public sector reforms.

There are alternative ideologies. For example, a recent emphasis on one-nation politics by Labour and the Liberal Democratic party advocates greater emphasis on financial, political and social equality. Such ideologies may reflect in policies which seek to maintain state welfare, education and health care provision at 'satisfactory' levels. Services may be increasingly paid by steady increases in taxation which might, in particular, be levied on high income groups.

However, change is omnipresent and environmental flux within the broader public sector is a reality which faces all employees, politicians and members of the public. Environmental change will ensure that public organizations will be called upon to change, sometimes radically, and the role of government in the economy will remain a contemporary issue for the foreseeable future.

QUESTIONS

1. Discuss the opposing ideological positions concerning the role of government in encouraging national competitiveness and technological development.

2. Identify the 'winners' and 'losers' if the government in the United Kingdom were to radically reduce expenditure and taxation.

3. What are the arguments for and against (a) reducing and (b) increasing, welfare expenditure in real terms?

CONCLUSION

In this chapter we have focused on many of the environmental factors outlined in this text and on the increasing dynamism and uncertainty in the environment. We then explored the implications of this for organizations, groups, individuals and governments.

We have tried to resist the temptation to predict the future and have concentrated on examining currently developing trends which we expect to continue to have a significant impact. In so doing we hope to have created a book which does not date too quickly, at least in its main thrust. The tendency with much factual data, however, is for it to become obsolete very quickly. This will, undoubtedly, mean that when you read this book there will be some points which no longer hold true. For this reason we trust that the most lasting impact of the book will be on the processes which you use to examine the business environment.

In respect of these processes we have placed strong emphasis on ways of evaluating the business environment. For example, we have stressed the importance of examining problems at a range of geo-political scales – that is, from international, through regional and national to local perspectives. It seems to us that a business environment textbook cannot confine itself to examining environmental factors at any one of these levels. We have also indicated that the methods which organizations adopt to monitor their environments will, to a large extent, influence both what is seen and whether it is perceived as an opportunity or a threat. We have used the phrase 'perceptual filters' to describe this process. This, intentionally, placed the emphasis upon the human side of organizational activity.

SUMMARY OF MAIN POINTS

This chapter has focused upon the nature of change in the business environment and organizational, individual, group and government responses to environmental dynamism. The main points made are:

- The business environment is increasingly complex, dynamic, and uncertain (turbulent) for many organizations, individuals, groups and governments.
- Major economic, political, technological and social changes have transformed the business environment in the last two decades, necessitating organizational change and increased flexibility.
- There may be a trend towards high profile 'shock events' and non-linear chaotic patterns in many areas of the natural world (to some extent such patterns are also observable in the business world) which suggests that organizations might do well to make contingency plans.
- The nature of the business environment calls into question the validity of organizational approaches to long-term planning and suggests the need for processes which build in flexibility and adaptability.
- There has been a rapid increase in previously considered 'non-standard' temporal and contractual patterns of work such as teleworking, contracting-out, self-employment and temporary work.
- The position of many young people in the United Kingdom shows alarmingly large proportions are 'disconnected' from both the political system and from their local communities.
- Turbulent environments demand government attention.
- The future role of government is likely to remain a fiercely debated issue for some time.

References

Beardwell, I. and Holden, L. (1994) *Human Resource Management: A Contemporary Perspective*, Pitman.

Bridges, W. (1995) 'The Death of the Job', *Independent on Sunday*, 5 February.

Burns, T. and Stalker, G.M. (1961) *The Management of Innovation*, Tavistock, London.

Cole, G.A. (1993) *Personnel Management* (3rd edn), DPP.

Curson, C. (ed.) (1986) *Flexible Patterns of Work*, IPM.

Davidow, W.H. and Malone, M.S. (1992) *The Virtual Corporation, Structuring and Revitalizing the Corporation for the 21st Century*, Harper Business.

Dickson, T. (1995) 'The fight against "Exclusion" – European corporate initiatives to help the long-term unemployed', *Financial Times*, 8 May.

Duncan, A. and Hobson, D. (1995) *Saturn's Children*, Sinclair-Stevenson.

'Flexible Working Patterns in Europe' (1993) *Issues in People Management*, no. 6, IPM.

Gleick, J. (1988) *Chaos, Making a New Science*, Cardinal.

Handy, C. (1989) *The Age of Unreason*, Arrow Business Books.

Handy, C. (1995) *The Empty Raincoat*, Hutchinson.

Hutton, W. (1995) 'High risk strategy', *The Guardian*, 30 October.

Johnson, G. and Scholes, K. (1993) *Exploring Corporate Strategy*, Prentice Hall.

Kettering General Hospital NHS Trust: *Business Plan 1994–95*.

Marquand, D. (1995) 'Political babble', *The Guardian*, 5 June.

Miles, R.E. (1980) *Macro Organizational Behaviour*, Sutt Foresman & Co.

Miles, R.E. and Snow, C.C. (1978) *Organizational Strategy, Structure and Process*, McGraw-Hill, New York.

Mintzberg, H. (1994) *The Rise and Fall of Strategic Planning*, Prentice Hall, New York.

Moore, S. (1995) 'Beware of dances with underwolves', *The Guardian*, 28 September, p. 2.

Pawley, M. (1974) *The Private Future*, Pan.

Perrow, C. (1986) *Complex Organizations: A Critical Essay* (3rd edn), Random House, New York.

Pollert, A. (1991) *Farewell to Flexibility?*, Blackwell.

Quinn, J.B. (1978) 'Strategic change: logical incrementalism', *Sloan Management Review*, Fall.

Quinn, J.B. (1992) *Intelligent Enterprise*, The Free Press.

Richardson, B. and Richardson, R. (1992) *Business Planning, An Approach to Strategic Management*, Pitman.

Schor, J.B. (1992) *The Overworked American*, Basic Books, New York.

Stacey, R.D. (1993) *Strategic Management and Organizational Dynamics*, Pitman.

Stanworth, J. and Stanworth, C. (1992) *Telework: The Human Resource Implications*, IPM.

Stevenson, H.H. and Moldoveanu, M.C. (1995) 'The power of predictability', *Harvard Business Review*, July–August.

Toffler, A. (1985) *The Adaptive Corporation*, Pan.

Watson, G. (1994) 'The flexible workforce and patterns of working hours in the United Kingdom', *United Kingdom Employment Gazette*.

PART II

CASE STUDIES

CHAPTER 10
BUSINESS ENVIRONMENT CASE STUDIES

10.1 Introduction

This section features **eight** business environment case studies which complement and support the material presented in the main body of the book. The cases have been carefully selected to illustrate an array of organizational types (e.g. manufacturing, service industries, public, private and not-for-profit sector) and operating environments (e.g. national and international). They comprise **four** commercial companies, a government service organization and a registered charity. Additionally, we have included one case which focuses on a 'type' of organization, that is small and medium-sized companies, and another which takes a closer look at an international region (South-East Asia). **Three** of the cases are ostensibly concerned with international organizations and/or issues, while just **two** primarily, but not entirely, focus on the environment in the United Kingdom.

Table 10.1 indicates the relationship between each chapter in the book and the case studies in this section and uses the following guidelines: * = minor relevance; ** = significant relevance; *** = prime focus.

Each case study includes a number of questions. It may prove beneficial to refer to the relevant chapter(s) when answering them.

TABLE 10.1   Indication of case study support for text chapters

Case	Chapter						
	2	3	4	5	6	7	8
Europe's largest employers: the National Health Service	*	*	*	**	*	**	***
The hotel industry: an Anglo-French perspective	**	**	*	**		*	
Worlds apart: the business environment of Oxfam	**	*		***	*	**	
H.P. Bulmer: cider, and a lot more besides	***			**			
Telecommunications: a changing industry	***		***	*		*	*
Environmental concerns: the case of Scania	*	*	**	*	***	**	
The industrialized countries of South-East Asia	*	**	*	**		*	
Small and medium-sized organizations	**	**	*			*	

Europe's largest employer: the National Health Service

Ian Brooks

> This case study discusses the highly complex and dynamic business environment facing the National Health Service (NHS) in the United Kingdom. It focuses, where relevant, on one particular Trust hospital, that is, Kettering General Hospital NHS Trust (KGH).

Introduction

KGH provides a full range of acute and midwifery services to a population of about 260 000, mostly in Northamptonshire. The hospital, which gained Trust status in April 1994, had an income of over £45 million in 1995/96. It employed over 2500 personnel, that is 1500 full-time equivalents, in 1996 (refer to Appendix 10.1A for extracts from KGH Business Plan).

This case study adopts a structured format by focusing on political, social, competitive and technological issues while briefly exploring ecological, legal and economic concerns.

10.1.1 Political environment

There is probably no area of public or private business that inspires such emotion as health care. The NHS lies close to the heart of the British public. Perhaps inevitably, the National Health Service is the subject of political contention and considerable academic debate. There is little which remains uncontroversial, accepting perhaps recognition that the technological, social, economic and political environment, all of which fundamentally influence the NHS, has undergone major change in the past two decades.

Most publicly funded health care systems, such as the NHS, operate in an environment in which demand exceeds supply. When a 'desirable' service, such as health care, is free at the point of use, this is always likely to be the case. Government, as the main provider of funds for the NHS, has a responsibility to the taxpayer and the health consumer to achieve value for money and to enhance the overall effectiveness of the service. During the 1980s and the 1990s to date, the UK government has attempted to control health care expenditure in the light of both its ideological stance and increasing demands upon the public purse. Escalating health care costs have become a major issue in many countries as most developed countries spend between 6 and 10 per cent of their gross domestic product (GDP) on health care. The United States is exceptional in spending about 14 per cent of its GDP in this area, much of which is accounted for by private health care. In many countries increases in health care expenditure have been facilitated by economic growth and consequent increases in receipts from taxation.

Partly as a result of escalating costs to the UK exchequer, government plays an influential role in most aspects of NHS activity. Despite technological and social dynamism, it is the political environment which most influences the NHS. Although influence is exerted at a number of tiers it is central government which acts as a powerful environmental actor. Central government provides the vast majority of funds for the NHS through various mechanisms. However, it is at the local level where 'environmental dialogue' is most intense. Local health authorities largely manage the allocation of resources and the local response to regional and national measures. Hence, for example, Northamptonshire Health Authority is the most immediate and powerful political actor in KGH's environment. That authority also oversees Northampton General Hospital NHS Trust and Rockingham Forest NHS Trust and has an overall responsibility to meet the needs of the local community and provide value for money to the taxpayer; two objectives which are not entirely mutually consistent.

The last decade has witnessed an emphasis within the public sector upon 'market' conditions and consumerism. This is evidenced in most areas of public service and notably in the NHS. An element of competition has been introduced within, and between, NHS Trusts. Self-governance has also blurred the boundary between the private and public sectors. Competition between Trusts and private hospitals is seen, largely by government, as a mechanism for increasing efficiency and patient choice.

Within the public services generally, and the NHS specifically, a top-down invasionary model of change has predominated, inspired by political agendas and prevailing socioeconomic conditions. Health care is rationed via a quasi-market in which GP fundholders (general practitioners) and health authorities purchase services from providers (NHS Trusts and other regional health authorities). Hospitals grow or decline, it is argued, according to their success in providing value for money. However, many aspects of health care do not fully lend themselves to market economics, hence effectiveness is often questioned and controversy is rife. Most changes in the NHS have met with considerable resistance.

In the United Kingdom, NHS Trusts have been established in which managers experience greater decentralized authority in return for further accountability. A strong general management spine was introduced within the NHS and its Trust hospitals during the 1980s and early 1990s, so reducing the influence of powerful professional groups such as medical consultants. Salaries for these 'new' managers are generally higher than those given to previous 'administrators'. Many senior managers, such as NHS Trust chief executive officers (CEOs), are largely employed on 'rolling contracts' and so have little job security. Many, therefore, face strong personal incentives to manage organizational change. Additionally, a non-elected board of directors, including a number of non-executive members, is responsible for the appointment of senior staff and for meeting the objectives of the Trust. Their role resembles that of a board of directors of a private company.

Central government change initiatives in the last decade include:

- the establishment of an internal market within the NHS involving the separation of purchasers and providers;
- encouragement for hospitals and other discrete NHS services to seek Trust, or quasi-independent, status in response to the National Health Service and Community Care Act 1990;
- the Patient's Charter which has established waiting times and other patient 'rights';
- the new deal for doctors which is attempting to reduce the hours of work and alter other conditions, especially for junior doctors;
- Community Care (Caring for People);
- the Carmen Report on the training and career structure of medical staff;
- the Griffiths report covering, among other issues, the restructuring of NHS management;
- the private finance initiative which has sought to encourage greater involvement of private organizations in capital projects and increasingly in operational initiatives;
- a requirement to market test and encouragement to contracting out non-core services, such as catering;
- the establishment of an efficiency index by the Department of Health which attempts to assess value for money;
- *The Health of the Nation* (1995) report which remains a central plank of government policy for the NHS as it provides a strategic approach to improving the overall health of the population, setting targets for improving health in five key areas and emphasizing disease prevention and health promotion (refer to Appendix 10.1B for sample targets).
- Attempts to signal a shift in resources towards primary care (Appendix 10.1C).

Implementing these initiatives, and dealing with the consequent operational and strategic changes, has many social and structural implications and involves considerable management effort. Collectively, these and other initiatives act as major forces for change within the NHS. On the ground each initiative has differential effects across the NHS as regional authorities 'interpret' central requirements and directives often independently of one another.

The NHS Executive, in its circular to all NHS authorities and units entitled *Priorities and Planning Guidance for the NHS: 1996/97*, argued for six 'baseline' requirements to guide the planning processes of all health authorities and individual Trusts. These baseline requirements were:

- progress towards *The Health of the Nation* targets;
- Patient's Charter standards and guarantees;
- waiting time targets and guarantees;
- national and local efficiency targets;
- agreed financial and activity targets;
- control of drugs expenditure.

The medium-term priorities for the NHS, extracted from the same document, are summarized in Appendix 10.1C. These targets and priorities are inevitably established by government and its agencies. Individual Trust hospitals, such as KGH, have little room for manoeuvre within the prescribed guidelines.

Intervention measures, such as those listed above, are largely consistent with priorities, and other changes within the public sector, instigated by the Conservative governments of the 1980s and 1990s. They directly influence the strategy, structure and operations of all aspects of NHS activity and, paradoxically, these interventionist policies tend to contrast with the Conservative party's espoused, *laissez-faire* values.

Political influence in health care is largely considered to be one-way – that is, there is a deterministic relationship between government and NHS practice, with the former significantly influencing the latter. However, as health care is very much in the public domain governments are concerned with public perception of the quality of service and value for money.

There is also international pressure placed upon national health care systems. The World Health Organization (WHO) has successfully managed the eradication of many global diseases, most notably smallpox; they also control many others. In the international context influence is largely non-binding guidance, as opposed to coersive legislation. For example, diabetes is the subject of considerable international debate. Careful management of diabetes can lead to a large reduction in its, often serious, consequences. The *St Vincent Joint Task Force for Diabetes* report (1995) established a set of guidelines and targets for health care providers to employ; as such, it was a good example of international pressure to move a health care agenda forward. Unfortunately for some, the targets have little bite and there are no international sanctions for failure; however, it represents one of many measures which seek to promote the better management of major global illnesses.

The European Union has little influence upon the NHS's core business of health care provision. However, the NHS buys an enormous quantity of equipment and each local health authority and Trust is obliged to tender, within the EU, for the supply of that equipment. Hence, for example, KGH cannot offer a local supplier the contract to supply expensive medical equipment to refurnish its operating theatres without first advertising for tender and, hence, opening it to producers in other EU countries.

10.1.2 Social and demographic environment

Flexible working at KGH

Sixty-two per cent of employees of KGH work part time while over 80 per cent of all personnel are female. Forty-three per cent of staff have over five years' tenure. The staff turnover rate is rather low compared to many urban hospitals and is declining. Absenteeism, for sickness, currently stands at 3.6 per cent, which compares favourably with many hospitals and other public and private sector organizations. Absenteeism among ancillary staff is about double the hospital average. About 80 per cent of the hospital budget is accounted for by wages and salaries. Increasing emphasis is being placed on flexibility and multi-skilling within the hospital. Moves towards greater flexibility include attempts to combine the roles of porters, cleaning staff and catering assistants to form a single role of ward assistant. Such moves are driven by the need to demonstrate efficiency improvements and to compete with commercial organizations who may, following market testing, manage the service currently run by in-house staff. Moves towards multi-skilling and flexible working are proceeding afoot within the private and public sector.

Consumerism

The general public were, prior to the 1980s, often reluctant to complain about the quality of service experienced within the NHS. However, a culture of dignified acceptance has slowly given way to one increasingly influenced by consumerist values. As a consequence of this, together with the provision of simpler mechanisms of complaint, there has been an increase in the number of complaints from the general public to almost every hospital and NHS service in the past decade.

The role of the media in this respect is not inconsiderable. Examples of poor practice are frequently exposed within national and local newspapers and television news programmes. Partly as a consequence most hospital Trusts, and KGH is certainly no exception, are concerned how they are portrayed in the local press. In fact KGH actively manage their public relations. Interestingly, KGH Trust also 'uses' the media, and subsequent public support, to help ensure that the scale of services offered locally, as opposed to in Northampton, is at least maintained.

Expectations of the quality of life experienced by individuals within society have increased. Fostered by the changes in national culture, by consumerism and by the Patient's Charter, people are less accepting of levels of disablement that they once were. This manifests itself in high levels of demand for many specific health care services, such as hip and other joint replacements and cataract operations, which improve mobility. Additionally, people demand such items as hearing aids that are cosmetically acceptable. Consumerism, in part encouraged by government in the 1980s and 1990s, acts as a pressure to improve the quality of the service and leads to an increase in the demand for the service. The latter characteristic ensures that greater rationing is essential and/or additional spending on health care is required.

Demography

Changes in the age and gender structure of local and national populations have far-reaching effects on the providers of NHS services. Accurate demographic data is fundamental to the planning process. For any hospital Trust, such as KGH, it is important to understand what is happening to the population in its catchment area. For example, if a large new housing estate is built which contains mainly starter and family homes, then it is likely that the number of women requiring maternity services will increase accordingly. Alternatively, if new sheltered housing for the aged is under construction, the hospital may well experience an increase in the demand for services more frequently demanded by this age group. The emphasis given to particular specialisms within a hospital, such as maternity care or rheumatology, is related to demographic conditions. For example, rheumatology services cater more for old age groups, as does chiropody. Also of significance in this regard is the political influence of different groups in society. Elderly people tend to be less mobile and appreciate local accessibility to NHS services. As the proportion of elderly patients increases in society then their influence over policy decisions may also increase.

The United Kingdom has an ageing population. Generally speaking, as people grow older they require greater medical care. There is little doubt that a significant element of the increase in the demand for NHS service experienced in recent decades is due to demographic ageing. This is a global phenomenon and one which has, in part, been created by improvements in health care which have progressively increased life expectancy and contributed to reductions in fertility rates. Increasing sophistication in drug regimes, surgery, and other technologies and medical knowledge has contributed to increases in life expectancy.

Racial mix within the local community served by a hospital is also an important characteristic which influences the nature and priority of services on offer. There are a number of ethno-specific illnesses. For example, mouth cancer is far more common in areas with large numbers of Asians who chew a plant root containing cancer-forming agents. In contrast, alcohol-related illnesses, for example, are far less common among Muslim populations. Additionally, many illnesses are related to social class and to occupational group. Hence the range of services offered by any hospital trust is influenced by a series of demographic and social variables.

10.1.3 Competitive environment

Funding for KGH and other Trusts comes from a variety of sources. About 50 per cent of general practitioners (GPs) are 'fundholders' who can 'purchase' services for their patients from any suitable 'provider'. KGH is a provider. GP fundholders are becoming increasingly important as a source of income. Trusts can also compete for the income derived from treating private patients. Additionally, individual patients can, in specific circumstances, choose the provider of certain health care services. For example, maternity care is one of the most competitive services offered by KGH, and many expectant women are 'free' to choose which hospital they would like to attend, or whose services they require, to provide pre-natal, birth and post natal care. In Northamptonshire, for example, both Kettering and Northampton hospitals run maternity units and hence 'compete' for patients.

There are many medical charities and local organizations who contribute to hospital income, most notably in providing specific pieces of equipment. However, the largest element of funding still originates from the local health authority which 'purchases' services 'in bulk'. In the case of KGH, about two-thirds of income comes from Northamptonshire Health Authority.

Price is usually not the prime 'order winning criterion' or reason for purchasing a service. Of greater importance in most cases is local accessibility and availability; in other words, people living in or around Kettering generally prefer to use KGH rather than travel to Northampton (about 25 kilometres) or Leicester (about 35 kilometres). Individual patients often view the service provided by a hospital as largely homogeneous and, of course, free at the point of delivery, suggesting that other criteria, such as accessibility, are of prime importance. Offering direct access – for example, providing facilities for fitting hearing aids without prior referral from a specialist consultant – can give a hospital a competitive advantage. Especially in serious or more debilitating cases, timely availability of care is a crucial determinant in the choice of provider.

Many NHS managers would argue that the establishment of the internal market within the NHS has sharpened managerial focus on the nature and quality of services offered. However, the mechanisms which would enable purchasers to differentiate fully between providers are still relatively unsophisticated.

Rather than permitting purely competitive pressures to dictate the nature of services offered by any one provider, local health authorities often act as the arbiter in such cases. For example, in Northamptonshire where there were three providers of vascular services in the early 1990s, the local health authority decided, largely on cost grounds, that two providers were sufficient. They felt that the duplication of these services did not represent value for money. The decision enabled some centralization of expertise, equipment and other facilities and economies of scale to be realized. However, it has reduced accessibility.

In the absence of an efficient market, together with the political unacceptability of such a phenomenon in health care, the local and regional health authorities, and the Department of Health centrally, intervene to influence both the availability and accessibility of NHS services. These authorities undertake, for example, considerable analysis of cancer services and attempt to assess their effectiveness. This is being driven centrally and may lead to some providers being encouraged to relinquish this service so that more efficient providers can further concentrate upon their areas of expertise. If this principle of concentrating resources in centres of excellence continues, then greater centralization of NHS services will ensue. As a consequence, local accessibility to a wide range of services will be diminished. There appears to be a trade-off, therefore, between efficiency and effectiveness on the one hand and the general public's desire for accessibility on the other.

Generally, there is little evidence to suggest that individual patients influence purchasing decisions. The Community Health Councils represent the needs of patients but many practitioners and academics have questioned their effectiveness in altering purchasing decisions or patterns of delivery.

Finally, there are new sources of direct competition for many of the services offered by a typical NHS Trust hospital. Firstly, the growth of private health care and insurance (e.g. Bupa) proceeds apace. Curiously, the NHS itself provides facilities and other resources for private users. Additionally, GPs do some minor surgery and nursing homes have removed many old people from hospitals; however, these changes are seen as largely complementary and in the best interests of patients. Rather, the major 'threat' of competition currently comes from other major NHS providers. Hence, in Northamptonshire, both KGH and Northampton General Hospital provide many services in common and, consequently, directly compete for continued funding from GPs and their mutual political masters, the local health authority. The local community in and around Kettering fear the reduction of services locally and the switch of resources to Northampton (the larger town). Although there may be some cost advantages for the providers, local accessibility to services would be denied if facilities are switched to the county town. The local political consequences of such an action are not inconsiderable.

10.1.4　Technological environment

Scientific breakthroughs and technological advances have made available new diagnostic methods and treatments for innumerable conditions which were not amenable to medical intervention in the past. Genetic science has developed, and continues to explore, a virtually endless array of possible treatments. Partly as a consequence of technological advance, and also the contribution made by changing demographics and increased customer awareness and expectations, health care specific inflation exceeds both retail price inflation and economic growth in the United Kingdom. For example, many more drugs have become available, some of which are very expensive, such as Beta Interferon for treating multiple sclerosis. In this case the existence of the new drug has raised the expectations of MS sufferers and necessitated its being rationed by health authorities.

Paradoxically, other technological changes have led to a reduction in the need for some treatments as new drugs, for example, can remove the need for more resource intense care or hospitalization. The increasing sophistication of many haematological treatments via a drug regime, which reduces the need for hospitalization, is a point in case. Other improvements in medical and surgical techniques have significantly reduced the time patients spend in hospital. For example, minimal access surgery reduces recovery periods. Consequently, such improvements, which obviously improve patient care and reduce rehabilitation time and discomfort, also reduce the demand for many hospital services, such as the provision of hospital beds. Preventative medicine would also reduce demand for hospital services, other things being equal. However, the NHS invests sparingly in preventative medicine, partly because of the political issues involved in persuading people not to smoke, for example. *The Health of the Nation* (1995), a preventative health campaign, is unlikely to achieve all of its rather modest targets.

Legal environment

Trust status has significantly altered the level at which legal responsibility lies. As a self-governed organization, each NHS Trust now carries liability for all its activities. Hospitals use the services of legal advisers on a very frequent basis for advice on actions against the hospital, statements to the press about hospital activity and for the assessment of risk in such matters as access to property. Additionally, Trusts have many contractual and service agreements with providers of contracted-out services. Although NHS contracts between purchaser and provider have no basis in law, as they are merely service agreements, disagreements often go to arbitration or appeal via an array of established mechanisms.

Ecological environment

KGH is a very large user of energy; it employees about 2500 people and produces considerable waste, e.g. radioactive materials from radio physics and X-ray and clinical waste including body fluids. It interacts with its ecological environment in very many respects.

CONCLUSION

Change in the NHS has been omnipresent since its establishment in 1948. However, few would disagree with the assumption that the pace of change has escalated in the last decade and taken the NHS in new directions. This has created many demands on management and staff.

At the local level, the internal market and the growing sophistication of financial and information systems have provided far more data on how resources are being used. Each Trust hospital is now 'closer' to the environment, and accountability for the consequences of its decisions is greater than in the past. This 'closeness' is demonstrated in the business planning process. For example, the NHS Executive, Anglia and Oxford region, require Trusts, such as KGH, to consider all possible environmental influences on their activity when undertaking their planning processes. The Executive suggested in 1995 that these influences may include:

- advances in medical and surgical practice (technological environment);
- public awareness and expectations (social environment);
- demographic changes (social and demographic environment);
- the economic outlook (economic and political environment);
- the local health care market and other related markets (competitive environment);
- national priorities including *The Health of the Nation*, *Caring for People*, Patient's Charter and *Value for Money* (political environment);
- local health commissions' and GP fundholders' priorities and future purchasing power/capacity (competitive and political environment).

Despite this guidance (although some might argue because of it) uncertainty within the NHS is rife. Meanwhile, the notorious short-termism in the NHS still prevails. Short-termism goes hand in hand with a growing recognition of political realities. Uncertainty about whether there will be a growth in private health care or the 'privatization' of parts of the NHS prevails. Additionally, there is constant media attention and individual Trusts are continually subjected to public scrutiny. In the 1992 general election the NHS was 'used' as a 'political football' such that despite attempts to make NHS activity apolitical, there seems little chance that this will occur.

QUESTIONS

1.   Conduct a stakeholder analysis of Kettering General Hospital NHS Trust. Map the relative power and interest of the stakeholders. Based upon this analysis assess which stakeholders are most likely to influence the direction of change in the NHS and attempt to assess in which directions you think the NHS may move in the next decade.

2.   What are the necessary conditions for perfect competition to thrive? Analyse the NHS internal market and assess the likelihood of perfect competition becoming established within the health care industry.

3. What are the consequences of demographic changes for the NHS?

4. Establish a small number of feasible scenarios for how the health care industry in the United Kingdom might develop within the next two decades.

Appendix 10.1A

Extracts from Kettering General Hospital NHS Trust Business Plan

Kettering General Hospital NHS Trust mission statement

Mission

'To deliver the best possible health care to our patients.'

The mission statement is founded on a set of values which seek to ensure that:

- quality care is provided in a caring and responsible way;
- the hospital retains the pride and loyalty of the local people;
- the health care provided meets the needs of the local people;
- the hospital's services stand favourable comparison with other hospitals;
- the hospital environment allows staff to work and train with dignity and pride to develop their individual excellence and, thus, the quality of care.

Source: 1995–96 Business Plan.

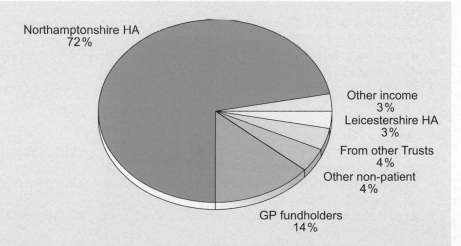

Figure 10.1.1 KGH contracted income by purchaser 1995–96. (*Source*: Business Plan, 1995–96.)

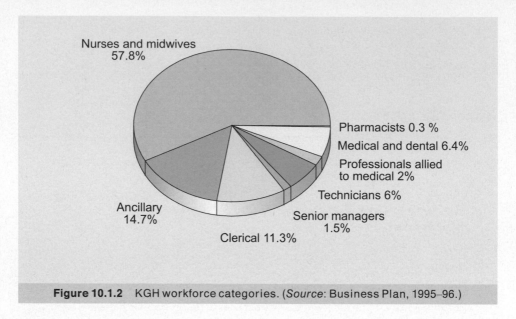

Figure 10.1.2 KGH workforce categories. (*Source*: Business Plan, 1995–96.)

Appendix 10.1B

The Health of the Nation: *baseline requirements and objectives*

The baseline for targets is 1990 unless otherwise stated.

CHD/Stroke
- Reduce death rates from CHD/stroke in people under 65 by at least 40 per cent by the year 2000.
- Reduce death rates from CHD in people aged 65–74 by at least 30 per cent by the year 2000.
- Reduce death rates from stroke in people aged 65–74 by at least 40 per cent by the year 2000.

Cancers
- Reduce death rates from lung cancer in men under 75 by at least 30 per cent and women under 75 by at least 15 per cent by 2010.
- Reduce death rates for breast cancer in the population invited for screening by at least 25 per cent by the year 2000.
- Reduce the incidence of invasive cervical cancer by at least 20 per cent by the year 2000 (baseline 1986).
- Halt the year-on-year increase in skin cancer by 2005.

HIV/AIDS and sexual health
- Reduce conception among under-16s by at least 50 per cent by the year 2000 (baseline 1989).
- Reduce percentage of drug misusers reporting sharing of injecting equipment by at least 50 per cent by 1997 and at least a further 50 per cent by the year 2000.

Source: Abstract from *The Health of the Nation* (1995).

Appendix 10.1C

Milestones for the medium-term priorities

A. Work towards the development of a primary-care-led NHS, in which decisions about the purchasing and provision of healthcare are taken as close to patients as possible.

B. In partnership with local authorities, to purchase and monitor a comprehensive range of secure, residential, inpatient and community services to enable people with mental illness to receive effective care and treatment in the most appropriate setting in accordance with their needs.

C. Improve the cost effectiveness of services throughout the NHS, and thereby secure the greatest health gain from the resources available, through formulating decisions on the basis of appropriate evidence about clinical effectiveness.

D. Give greater voice and influence to users of NHS services and their carers in their own care, the development and definition of standards set for NHS services locally and the development of NHS policy both locally and nationally.

E. Ensure, in collaboration with local authorities and other organizations, that integrated services are in place to meet needs for continuing health care and to allow elderly, disabled or vulnerable people to be supported in the community.

F. Develop NHS organizations as good employers with particular reference to workforce planning, education and training, employment policy and practice, the development of teamwork, reward systems, staff utilization and staff welfare.

Source: Main priority headings directly quoted from NHS Executive, *Priorities and Planning Guidance for the NHS: 1996/97*.

CASE STUDY 10.2

The hotel industry: an Anglo-French perspective

Jon Stephens

This case looks at some of the major factors affecting the business environment of hotels in both the United Kingdom and France and the extent to which the factors are common to both countries. From this the comparative nature of the industries will be assessed.

The hotel industry is significantly affected by changes in the national and international business environment and as a result tends to operate in a dynamic, rapidly changing situation which demands proactive responses from hotel owners if they are to maintain competitive advantage in the market.

The market for hotels in Europe is a significant one, given the fact that Europe remains the Number 1 holiday destination in the world and also that the impetus of the Single Market has led to increased business travel in Europe. The United Kingdom and France are two of the major hotel markets with the UK having 870 000 rooms compared to 1.2 million in France.

While the hotel industry is usually linked with the leisure industry, it must not be forgotten that essentially it serves two main groups of customers – namely business and leisure users – and thus there are two distinct markets that should be examined to assess the critical factors that will affect the hotel industry in the two countries.

10.2.1 The tourism and leisure markets

The hotel industry is often classified as part of the leisure industry and is particularly linked to tourism, especially in certain times of the year. Tourism already accounts for 6 per cent of GDP in the United Kingdom and is even more significant in France. This is reflected in the profile of hotel users in the two countries.

In the United Kingdom, for example, business users in 1993 accounted for 45 per cent of market share and conferences for 11 per cent of the market, leaving about 44 per cent of the market accounted for by leisure travellers. By contrast, in France there is a much greater reliance in the hotel industry upon the leisure traveller as, in 1993, 76 per cent of demand was for leisure travellers and 59 per cent of these were overseas residents. This suggests a higher reliance on the tourist trade from overseas in the French hotel market. This is accentuated when one considers that the average stay of a client in a French hotel is about 6 to 7 days whereas in the United Kingdom it is only 2 days, which indicates the potential of leisure travellers for longer stays, although the business traveller is likely to pay the higher premium.

Tourists can be very sensitive to instability in a particular area and demand can drop quite dramatically when there is a risk of danger or unrest in a region. For example, the outbreak of the Gulf War saw hotel occupancy levels drop to 60 per cent of normal in London and Paris, primarily as a result of American tourists staying away because of concerns about travelling to Europe. More dramatic examples can be seen in Dubrovnik in Croatia which used to be a prime tourist resort before the outbreak of the Balkan conflicts and in Egypt where terrorist activity has severely damaged the tourist trade, although it is now beginning to recover. In the 1990s bombing campaigns by the IRA in London and Algerian fundamentalists in Paris have caused short-term fluctuations in demand.

On the other hand, increased political stability can have the reverse effect by encouraging tourism and hence increasing the demand for hotel accommodation. This has recently been the case in parts of Eastern Europe, such as Prague and Budapest, which have seen significant increases in tourist inflows and, on a smaller level, this has been identified in Northern Ireland as part of the 'peace dividend' (now under threat).

The demand for travel and tourism, and hence for hotel spaces, will also be significantly affected by the economic conditions in both the host country and the visitors' home countries. Some of the key economic indicators of France and the United Kingdom can be seen in Table 10.2.1.

The relative levels of wealth and rates of economic growth will either encourage or discourage increased travel and tourism and use of hotels. In a recession people will have less disposable income for holidays or may be forced to substitute alternative and cheaper forms of accommodation when travelling, such as camping, *gîtes* and villas, rather than using the more expensive hotel accommodation. Alternatively they may look for greater discounts or cheaper hotels when they travel. This has led to the formation of cheaper hotel chains in both the United Kingdom and France such as the 'Formule 1' range where facilities are clean but minimalist and thus offered at a cheaper price. Conversely, with higher income levels, there would tend to be a higher demand for tourism and travel and perhaps a move away from, say, camping to a hotel-based vacation or to higher quality hotels.

TABLE 10.2.1   Key economic variables in France and the UK

		1994	1995	1996 (est.)
Economic growth	UK	3.4%	2.7%	3.0%
	France	2.3%	2.7%	2.6%
Inflation	UK	2.4%	3.5%	3.0%
	France	1.7%	1.9%	2.3%
Interest rates	UK	5.5%	6.8%	7.0%
	France	5.8%	6.6%	5.8%
Current account ($bn)	UK	−2.6	−9.8	−9.0
	France	8.1	12.0	8.5
GDP/head ($)	UK	18 950	20 490	n.a.
	France	23 550	27 000	

Source: OECD.

One factor which can have a very significant impact upon the demand for hotel space from the leisure traveller will be the rate of exchange between countries. This will be particularly significant for hotel industries that have to rely for a substantial amount of their business from the overseas traveller. A substantial appreciation of an exchange rate will force up the cost of hotel stays and could even offset the impact of income gains discussed previously with negative consequences for the industry.

The period from 1993 has seen particular emphasis laid by the French government on its 'le franc fort' policy which has deliberately kept the value of the French franc high for a range of economic and political reasons. The consequence has been a substantial reduction in British holiday makers visiting France. The United Kingdom, with its relatively weak currency on the European stage, has fared better and is becoming an increasingly attractive holiday destination with increased demand for hotel spaces.

One factor common to both countries is the trend for the leisure customer to demand better amenities and value for money. The general increase in health awareness is leading to an increased demand for additional facilities such as fitness centres and swimming pools, together with special facilities for younger children. Many of the leading hotel chains, such as Accor and Forte, have responded to these demands but it does have cost implications for the smaller independent hotel.

Both the United Kingdom and France have a population that is significantly ageing and this, coupled with the move towards earlier retirement, has resulted in a significant number of people of 'the third age' who are not only much more healthy and interested in travelling, but they also have a much greater spending power than ever before which will enable them to undertake more travel. If one adds to this the anticipated increase in the numbers of people aged 45 to 59 in each country, caused partly by the 'post-war baby-boomers', then it can be seen that this group will be a significant market in the future for the hotel industry and where the competition from areas like camping will be less. Already some groups are responding, such as the new chain in France, called 'Hotelier', which caters specifically for this group.

10.2.2 The business market

It has already been identified that the business sector is also a significant group served by hotels and hotel chains. This is the case for businessmen and women who are travelling from one destination to another but also hotels are often used as a place to conduct business meetings and in many cases as a location for presentations, development workshops and conferences.

With the advent of the Single Market there has been an increase in the cross-border utilization of hotels as more companies seek closer European contacts or alliances in order to develop a European presence. The issues of costs, value for money and quality of accommodation are just as significant for this sector as for the leisure traveller, although the corporate customer is increasingly demanding more business facilities such as seminar rooms and conference facilities. Some hotels, especially in the well-established hotel chains, are developing facilities such as teleconferencing, video conferencing and even satellite conference facilities in a bid to attract this market.

The Atria group of hotels in France are specifically aimed at the business sector and Forte in the United Kingdom have developed business television networks with British Telecom which use satellite transmissions to allow global conferencing.

10.2.3 Industry structure in France and the United Kingdom

The structure of the hotel industry in France and the United Kingdom, and indeed most of the rest of Europe, can be split into two groups; the *independent hotels*, often family-run and based in a specific or a limited range of locations, and the *hotel chains* run by well-known companies, having a wide portfolio of different types of hotel to suit different needs and frequently having a wide national and often international distribution of hotels. Examples of these hotel chains would be the Accor Group in France and the Forte Group in the United Kingdom, who are both market leaders in their respective countries but also compete globally. Table 10.2.2 indicates the range of hotel types available in these chains.

Independent hotels

The independent hotels still make up about four-fifths of the market in France and are still in the majority in the United Kingdom. These traditional hotels, often aiming at the leisure traveller in specific locations, are numerous for many reasons.

TABLE 10.2.2   Positioning of selected hotel chains in the UK and France

	France	UK
Economy and budget	Formule 1 Primo Arcade Ibis Fimotel	Campanile Granada Lodge Travelodge
Mid-market	Best Western Inter Hotel Mercure Novotel	Garden Court Post House Toby Hotels Novotel
Upper market	Concorde Sofitel Relais et Chateaux Holiday Inn	Country Court Crest Hilton International Holiday Inn

Source: Parnell-Kerr Associates.

One key factor is that there are limited entry barriers to setting up a hotel. There will be the original land and construction or conversion costs and limited marketing costs. Labour costs tend to be low as many of these hotels will be family-run businesses and additional labour costs tend to be very low in this sector given the part-time and seasonal nature of much of the employment.

In France the deregulation of the financial markets has led to easier access to finance and has encouraged investment in hotels at this level, although the Voisin Law does control the number of constructions at local level.

One advantage the small independent French hotels have over their United Kingdom counterparts is in the VAT rates they have to pay, which are significantly lower in France than in the United Kingdom for hotels, as can be seen in Table 10.2.3.

TABLE 10.2.3   Levels of VAT applied to hotels in the European Community (% rate, 1993)

Country	Standard rate	Hotel rate
Belgium	20.5	6
Denmark	25	25
France	**18.6**	**5.5**
Germany	15	15
Greece	18	8
Ireland	21	12.5
Italy	19	9
Luxembourg	15	3
Netherlands	17.5	6
Portugal	16	5
Spain	15	6
United Kingdom	**17.5**	**17.5**

Source: British Tourist Authority.

However, the United Kingdom independent hotel sector benefits to some extent from the fact that the United Kingdom had an opt-out clause in the European Social Charter. In an industry which is labour-intensive by nature and which employs a considerable number of part-time workers, the United Kingdom has been less affected by legislation concerning part-time workers' rights and hours of employment and by National Minimum Wage levels than in France.

It has already been seen that demand can be volatile in the sector and this may frequently have a regional dimension – that is, national demand may rise but regional demand could fall because of factors specific to the local or regional business environment.

One economic factor that may be significant for the independent hotel operator is the rate of interest, as not only will this have a bearing on consumer demand but it will directly affect hotels where they have had to borrow money for, say, expansion or to comply with tighter health and safety regulations. These highly geared hotels are at risk from any increases in interest rates. They particularly suffer in recessions when there is intensive competition to attract customers and there is a general increase in buyer power in terms of demands for bigger discounts and more value for money. In addition, they are considerably at risk from consumers using alternative sources of accommodation such as camping, holiday centres or bed-and-breakfast establishments, and in a market with elements of over-capacity their profit margins get squeezed and many struggle to survive.

The hotel chains

The rest of the hotel industry consists of the hotel chains which have been significantly increasing their share of the French and British markets. In France the top five hotels control 17.5 per cent of the market with the Accor Group alone controlling 12 per cent. In the United Kingdom the top five hotel chains control one-third of the market, making it one of the most concentrated hotel markets in Europe.

One of the main reasons for the growth of the hotel chains is the advantages that accrue to them through economies of scale. These are seen especially in the areas of purchasing, marketing and financing. For example, with purchasing, the major chains are able to own or control their chief suppliers, thus achieving the advantages of vertical integration. The Forte Group owns most of its suppliers and, like Accor, has a computerized purchasing database. In marketing the larger chains are able to advertise extensively and support the wide range of brands of hotels they own, thus enhancing brand loyalty among targeted segments of current and potential hotel customers. They use database-driven marketing, often linked up to a computer reservation system, such as the Resinter system at Accor, which makes the whole process of booking into a hotel considerably easier for the client.

In addition they can offer consistent quality in a range of locations and at different classes of hotel. This has undoubtedly attracted custom from the business traveller and conference markets and may have also benefited from such legislation as the EU Package Tour Directive which makes organizers of package holidays legally liable to the customer for all aspects of the package offer; and as this includes hotels, customers may benefit from the guaranteed quality the hotels can provide.

On the whole, the prospects for the industry in France and the United Kingdom look good with the continuing move towards leisure-based activities, but the market remains very competitive and is prone to over-capacity. The challenge for both the independents and the hotel chains will be to retain competitiveness in such a rapidly changing business environment.

QUESTIONS

1.   Compare the business environment for hotels specializing in the business market with those in the leisure market. Which of these is the more volatile and why?

2.   Assess the extent to which the business environment for the hotel industry varies between the United Kingdom and France. Is this a market where national tendencies dominate or is there evidence of a European market?

3.   Compare an independent hotel in your home location and one in an overseas location that you may have visited and evaluate the key differences in their business environment.

4.   To what extent do you feel that the hotel industry is becoming more concentrated in the United Kingdom and France and what are the likely consequences of this? What do you feel are the main competitive forces affecting the industry?

Worlds apart: the business environment of Oxfam*

Ian Brooks

This case study explores the business environment facing a not-for-profit organization. It takes a closer look at both its income generating and expenditure activities and assesses the nature of numerous environmental variables that influence its well-being. The case also explores the breadth of activity undertaken by Oxfam.

10.3.1 Oxfam's structure and objectives

Oxfam is a registered charity based in Oxford, England employing about 30 000 volunteers and about 1250 other staff in the United Kingdom and Ireland. In addition there are about 1600 staff employed outside the United Kingdom and Ireland in field offices in over 70 countries. It has an ambitious and far-reaching organizational objective, outlined below.

Oxfam's main objective

To relieve poverty, distress and suffering in any part of the world (including starvation, sickness or any physical disability or affliction) and primarily when arising from any public calamity (including earthquake, pestilence, war or civil

---

* This case study is based upon information supplied by Oxfam, 274 Banbury Road, Oxford, OX2 7DZ, tel. 01865 313600, for which the authors extend many thanks. For more details about Oxfam contact Support Services at the above address. There is a wide range of information available from Oxfam, including leaflets, pamphlets, posters and books.

disturbance) or the immediate or continuing result of want of natural or artificial resources or the means to develop them and whether acting alone or in association with others; and in particular but without prejudice to the generality of the foregoing for that purpose to provide food, healing, clothing, shelter, training and education and to undertake or assist in work calculated directly to achieve that purpose; and in connection therewith to educate the public concerning the nature, causes and effects of poverty, distress and suffering as aforesaid, to conduct and produce research concerning these and to publish or otherwise make the results thereof available to the public.

The Director of Oxfam is responsible to Trustees for the management of the organization. There are four deputy directors each responsible for one of the four divisions (refer to Table 10.3.1 below).

TABLE 10.3.1   The four divisions of the Oxfam organization

International division	*Trading division*
Implementation of Oxfam's overseas programme;	Shops;
Emergencies department;	Oxfam Trading;
Programme services department;	Bridge programme;
Policy department	Wastesaver
Marketing division	*Management services division*
Fundraising;	Finance;
Communications;	Administration;
Campaigns;	Central human resource services;
Public advocacy;	Computing;
Education work	Printing and design

10.3.2 Fundraising

Oxfam raises funds in the United Kingdom and Ireland with the help of about 30 000 volunteers who run Oxfam shops and assist in other activities. A considerable amount comes from governments, bilateral agencies and other institutional sources. Oxfam raised nearly £100 million in the year ending 30 April 1995, which represented an increase of 15 per cent on the previous year. The charity's net assets are £34.5 million (1994–95).

A major source of income derives from the sale of goods donated from the public. Oxfam shops enjoyed a net income of £17.8 million in the year to April 1995, up over £3 million from the 1994 figure; there are 850 shops, the largest charity chain in the United Kingdom. The shops' operation and trading activities are a distinct part of the organization, bearing their own operating costs.

Donations from the public, primarily given on a regular basis by covenants or

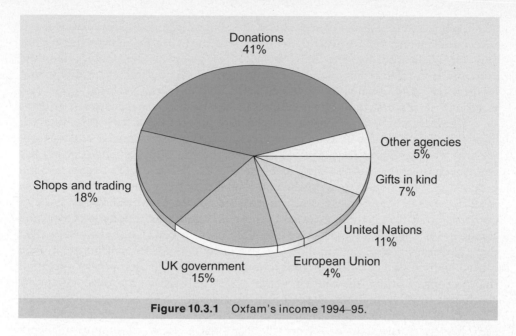

Donations
41%

Other agencies
5%

Gifts in kind
7%

United Nations
11%

European Union
4%

UK government
15%

Shops and trading
18%

Figure 10.3.1　Oxfam's income 1994–95.

bank standing orders, form a substantial source of funds. These donations, which raised almost £39 million in 1995, may be tax deductible for the donor. Other donations are received in response to press and postal appeals and fundraising events. Donations and gifts in kind showed a sizeable increase between 1994 and 1995.

As Figure 10.3.1 indicates, Oxfam also receives funds from government, the European Union and UN Agencies under their co-funding schemes and from their disaster relief funds. It was from these sources that significant increases have been achieved in recent years – that is, from £14.4 million in 1993 to £24 million in 1994 and to almost £29 million in the year to April 1995.

Oxfam's subsidiary company, Oxfam Activities Ltd, has continued to trade throughout the year as Oxfam Trading and Oxfam Wastesaver. Oxfam Trading purchases goods from producers in the developing countries through Oxfam's Bridge Scheme. It also purchases goods from commercial suppliers and through the Good Neighbour Scheme, working with people who have physical or learning disabilities and at the training centres teaching young people new skills. These goods are sold through Oxfam Trading's mail order catalogue and Oxfam shops. Oxfam Wastesaver in Huddersfield processes textiles and aluminium for subsequent industrial recycling. Oxfam's Memorandum of Association gives the trustees wide-ranging powers of investment, including stock, shares and debentures, in any part of the world.

There are numerous fundraising charities in the United Kingdom all competing with one another for donations from the general public. A large number of these now manage charity shops adopting a similar format to the Oxfam stores which pioneered the idea of charity shops. It is not uncommon to find half a dozen such outlets along a high street or within a small urban area. They compete not only for quality products to sell but also for customers. Naturally, when the economy is in relative boom and unemployment on the decline charitable giving tends to rise. Additionally, most charity shops tend to follow the 'retail cycle' and experience an increase in turnover in times of significantly rising economic growth.

Charities which hope to raise a substantial proportion of their revenue from public donations are also in indirect competition with other producers of goods and services which compete for people's disposable income. The National Lottery has enjoyed considerable success since its birth in 1994. Evidence now suggests that a proportion of the monies spent by the public on lottery tickets might otherwise have been donated to charities. However, there is no consensus regarding this issue as numerous charities, including Oxfam, reported an increase in donations from the public in 1995. The National Council for Voluntary Organizations claimed in 1995 that charities will lose £276 million due to a decline in donations from the public caused by increased spending on the National Lottery. In its first year of operation the National Lottery distributed about £250 million to charities. A survey conducted by NOP in 1995 revealed that the general public believe that about 20 per cent of Lottery monies are donated to charities. The actual figure is just 5.6 per cent. Oxfam received money from the National Lottery to support its work programme with poverty in the United Kingdom and Ireland in Autumn 1995.

Additionally, alterations in income tax and VAT which change levels of disposable income, influence charitable giving. Finally, the UK government varies its contribution levels according to numerous, sometimes unrelated, criteria such as the state of the economy in the UK.

The impact of 'compassion fatigue' and an increase in the demand for aid has forced many charities into longer term, more strategic, marketing activities. Many experts believe that greater emphasis needs to be placed by national and international charities on marketing and branding if they are going to compete successfully for private and corporate funds against a host of new, local organizations, such as hospital trusts, schools and parent–teacher associations.

Oxfam are constantly looking for new ways of reaching new donors. They have recently introduced successful television and radio advertising and market directly through mail and press advertising. Additionally, Oxfam is supported by a number of major organizations such as the Cooperative Retail Society and Northern Foods.

10.3.3 Oxfam's aid work

Oxfam aims to spend annually what it raises and to keep a very low level of reserves to protect forward commitments to the development programme. Oxfam produces a strategic plan which outlines the programme activity for the forthcoming five years. Oxfam's Chair in 1993/94, Mary Cherry, suggested that the constant challenge facing the charity was 'to change to meet the needs of the times and yet to retain our core values undiminished'.

Much of Oxfam's development programme is carried out through grants to local organizations which support long-term, sustainable development for a community. Additionally, support is made available for immediate emergency relief provision in times of crisis. Oxfam's own staff, both in the United Kingdom and Ireland and overseas, provide specialist services, for example assistance with the water and sanitation needs of refugees, and engage in training and networking with local organizations. Considerable support is given to programmes through local organizations. Oxfam's information, campaigning and education programme aims to share its experience of the overseas programme with various interest groups, such as schools, direct supporters and the wider public.

Oxfam aim to contribute to the public debate and policy making in the United Kingdom, Ireland and the European Union in the interests of alleviating poverty, distress and suffering. They engage in lobbying activity at many levels, for example at the UN and World Bank level, at national and continental tiers and by committed campaigners working at constituency level. They were, for example, able to get African debt onto the agenda of the G7 summit in Tokyo in 1994. They have also influenced the UK government's policy in Bosnia towards aid.

Figure 10.3.2 indicates Oxfam's expenditure by broad category while Figure 10.3.3 illustrates a more detailed breakdown of their spending (1994–95). Figure 10.3.4 shows the geographical focus of their efforts.

Despite statements of commitment from government and other official agencies such as the World Bank, Oxfam are saddened by the lack of genuine

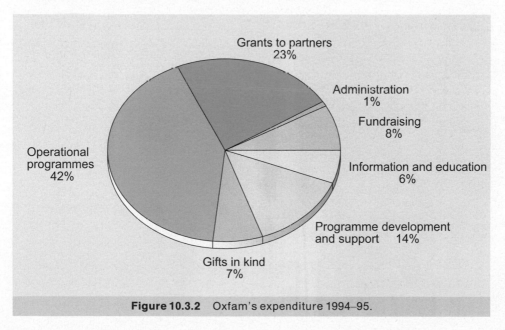

Figure 10.3.2 Oxfam's expenditure 1994–95.

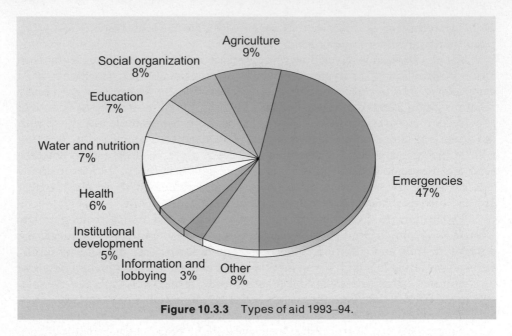

Figure 10.3.3   Types of aid 1993–94.

commitment to the alleviation of poverty on the ground. Although, for example, governments have committed themselves to apportioning 0.7 per cent of gross national product (GNP) to aid, most have failed to deliver. Countries like the United Kingdom, Italy, Japan and the United States contribute less than one-

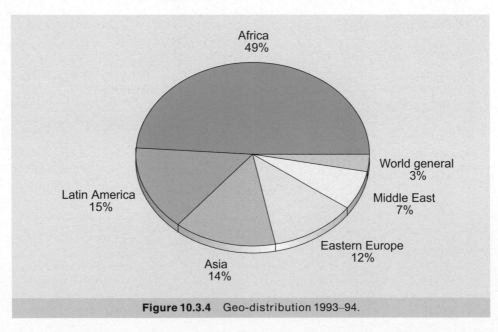

Figure 10.3.4   Geo-distribution 1993–94.

third of 1 per cent of their GNP to overseas aid, and only Denmark, Sweden, Norway and the Netherlands currently exceed the above-stated target.

Oxfam are attempting to strengthen their voice by publishing a 'hard-hitting' book, entitled *Words into Action*, which demonstrates the relative lack of commitment from governments and international bodies. They have also increased their links with other agencies and charities, for example with the 21 like-minded agencies in Eurostep. In 1995 international links were consolidated by the formal establishment of Oxfam International which brought together Oxfam organizations in Canada, the USA, Australia, New Zealand, Hong Kong, Belgium and the Netherlands.

Oxfam operate in about 70 countries, although over half (58 per cent) of their overseas programme expenditure goes to continental Africa. Within that continent many economic reforms have failed to generate economic recovery while imposing huge social costs. For example, recent measures imposed by the World Bank and the IMF in Burkino Faso led to the near collapse of social services such as health and education, one consequence being the swelling of numbers of school-age street children in the cities. In Oxfam's experience, many market-based reforms have increased income disparities because of the failure to address unequal power relations and poor people's lack of access to markets. A constructive dialogue on policy has been established with senior staff in the World Bank and an Oxfam policy adviser participated, with considerable success, in a World Bank assessment mission in Zimbabwe. A major lobbying success was recorded in 1994/95 which succeeded in enabling major agencies, like the World Bank, to realize that protection of fundamental social services, such as health and education, was a necessity in times of economic restructuring.

Possibly the change which has most directly affected poor people in the past two decades has been the accelerating movement of people towards the cities as life becomes less viable on the land. Economic recession, structural adjustment programmes, natural disasters, conflicts, breakdown of traditional lifestyles and lack of access to land all contribute to this rural–urban migration. The loss of old community support systems and the breakdown of families can leave people isolated and vulnerable to exploitation. Poor housing and unemployment is a reality for the majority.

Oxfam also supports organizations working to make sure that elections are 'free and fair'. In South Africa in 1994 grants covered the costs of a UN election observer in Sekhukhuneland and paid for outside observers to travel to conflict-ridden rural areas.

Oxfam's aid is not destined exclusively to recognized developing world countries. Many parts of the former Soviet Union and Eastern Europe have undergone substantial political and economic change during the past five years, resulting in considerable hardships for certain groups. Free market doctrines have led to reductions in welfare programmes leaving many people in desperate poverty, disillusioned with their governments and fatally responsive to ethnic hate-mongering.

Changes in trading patterns have continued to have profound effects on many of the people Oxfam works with. The North American Free Trade Agreement (1994), for example, sparked an uprising in southern Mexico. For more than one million peasant farmers this agreement meant the loss of an important market for their crops as it put them in direct competition with huge mechanized maize farms in the USA. Oxfam promote fair trade. Cafedirect, the fairly traded coffee promoted by Oxfam and three other organizations, is now outselling many other ground coffees and has 4 per cent UK market share. The first goods bearing the Fairtrade mark went on sale in most major supermarkets in 1994. Part of the lobbying, campaigning and advocacy work in the United Kingdom aims to make people fully aware of the wider consequences of their purchasing activities.

QUESTIONS

1. Using the acronym LE PEST as an analytical framework, conduct an analysis of the fundraising and campaigning side of Oxfam's business (primarily the Marketing and Trading divisions). You may need to draw upon other secondary sources of information, for example, regarding the legal framework under which charities operate. What changes are taking place within Oxfam's business environment?

2. Explore the competitive position of Oxfam *vis-à-vis* other charities and other forms of competition for funds. You may find Michael Porter's structural analysis (Chapter 2) of value.

3. Who are the stakeholders of the Oxfam organization? Comment on the relative power each stakeholder possesses and the interest they are likely to show in Oxfam's activity.

4. Are the models and concepts of environmental analysis outlined in this book and other sources suitable for dealing with the environment in which Oxfam administer their aid programme? Attempt to illustrate how Oxfam intervene to influence the environment. In what ways does the environment in which they operate determine their activity?

CASE STUDY 10.4

H.P. Bulmer: cider, and a lot more besides

· John Reast

> This case explores many of the areas within the business environment, specifically focusing upon the competitive factors facing the Bulmer organization.

10.4.1 The company: background

H.P. Bulmer (HPB) is a leading independent drinks company, based in Hereford, with a turnover of £247 million and an operating profit of £27.4 million in 1995. HPB is best known as the UK market leader in cider with brands such as Woodpecker, Strongbow and Scrumpy Jack (see Table 10.4.1). HPB also sell a range of premium branded beers and had significant interests within the mineral waters and fruit-based non-alcoholic drinks sectors of the market. A further significant source of HPB income has been derived from the sale of pectin, a natural product extracted from citrus fruit peel and apples, and used as a gelling agent and stabilizer in a variety of foods and pharmaceuticals. Some of the well-known food products which have used HPB pectin include McVitie's Jaffa Cakes, Ski Gold Yoghurt and Robertson's Jam.

HPB operations are primarily based in the United Kingdom, with other operations in Australia and, more recently, in Belgium and other parts of Europe. HPB gains 84 per cent of its operating profits from its UK drinks operation, with the bulk of this coming from its cider sales (see Table 10.4.2). Sales projections for the UK cider market are rosy (see Table 10.4.3). They have grown from 62 million gallons in 1989 and are expected to exceed 110 million gallons by the year 2000.

Few parts of the drinks industry can claim to have increased sales by 50 per cent in five years. This dramatic increase in cider sales is largely due to the efforts of H.P. Bulmer. In 1989, HPB took the decision to spend huge sums on

TABLE 10.4.1   Cider portfolios

Showerings	Taunton	Bulmer	Merrydown	Inch's
Gaymers Old English	Diamond White	Woodpecker (sweet)	Merrydown Original	Stonehouse
Gaymers Finest Special Cider	Blackthorn	Pomagne	Longman	White Ligthning
Coates	Dry Blackthorn	Strongbow (dry)		Edson
Somerset LA	Blackthorn Super	Scrumpy Jack		Appledure
K	Blackthorn L.A.	MAX		Iron Oak
Ice Dragon	Blackthorn Sweet	Strongbow White		Calva Sidro
Addlestones Vintage (cask)	(formerly Autumn Gold)	Strongbow Ice (Dec. 94)		Frizzante (vs wine)
Copperhead	Blackthorn Cidermaster	Strongbow LA		Red or white sparkling
Copperhead Plus	Red Rock (1989)	Strongbow Super		
Kells Edge	Brody (1991)	Crispen (light alcohol)		
VOX	Diamond Blush	Original (premium traditional)		
	Applewood			
	Moonstone	Black Jack (beer/cider) Jan. 93		
	Fres			
	Rooster	Bulmers Fine		
	CID	Hockhams		
	First Edition	Discovery		
	Old Somerset (economy)	Black Oak (economy)		
		Great White (strong economy)		
		Scrumpy Jack – Old Hazy (cask conditioned cloudy)		
		Strongbow Lemon White (flavoured – from Australia)		
		Compte de Balvielle (premium continental sparkling cider)		

advertising. The company realized that profits would take a knock in the short term, but it was felt that strong marketing was the only way to lift the cider market out of what threatened to be a terminal decline. This policy was successful. Sales went up; margins, eventually, rose sufficiently to compensate for the money spent on advertising. The cider industry in general, and HPB in particular, prospered.

TABLE 10.4.2   Operating profit by region

	1995 (£000)	1996 (£000)
UK	22 966	21 457
Australia	3 654	2 967
Belgium	811	1 339
	27 431	25 763

Source: HPB Holdings 1994/95 Annual Company Reports.

TABLE 10.4.3   UK cider market (millions of gallons)

1989	1994	1995
62	92.5	99

However, despite the successes within the cider market, other problems have meant that HPB profitability had been unimpressive in the early 1990s. The reasons will be explored within this case.

10.4.2 Bulmer and its markets 1989–92

In 1989 H.P. Bulmer's fortunes were almost universally tied to UK cider sales, which were in long-term decline (see Table 10.4.4). This decline was partially due to the rise in popularity of lager drinking during the 1980s. Traditionally cider drinking was associated with younger, heavier drinking males, which was the same target audience as for lager and other beers, fuelling severe competition. The shift to premium bottled beers and lagers, the historically low level of cider promotion, and a decline in the number of young people meant that cider was increasingly being squeezed – and something had to change.

TABLE 10.4.4   Geographic analysis of turnover by region

	1995 (£000)	1994 (£000)
UK	210 302	219 971
Australia	18 851	16 375
Belgium	5 880	5 246
USA	863	2 006
Far East	260	721
All other countries	10 899	10 258
	247 055	254 577

Source: HPB Holdings 1994/95 Annual Company Report.

HPB, realizing that its performance was so closely linked to the performance of this market, took steps to expand sales. HPB was partially able to take the decision to accept short-term profit falls as more than half the equity capital of the company was controlled by the Bulmer family itself. The company also made other major strategic decisions. They decided to further develop their business in other product markets and also other geographic markets around the globe.

10.4.3 The position in 1992

The United Kingdom cider market

HPB held just under half the £720 million UK cider market with its key brands Strongbow, Woodpecker and Scrumpy Jack. The market had grown from under £600 million in 1989. Competition in the UK was strong, Taunton had just over one-third of the market and Showerings had over 10 per cent. So the big three players controlled over 90 per cent (CR3 90) of the market. The key pressures within the market in 1992 were not only between the big three players who increased the number of new product launches, but also from other sectors of the drinks market including beers, lagers and wine. There also appeared to be a growing trend among young people to reject alcohol.

Red Rock, Brody and Diamond White (Taunton), Scrumpy Jack, MAX, Strongbow White (Bulmer) and K (Showerings) were all trying to make the cider market more appealing to a premium audience. Not only were the companies raising the competition stakes among themselves, but also with other alcoholic drinks. One of the reasons why the cider market was seeing a focus on premium launches and increasing promotional spends was because cider had, traditionally, been a highly price-sensitive product, associated with a young, down-market, low income, male drinker. This factor meant that cider demand could be severely threatened by issues which pushed prices relatively higher or reduced the spending capacity of the target audience. Concerns included United Kingdom or European Union excise duty increases in comparison with other drink categories, increased promotional spends in other drinks markets, unemployment, the impact of recession upon disposable incomes, and declining public house traffic. An indication of the power of the lager and beer rivals can be gleaned from the advertising spend levels in 1990 (see Table 10.4.5).

The international picture

Bulmer exports its principal brands to over 30 countries in both draught and packaged formats, and is the major force in the expansion of 'UK style' ciders throughout the world.

TABLE 10.4.5 Advertising spend

	1990
Cider	£10.3 million
Beer	£27.0 million
Lager	£73.0 million

Cider – Australia

While most of Bulmer's profits came from the UK cider market, they also have other cider interests outside the United Kingdom. HPB dominate the Australian cider market with its Strongbow, Woodpecker and newly introduced Strongbow White and Strongbow Lemon White brands. HPB gained 8 per cent of its 1992 profit from the growing Australian market. Bulmer Australia delivered a profit of £3.7 million in 1994/95, an increase of 23 per cent on the previous year (see Table 10.4.2).

Cider – Europe

In September 1992, HPB purchased the leading Belgian cider manufacturer, Cidreric Stassen. It was hoped that Stassen would form a bridgehead for an assault upon the European market. Stassen had strengths within the French and Dutch markets in addition to the Belgian cider market. The purchase also enabled HPB to bring Continental-style, fruit-based ciders and beers to the United Kingdom from Belgium. Stassen exports a wide range of products principally to the Netherlands, France and Germany.

10.4.4 Bulmer's other products

Beer

HPB not only operates as a manufacturer of cider, but also acts as a distributor for other categories of drinks. Such distribution not only generates profit in its own right, but also leads to economies of scale and improved efficiency for the Bulmer warehousing and distribution system. In addition, an expanding portfolio of brands across different drinks categories provides more power for HPB when dealing with major customers, such as the UK supermarkets.

In 1992 HPB held the exclusive UK distribution rights for Redstripe and Crucial Brew Jamaican lagers, DAB premium lager from Dortmunder Actien-Brauerei and for San Miguel, a leading brand in the premium sector of the Spanish market. HPB undertook no manufacturing within this sector. In 1994 HPB also gained the UK distribution rights for Amstel, a Dutch lager, which is one of the top five selling European brands.

Soft drinks

HPB was the exclusive sales and distribution agent for the Perrier range of natural mineral waters which includes Volvic, Buxton Spring, Ashbourne, Vittel and the main Perrier brand. HPB, as distributor, had to handle the Perrier product recall in the United Kingdom, following a benzine scare at the European production plant in the early 1990s.

HPB also held the sales and distribution agreement for Orangina in the United Kingdom, where it was manufactured under licence.

In addition, HPB produced and marketed a range of its own soft drinks including Kiri sparkling apple juice, and Sao'Rico and Giardini, two new drinks targeted at the booming adult soft drinks market, competing against rivals such as Purdeys and Aqua Libra.

Pectin

Bulmer was the sole manufacturer of pectin within the United Kingdom and exported all over the world. HPB also had a 50 per cent interest in Braspectina SA, a Brazilian company which produces and markets in South America. While the world-wide pectin market was becoming increasingly more competitive, it still generated 12 per cent of the company profits in 1992.

10.4.5 The competitive environment post-1992

Having considered the HPB company profile, broad portfolio and important areas of profit generation, attention will now be focused upon the competitive pressures faced by HPB over the following period. The case will indicate that, while competitive pressure has always been present in the cider and beverages market, these pressures have never been greater or more intense. Not only do HPB have to contend with competition from other cider and beverage manufacturers, but also other distribution specialists and supply chain customers.

The UK cider wars

As the cider market expanded in the early 1990s, with increased promotional activity and a plethora of expensive up-market brands hitting the shelves, competition from more down-market competitors was stimulated. There has been a sharp increase in the number of rivals prepared to sell cider at rock-bottom prices. As a result, the HPB share of the cider market slipped back in 1993, largely due to the company's refusal to resort to price cutting to protect its market share. HPB responded with generous multibuy promotions on their two volume brands, Strongbow and Woodpecker (three litres for the price of two). However, despite the promotional efforts of the company, they have still to arrest the decline of the sweet cider Woodpecker brand. While the company has sought to differentiate itself from competitors with launches of new premium products – many have been entirely new branded offerings or line extensions from the Strongbow brand – these have not helped the Woodpecker brand.

HPB has come through a period of intense competition within the cider market relatively unscathed; however, some of the smaller competitors such as Merrydown failed to make a profit in the latter half of 1993 and have been struggling due to price competition within the cider market.

Who are the cut-price competition?

The price competitors are from two sources: economy brands produced by manufacturers and own-label products carrying supermarket brand names. The influx of low-price competitors has been prompted not only by growth in a large, profitable market, but also by the recessionary environment and a desire among many consumers to achieve value for money.

A further form of price competition which has indirectly impacted upon all UK alcoholic drink manufacturers, is the trade in cheap drinks coming across the Channel by sea, and now land, from Europe. Merrydown chief Richard Purdey, speaking in December 1994, denounced the flood of cheap beer from France, claiming 'this invasion had hit the domestic cider market'. The cider price wars, plus the foreign beer influx, had again left Merrydown reporting vastly reduced profits in 1994. Purdey proceeds: 'Shareholders should continue to be aware of the highly competitive nature of the markets in which we operate, especially cider.'

Taunton's chief executive, Peter Adams, indicated in 1994 that he believed that price competition would be 'a permanent feature of the market'.

Intensified competition among key competitors

Not only have Bulmer faced an assault at the bottom end of the market, but they have also faced renewed launches from Taunton and Gaymers within the premium bottled and draught sectors of the marketplace. A relatively 'new' national contender, Inch's Cider Ltd, has shown impressive growth recently. It is a family-owned Devon producer of traditional ciders, sold to management in 1989, and has a mission to become a national brand with exciting product developments. The policy has been to produce quality ciders using traditional methods, for example using oak rather than stainless steel in production and storage.

While Inch's only had around 3 per cent of the national market in 1994, this had grown from only 1 per cent in 1990 and was equal with Merrydown as the fourth largest supplier.

In November 1995, Merrydown recorded a record financial performance, reversing its downward profit trend. The results have been dramatically helped by their decision to introduce the first alcoholic lemonade into the UK market. The distribution agreement has, so far, paid great dividends, but already several large brewers have introduced their own versions of this new drink. At least in the short term, the launch has compensated for the harsh competitive position they face within the cider market. Such product launches serve to compete with HPB's claim on consumer spending on premium bottled drinks.

Distribution channels

Over time supermarkets have been responsible for an increasing share of the take-home trade. It has been largely due to HPB's strong presence within the 'on-trade' (pubs and clubs) that the company is not totally at the mercy of the grocery multiples. The multiples not only threaten the major brands with increasingly sophisticated own brand offerings, but they are also able to exert significant downward pressure on manufacturers' prices. Given the dominance of own-label in many food and drink categories, most of the big players in the cider industry are placing each-way bets – supporting their branded products as well as supplying a large proportion of own-label business. Indeed, approximately 90 per cent of own-label production is accounted for by HPB and Taunton. However, while grocery brands are obviously a concern, the own-label penetration of 16 per cent in 1994 is relatively low compared to many other product categories.

    However, it has not just been the supermarkets which have been causing the major cider manufacturers' problems. The big brewers, who still control vast swathes of Britain's pubs, were accused by John Rudgard, former chief executive of H.P. Bulmer, of 'deliberately inflating the price of cider to keep it a fifth higher, on average, than the products they brew'. John Rudgard stated in 1994 'that based on the cost of production and the amount of duty levied, there is no reason why a pint of cider should not be priced the same as a pint of ale'. The growth in the cider market at the expense of beer has meant an increasing level of hostility between the cider manufacturers and the big brewers. The latter are lobbying for the tariff levels on cider to be increased in line with beers and lagers.

The world-wide picture – competition

The purchase of Cidererie Stassen in Belgium has provided HPB with benefits in its strategic advance into the European marketplace. Stassen produced an operating profit of £0.8 million in 1995. One such advantage has been the development of a 'continental sparkling cider', Compte de Balvielle, for the UK market. However, the acquisition has not been without its problems. Traditionally cider is thought of as a substitute for sparkling wine within the European marketplace. HPB is attempting to sidestep this cultural issue, trying to present cider as a substitute for beer. Part of the thinking behind this strategy is the desire to create an 'international brand' to carry its product world wide. In 1994, John Rudgard stated 'that it would take at least two years to decide whether Strongbow had become Europe's "new wave" beverage', but indicated that the group's new European partners, the Stella Artois company Interbrew and Heineken are enthusiastic. The issues are underlined by the reported fall in profits for Stassen, declining by almost £0.5 million – a figure which the group says reflects investment costs such as expanding its marketing spend, boosting its salesforce and opening a new bottling hall.

In addition, in 1995, HPB concluded an exclusive agreement with Oy Hartwall AB, Finland's largest brewer, to distribute ciders within the market.

Overall, in 1995, the European export trade is showing positive signs, with markets such as Spain and Ireland showing sales increases of 40 per cent or over.

HPB is also facing competition within some of its other important international markets. It is a clear market leader in Australia and derives 13 per cent of its operating profits from the market in 1995 (see Table 10.4.2). However, in 1994, Taunton Cider announced its major initiatives within the Australian market – indicating that it was seeking partnership agreements to open up distribution for its products there.

The move came only shortly after Taunton signed a distribution agreement in America with Molson Brewing. This partnership has seen Taunton brands, such as Red Rock, Brody's and Fres, on prominent display in the bars of Washington DC and Boston.

Such initiatives may mean that HPB will face a more difficult competitive environment when seeking to establish itself in foreign markets in future.

The Bulmer portfolio post-1992

Throughout the 1980s, and at the beginning of the 1990s, HPB had a strategy of diversification. It not only operated within its traditional core area of the United Kingdom and international cider sales, but was a major operator within the world-wide pectin industry, a manufacturer and distributor of wines, sprits, soft drinks and waters, and a distributor of premium beers within the UK market.

As competition intensified during the 1990s, HPB increasingly realized that many of its diversifications had led to lower margins and also a reduced strategic focus upon its core business activities. In addition, the world-wide pectin market was in severe decline with the break-up of the Soviet Union and world-wide recession increasingly hitting sales and profitability.

Not only was HPB facing problems in pectin, it also found that certain distribution contracts were difficult to hold on to. For example, it had lost the Perrier distribution rights to Coca-Cola Schweppes Beverages in the early 1990s.

The new strategic focus

In 1993 the group disposed of its pectin operations, having already withdrawn from the US apple juice market and the wine and spirits distribution business within the United Kingdom.

In 1994 HPB formally announced its new strategic focus. It decided to withdraw from the soft drinks market in order to focus on its cider and beer activities. Withdrawal meant selling its own brands and relinquishing distribution contracts.

John Rudgard said that 'this was the final step in the strategic repositioning of the group – which involved pulling out of small, low-margin businesses'. As a result of the strategic shift in its portfolio, the company has succeeded in increasing group operating margins from 10.4 to 11 per cent in 1995. This reflects the lower cost base, reduced soft drinks sales and a higher proportion of premium ciders within the sales mix.

QUESTIONS

1. Analyse the competitive environment facing HPB, applying industry competitive tools or frameworks.

2. Consider how demographic changes within the environment will have an impact on HPB in the future.

3. Consider how the HPB portfolio has been changed over the period of the case in response to competitive pressures within the environment.

4. To what extent does the picture portrayed within the cider and beer market approximate to a situation of 'perfect competition'?

5. Establish what market you feel HPB are in, and therefore who are their key competitors. Has this changed during the period of the case?

CASE STUDY 10.5
Telecommunications: a changing industry
Hugh Davenport

This case study of the telecommunications industry in general and British Telecom in particular focuses on some of the regulatory, technological and competitive issues which pervade the industry. The overall theme is one of rapid and all-consuming change, both nationally and globally. The scope of this change in the United Kingdom is tempered by a certain amount of governmental regulation.

10.5.1 The telecoms sector

Lehman lures top BZW guru for £1m

A new salary benchmark for top-rated City analysts has been set by Lehman Brothers, the Wall Street investment house, which has hired Paul Norris, BZW's telecommunications guru, for a package understood to be about £1 million a year.

'Telecoms is a lucrative sector because there is so much deal flow,' said a City source. 'European countries are privatising their telecoms industries; and for an investment house to be a credible adviser it has to have a star analyst.' (Jeff Randall, *The Sunday Times*, 16 July 1995)

The above news item came and went and, in itself, is not a particularly fascinating piece of information. Although the size of the 'package' used to 'lure' Paul Norris could be viewed with some wonderment, for many of the people working in this environment, the need to use a sum as large as £1 million did not come as a total surprise. The real beauty in this nugget of news is that it is a clear reflection of the changes and developments happening in and around the telecoms sector. It is a strong symbol and indicator of the value, worth and importance of the industry and of its elevated status within the business environment.

First, a bit of history

In August 1984, British Telecom was privatized in line with the Conservative government's ideology and subsequent policy. Prior to the formation of British Telecommunications Plc, the provision of telephony services was run as part of the Post Office. In 1977 the telecommunications arm of the Post Office was separated. Following the British Telecommunications Act of 1981, British Telecom became an entity in its own right. Network competition was allowed for the first time and the Secretary of State for Trade and Industry was given authority to grant licences to alternative operators. In 1983 Mercury Communications Limited started operating in Britain. Their licence to operate was issued as part of a duopoly policy with an agreement that no further licences would be granted for a further seven years. This allowed Mercury protection from other potential new entrants. A White Paper ended the duopoly, thus promoting and facilitating more competition. The government stated that it would consider applications from any applicants for licences to offer public fixed-link UK local and long-distance telecommunications services, and agreed to allow cable television companies to provide local fixed-link services.

The United Kingdom is generally viewed as the most open market in the world. Britain became the only country in the world to allow cable companies to get into the telephony business. The 'wholesale' deregulation of the industry in the United Kingdom appeared to be on its way, except for BT. Although BT are technically capable of sending both messages and entertainment services down the same wires, they are not allowed to provide broadcast television services to homes under a policy which will not be reviewed for several years.

Regulation

When BT was privatized, the government established an independent non-ministerial regulatory body called Oftel (Office of Telecommunications) to assist the Director General of Telecommunications in the exercise of his or her duties. These included supervising telecommunications activities in the United Kingdom and promoting the interests of the consumers of those services. In other words, Oftel's key job is to promote competition. Initially, this was bound to be aimed at regulating and 'constricting' BT and shifting the balance of power away from them, in an attempt to spread it a little more evenly. The regulatory framework imposed has slowly introduced a level of competition. Oftel's main weapons for doing this are:

- its powers to set prices, not only a ceiling on those prices but also a floor, so that BT is precluded from predatory undercharging;

- to issue the licences under which both BT and its competitors are allowed to operate;
- to set the terms (and charge rates) at which those competitors can demand 'interconnection' with BT's own expanding network.

Oftel has become doubly important. It has managed, through its regulatory processes, to encourage, 'help' and facilitate competition. But possibly of more importance, now that there are a number of entrants into the telecommunications market, is the effective regulation of the whole industry. With current deregulation offering potential market entrants licences to offer telecommunications services, liberalization has led to necessary effective regulation.

10.5.2 Competition and change

With the flick of a wrist, a name on a dotted line, the signing of another contractual agreement or operating licence and the laying of more optic fibres and network, what were '160 telecom companies licensed to compete against BT in particular sectors' (*Marketing Week*, 4 August 1995) soon becomes 165 ... 170 ... 175. The list of established or potential operators (and hence competitors) of telephony services is 'endless'.

This case study could proceed with a variety of statistics to demonstrate and reflect the speed with which the whole industry is changing and growing. The quoted figures could be out of date by the time you read this! This is an important issue facing the industry, how to plan for and predict a future which was out of date yesterday, never mind tomorrow (or possibly the day after tomorrow)!

It is the rate of this change which is one of the more significant factors for the telecommunications industry, and individual companies, to deal with. Fifteen years ago the choice customers had was BT ... or ... BT. A decade ago it was BT or Mercury; in 1990 we were faced with a handful of 'choices'. In 1995 we not only have a whole basket of providers, we also have a whole range of services to choose from – Option 15, Business Choice level 4, Volume-Link 3, Automatic Discount Plan, Bonuscall. Competition has certainly brought with it a confusing array of rates and products.

The mobile phone market, too, continues to grow so fast that analysts struggle to keep up. Today 5 million people, or 8.5 per cent of the population, own a mobile phone. It is generally accepted that this figure will triple within five years to around 15 million people. The mobile phone market is also a good measure of how fiercely competition is fought in every sector of the industry. In November 1995 Vodafone, the industry leader, issued Orange with a writ alleging 'malicious falsehood and trademark infringement'. This writ centres around Orange's aggressive £10 million advertising campaign in the build-up to Christmas 1995.

At the same time (21 November) the shares of Vodafone slumped, despite stronger half-year results, a 20 per cent rise in the interim dividend and a lower disconnection rate. The City voiced concerns that intensifying competition will reduce future growth.

Clearly, it is not just the growth of competition which is of significance for the industry. It is one of the most dynamic industries in the world, encapsulating rapid technological developments and innovations, global growth and reorganization and political and regulatory differences.

No industry better reflects the complexity of operating in the mid-1990s than telecommunications. It has become an industrial icon for the twenty-first century, representing the key issues of technological change and progress, globalization and increasing organizational complexity and development. It is moving, and moving with speed.

10.5.3 Technology

With the continuing liberalization of the industry in the United Kingdom and the increasing number of licences being granted to potential operators, the competitive edge (for BT?) shifts towards the development of new (technology) products and services. After 'caller identification' and 'call waiting' will come 'call minder' and other 'select services'.

We have now all heard about, or even seen, the video phone. Companies such as BT, IBM, Intel and Picturetel have all developed systems which convert a PC into a videophone. Videoconferencing by PC may soon be commonplace, so look smart before you telephone!

As part of a trial, more than 150 BT public payphones in Swindon can now be used to charge up Mondex 'smartcards' with 'cash' units. Cable & Wireless, through its British subsidiary Mercury Communications, will soon be launching Britain's first 'thinking' communications network linking voice, e-mail and fax messages with new information and shopping services around the world.

In an attempt to counteract the cable-TV companies, who are eating into the traditional telephony market, BT is creating what is claimed to be the world's most advanced and comprehensive interactive TV service, currently on trial in Ipswich and Colchester. However, so is Videotron in London, Bell Cablemedia in Peterborough, Nynex in Manchester and Cambridge Cable in (not surprisingly) Cambridge.

Advances in technology will certainly create, or tap, new markets for the operators within the industry, but these advances may also 'wipeout' the traditional stronghold markets for the telephony companies. As an example, Internet users can now buy software which 'turns' their personal computer into a voice-based telephone. All one needs is a microphone, a modem, a soundcard and access to an Internet gateway service. You can then dial anyone who has the same software for the cost of calling your local Internet gateway. Once on the Internet there are no other charges, regardless of distance or time. If Internet Phone takes off, it could severely cut the income phone companies make from international calls.

10.5.4 Alliances, mergers and partnerships?

On a global scale, competitive advantage is being achieved through forging a number of partnerships and alliances with other telecommunication companies overseas.

> Competition will not become easier and regulation will remain a fact of life. The future lies in making money abroad. (Roger Eglin, *The Sunday Times*, 4 December 1994)

BT has these global ambitions. Their partnership with MCI, America's second biggest carrier of long-distance telecoms services, has cleared the final regulatory hurdles. They now have a 20 per cent stake in this US long-distance telephone operator which, early in 1995, struck a deal with Rupert Murdoch by purchasing 13 per cent of News Corporation stock and injecting £200 million into the company. The overall aim is to create a US-based joint subsidiary to distribute electronic information, education and entertainment material world-wide. With such large and complex joint ventures we can readily start to recognize increasing organizational complexity, development and change as the key issues and challenges for telecommunication companies entering into the next millennium.

BT and MCI have also launched Concert, their joint-venture company, which offers seamless voice links between the countries in which it now operates and global networking solutions to a range of multinational customers.

The telecommunications industry in many European countries, though, is still controlled by state-owned monopolies and the market will only open up if pressure for liberalization is maintained. Having said this, BT are still establishing a presence in many European countries. Through their deal with VIAG in Germany, and in anticipation of deregulation, they hope to compete against Deutsche Telekom AG. In Italy, through a joint venture with the Banca Nazionale del Lavoro, they now have an interest in one of the country's largest private telecoms networks. Prior to this, BT moved into Spain in an alliance with Banco Santander to distribute Concert products. The bank already has a big data network and the partnership will invest £400 million in developing this. They have also set their sights on territories further afield – Israel, India and China. The strategy is clear.

> Customers will be offered an all-embracing service. Starting with the United Kingdom and America, and spreading into Europe and the Asia Pacific region, BT will provide the complete communications package for data, voice or vision from desktop to desktop. (Roger Eglin, *The Sunday Times*, 4 December 1994)

All we have to do is sit tight and wait for the rapid communications ride of a lifetime! This may not happen as easily as BT, or others, would like it to. Having recognized some of the forces which are driving the changes in the industry (i.e. deregulation, liberalization and hence competition) it is, ironically, the very same mechanisms which may frustrate BT's intended strategy. As mentioned earlier, BT is currently forbidden from broadcasting moving picture entertainments until at least the year 2001.

Compared with the wide-open British and American markets, telecommunication markets in many European countries are still tightly guarded against overseas invaders. It is not until 1998 that the European Union is committed to imposing full 'liberalization' on its members' telecommunication arrangements. In Asia Pacific, a number of countries have no plans this century for deregulation.

BT are not alone in their quest for global connections. BT's activity with MCI and, in particular, the formation of Concert have shaken their rivals into similar action. Inevitably, other alliances and combinations have sprung up: in June 1994, Worldsource, a venture led by the American giant AT&T, with Japan's KDD; Singapore Telecom and Australia's Telstar, linked with Unisource; a combination of the national operators of Switzerland, Sweden and the Netherlands together with the partially state-owned Spanish carrier, Telefonica. Likewise, Deutsche Telekom and France Telecom, together with Sprint, America's third largest long-distance carrier, have formed Atlas. Mercury are only the British subsidiary of the much larger and more widely spread Cable & Wireless. C&W owns a 57.5 per cent stake in Hong Kong Telecom and is negotiating a joint venture with the German energy conglomerate Veba as a means for breaking into the German telecoms market.

CONCLUSION

The telecommunications business is an increasingly international and global one. BT used to envy the large home markets of the Americans and Japanese, but they now see a Europe of 340 million people as their home territory.

Technology is lowering the entry barriers; many of today's companies could not have existed several years ago, but will they still be around for the next few years?

It is difficult to write more in a conclusion for an environment which is changing on an almost daily basis – maybe that is the conclusion!

QUESTIONS

1. Using the information in the case study map out BT's business environment.

2. Using Porter's five-force model outline BT's competitive environment.

3. How successful has Oftel been in:
(a) 'promoting the interests of consumers of telecommunications services' and
(b) encouraging and promoting competition within the telecommunications industry in the United Kingdom?

4. How successful has the privatization of BT been in creating a truly competitive market in telecoms?

5. In work groups, choose one of the main providers of telephony services and review the opportunities and threats which exist for them in their business environment.

6. In work groups, find out more about Interactive TV.

7. Brainstorm some of the technological innovations and ideas which may appear in the next century.

8. Which groups of people have been affected by the privatization of BT and how?

9. What does the overall future of the telecommunications industry look like?

Environmental concerns: the case of Scania

Ian Brooks

> This case study focuses on the ecological or 'green' issues facing Scania, a lorry manufacturer. Because of the integrated nature of environmental forces, other areas – including technology, legal and political issues – are also addressed. It discusses some of the issues central to the heated debate concerning the growing use of road transport in the United Kingdom and Europe.

Introduction

Scania is a Swedish-owned manufacturer and distributor of lorries, buses, coaches, aircraft and marine engines. Its sister company, Saab, manufactures cars. The lorries, or trucks as they are referred to in the industry, are manufactured and assembled in Sodertalue in Sweden, Zwolle in Holland and Angers in France. They produce heavy trucks and operate across Europe and in other world markets. Scania trucks have been referred to as the Rolls-Royces of the truck industry. Trucks of this nature cost in excess of £50 000 excluding a trailer. In 1995 Scania plan to sell over 5000 units in the United Kingdom alone, which represents about 16 per cent market share. This will make it the second major company in the market. Other major European manufacturers include Volvo (20 per cent market share in the United Kingdom), Mercedes, Leyland–Daf, Renault and MAN. It is a highly competitive market place. In 1960 there were 59 truck manufacturers in Europe of which only a dozen remain (see Figures 10.6.1 and 10.6.2).

Trucks are primarily marketed through franchised dealers, most of whom are separately owned companies. Each commands a territory and directly serves the customer. Their prime business comprises the sale of new and used trucks, servicing and repair. It is the lucrative after-sales market which yields the lion's share of their business profits. This marketplace is rapidly changing with the

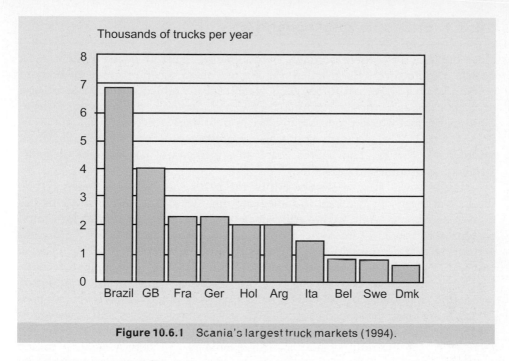

Figure 10.6.1 Scania's largest truck markets (1994).

development of different forms of competition and a changing customer base. There has been a decrease in the importance of small haulage operators and a rise in fleet sales to large organizations. Contract hire and truck leasing are also rapidly expanding.

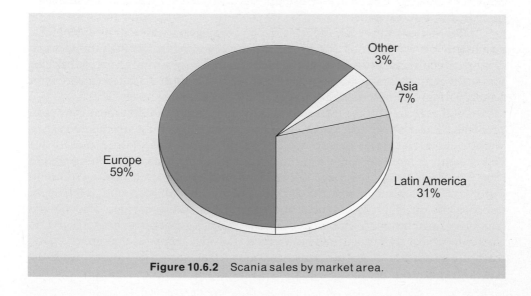

Figure 10.6.2 Scania sales by market area.

10.6.1 Environmental concerns

Until the mid-1960s there were few environmental issues at stake for commercial vehicle manufacturers. Legislation was limited, there was no significant body of opinion voicing concern and few facts were available which demonstrated that a problem existed. In those circumstances the manufacturers' prime concern was to build trucks that would prove competitive in their marketplaces. In the late 1960s West Coast (USA) laws were established which began to regulate pollution from commercial vehicles. The United States of America still has some of the most stringent environmental legislation.

Progress was slow in Europe during the 1970s and the 1980s, hampered by the lack of clear-cut evidence and adequate methods of measurement. This has now changed, and while we are still a long way from the harmonized legislation sought by Scania and some other manufacturers, many standards for the present and future have been established. To a large extent these standards drive change, although some 'environmentally friendly' activity also improves competitiveness. Leif Ostling, the general manager of Scania Trucks and Buses, argues that technology improvements linked to emissions will have competitive pay-offs. Methods are being developed to improve the efficiency of engines and non-engine-related improvements can also reduce emissions and fuel consumption by increasing aerodynamic qualities. Improvements in aerodynamics, rolling resistances and weight reductions have reduced energy consumption by up to 50 per cent in a little over two decades, Ostling argues.

Scania regards the integration of environmental work into all of its processes as a key competitive factor. Nearly half of Scania's product development work occurs in fields related to the environment. These include materials selection, exhaust emissions, noise, fuel consumption, alternative fuels and recycling of components and materials.

Nevertheless, the truck industry is an obvious target for environmentalists who brand it as a polluter of urban areas and the countryside. Yet road transport is, in most circumstances, the most economic form of transport for goods. It has also adapted well to changing economic and competitive conditions and to a variety of legal constraints imposed at both national and international levels.

Total road freight has increased rapidly in recent decades in most European countries. This rise is particularly significant when compared with the dwindling importance of rail in some countries. Yet in many ways rail transport, especially for bulk freight, is more acceptable to the environmentalist lobby. Switching freight from road to rail would reduce both road congestion and atmospheric pollution. Table 10.6.1 shows the relative growth and decline of road and rail freight transport in the United Kingdom and other European countries. The United Kingdom, together with France, 'head' the table, a position of some regret to environmentalist groups and rail authorities. This decline is made more dramatic when one considers that total freight movement has increased vastly during the same time period. The increasing importance of road transport for industrial and

TABLE 10.6.1   Change in total road and rail freight (tonne/kilometre) 1977–92

Country	Road % change 1977–92	Rail % change 1977–92
United Kingdom	+43	−24
France	+48	−24
Spain	+83	−18
Sweden	+50	+19
Germany (West)	+94	+26
Italy	+150	+26
Portugal	+5 (est.)	+109

Source: IRF.

consumer goods is particularly marked in those countries which have enjoyed sizeable growth in their economies.

In 1993 over 1600 million tonnes of goods were transported on roads within the United Kingdom while a little under 110 million tonnes went by rail. Coastal and inland waterways accounted for a further 135 million tonnes of freight in and around the United Kingdom in 1993. Thus, excluding materials carried within pipelines (125 million tonnes in 1993), road transport in 1993 accounted for almost 87 per cent (by weight) of total freight movement within the United Kingdom. That proportion is likely to increase as the decade draws to a conclusion.

Throughout Europe there is concern about road congestion. The European Union forecast that Europe's roads will carry 16.5 billion tonnes of freight by the year 2010. This would represent a doubling in a little over 20 years. In England, the M6 motorway north-west of Birmingham was built for a capacity of 80 000 to 90 000 vehicles per day. It now carries, and has carried for some time, in excess of 115 000 vehicles a day, although the majority of these are private motor vehicles. Meanwhile truck manufacturers, such as Scania, are pushing for an increase in the legally permissible size of lorries to 48 tonnes, arguing that this would reduce the number of journeys required. In Britain, hauliers are restricted to 38 tonnes maximum weight until 1999 and just 40 tonnes thereafter. The Freight Transport Association argue that increasing the permissible weight limit to just 44 tonnes would remove some 9000 trucks from Britain's roads and save 300 million litres of diesel fuel annually. Such a move, however, may require some road bridges to be rebuilt and speed restrictions and other safety measures to be reviewed. Additionally, public perception of the effects of an increase in the size of lorries is far from favourable.

Considerable pressure is placed on governments across Europe to reduce their reliance on road transport and to improve public and rail freight services. The United Kingdom government between 1995 and 1997 provided grants for companies to establish private rail freight terminals. They have also shown some commitment to raising the price of fuel to further encourage movement off the roads. Critics argue these measures do not go far enough. Governments, for their part, have been reluctant to impose extra costs on industry for fear of damaging its competitiveness overseas. For this reason the Conservative government in the mid-1990s rejected European Union proposals for a carbon tax. However, at the 1992 Rio Earth Summit the United Kingdom agreed to reduce carbon dioxide emissions to 1990 levels by the year 2000.

The Royal Commission on the Environment Report, published in 1994 (*Transport and the Environment*, Cmnd 2674, HMSO, 1994) made a significant contribution to the sometimes heated debate concerning the increasing reliance on the use of roads in the United Kingdom for both passenger and goods transport. It contributed to a reduction in the road-building ambitions of the government of the day. The report argued that 'pollutants from vehicles are the prime cause of poor air quality that damages human health, plants and the fabric of buildings'. It continues, 'noise from vehicles and aircraft is a major source of stress. The transport system must already be regarded as unsustainable.' The commission made a series of firm recommendations to government to ensure that World Health Organization guidelines for the year 2005 were met. These included the encouragement of the use of natural gas and electric-powered vehicles, stronger emission controls and encouragement to use rail for freight transport. The commission argued for a target for rail's share of total freight movement within the United Kingdom to rise from 6.5 per cent in 1994 to 20 per cent by 2010. One proposed mechanism to achieve this is the encouragement of attempts to further extend the use of 'piggybacking', where truck trailer loads are lifted on to rail carriages and transported by rail. This may encourage some long-distance and Continental loads off the roads.

10.6.2 Scania's environmental policy

A growing number of national and international organizations have developed an environmental policy which sets out their ecological position. Scania have long recognized that industrial production and ecological concerns often conflict. When that industry is primarily concerned with the manufacture of vehicles which burn fossil fuels and contribute to traffic flows on land, air and sea the environmentalist lobby is particularly watchful and active. However, partly perhaps due to their liberal and sensitive Swedish cultural origin, Scania is renowned within the truck industry for the attention it pays to environmental[1] concerns. Scania's environmental policy is enshrined in its mission statement, explicitly stated below.

It is of interest to note that Scania claim to match or improve upon all statutory environmental standards despite the inevitable cost of following such a policy. However, of equal certainty are the competitive benefits that ensue from the application of technology to forge a bridge between ecological concerns and

---

[1] The term 'environmental' refers to 'ecological' aspects of the wider business environment.

> ### *Scania's environmental policy*
>
> - We shall maintain a lead in commercially applicable technology within our field of competence in order to promote a better environment.
> - We shall strive towards the establishment of internationally harmonized and effective environmental regulations.
> - We shall ensure that our production causes a minimum environmental impact by developing our products and production processes.
> - We shall design and manufacture our products so as to facilitate effective recycling.

competitive pressures. For example, Scania's designers have achieved a steady reduction in fuel requirements from the application of aerodynamic technologies. The 'Scania Streamline' has achieved reductions of up to 15 per cent in the coefficient of drag (C_d) compared with standard models. The resultant C_d is around 0.5 compared to over 0.8 in the mid-1970s. This has led to a reduction in fuel requirements, as illustrated by Figure 10.6.3.

Additionally, engine designs have sought to reduce fuel consumption and exhaust emissions. Measured under laboratory conditions and expressed in grams per kilowatt hour (g/kWh), specific fuel consumption (sfc) is the number of grams of fuel an engine consumes for a power output of 1 kW over a period of one hour. Compared with family motor vehicles or light commercial vehicles, lorries are energy efficient. For example, an average car (weighing a tonne) will require about 8 litres of fuel to travel 100 km, while a 40 tonne truck will only need about 0.8 litre for each tonne of its weight over the same distance. That is, the heavy truck is about 10 times as efficient as the family car.

As Figure 10.6.4 shows, sfc has fallen by 16 per cent since 1970. Another dramatic downward shift is seen in truck exhaust emissions. Figure 10.6.5 indicates the reduction in outputs of nitrogen oxides (NOx), hydrocarbons and particulates during the 1980s by Scania.

Of course, given the clear improvements in exhaust emissions, fuel consumption and noise levels, the question still remains: has the truck industry gone far enough? Across the globe, although particularly in Europe, social protest against heavy lorries and road transport in general has increased in recent years. The wondrous Taj Mahal in Agra, India, is being dangerously affected by pollutants created as a result of increasing industrialization and use of road transport. This has necessitated urgent repair work. Similarly, the Parthenon in Athens is showing signs of rapid deterioration due in large measure to road vehicle emissions. High levels of exhaust emissions have been linked to all manner of human illnesses, not least asthma and lung disease, and significant increases in these and other medical conditions have been recorded in many urban areas in the United Kingdom.

Noise pollution ranks highly among concerns of those living and working

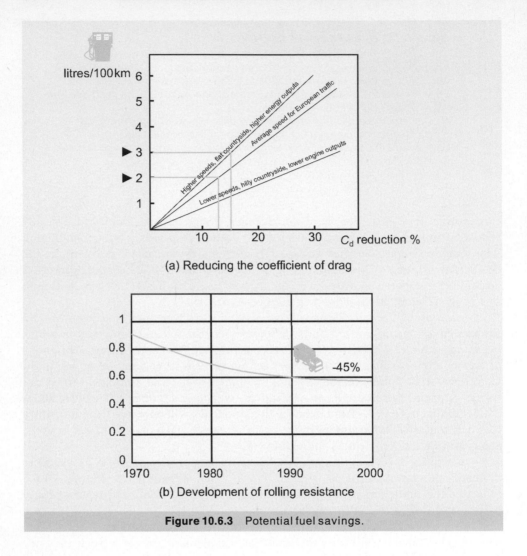

litres/100km

(a) Reducing the coefficient of drag

Higher speeds, flat countryside, higher energy outputs

Average speed for European traffic

Lower speeds, hilly countryside, lower engine outputs

C_d reduction %

-45%

(b) Development of rolling resistance

Figure 10.6.3   Potential fuel savings.

close to busy roads. Scania, too, have made considerable progress in reducing noise levels, although progress in future may be slowed as much of the remaining problems lie with road surfaces and the inevitable noise created by contact with that surface. However, new Scania trucks are fitted with air brake silencers to avoid the often ear-shattering hiss of air brakes. These limit sound emitted to 72 decibels (dB(A)). With regard to engine sound levels it now takes eight engines to produce the same noise as one from 10 years ago. *Coach and Bus Week* magazine reported that 'a Scania coach whispered along at 70 mph with 61 dB(A) measured throughout the top deck', while comparatively a typical family car registers 70 dB(A) at 50 mph while a passenger train at 70 mph registers at 98 dB(A).

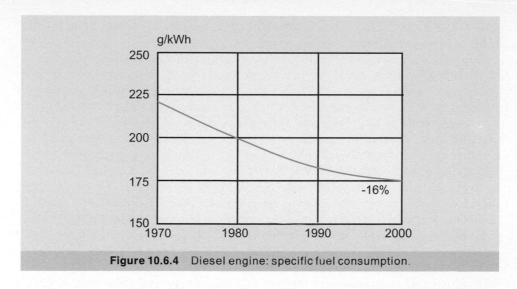

Figure 10.6.4   Diesel engine: specific fuel consumption.

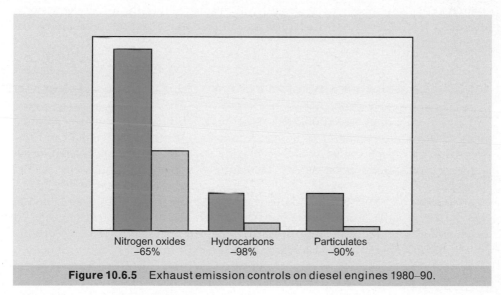

Figure 10.6.5   Exhaust emission controls on diesel engines 1980–90.

10.6.3 Alternative fuels

It is sulphur in diesel and other fossil fuels which causes particular pollution worries. During burning the sulphuric acid which is created damages and renders inoperative any catalytic converter. The 'cat' is there to catch the particulates. Lowering the sulphur content down to a maximum of 50 parts per million, or 0.005 per cent, reduces acid production enabling the after-treatment to take place.

The OK Petroleum Company in Sweden now markets low-sulphur diesel and Shell has joined them by opening the world's first ultra-low-sulphur diesel refinery which produces fuel with a sulphur content of just 0.001 per cent.

Alterative fuels come in all shapes and sizes; however, ethanol and compressed natural gas (CNG) are already widely used. Scania engage in considerable research in examining alternative future fuels. They conclude that diesel will continue to provide the optimum business solution for the long term. Next on their favoured list is ethanol (alcohol), with CNG taking third place. In Sweden the wood-pulping industry produces ethanol as a byproduct of its operations, a factor that led SL, the Stockholm equivalent to London Transport, to start trials with 30 ethanol-powered Scania buses. By the year 2000 SL Bus will have 150 ethanol-powered buses in its fleet. This fuel reduces a number of harmful emissions when compared with diesel, including nitrogen oxides and sulphuric acid. However, currently ethanol is not as efficient a fuel as diesel. In a related development, Scania is now supplying 250 CNG-powered buses to Sydney, Australia, and British Gas have shown an interest in further developing and marketing CNG as a fuel source for domestic and commercial vehicle users. CNG is an effective suppressor of noise and will dramatically reduce NOx emissions; however, it is still a fossil fuel product with all the inherent difficulties this involves.

10.6.4 Legislative emission control: the European Union

The European Union has established numerous environmental control standards, many of which directly apply to the truck industry. Whereas individual countries have targets for such things as carbon dioxide emissions, more specifically truck engine manufacturers must satisfy increasingly stringent, legally enforceable, standards.

The 'Euro 1' emissions standards were introduced by the European Union in October 1993, while 'Euro 2' were initiated in October 1996. 'Euro 2' represented a tightening of limits compared to 'Euro 1'. 'Euro 3' standards are now driving developments. These standards require reductions in emissions of nitrogen oxides, which contribute to acid rain, carbon monoxide and particulates, principally diesel soot. Achieving these standards relies upon cooperation from the petroleum industry which needs to reduce the sulphur content of diesel fuel. Standards for measuring emissions are currently being prepared for the turn of the century. These will require trucks to undergo a new driving cycle which reflects 'real life' road conditions in Europe rather than the current, rather artificial, test conditions.

Scania, together with its rival Volvo, are influential players in the European truck market. Their Swedish origin has assisted both companies in coming to terms with European environmental legislation. For many years successive Swedish governments have been at the forefront, within Europe, of legislative controls concerning all manner of environmental issues. Hence, Scania has 'grown-up' in an ecology conscious environment. Scania engines met the 'Euro 2' standards some two and half years prior to the 1996 deadline. However, the competitors had also responded effectively. Cummins, Volvo, Daf, MAN and Mercedes all produce engines which match up to new environmental regulations.

10.6.5 Recycling

In a recent report entitled *The Greening of the Automotive Industry*, consultants Coopers & Lybrand stated* that vehicles are already surprisingly recyclable. Approximately 87 per cent of the materials in a Scania truck can be reused in some way or another. The report expressed concern, however, that a residue of glass, plastics, rubber, fibres and various fluids cannot be profitably recovered and is, therefore, buried in landfill sites. In Europe this mountain of 'auto crusher residue' represents close to 5 million cubic metres a year; this is the equivalent of burying a waste tip the size of Wembley stadium every 12 months.

One potential solution to the problem is to establish automotive disassembly plants which would provide a recycling structure to match current production and assembly systems. However, if not driven by legislation the viability of this idea will be governed by cost effectiveness. In the United States, which actually produces less auto waste than the European Union, the big three manufacturers – GM, Ford and Chrysler – have formed a vehicle recycling partnership. In Switzerland a recycling levy of £30 is now placed on vehicles to cover the cost of incineration plants to render harmless parts that cannot be reused. One thought to ponder is that eventually manufacturers may have to guarantee that there are disassembly plants to dismantle every vehicle they construct. Table 10.6.2 shows the material make-up of a Scania truck.

TABLE 10.6.2   The Scania recipe: the make-up of a truck

Components[1]	kg
Steels (e.g. forgings, crankshaft, springs)	2400
Cast iron (engine block, brake drum)	1300
Sheet steel (cab shell, chassis frame members)	1200
Rubber (tyres)	600
Aluminium (flywheel housing)	1300
Plastics (wings, interior fittings)	30
Lead (batteries)	50
Copper (electric cables)	30
Zinc	4

[1] Typical ex-factory truck comprises 8000 parts weighing 5.75 tonnes of which 87 per cent is recoverable. From the metal components, forgings, iron castings, steel, aluminium, lead and copper are all recyclable. All rubber and plastic components are now marked in accordance with German VDA 260 standard enabling them to be sorted easily after scrapping.

CONCLUSION

The debate concerning the increasing use of road freight transport is set to continue. If the industrialized nations are sincere in their espoused intent to reduce or even maintain current levels of traffic on roads and reduce carbon dioxide and other emissions, nothing short of drastic government action will be required at national, European Union and international levels. The role played by the major truck manufacturers and car producers will be important in influencing future decision making in this regard. The future profitability and growth of manufacturers, such as Scania, and their hundreds of distributors across the globe are in balance.

QUESTIONS

1.   Is road transport of manufactured goods the most ecologically sound form of transport? Discuss your answer with reference to alternative transportation methods.

2.   Why is it important for Scania to publish and otherwise promote the ecologically relevant improvements it has made to its truck designs?

3.   How can a concern for the environment act as a source of competitive advantage to Scania? How might that concern, if taken to greater extremes, prove to be a liability?

4.   Why do you think companies like Scania are concerned to achieve a harmonization of environmental legislation across the globe?

5.   To what extent is collaboration between governments and industry needed to tackle environmental concerns? How can collaboration between companies in the same sector (e.g. manufacturers of trucks) and manufacturers in different sectors (e.g. Scania and Shell) make progress in environmental protection?

6.   Discuss the potential consequences in terms of global competitiveness of the United Kingdom government enforcing controls to ensure far greater use of rail transport for freight.

The industrialized countries of South-East Asia

Ian Brooks

This case study will explore the characteristics of the newly industrialized and rapidly expanding economies of South-East Asia and outline the environmental opportunities and constraints these countries face. We will open by identifying the countries concerned and outlining the scale of their successes of late. The case will then take a closer look at the competitiveness of these countries and finally focus on four countries in further detail and explore their unique characteristics and environmental influences.

10.7.1 The scale of economic growth in the newly industrialized countries

There is little agreement concerning which countries in this region can legitimately be referred to as newly industrialized countries (NICs). In order to avoid this largely technical and historical debate, for the purposes of this case study we will refer to the newly industrialized economies of Taiwan, South Korea, Singapore and Hong Kong, 'the four tigers', and Malaysia and Thailand referred to as the ASEAN-2 (Association of Southeast Asian Nations). These six countries known by the acronym DAE (Dynamic Asian Economies), together with Indonesia and Japan, are often referred to as the eight high-performing Asian economies (HPAEs). Table 10.7.1 clarifies these categories.

Japan is generally considered to be an 'old' industrialized country and hence not classified as an NIC. Joining the ranks of the HPAEs in the recent years are two other economic dragons, the gigantic China and an enterprising Vietnam.

In the period 1965–90, the eight HPAEs averaged a per capita rise in GNP of 5.6 per cent per year compared with just 2.3 growth for all OECD economies (World Bank, 1993). The rate of growth in 'the four tigers' was closer to 8 per cent and remains at that level (e.g. Singapore 8 per cent in 1994–95).

TABLE 10.7.1   HPAEs, NIEs, ASEAN-2: clusters of countries

High performing East Asian economies (HPAEs)	Newly industrialized economies (NIEs): 'the four tigers'	ASEAN-2	Latest additions to high economic growth countries
Japan[1]			
Hong Kong	Hong Kong		
Singapore	Singapore		
Taiwan	Taiwan		
South Korea	South Korea		
Malaysia		Malaysia	
Thailand		Thailand	
Indonesia			
			China
			Vietnam

[1] Data from Japan is not included in figures which refer to South-East Asia, the NIEs or ASEAN.

Economic prospects for the industrial countries of South-East Asia are promising; for example, if current growth rates are maintained, the Asia–Pacific region (including Japan) will be larger in GDP terms than the European Union by the year 2000. In the year 2025, it will be twice the size of both North America and the EU (*Business Week*, 29 March 1993). Per capita incomes in Hong Kong and Singapore, for example, already exceed those of a number of European Union countries. In 1994 per capita incomes in Hong Kong and Singapore were $US18 634 and $US17 414 respectively (*Asia Magazine*, 5–7 August 1994).

Growth in China and Vietnam, the two most recent 'entrants' justifying the newly industrialized label, has been impressive in recent years. China began its process of reform and opening itself to the outside world, a process referred to as *gai ge kai feng*, with historic policy shifts in December 1978 under the leadership of Deng Xiao Ping. Subsequently, the annual average growth in GNP of 9 per cent has captured the attention of economists and politicians world-wide. In 1993, for example, China approved a record 83 265 foreign investment projects amounting to over £70 billion (actual investment totalled £36 billion). These figures were equivalent to the accumulated total of all foreign investments attracted to China in the preceding 14 years. Given the difficulties of accurate measurement and inter-country comparisons, some considerable debate exists concerning the current size of the Chinese economy. However, China's economy is now considered to be in excess of 45 per cent of the size of the United States of America (*The Economist*, 28 November 1992). In 1993 the International Monetary Fund ranked China as the third largest economy in the world behind only the USA and Japan.

Since the introduction of the 'Doi Moi' (renovation) policy in 1987, Vietnam has attracted considerable international investment. It achieved its first recorded trade surplus in 1992 and an economic growth rate of 9 per cent in 1994.

The export-driven manufacturing sector has been particularly dynamic in the newly industrialized countries of South-East Asia. The four tigers together with Malaysia and Thailand accounted for over 10 per cent of world exports in 1990, an increase from just 4 per cent in 1975. Additionally, by 1989 Hong Kong, Taiwan, Singapore and South Korea had joined Japan and China in the world's top 20 exporters. In more recent years these countries have experienced significant growth, although not yet comparable to many developed OECD countries, in service industry.

This rapid growth has contributed to a dramatic upgrading of human welfare measures. Just two or three decades ago all South-East Asian countries would have been considered to be impoverished Third World nations. Life expectancy in the HPAEs has increased from 56 years in 1960 to 71 years in 1990. Life expectancy in Hong Kong, Taiwan and Singapore, for example, is now comparable to that found in Western Europe. The proportion of people living in absolute poverty, lacking such basic necessities as clean water, food and shelter, has dropped substantively – in the case of Indonesia from 58 per cent in 1960 to 17 per cent in 1990, and in Malaysia from 37 per cent to less than 5 per cent in the same period (World Bank, 1993). Such poverty is virtually non-existent within 'the four tigers'. Birth rates have declined significantly throughout South-East Asia. South Korea, Taiwan, Hong Kong and Singapore, the core NICs, had a birth rate of about 15 per 1000 in the early 1990s, again very similar to that found in Western Europe. These countries are now experiencing a rapidly ageing population. The decline in fertility rates is partly due to birth control, which typically accompanies economic growth, but also due to measures to further encourage women into the workplace. Female representation in the labour force within 'the four tigers' and the ASEAN-2 countries averages over 40 per cent, just a little below that of the European Union. Additionally, partly due to rapid economic growth, unemployment tends to be low, especially in Hong Kong and Singapore (<3 per cent) and skill shortages are common. By as early as the mid-1970s, Hong Kong, Singapore, Taiwan and South Korea had passed the so-called 'Lewis turning point', going from unlimited to limited labour supply. This has exerted an upward pressure on wages but has not, noticeably, slowed economic growth.

10.7.2 Competitiveness

The Swiss-based World Economic Forum (WEF) analyses national competitiveness on an annual basis. They utilize a wide range of data in order to 'score' and rank 48 countries. Thus, data ranging from GDP to gold reserves is combined with feedback from 3000 business managers responding to 130-item questionnaires. Although competitiveness is a notoriously contentious concept, the results of the WEF report are generally held in high regard. They showed in 1995, for example, that Singapore and Hong Kong were second and third, respectively, in the world (behind the USA) and Taiwan was 11th. The UK was in 18th position. Each of the industrialized countries of South-East Asia had either entered the rankings for the first time in 1995 or had been promoted to a higher position.

Taiwan

Taiwan is an island with a population of 22 million (1996). Like Japan it has few economically viable natural resources and is highly mountainous. Nevertheless, one-third of the total area consists of arable land and this has supported intense agricultural production and was a springboard to economic growth.

The economy was badly damaged during the Japanese occupation and the subsequent Pacific war in the early 1940s. However, the Japanese had left behind a modern rail network and communication system and improved literacy and technology training facilities. When Chiang Kai-shek brought over a million mainland Chinese refugees, including many educated 'technocrats', to Taiwan in 1949 there was neither a plan nor an existing base for the industrialization of the island. Initially Chiang's Kuomingtang party focused on upgrading agriculture and supporting an import substitution policy. American aid in the mid-1950s stimulated growth in the agricultural industry and significantly improved the country's infrastructure. Despite impressive economic developments, for 30 years power remained in the hands of the unelected Kuomingtang.

However, the post-1949 political story of Taiwan is complex and has involved delicate and often frayed relationships between the Americans and mainland China. Democracy was not openly advocated in Taiwan until the 1980s. Both Taiwan and China have long laid claim to each other; however, a new separatist government in Taiwan seeks to gain recognition for itself as an independent nation. This aspiration is causing considerable anxiety in the People's Republic of China. For politicians in Beijing, Taiwan is an inalienable part of China. The Chinese armed forces conducted extensive military manoeuvres off the coast of Taiwan during the Taiwanese election campaign in the spring of 1996.

In order to further develop the country, reduce its isolation and enhance its political security, Taiwan encouraged investment from multinational companies (MNCs) in the 1970s. The MNCs invested heavily, which promoted technological and management advances and led to rapid economic growth.

Most Taiwanese are Han Chinese, which is the major ethnic group on the mainland. They speak Mandarin and a few other dialects. Culturally families are close social units with strong traditional practices and beliefs. Despite enormous Western influence, most Taiwanese remain essentially Chinese in their cultural orientation. Education is valued highly with stiff competition for university places. Government actively intervenes in the education system to ensure that technical and entrepreneurial skills are incorporated into the educational system.

Taiwan has developed into a highly successful economy with a per capita income in excess of that of some European Union countries (e.g. Portugal) and an unemployment rate of less than 2 per cent.

South Korea

South Korea has a population of 45 million (1995), placing it among the most densely populated countries in the world.

Like Taiwan it experienced a turbulent political environment in the mid-twentieth century. Japanese colonization, which was particularly brutal, and a major civil war, which ended in 1953, created untold human and economic suffering. North and South Korea are artificially separated by a 2000 kilometre demilitarized zone and there has been an ever-present threat of military action from the North. However, it emerged from civil war with the active support of the USA and many non-communist countries. The military government in the 1960s embarked on export-led industrialization built upon Japanese-styled organizations (known as *kairetsin* in Japan and *chaebol* in South Korea).

The Korean government has actively intervened in the management of the business environment, for example in establishing the Korean Advanced Institute of Science and Technology which seeks to train researchers and to transfer technology to Korean companies. With strong state support the *chaebols* grew into large and integrated organizations which continually sought new capital-intensive expansion opportunities during the 1970s. Rapid economic growth in South Korea has created an acute shortage of qualified people which, in turn, has stimulated government into providing resources to produce many more graduate engineers and scientists.

The Koreans are thought to be a disciplined and enduring people, extremely patient and tolerant of hardship. They enjoy a strong sense of ethnic nationalism and a rich cultural heritage. The Korean approach to education has been largely Confucian-based, which has not acted as a major causal factor in influencing economic growth. Nevertheless, Confucianism has helped create a meritocracy and an obedient, almost subservient, population.

However, the militarized orchestration of industrialization is characteristic of a few nations in this region, as they emerged from war and colonization. As modernization sets in and quality of life improves, societal pressures have tended to remove military governments.

Singapore

Of the four newly industrialized economies ('the four tigers') Singapore has the smallest population of about 3 million in 1995 and the fewest natural resources. Like Hong Kong, Singapore is at the cross-roads of international trade routes. However, despite having an ethnically diverse population (77 per cent Chinese, 14 per cent Malays, 7 per cent Indians) and hence little ethnic identity as a nation, it has been able to achieve political unity and has enjoyed a highly successful industrialization programme. Additionally, the state has assumed responsibility for social welfare, such that the standard of living and per capita income of most Singaporeans exceeds that of very many Europeans.

Singapore developed into a successful commercial centre in the late nineteenth century; however, this was shattered by the Japanese occupation (1941–45). Following independence from the British in 1965, the pragmatic leadership of Lee Kuan-yew has successfully planned the industrialization of the country. Politics have been dominated by his ruling People's Action Party. Lee and his team of planners actively encouraged multinational companies from the USA, Japan and Europe to invest in Singapore and selected those that would offer both jobs and technological progress. They have flooded in since the 1960s, bringing with them capital, technology and the essential new overseas markets that were necessary if industrialization was to succeed in the lightly populated Singapore. The Singaporean government had adopted a highly interventionist policy towards industrialization, including the development of modern infrastructure, the establishment of key industries and direct participation in business and industry. Since the late 1980s some of the government-owned 'statutory boards' that run public utilities, transport services and telecommunications, have been privatized.

In the 1990s the government has been directing its efforts towards economic restructuring, encouraging less labour-intensive and more value-added, skills-focused, high-technology industry. Education and training are high priorities for the Singaporean government, as is the encouragement of inward migration of skilled personnel.

For welfare purposes the government established the Central Provident Fund Scheme which extracts a sizeable proportion of wages from both employers and workers. These monies can be used by individuals who have contributed to secure mortgages and to meet pension, welfare and medical expenses. Additionally, the central fund was used to finance the development of industry, infrastructure, housing and parks. This scheme has enabled Singapore to achieve one of the highest savings and investment rates in the world.

Hong Kong

Hong Kong has a population of over 6 million and a population density of 5700 per square kilometre (1995). It comprises a number of small islands and a part of the 'Chinese' mainland. Hong Kong harbour is the only deep-water harbour between Singapore and Shanghai. It is located in the centre of major sea and air routes. Hong Kong has long benefited from its proximity to a huge Chinese market, a sizeable domestic demand and its prime location and reputation as a regional and international financial centre and distribution point. It has also benefited from associated finance, shipping, insurance, information and other services related to its long-established and highly successful port activities.

Hong Kong is, until 1997 when it reverts to Chinese control, a British colony. It was ceded to the British in 1841 and extended on a 99-year lease in 1898.

Many of the Hong Kong Chinese have migrated from Guangdong in China, an area that had been commercialized for some time. It was not, however, until the

1970s that the government notably increased investment in the construction of infrastructure and in education. Many would argue that Hong Kong has the best of both worlds, Western experiences of a developed modern society (Britain) and an oriental culture (Chinese) rich in traditions like respect and hard work.

Hong Kong is widely regarded as a successful economic model which broadly adheres to the *laissez-faire* principle. There has been some government assistance, mainly in export promotion and representation in international trade negotiations and in maintaining order and stamping out corruption. The province now enjoys an average per capita income in excess of many European Union countries and is a major, and growing, industrial and commercial centre in South-East Asia.

CONCLUSION

> Most of the high-growth countries of South-East Asia have developed not by the invention of new products but by experiencing changes in their productive structures utilizing existing technology. Additionally, they have experienced, at various times, government-led industrial and development policies which have sought to attract technology and investment. These include offering 'tax holidays' to investors, the development of industrial estates and export subsidies. Many have, since the mid-1980s, initiated substantial economic reforms due to a combination of domestic pressures and international competition. Many have particularly endorsed privatization and market-oriented competition.

QUESTIONS

1.   (a) What are the prime characteristics of the different approaches adopted by governments in South-East Asia to achieve economic growth?
(b) What appear to be the merits and drawbacks of each approach?

2. What may be the (a) political, (b) social and (c) other consequences of rapid growth in Asia during the next two decades for:
(i)   the countries themselves, and
(ii)   Europe and North America?

Reference

World Bank (1993) *The East Asian Miracle: Economic Growth and Public Policy*, World Bank Policy Research.

Small and medium-sized enterprises

Mark Cook

> This case study focuses on the importance and growth of small and medium-sized enterprises (SMEs) within the international environment, concentrating in particular on SMEs within the European Union (EU). It outlines their role in contributing to the economic growth, competitiveness, innovation and job creation while at the same time discusses the constraints they face from their business environment.

Introduction

In the past, small businesses were considered to be the poor relations of their larger counterparts. A casual glance at the quality press, with its focus on large enterprises, might suggest that small firms hardly exist in developed economies. However, small businesses make up the majority of enterprises in the economies of all countries. A perception that they are likely to be small family-run concerns, making low-grade products/services, is a misconception. Today a small business may be a biotechnology business, a software house, a high-quality design company or a manufacturer.

Within the European economy over 95 per cent of firms are defined as small businesses. These provide more than half of all the jobs in the European Union. Indeed, the European Union sees the small firms as providing the fast-moving and adaptable businesses that will (a) improve its competitive position in the future, (b) be the main provider of new jobs and (c) enhance the growth performance of the Union.

It is possible that small enterprises face greater degrees of uncertainty than large firms, especially when considering the environment. They may perceive themselves as being much more vulnerable than large firms, since they may be dependent on dominant customers and lack the power to influence the marketplace.

TABLE 10.8.1

Type	Number of employees
Micro	0–9
Small	10–99
Medium	100–499
Large	More than 499 employees

Source: European Commission.

10.8.1 Small and medium-sized enterprises

Defining SMEs

The European Union defines small and medium-sized enterprises (SMEs) as private enterprises outside the agricultural sector, employing less than 500 persons. This can be further disaggregated as shown in Table 10.8.1.

This, however, is only one method by which SMEs can be defined. They can also be described in terms of sales turnover, profitability, net worth or – as in the case of the transport sector – number of vehicles. Defining SMEs in this way leads to a situation where a small firm in the transport sector is likely to differ in terms of sales and other factors from a small firm in the petrochemical industry. This means that in some sectors there may exist few, if any, small firms while in another the majority of firms may be defined as 'small'.

Although there is some consistency between the definition of the SME across the European Union the definition in the wider international field differs. For example, a small firm in the United States is defined as one with less than 1000 employees. Bearing these definitional issues in mind, Table 10.8.2 indicates that the number of small firms appeared to be less in the United Kingdom than in other advanced industrialized countries during the early 1980s.

TABLE 10.8.2 Number of small firms relative to population – selected countries (1980)

Country	Small firm population (millions)	No. of small firms per 1000 of population (UK = 100)
Netherlands	1.2	370
France	3.1	250
Japan	5.4	202
United States of America	8.0	157
West Germany	1.9	133
Canada	0.6	109
United Kingdom	1.3	100

Source: Bannock (1980).

This situation had altered by the end of the 1980s, but the United Kingdom still possessed a slightly greater proportion of larger organizations, which may be associated with the remnants of its industrial past.

The importance of SMEs

Within the European Union more people work in micro enterprises (with 10 or less workers) than are employed in large enterprises employing over 500 people. In fact 75 per cent of total private sector employment in Europe is in SMEs. Hence, we can see the importance of this sector as a generator of jobs. Even during the recession in Europe, between 1990 and 1993, only small and micro-enterprises showed any marked growth in employment. In particular, in Europe's disadvantaged regions, the Objective 1 regions, SMEs outperformed their larger contemporaries in terms of maintaining and increasing employment.

Employment in SMEs varies from country to country and by region. The greatest regional variation exists in the Netherlands, Finland, Norway, France, Spain and Portugal. Perhaps even more important on a structural basis is the fact that the regions with the highest proportion of SMEs are also those with the highest level of self-employment. This contrasts with those regions which have been traditionally dominated by larger declining industries which have much lower levels of self-employment. It is important to understand the nature and determination of regional trends in SME development if national and European Union SME policies are to be effective at the regional level, and regional policies are to assist in reducing existing regional disparities in economic performance.

Distribution of SMEs within the European Union

In a large number of European Union countries, particularly Greece, Ireland, Spain and Portugal, a substantial proportion of employment and output is within the SME sector. In the European Union half those in employment work for companies employing less than 50 people. In Italy, for example, 64 per cent of enterprises employ fewer than 50 people. In Belgium, France, the United Kingdom and Germany, however, the proportion of the workforce in SMEs, of 50 employees or less, is much lower.

Table 10.8.3 indicates that in 1990 enterprises with fewer than 50 paid workers represented almost 99 per cent of the total number of enterprises in the EU-12 and 99.8 per cent of enterprises had fewer than 250 paid workers.

A sectoral approach to SMEs in the European Union

The industrial sectors which include organizations with the greatest numbers of workers are energy and transport equipment, while textiles, printing and the food industry include firms which are generally smaller. On a national level there has been a movement from dependency on and employment in, the manufacturing

TABLE 10.8.3 Weight of employment-size classes by country in terms of enterprises (selected countries), 1990, percentages

Country	Size classes			
	<50	<250	50–250	250+
EU-12	98.8	99.8	1.0	0.2
Belgium	98.9	99.8	0.9	0.2
Denmark	98.3	99.8	1.5	0.2
Germany	97.9	99.6	1.7	0.4
France	98.7	99.8	1.1	0.2
Italy	98.9	99.8	0.9	0.2
Portugal	98.9	99.8	0.9	0.2
United Kingdom	98.6	99.8	1.2	0.2
Netherlands	98.7	99.8	1.1	0.2

Source: Eurostat.

sector, towards economies becoming more service oriented. At the EU-12 level, and in Belgium, France, Italy, Portugal and Norway in particular, service sector organizations are usually SMEs. More than 99 per cent of these enterprises had fewer than 50 employees. Germany and the United Kingdom were the only countries where there were a significant number of firms employing more than 250 people. This may indicate the existence of a different type of service sector, for example a highly developed financial services industry, in Germany and the United Kingdom.

10.8.2 Why the interest in small firms?

It has been stated, on more than one occasion, that the relatively poor performance of the United Kingdom economy could be related to the historic lack of SMEs in the economy. Lloyd (1993), however, sees the problem as mainly due to the dearth of middle-sized SMEs rather than less SMEs as a whole.

By the 1970s, an increasing number of studies appeared to indicate that the emphasis on developing large-scale organizations had been misplaced. Large firms were seen as less innovative than at first believed. It was true that they were still growing but this tended to be through the process of merger and takeover rather than organic growth. There was a growing body of evidence to suggest that mergers and takeovers did not enhance the performance of the newly merged company. Profits were often not larger and the new organizations appeared to suffer from negative synergy.

In addition, small firms appeared to be playing an increasingly important role in the innovation process, particularly instrument engineering, electronics and high-technology sectors.

Prais (1976) also produced evidence to suggest that, even though some firms had grown, it was not necessarily due to an increase in the size of their plants, but rather in their number. This would suggest that economies of scale are less important and that small firms using similar sized plants could become equally competitive.

Smaller firms also appeared to be generators of greater levels of employment during the 1970s and 1980s, while larger firms had been shedding labour. Finally, small firms also appeared to be taking an increasing role in international trade, particularly in manufactured products. Nonetheless, it should be noted from studies undertaken by Blackburn and Curran (1993) and Cook and Weatherston (1995) that many service sector SMEs are not particularly active in export markets.

10.8.3 The micro-evidence for small firm growth

As we can see from the above, the benefits that accrued to large firms and to society were increasingly being questioned. This led to a resurgence in the study of the small firm sector. The evidence is not always conclusive but it suggests that certain environmental factors lie behind the general re-emergence of the small firm. Some factors have pushed small firms into existence (supply side) while others have pulled small firms to grow (demand side).

Technological factors

When economists consider the various cycles through which an economy progresses the Kondratief cycle has the longest wavelength. It has been recognized that in this cycle, which has a period of 50 years, the early years are distinguished by new technologies being cultivated and dispersed by smaller enterprises. In this early period of the cycle small enterprises become relatively more important to an economy. As the cycle develops some small firms become larger enterprises and at the same time some existing larger enterprises acquire some of the small firms. Only towards the end of the cycle do large firms become the dominant force again. The previous cycle, which started in the 1920s/1930s with the development of the car and other electrical goods, has now come to an end and a new Kondratief cycle is in motion based upon electronics, new technology and information. There has been a large growth in the number of small firms that are involved in new technology and information services, but if the Kondratief cycle is to be believed, then the growth of new small firms is but a temporary phenomenon.

There are also demand-side factors which are leading small firms to be involved in the service/information technology sector. On a national level many of the economies within Europe are becoming more service oriented. For example, in the United Kingdom almost two-thirds of the workforce are employed in this sector. Thus the growth in service sector SMEs is also associated with the rise in the demand for services from a post-industrialized economy and may be a reflection of Europe's comparative advantage in this sector.

Cost factors

On some occasions it may be less costly to use outside contactors for a particular task than 'in-house' expertise. There are many examples of firms which have put part of their production processes out to external tender; large firms can, in this way, reduce costs, remain competitive and create opportunities for other businesses. Whatever the reason, extensive contracting out makes a firm more flexible – an essential quality in the dynamic and complex environment in which most operate. However, the growth in small firms may also be symptomatic of a decline in larger organizations which now have reduced their manning levels and moved themselves into the SME category.

10.8.4 Impact of the labour market

There are characteristics which are said to distinguish the self-employed from the employee. They are more likely to be male than female; generally older than the average age of the employed population; influenced by their family background, ties and culture. However, studies do not show conclusively that the self-employed are different from employees. One other factor that may influence the move to self-employment is unemployment. Unemployment may provide the impetus to set up in self-employment as it reduces the opportunity costs of becoming self-employed. In this case the change in the labour market may have a positive impact on the creation of SMEs. However, becoming unemployed might also imply that the individual has redundant skills and is therefore not in a position to establish a business.

10.8.5 The role of the state

The role of privatization or contracting out could be expected to benefit the SME sector since contracts that were undertaken in-house by local government, Civil Service agencies or NHS Trusts can now be expected to be offered to the private sector. Although this process of contracting out may be expected to lead to an increase in the number of firms in an economy, it is not necessarily the case since public sector organizations often appear more willing to deal with larger organizations.

Government influence on the firms' environment can also be through the tax and social security systems (or their equivalents). It might be expected that higher personal taxation would lead to some individuals removing themselves from employment into self-employment to minimize their tax bills. During the 1980s, however, the rate of direct taxation fell when the number of SMEs rose, so this cannot provide a complete explanation. The role of state welfare payments might provide a more suitable answer. Work undertaken in the United Kingdom,

Germany, France and Denmark during the 1980s suggests that only in the latter did the numbers of self-employed not rise and this may be linked to the greater level of welfare payments in that country. Governments have also sought to encourage people into the enterprise culture via various allowance schemes, such as the enterprise allowance in the United Kingdom. It is also possible for governments to reduce the stigma attached to business failure by altering legislation to allow individuals, whose businesses have failed, a shorter period of time before returning to managing and owning a business.

10.8.6 Level of development

There appears to be a link between the level of development of an economy and the number of self-employed individuals. The more developed the economy, the smaller is the amount of self-employment in the total workforce. This is probably explained by the greater dependency the less-developed economies have on their agricultural sectors. It is generally the case that a greater number of self-employed units are to be found in the service sector of the economy; nonetheless, in the United Kingdom, the highest rates of self-employment are to be found in construction and agriculture.

10.8.7 Niche markets

As an economy develops it is highly likely that specialist services and goods will be required to cater for the growth in the population's real income. These goods and services are not dependent on scale economies and therefore provide the sorts of markets that can be filled by small firms. Thus, as demand changes it is the flexible specialization of the small firms that is paramount. This is particularly the case for the north-east central region of Italy where many small firms specializing in textiles, ceramics and footwear are situated. This form of specialization is linked to quality products and enables the Italians to be one of the few developed countries which have increased their world share of these markets. Why have other areas on the Italian mainland, and throughout the rest of Europe, not developed similarly?

Factors affecting existing small firms

On a macroeconomic level, there are a number of factors which can play their part in developing or constraining the small firm sector. Access to capital has always been an issue. Small firms argue that they do not have long enough track records to raise finance themselves. Moreover, this can militate against obtaining loans from the banking sector. Governments have sought to reduce these financial constraints through a variety of schemes. In the United Kingdom the government has used the enterprise allowance scheme and loan guarantee schemes. In addition, a further securities market, the unlisted securities market (USM), was established in 1980 to enable small firms to tap into venture capital. The advantages of the USM over the conventional stock exchange was its cheapness. However, relaxation of the rules on the full stock exchange meant that the attractiveness of the USM waned during the early part of the 1990s and a new market called the alternative investment market (AIM) has been developed in its place.

Existing small firms are also helped with tax allowances and grants. Reductions in corporation tax and various schemes to encourage business start-up have helped the longevity of the small firm. Governments have also sought to reduce the amount of red-tape facing the small firm. The Deregulation Initiative reduced the constraints faced by industry and there were further changes to ease the auditing procedure. Training, too, was given help through the provision of the Training and Enterprise Councils in the United Kingdom and the development of Business Link.

However, even with this assistance, SMEs still face a number of further constraints to growth. Interest rate policies and, in particular, increases in interest rates or interest rates that stay at a high level for an appreciable length of time, have resulted in the closure of many small businesses. Skills deficiencies have also been noted with regard to management and marketing skills. The impact of economic activity and government policy are also important factors, in particular the lack of consistency of policy which inhibits planning. Perhaps one of the major problems, however, is the role of finance as highlighted earlier. We need to consider the relationship of small firms with banks, their reliance on short-term finance, their difficulties in raising equity and the use of alternative forms of funding.

The small firms sector, therefore, can be looked at from a number of perspectives. We can disaggregate it at the sectoral level into manufacturing or service companies, and we can divide it up regionally. However, a major difference also exists between new SMEs and more mature small firms. The problems and constraints they face from the business environment can be quite different. We should also recognize that even these segments can be further divided so that there are growth segments and those in decline. For example, in any sector of the economy we need to consider each individual firm to assess the level of management training, whether the owner manager has run a successful business before, the objectives of the management team, the kind of products the small firms produce, the level of competition in their markets, etc. Thus developing an overall policy for this increasingly important sector of the European economy is fraught with difficulties.

QUESTIONS

1. What advantages does an economy obtain from a large SME sector?

2. To what extent will changes in technology, which lead to smaller and more efficient plants, influence the small firms sector?

3. Consider your local economy. Which sectors are most buoyant? Are these sectors constituted from a large number of small firms? Account for the patterns found.

4. In Europe why is the small firms sector so important?

References

Bannock, G. (1980) *The Promotion of Small Business: A Seven Country Study*, Vols 1 and 2. Prepared by the Economists Advisory Group for Shell UK.

Blackburn, R. and Curran, J. (1993) 'In search of spatial differences: evidence from a study of small service sector enterprises', in J. Curran and D.J. Storey (eds) *Small Firms in Urban and Rural Locations*, Routledge, London.

Cook, M. and Weatherston, J. (1995) 'The exporting potential of SMEs: improving the skills gap?', *Paper presented at the ICSB Conference*, June, Sydney, Australia.

Lloyd, T. (1993) 'Corporate giantism: a suitable case for treatment', *Quarterly Enterprise Digest*, February, pp. 8–11.

Prais, S.J. (1976) *The Evolution of Giant Firms in Britain*, Cambridge University Press, Cambridge.

GENERAL INDEX

ORGANIZATION AND SECTOR INDEX

INTERNATIONAL AND PLACES INDEX